RED EARTH NATION

The Environment in Modern North America

Red Earth Nation

A History of the Meskwaki Settlement

ERIC STEVEN ZIMMER

Foreword by Johnathan L. Buffalo and Dawn Suzanne (Wanatee) Buffalo

University of Oklahoma Press: Norman

This book is published with the generous assistance of the Kerr Foundation, Inc. and the Center for Global and Regional Environmental Research at the University of Iowa.

Library of Congress Cataloging-in-Publication Data

Names: Zimmer, Eric Steven, author.
Title: Red Earth Nation : a history of the Meskwaki Settlement / Eric Steven Zimmer ; foreword by Jonathan L. Buffalo and Dawn Suzanne (Wanatee) Buffalo.
Other titles: Environment in modern North America ; v. 10.
Description: Norman : University of Oklahoma Press, [2024]. | Series: The environment in modern North America ; volume 10 | Includes bibliographical references and index. | Summary: "Environmental and tribal history of the Meskwaki Nation since the 1850s and the tribe's struggle for sovereignty"— Provided by publisher.
Identifiers: LCCN 2023057773 | ISBN 978-0-8061-9386-1 (hardcover) | ISBN 978-0-8061-9387-8 (paperback)
Subjects: LCSH: Fox Indians—Iowa—History. | Sac & Fox Tribe of the Mississippi in Iowa—History.
Classification: LCC E99.F7 .Z57 2024 | DDC 977.7/00497314—dc23/eng/20240220
LC record available at https://lccn.loc.gov/2023057773

Red Earth Nation: A History of the Meskwaki Settlement is Volume 10 in The Environment in Modern North America series.

The paper in this book meets the guidelines for permanence and durability of the Committee on Production Guidelines for Book Longevity of the Council on Library Resources, Inc. ∞

Copyright © 2024 by the University of Oklahoma Press, Norman, Publishing Division of the University. Manufactured in the U.S.A.

All rights reserved. No part of this publication may be reproduced, stored in a retrieval system, or transmitted, in any form or by any means, electronic, mechanical, photocopying, recording, or otherwise—except as permitted under Section 107 or 108 of the United States Copyright Act—without the prior written permission of the University of Oklahoma Press. To request permission to reproduce selections from this book, write to Permissions, University of Oklahoma Press, 2800 Venture Drive, Norman OK 73069, or email rights.oupress@ou.edu.

For Sam and Stevie

Contents

List of Illustrations — ix
List of Maps — xi
Foreword, by Johnathan L. Buffalo and Dawn Suzanne
    (Wanatee) Buffalo — xiii
Preface: Don's Advice — xix

Introduction: This Land Is Our Fortune — 1

Part I. The Red Earth People on the Emerald Horizon
    Chapter 1 Wisaka's Arrow — 25
    Chapter 2 Reconfiguration — 53

Part II. Settlement Sovereignty
    Chapter 3 Renegades — 81
    Chapter 4 Pressure — 104

Part III. Erosion
    Chapter 5 *Peters v. Malin* — 125
    Chapter 6 Living on the Land — 147

Part IV. Rebuilding
    Chapter 7 Testing Ground — 173
    Chapter 8 Strategic Embrace — 202

Epilogue: Recovery	228
Acknowledgments	243
Sources and Abbreviations	249
Notes	251
Artist's Statement	321
Index	323

Illustrations

"No Dancing Letter"	xvi
Donald Wanatee	xx
Connecting Meskwaki Land and Population	14
Pushetonequa	111
Indian Industrial School at Toledo (Meskwaki Boarding School)	127
Meskwaki Wickiup	137
Meskwaki Musicians	150
Jonas and Ruth Poweshiek and Their Child	153
Ida Snowball Poweshiek	154
Young Bear	160
Sam Slick	169
Meskwaki Children's Poultry Club	180
Meskwaki Crafts Stand	181
Ada Old Bear and Marie Jefferson	195
Adeline Wanatee	208
Sam Slick's Bear Claw Necklace	238

Maps

Meskwaki Land Reclamation, 1857–2020	15
Meskwaki and Sauk Migrations, 1600–1870s	26
Dispossession of the Meskwaki and Sauk Nations	50
The Red Earth People's Presence in Iowa, 1805–1842	66

Foreword

Proper context is everything in history. Proper context makes history real. Proper context is what makes historical information valuable, it's what makes history meaningful, and ultimately it is what makes history useful. Finding the "big picture" is always key to finding the proper context.

From time immemorial, our community has consistently identified itself as being Meskwaki, or the "Red Earth People." Yet we have commonly been misidentified throughout written history: we were "les Renards" to the French and were known later to English speakers as "the Foxes." Why? One theory floated by academics is that when the tribe first met the French in 1666, the French encountered a group from our Fox Clan and mistakenly identified the entire tribe as "the Fox." Today, visitors routinely ask us why we changed our name from Fox to Meskwaki. When we respond that we don't really know why we were called Fox in the first place, some people jump to the conclusion that we have forgotten our own history, or they assume the French put the name on us because they viewed us as being very smart.

But there is a different theory, one that relies heavily on proper context. It was during the reign of the French king Louis XIV, to whom traders and Jesuit priests first reported back about the growing troublesomeness our tribe posed to them. Many people in America today are unaware that in Europe, fox hunts were an enjoyable pastime for the elite. These were blood sports intended to exterminate vermin such as foxes, which were commonly seen as bloodthirsty thieves, indiscriminate killers, and vicious slayers of domesticated fowl and young livestock.

No, we don't believe "Fox" was a term of admiration bestowed on us by the French. When we first met the French, they did not refer to us as "Renards"—that came about after we got to know each other better and discovered our differences, mostly economic and religious. Context is everything. Then we had a forty-year war with them, with the French king (Louis the XV by that time) issuing a decree commanding the death of every single one of our people. Every man, woman, and child—and even our dogs. Today, we are still alive as a people, we are still calling ourselves Meskwaki, and there is no more French monarchy. Why were we called "Renards" by the French king? We can only guess, but we do know that proper context makes for a more meaningful perspective on history.

Eric Zimmer came to our Settlement looking to do his dissertation about the Meskwaki, and he could not have selected a more unaccommodating group of people. Over the past hundred years at least, the Meskwaki have become apprehensive of scholars wanting to use the tribe as a step up in climbing their personal educational and professional ladders, or to prove theories they had already formed. The tribe had learned not to invest too much in such relationships, as there was little benefit for them for the expense in time and energy. Good relationships with scholars have been possible. But the successful relationships, from the view of the tribe, were few and far between. Often, when a project was over, we would never hear from the scholar again. And today their work sits on some obscure, dusty shelf somewhere in academia and is never read by any Meskwaki people, nor is it beneficial to us in any way. Other times when a project ended, we were surprised by how incomplete or flawed the research findings and conclusions were. The resulting piece of dangerous work would never fail to resurface over the years, for us to deal with all over again, when a new researcher wholly or partially integrated the poor information into their writing or preformed perceptions of us before arriving.

We met Eric in September 2011 when he accompanied Mary Bennett on a trip to the Meskwaki Settlement. Mary, a dear and trusted longtime friend, was the special collections coordinator for the State Historical Society of Iowa. Before arriving, Eric had already gained praise from professors we knew and respected at the University of Iowa. After meeting him, we decided to support him and his dissertation. If anything, we thought a new dissertation on the Meskwaki would be good, especially one created with the additional benefit of more and more government records being available online and fresh reference material that, only a few years earlier, was very difficult and labor intensive to find. Eric did not rush on his dissertation research. He took the time to learn about the people he planned to write about, explored many perspectives, and became a collaborator in our work.

One example of this is that he was one of the volunteers who painted the ceiling of the first Meskwaki Cultural Center and Museum, a refurbished part of an old tribal building. We were so excited to finally have space to set up a tiny museum, but with little to no funds the workload and finding supplies fell heavily on volunteers—from the tribe and friends of the tribe—and we were grateful to those who stepped forward to help. Eric also helped organize a conservation lab in the museum. The genuine friendships that developed went beyond his research and remain strong to this day.

When it came to his dissertation research, Eric did excellent scholarly work, as other peers and academics have noted. But he also talked to many tribal members to learn what they knew of the events he researched and what impressions, thoughts, or memories they had. Eric collaborated with the Meskwaki and gave us valuable insight into our own tribal history. Often researchers separate us from their projects, as if we have no relevance to our past. His master's thesis on tribal history and his *Annals of Iowa* article brought us new insights. And we learned to trust him with our history and the proper contexts he employed.

His dissertation was full of tremendous promise as a book, one that could offer a fresh viewpoint on our history to all audiences, including us, the studied. We have indeed benefited from Eric's—now *Dr.* Zimmer's—work. We benefited from his diligence and his methodical search for the pieces of evidence that combine to form a picture bigger and more realistic than the pinhole views more frequently portrayed of tribes. He focused on a time period prone to oversimplification and underestimation, ulterior motives and shadowy figures, rife with political thuggery and very real threats with potentially catastrophic social and economic consequences. It was a time that saw the steady incremental layering of policy upon policy on tribes. Some policies were reformative, some punitive, and some simply by-products of indifference. Tribes debated how to respond, or not, and how much, if at all, to invest in change, knowing that the political

DEPARTMENT OF THE INTERIOR
OFFICE OF INDIAN AFFAIRS
WASHINGTON

A Message

TO ALL INDIANS:

Not long ago I held a meeting of Superintendents, Missionaries and Indians, at which the feeling of those present was strong against Indian dances, as they are usually given, and against so much time as is often spent by the Indians in a display of their old customs at public gatherings held by the whites. From the views of this meeting and from other information I feel that something must be done to stop the neglect of stock, crops, gardens, and home interests caused by these dances or by celebrations, pow-wows, and gatherings of any kind that take the time of the Indians for many days.

Now, what I want you to think about very seriously is that you must first of all try to make your own living, which you cannot do unless you work faithfully and take care of what comes from your labor, and go to dances or other meetings only when your home work will not suffer by it. I do not want to deprive you of decent amusements or occasional feast days, but you should not do evil or foolish things or take so much time for these occasions. No good comes from your "give-away" custom at dances and it should be stopped. It is not right to torture your bodies or to handle poisonous snakes in your ceremonies. All such extreme things are wrong and should be put aside and forgotten. You do yourselves and your families great injustice when at dances you give away money or other property, perhaps clothing, a cow, a horse or a team and wagon, and then after an absence of several days go home to find everything going to waste and yourselves with less to work with than you had before.

I could issue an order against these useless and harmful performances, but I would much rather have you give them up of your own free will and, therefore, I ask you now in this letter to do so. I urge you to come to an understanding and an agreement with your Superintendent to hold no gatherings in the months when the seed-time, cultivation of crops and the harvest need your attention, and at other times to meet for only a short period and to have no drugs, intoxicants, or gambling, and no dancing that the Superintendent does not approve.

If at the end of one year the reports which I receive show that you are doing as requested, I shall be very glad for I will know that you are making progress in other and more important ways, but if the reports show that you reject this plea, then some other course will have to be taken.

With best wishes for your happiness and success, I am

Sincerely yours,

Commissioner.

February 24, 1923.

The "No Dancing Letter" discouraged Native American tribes across the United States from engaging in cultural celebrations. Today, the Meskwaki Historic Preservation Office displays the document in its museum, at the annual powwow, and during other public events. It serves as an educational tool and reminder of the challenges the Meskwaki Nation has overcome. Courtesy of the Meskwaki Historic Preservation Office, 2023.

FOREWORD

machinery of the United States was a fragile thing and prone to abrupt accelerations, decelerations, breakdowns, and collective amnesia. Most tribes suspected there was much more behind the forces at work. Some thought the enemy was not foreign but domestic and aimed the cannons in, not out. What did the Meskwaki do, in the center of the country during this complicated period in American history, and why? That is the question Dr. Zimmer uncovers in this book.

It is time to bring this part of our story outside the walls of academia and out to the rest of the world. This effort, guided by Dr. Zimmer's talent for relating proper contexts, can only enrich the reading experience of every Meskwaki, as well as scholars and the general public. We are pleased to finally have this book, *Red Earth Nation: A History of the Meskwaki Settlement*, which offers an overview of our migration to Iowa and focuses on the period from the mid-1800s forward, with an emphasis on the story of our Settlement. Dr. Zimmer's book has joined the ranks of what we feel are the best written works regarding the Meskwaki Tribe: David Edmunds and Joseph Peyser's *The Fox Wars: The Mesquakie Challenge to New France*, covering the late 1600s to the mid-1700s; Judith Daubenmier's *The Meskwaki and Anthropologists: Action Anthropology Reconsidered*, covering the Sol Tax period; and Douglas Foley's *The Heartland Chronicles*, which looks at more contemporary days.

There is a document we simply call the "No Dancing Letter." It was issued by the Department of the Interior's Office of Indian Affairs on February 24, 1923. It was sent to tribes across the United States, reminding them of federal prohibitions on Native American dances, ceremonies, and the like. We still have our original letter. It is in the museum that Dr. Zimmer helped us make. Every American who thinks they already know American history should read this letter. As you read, an aperture into those days immediately opens up, and then snaps closed again at the end of the letter. This letter was written during the not-so-distant time period of the Meskwaki Nation that Dr. Zimmer writes about: that of our great-grandparents, grandparents, and parents. That letter represents the deep challenges they faced, and we regularly show it to visitors to the museum and tribal events as a reminder of the history most people have forgotten.

On behalf of the many Meskwaki who had long conversations with Dr. Zimmer and the great friends who shared their insights and information learned from their own studies, we thank Dr. Eric Zimmer for sharing part of his life with us.

> Johnathan L. Buffalo
> Tribal Historian, Sac & Fox Tribe of the
> Mississippi in Iowa (Meskwaki Nation)
>
> Dawn Suzanne (Wanatee) Buffalo
> Meskwaki tribal member

Preface
Don's Advice

More than a decade ago, I left my home in western South Dakota for the University of Iowa. Shaped by my concern over the troubling history of tension between Native and non-Native people in my home state, I arrived in Iowa City interested in the history of federal and state Indian policy. Since Iowa taxpayers funded my graduate fellowship, I also wanted to undertake a local research project. After some preliminary reading and conversations with my advisor, Jacki Thompson Rand, I approached Mary Bennett at the State Historical Society of Iowa, who, I was told, had long-running relationships with members of the Meskwaki community. She offered to take me on her next trip to the tribe's land, which they call the Meskwaki Settlement, where she was helping the staff convert an old government building into a new tribal library and museum.

In the months that followed, I spent many hours in that facility chatting with the tribal historian, Johnathan Buffalo, his wife Sue, and colleagues like the museum conservator, Mary Young Bear. One day, I told Johnathan about my background and interests and asked if there was a project I could work on for my master's thesis that the tribe might find useful. He thought for a moment then told me that I should probe the origins of the Meskwaki Constitution. Although the topic was a subject of regular debate in the community, he said, most people knew little about how it came to be. Over the next five years, my master's thesis grew into a dissertation as I realized that to explain the origins of the Meskwaki Constitution in the 1930s, one first had to recognize that event as part of an ongoing, multigenerational political strategy that was rooted in the community's 1857 Settlement purchase.

Donald Wanatee (1933–2021) was a politician, advocate, activist, veteran, and respected leader within the Meskwaki community. He shared cultural knowledge and provided early encouragement for this book. Photo courtesy of Edda Taylor Photography.

A few years into my dissertation research, I shared some chapters focused on the 1930s and 1940s in an evening talk at the tribal museum. After I finished, Meskwaki elder Donald Wanatee approached me. An octogenarian who was recovering from major surgery, he made a slow beeline to the podium. Braced by his cane, Don reached up and patted me on the shoulder. He had lived the history I was writing about. He offered what was, for Don, a high compliment: "You got a few things right," he teased in a wry whisper. "You should keep going."

So I did. What follows is the result, framed and reframed in fits and starts over the course of a decade, during late nights between consulting projects and infant feedings and, most recently, as a guest in the history department at the University of Montana. Over the years, I have given a copy of my finished dissertation to the Meskwaki library and shared copies with anyone who asked. I solicited feedback from Sauk and Meskwaki people, members of other Native nations, and fellow historians. As I developed this book, professional, community, and family obligations pulled me away time and again. These lapses proved invaluable to the process. Each time I found a moment to return to Meskwaki history, the story revealed something new.

Make no mistake—I am an outsider to the Meskwaki community. So were the authors of most of the sources I used to reconstruct this story. Many of these documents were created by and reflect the perspectives and biases of the non-Natives who wrote them. Cognizant of this fact, I have attempted to situate Meskwaki people at the center of their story while also treading carefully around issues like spirituality and intertribal politics. I offer only glimpses into Meskwaki worldviews and how custom and ceremony have shaped the tribe's systems of governance and Meskwaki people's relationship to the natural world. I did not dig for details about clans, ceremonies, or religion, nor have I sought to intervene in long-standing disagreements over issues of leadership and tribal membership that have been examined by many authors over the years. Simply put, that is not my place.

This approach—and, indeed, the work of any non-Native historian exploring Indigenous history today—has its boundaries and pitfalls. As a function of time, geography, war, and policy, Meskwaki history is American history and is open to academic inquiry. Yet I do not view this as license to go poking around just anywhere. In the 1960s, Vine Deloria Jr. chided the legions of "anthropologists and other friends" who flocked from universities to Native communities, where they spent long summer breaks capturing Indigenous knowledge and telling stories that advanced their careers. This work, in Deloria's view, rarely benefited Native peoples.[1] More recently, a lively scholarly discussion about the ethics and limitations of doing Native history has taken place in the pages of major academic periodicals. Several authors have criticized non-Native academics whose work has influenced policies and social attitudes that contributed directly to the systematic oppression of Indigenous peoples.[2]

I do not wish to replicate these patterns. I worked most closely with folks like Mary and Johnathan, largely because they are warm and wonderful people who share my interests, but also because their tribe has tasked them, by virtue of their jobs, with engaging with scholars like me. I have done my best to listen carefully to them and others and hear the explicit and more subtle signals about which subjects the community might consider appropriate, and then balance those against the ethics and expectations of the historical profession.[3] As an extension of this ethic, I will also donate whatever royalties this book earns to causes that support Meskwaki people, decided under the guidance of folks on the Settlement.

I have come to call this general approach "working in a good way," a phrase I borrow from Native friends and collaborators in South Dakota. For them, this means starting meetings in prayer, taking the time to hear everyone's perspective, and keeping a general eye toward the well-being of the collective. Over the years, some academic colleagues, all with my best interests in mind, have worried that being sensitive in or candid about my approach might lead peers in the field to perceive my work as less rigorous or insufficiently critical. For me, working in a good way has meant trying to produce work that is maximally constructive and minimally harmful. Working in a good way requires its own kind of rigor, a stout challenge given the long legacy of scholarship that has reinforced the destruction and marginalization of Indigenous Americans. Historians make all kinds of choices as they write and revise their work. I am a public historian at heart, and for me, public history is a methodology characterized by reciprocal partnership as much as it is an attempt to share history with broader audiences.[4] I have chosen to listen to the community and do my best to write in a way that hopefully does less harm than good.

My approach, meanwhile, has also allowed me to step back from the minutiae to ask bigger-picture questions about the history of the Meskwaki Nation. Readers interested in detailed analyses of Meskwaki culture, religion, or political disagreements within the tribe can look to my notes for a roadmap to the generations of government officials, anthropologists, historians, tribal members, and others who have opined on these matters. Many observers have produced smart and compelling studies about Meskwaki history and issues. Their work certainly provides a factual and intellectual foundation on which I have tried to build. Yet, in hindsight, it is difficult to imagine that Meskwaki people did not find some of this work rather intrusive—especially when it came to government agents or anthropologists tracking their every move and, sometimes, the most intimate parts of their lives. In some cases, it probably inflamed tensions within the tribe. Indeed, scholars' fascination with the inner workings of Meskwaki life has sometimes distracted them from important developments in the tribe's history. Like, for example, the remarkable story of how the Meskwaki Nation reclaimed its land in the 1850s, how that decision influenced the tribe's long-term recovery, and how that story serves as a harbinger of other Indigenous reclamation histories.

With all of this in mind, my writing reflects the preferences of the time and places in which I have been working. In my experience, the terms "Indigenous," "Native American," and "Indian" are informally used in daily conversation by Native and non-Native people in South Dakota, Iowa, and Montana, and on the Meskwaki Settlement. I respectfully use these terms interchangeably, though "Indian" rarely, and only for the sake of variety. Wherever possible, I refer to Native communities using the words they use to describe themselves. For example, although the Meskwaki Nation is federally recognized as the "Sac and Fox Tribe of the Mississippi in Iowa," a tribal resolution prefers the use of "Meskwaki Nation." So I use "Meskwaki" and its English translation, "People of the Red Earth" (which I shorthand as "Red Earth People") instead. I avoid the plurals "the Meskwaki" or "Meskwakis" because some members of the Meskwaki community asked me to. My goal here is to be respectful and precise but not overly repetitious.[5]

In some parts of the book, my description of the actions of the "Meskwaki Nation" may give the impression that the tribe was more monolithic and uniform in its decision-making than any community ever really is. My intent is not to diminish the agency of individual Meskwaki people or to flatten out the nuance of internal tribal debates. Instead, I recognize that much of Meskwaki history was shaped by the tribe's collective response to the actions of European and American national governments in earlier eras and, more recently, by a complex interplay of tribal, federal, state, and local politics. The Meskwaki Nation is a small community, and I have focused much of my analysis at the nation-to-nation level in order to navigate some limitations in the source material, resist the urge to wade unnecessarily into fine and potentially intrusive details, and elevate the sovereignty of the Meskwaki Nation.

On that last point, there also exists a lively discussion about the applicability of the terms "sovereignty" and "self-determination" across Indigenous history. I use "sovereignty" as an imperfect shorthand for the inherent rights that the Meskwaki Nation (and other tribes) have to control their land, systems of governance, cultures, identities, spiritualities, and other elements of their nationhood.[6] Similarly, regardless of time period, I use variations of the terms "Native Nation" and "tribe" throughout, and all out of respect for tribal sovereignty. I use "self-determination" when describing the specific execution of the rights that tribes enact as sovereign nations. For example, the Meskwaki Nation had a (sovereign) right to negotiate with the State of Iowa for social services in the 1960s. The tribe's decision to use federal funds and contract with the state for those services, on the other hand, was an exercise in working within the American policy framework (self-determination) to administer those programs.

Shaped by this approach, my intention is that this book adds something of value to the way we think about Meskwaki history, the Red Earth People's role in the broad processes that shaped the American Midwest and West, and how all this connects to Indigenous issues past and present, while minimizing interpretive mistakes. I acknowledge that my process may have overlooked individuals and families whose stories and knowledge might add to or diverge from the story told here. Where disagreements occur or gaps exist, I hope they inspire future work that adds rich new insights and perspectives gained, whenever possible, from members of the Meskwaki community themselves.

Don Wanatee passed away in 2021. He was an inspiration. Had he gotten a chance to see the finished product, I hope he would have appreciated the things I got right, corrected the things I got wrong, and encouraged others to continue to rethink and expand upon Meskwaki stories. In that spirit, I invite anyone, Meskwaki or otherwise, to write to me at ericszimmer@gmail.com with any questions or critiques.

EZ
Missoula,
Montana
2023

Introduction
This Land Is Our Fortune

In the spring of 1857, a Meskwaki man mounted his horse and made a slow but deliberate trek to the doorstep of Isaac and Susan Butler, who had settled along the Iowa River five years earlier.[1] Sent by the leaders of the Meskwaki Nation, he arrived with an unusual request: would the Butlers, a white family, sell a portion of their land to the Meskwaki Nation, a Native American tribe that, as Butler would have found if he had checked with a federal official, was not even supposed to be in Iowa? The conversation that followed brought about a critical shift in Meskwaki history. It also presaged ripples of Indigenous action that would follow in centuries to come.

We know very little about this Meskwaki diplomat. We do know, however, that he and the Butlers did not complete their business that day. Instead, the Meskwaki man "went away and came again, about three times," presumably taking the Butlers' proposed price back to the Meskwaki Nation and returning with counteroffers.[2] On his final trip, the Meskwaki man struck a deal: the family agreed to sell 80 acres along the Iowa River to the tribe for $1,000. Their agreement did not complete the transaction, however. That would have required the Meskwaki Nation to overcome some tall political and bureaucratic hurdles.

A few months later, in July 1857, the Meskwaki Nation dispatched a contingent of five diplomats to Iowa City.[3] At the time, Iowa City was still the state capital, although Des Moines would become the seat of the Iowa government just a few months later.[4] These men, like the interlocutor sent to visit the Butlers, were on a mission to secure a land base that would be collectively owned by all of the Meskwaki Nation. On that day, they signed a deed for 80 acres of the Butlers' land in Tama County, about 65 miles northeast of Des Moines. It was a cramped space for 250 people to share, half the size of the tracts that individual settlers would start to receive after the 1862 Homestead Act was passed. But, exhausted from decades of movement and uncertainty, the Red Earth People welcomed the chance to reclaim that small riparian plot. It offered a crucial foothold. In the 165 years since, the Meskwaki Nation has grown to around 1,450 members, and their Settlement encompasses over 8,600 acres and counting. With each new acquisition, reclaiming land has been an affirmation of Meskwaki sovereignty. As the Red Earth People and their land base have grown, the Meskwaki Nation has recovered.

LANDBACK

Across the United States, Indigenous Americans are reclaiming their land. It seems that every few months, a new headline blares a story about how, in some corner of the country, a Native American tribe has acquired some real estate. Recently, this phenomenon has been branded—as everything in the 2020s must be—with a hashtag. Known as #Landback, the movement is wide ranging and takes many forms. As the Indigenous philanthropy and advocacy organization NDN Collective puts it, "LANDBACK is a movement that has existed for generations with a long legacy of organizing and sacrifice to get Indigenous Lands back into Indigenous hands."[5] The Choctaw writer B. "Toastie" Oaster, meanwhile, argues that Landback "is less about a mass real estate transaction than it is about sovereignty, recognition of treaties, and, ultimately, the abolition of the United States concept of real estate altogether."[6]

Examples of Landback abound. Some mirror the Meskwaki Settlement purchase in the 1850s. In January 2022, for example, a consortium of Native American tribes called the Intertribal Sinkyone Wilderness Council reclaimed 523 acres of redwood forest in Northern California known as Tc'ih-Léh-Dûñ (Fish Run Place). That property was purchased by a nonprofit organization, Save the Redwoods, and donated to the tribes. This acquisition expands the approximately 4,500 acres already reclaimed by the consortium since its first reclamation in 1997.[7] On the opposite coast, in 2021, the Passamaquoddy Tribe bought a 140-acre island in Maine called Kuwesuwi Monihq (Pine Island) for $355,000. Passamaquoddy people had inhabited the island for some 10,000 years, and a deal with Massachusetts protected it as treaty land in the 1790s. When Maine achieved statehood a few decades later, settlers voided the agreement. By the 1860s, there were no Passamaquoddy people left on Kuwesuwi Monihq. A century and a half later, as reclamation was underway, tribal members and their supporters deployed #IslandBack to celebrate the Passamaquoddy achievement.[8]

The list goes on. In 2020, the Esselen Tribe worked with the California government and a nonprofit group called Western Rivers Conservancy to reclaim a 1,200-acre ranch in Northern California.[9] In 2016, four tribes of the Oceti Sakowin (often called the Great Sioux Nation) purchased Pe' Sla, a 2,300-acre sacred site in the Black Hills of western South Dakota.[10] As of this writing, another reclamation effort, supported by the tribes but led by members of the urban Indigenous community, is going on just a few miles from Pe' Sla, in my hometown of Rapid City. Directed by a group of intrepid Lakota and Dakota women, the Rapid City Indian Boarding School Lands Project has been working with local and federal stakeholders to reclaim land within Rapid City since 2012. Their goal is to honor and protect the graves of children who died at the boarding school and resolve inequities that arose when the Department of the Interior began dispersing the boarding school's property in 1948.[11]

Tribes also reacquire land through transfers authorized by Congress. In June 2021, for example, the Confederated Salish and Kootenai Tribes reclaimed the National Bison Range on the Flathead Reservation. To save the bison, the United States had stripped away more than 18,000 acres of tribal land in the spring of 1908. After decades of litigation, activism, and lobbying by Indigenous peoples and their advocates, Congress tucked a provision approving the return of the National Bison Range to the Salish and Kootenai Tribes into a COVID-19 relief bill. It passed and, in the months that followed, the Department of the Interior transferred the property to the tribes.[12]

More than a decade earlier, in 2009, the federal government settled *Cobell v. Salazar*, a massive, decades-long class-action lawsuit that Native activists used to force the United States to reconcile more than a century of mismanaged tribal assets. As part of the settlement, the Bureau of Indian Affairs (BIA) established the "Land Buy-Back Program for Tribal Nations."[13] The program enables tribes to draw from a $1.9 billion trust fund to buy small parcels of trust land from tribal members. By 2021, the BIA had consolidated some 700,000 interest cases, paying $1.2 billion to tribal owners to buy back some 2.1 million acres of land.[14]

Altogether, reclamation in all its forms has increased Native landholdings in the contiguous United States from around 47 million acres at the end of the 1950s to some 56 million acres today. If we count Alaska, this figure is much higher—around 114 million acres, although Alaska Native land has a different status than other Indigenous property in the United States.[15] In short, Indian Country is growing.

OF THE EARTH

Like many aspirational movements, Landback has multiple meanings. This book focuses on the actual physical reclamation of Native land. Yet, in many cases, Landback is less literal: spend any time in Indian Country, and you will quickly learn that the concept has a variety of meanings. For NDN Collective, Landback "is a political framework that allows us to deepen our relationships across a field of organizing movements working towards true collective liberation."[16] Some Indigenous peoples see land reclamation as supporting self-determination through economic development and capacity-building programs, or simply as a way to create economic benefits through real estate. Others view it as an avenue for reasserting legal rights or strengthening self-governance. Still others view land reclamation as one strategy within the broader, ongoing project of restoring balance to an Indigenous world upended by colonization.[17]

At the same time, land carries diverse meanings for different Indigenous peoples. Generations of scholars have explored how Indigenous peoples have understood the environments that surround them.[18] Native people knew what it meant to access, utilize, manipulate, and control territory—even when this knowledge differed from Western concepts of property ownership. And, as the example of Meskwaki history certainly bears out, whether or not tribes agreed with Western ideas about the land, or even believed in them, tribal members certainly understood and could work in and around the American land tenure system.

Indigenous discussions about land often emphasize relationality and stewardship over ownership. Stephanie Bad Soldier-Snow, education coordinator for the Meskwaki Nation's Workforce Development office, recently told me that whenever she gives public talks about Meskwaki history, she always takes the time to remind her audience that "we Meskwaki believe that we are created from the Earth, because our name [People of the Red Earth] literally means that we are *of* the Earth, and therefore have an intimate relationship with the Earth and everything in and on her."[19] The Cherokee scholar Clint Carroll extends this idea to the practice of Indigenous decision-making with and about the environment. In non-Native contexts, he observes, terms like "environmental governance" and "natural resource management" are about asserting control over and administering, usually for economic gain, the natural world and what it provides. For many Indigenous peoples, Carroll notes, "there is no artificial separation of human beings from the rest of creation." This is an objective that Indigenous decision-making about environmental matters, as both a process and a set of outcomes, often aspires to meet.[20]

The Yellowknives Dene scholar Glen Coulthard takes this beyond the internal management of nature and its resources, framing environmental relationships as central to the ways in which Native peoples ward off external threats. He asserts that Indigenous resistance "is best understood as a struggle primarily inspired by and oriented around *the question of land*—a struggle not only *for* land in the material sense, but also deeply *informed* by what the land *as a system of reciprocal relations and obligations* can teach us about living our lives in relation to one another and the natural world in nondominating and nonexploitative terms."[21] According to the Wabanaki writer Mali Obomsawin, the Passamaquoddy Tribe's reclamation of Kuwesuwi Moniqh was about "more than land return.... it [was] the return of a stolen family member."[22] Meanwhile, scholars such as Craig Howe (Lakota) and Rosalyn LaPier (Blackfeet/Métis) extend these relationships to the study of the past itself, noting that for many Indigenous peoples, histories are studied and told in relation to land, water, and sky.[23]

Often, relational Landback is not about buying land but protecting sites and resources. From 2016 to 2017, a huge protest movement on the Standing Rock Reservation sought to stop construction of the Dakota Access Pipeline, which would run petroleum products from northwestern North Dakota underground to Illinois. This movement comprised a diverse group of Native-led "Water Protectors," organized under the banners #NODAPL and "Water is Life." The pipeline was completed during the Trump administration, and, as of this writing, the Biden administration has not shut it down, while court challenges and environmental reviews continue. The #NODAPL movement broadens the possibilities of Indigenous land reclamation. The Water Protectors' goal was not necessarily to take back the property but to reclaim control of the land in a different sense, through an ongoing process of protecting land and water—including that beneath the surface—and, by extension, the downstream human and nonhuman populations that could suffer from contamination.[24]

Similarly, land reclamation can be about the maintenance of less tangible but still vital matters like tribal jurisdiction. In 2020, the US Supreme Court handed down its decision in *McGirt v. Oklahoma*, a capital murder case appeal that hinged on whether the state had criminal jurisdiction over historic treaty lands. Although *McGirt* did not literally return a huge swath of land in Oklahoma to the Creek Nation, the Court affirmed treaty-based reservation boundaries and maintained tribal jurisdiction over them—a crucial aspect of the Landback movement. Then, in the summer of 2022, the Supreme Court issued another ruling in a different criminal appeal, *Oklahoma v. Castro-Huerta*, this time narrowing its findings in *McGirt* by restoring some state jurisdiction over tribal land.[25] In between these two decisions—indeed, just three weeks after *McGirt*—a federal court of appeals affirmed the reservation status of the Oneida Tribe of Wisconsin, which had been challenged by the village of Hobart, a predominantly non-Native municipality located within the Oneida Nation's treaty territory.[26]

Landback can also be symbolic. Renaming places, for example, is a way to raise awareness about who and what society chooses to honor and remember. While there are many recent examples from around the world, prominent ones in the United States include the Obama administration's 2015 restoration of the Athabaskan name "Denali" to the tallest mountain in North America, which had previously been known as Mount McKinley.[27] In 2018, the largest lake in Minneapolis—previously called Lake Calhoun—was renamed Bde Maka Ska.[28]

The past few years have also seen the rise of "land acknowledgments." These usually include formal statements recognizing the history of Indigenous dispossession. They often appear on institutional websites or occur at the beginning of public lectures and other events. A sprawling debate ensued as this practice gained popularity in recent years, with some observers considering land acknowledgments an important first step in reckoning with inequitable pasts. For some, land acknowledgments create learning opportunities for non-Indigenous audiences and help lay the groundwork for meaningful consultations and the restoration of resources to tribes and Indigenous people. Critics, meanwhile, have derided the practice as performative and self-serving. Wrestling with these questions, some authors have produced guidebooks on how best to develop land acknowledgments and carry them forward as both symbolic acts and commitments to correcting historical misdeeds.[29]

From reclamation to acknowledgment, Landback is an encompassing and multidimensional project. It is a source of optimism and energy for Indigenous peoples and their advocates. It is also rife with deep historical challenges.

TRUST IN LAND

Despite the momentum of the Landback movement, the very idea of Indigenous land reclamation is conceptually fraught. After all, even successful examples are, at their core, stories about people forced to raise money and buy back that which was taken from them.[30] We must also bear in mind that the scale of successful Indigenous land recovery simply does not compare to the vast losses brought about by the dispossession and dislocation of Native peoples over many centuries. The fact that some tribes and urban Indigenous communities have reclaimed land and realized its benefits neither overshadows nor excuses the long history that placed tribes in this position in the first place. In the broad sweep of North American history, the dispossession of Indigenous land has been an abiding theme. It has also been a topic of great scholarly and public interest. The dispossession of Indigenous land has assumed several forms, and scholars have demonstrated that it was about more than land and property; it was also about the development of the United States as we know it. They argue that the systems that facilitated the settlement of North America and the extension of American democracy across the continent were inextricably intertwined with the taking of Indigenous land and the marginalization of Native people.[31]

In many places, these histories are barely even past. Even as the Landback movement builds momentum, Native lands are under threat. In April 2020, the Trump administration stripped the reservation status from 321 acres of Mashpee Wampanoag land in Massachusetts. After legal battles and the transition to the Biden administration in 2021, the Interior Department reversed its decision, keeping the land in Mashpee Wampanoag hands.[32] Meanwhile, Bears Ears and Grand Staircase–Escalante national monuments, two sites important to tribes in the Southwest, have been a political volleyball for several years, subject to intense lobbying at various levels of government. President Barack Obama afforded them federal protections in 2016. In 2019, President Donald Trump reduced the protected area. Then President Joe Biden restored and expanded the boundaries in 2021 and announced a tribal comanagement agreement for Bears Ears in 2022.[33] The Biden administration's actions at Bears Ears occurred as the Departments of Agriculture and the Interior were also rolling out a joint secretarial order aimed at protecting and restoring tribal homelands through co-stewardship agreements between tribes and the federal government.[34]

Together, these examples underscore how, in recent history, the status of Indigenous lands has often oscillated according to the whims of the executive branch—a common theme in a long tradition of capricious Indian policy.[35]

Scholars and Indigenous advocates have also shown how most Native American land fell into a confusing "checkerboard" of ownership. Federal Indian policy in the United States is anchored in Western European legal principles like the "Doctrine of Discovery," a 1493 papal decree that "allegedly granted Euro-Americans property and sovereignty claims over native peoples and native lands as soon as Euro-Americans 'discovered'" the Western Hemisphere.[36] The policy of "preemption" is an extension of that logic. It came into existence in 1763, when the British Crown issued a proclamation giving itself the right of first refusal to the sale of Native land in colonial America. A few decades later, and shortly after ratifying its Constitution, the new United States of America passed the Trade and Intercourse Act of 1790, which extended preemption and gave the federal government an exclusive right to buy tribal land. Sometimes described as a way to regulate westward expansion and prevent predatory speculators from getting

Native land, preemption quickly became a tool of control. Still today, tribes generally cannot sell their land without federal approval.[37]

In the 230 years that followed the Intercourse Act, the making and breaking of treaties, the creation of the reservation system, policies like allotment and termination, and a tortuous set of federal legal precedents—like *Johnson v. McIntosh* (1823), which enshrined the "Doctrine of Discovery" in American law—have created a complex web of Indian law and policy. Today, as the Indian Land Tenure Foundation notes, the acreages within a given reservation's outermost boundaries are often composed of a hodgepodge of "trust lands, fee lands, and lands owned by tribes, individual Indians, and non-Indians." This limits the ability of Native people to use their land for agriculture or economic development, creates all kinds of jurisdictional problems, presents barriers to accessing cultural and sacred sites, and poses other obstacles.[38]

When tribes reclaim land today, they often attempt to place it in federal trust, which is the status held by most reservation lands in the United States. Today, trust status is often viewed as a layer of protection that can shore up tribal jurisdiction, protect land from being taken by outsiders, or create economic incentives by avoiding things like state taxes and regulations. Trust status, however, produces its own challenges. States, for example, commonly resist trust applications, making it slow and often difficult for tribes to place newly acquired land into trust. Meanwhile, federal restrictions limit tribes' abilities to use trust land—including to borrow against or sell it.[39] This has led some observers to call tribal land "dead capital" or even to argue that "Indians can't own land, so they can't build equity," which "prevents American Indians from reaping numerous benefits."[40]

This is one of the issues that the federal government's recent "Land Buy-Back Program for Tribes" is trying to reconcile. Problems with "fractionated land" arise when each member of a group of descendants owns an "undivided interest" in a piece of land that was allotted under the 1887 Dawes Act. Today, after the land has been divvied up many times over many generations, each of these interests amounts to a tiny fraction of the overall property. Often, the administrative costs of maintaining fractionated land are higher than the property's value itself, and the system does not allow owners to sell or borrow against their fractions. Instead, descendants receive a regular (and often minuscule) payment from the federal government.

There were some 11 million acres of fractionated Indigenous trust land across the United States when the buy-back program began in 2013.[41] So, on one hand, consolidating it in tribal trust solves part of the problem. It could also be trapping large portions of Indian Country as dead capital.

Native Nations and their supporters will continue searching for legal remedies and policy revisions to resolve trenchant problems like these. Meskwaki history reveals how the Red Earth People viewed the Settlement's federal trust status in different ways at different moments in history. Sometimes they rejected it as an incursion into tribal sovereignty, and at others they embraced it to meet the needs of the moment. Significantly, the Meskwaki Settlement never became checkerboarded but has remained entirely in Meskwaki hands. As tribes consider issues like financial equity or other pros and cons of consolidating land in trust, the long view of Meskwaki history demonstrates what tribes stand to gain when they place their "trust in the land."[42]

RECLAMATION HISTORIES

Native America is vast and diverse. There are presently 574 federally recognized tribes in the United States. Many more are recognized by states or are processing recognition claims. Several of these tribes and communities have land histories that, like the Meskwaki story, push against the well-known narrative of dispossession. They demonstrate that the recently branded and rapidly accelerating project known as Landback has a deep and textured history in the United States. It emerged in myriad forms across various contexts, but almost always in pragmatic responses to the cascading effects of corrosive land policies.

Indigenous reclamation histories extend deep into the American past. In 1709, for example, the Indigenous peoples of Santa Ana Pueblo began to purchase land from neighboring Hispanos, many of whom had received Spanish colonial grants to land in what became New Mexico. In the centuries that followed, the Pueblos fought hard to ensure that some of these properties remained in Native ownership, even as control of the wider territory transitioned between the Spanish, Mexican, and United States governments, and as numerous outside interests tried to strip it away.[43] More than a century later, a group of Indigenous people representing seven New

England tribes formed the Brothertown Indian Nation and moved to Wisconsin in the early 1820s. They had acquired a permanent land base by 1832, and their story underscores the intimate linkages between the protection of Native land and the maintenance of Indigenous nationhood.[44] The terms of their forced removal from Georgia in the early 1830s afforded the Cherokee Nation some 4.5 million acres of fee-simple land in the "Indian Territory" of present-day Oklahoma. There, they established a "hybrid property system" to manage property in a new place and under rapidly evolving market pressures.[45] The Meskwaki Nation bought its Settlement in 1857. In the decades that followed, a few tribes in the Indian Territory, like the Osage Nation and the Ottawa Tribe of Oklahoma, sold treaty lands and used the revenue to buy other property in the Indian Territory. In some cases, this ownership slowed the process of allotting tribal lands.[46] And, in 1874, the Jamestown S'Klallam Tribe bought a 210-acre piece of land in Washington State, a purchase that, according to the tribe, "provided a geographical center of group identity and independence."[47]

Reclamation histories continued into the twentieth and twenty-first centuries. After a dam flooded their land in the 1930s, the people of the Barona and Viejas Bands of Mission Indians outside San Diego each chose to use federal funds to buy a collective land base and restore reservation status rather than divvy up the money and go their separate ways.[48] Around that time, the Indian Reorganization Act of 1934 created legal mechanisms through which tribes could restore allotments to tribal trust. The Rosebud Sioux Tribe in South Dakota was among the tribes that took advantage of these provisions, opening its Tribal Land Enterprise Office in 1943, an office that has been slowly buying up allotments and other property ever since.[49] The Confederated Tribes of the Warm Springs Reservation in Oregon and the Grand Traverse Band of Ottawa and Chippewa Indians in Michigan undertook energetic land repurchase initiatives in the 1960s and 1980s, respectively.[50]

Alongside tribes that restored property as collectives, individual Indigenous people, and sometimes families or groups of families, worked creatively to obtain land. They used the Homestead Act or provisions of the Dawes Act or other programs that opened access to public land under certain conditions, sometimes securing property outside their reservations.[51] Recent scholarship, meanwhile, has explored the complicated implications of the privatization of Indigenous land, demonstrating how Native people have subverted allotment policies and revealing how land ownership has been both a tool of dispossession and a site of Indigenous resistance in American and global history.[52]

All of these reclamation histories presaged the modern Landback movement. Studying each one on its own terms can tell important stories that add texture and dimension to the broader narratives of the expansion of the United States and the dispossession and removal of Native peoples. Comparing tribal reclamation histories and situating them within the larger paradigms of state and federal land policy, meanwhile, stands to generate new questions and sketch a road map toward policy solutions. Exploring these stories offers lessons to Indigenous communities seeking reclamation and recovery in the twenty-first century.

NATIVE HISTORY IN REVERSE

Set against this complex backdrop of history and contemporary action, *Red Earth Nation* is about land reclamation and its relationship to Indigenous recovery and resurgence. More specifically, it is a history of a people and their land. It has two goals: to offer a narrative update to the history of the Meskwaki Nation and to explore the Meskwaki story as a case study of Indigenous land reclamation. The book picks up roughly where R. David Edmunds and Joseph L. Peyser left off in *The Fox Wars: The Mesquakie Challenge to New France*. Although by no means comprehensive, *Red Earth Nation* builds upon the foundation of earlier works to offer an update to the last four centuries of Meskwaki history, interpreted through a blend of environmental, political, and social history. On the recommendation of several members of the Meskwaki community, the chapters that follow tell a chronological and narrative story to make this history as accessible to Meskwaki people and broader audiences as possible.

As this story unfolds, *Red Earth Nation* offers a series of arguments about the broad arc of Meskwaki history. First, it suggests that Iowa and the surrounding territory became a Meskwaki homeland because, over the last several centuries, successive generations of Red Earth People have found there a place of ecological, economic, and political refuge. After a long and disruptive migration, the woodlands and prairies in and around the

Upper Mississippi River enabled the Meskwaki Nation to stabilize its population twice. The first arrived after a war with the French had led to the near annihilation of the Red Earth People by about 1730. In the century that followed, the tribe rebounded by allying itself with the Sauk Nation and developing a place-based economy dependent upon a seasonal agricultural round, hunting, and participation in the regional lead mining and fur trade economies. The second period of stabilization in Iowa came when the Meskwaki Nation purchased its Settlement in 1857. In the half century preceding that event, the US government systematically dispossessed the Sauk and Meskwaki Nations. By the 1840s, the process of removal, compounded by economic and ecological pressures exacerbated by non-Native settlement, had reduced the Meskwaki population to its lowest point in a century.

Responding to these pressures, the Red Earth People sought a way to remain in Iowa. The 1857 Settlement purchase achieved that goal. Thereafter, residing in Iowa enabled the Red Earth People to stabilize and recover. In the 160 years since purchasing its Settlement, the Meskwaki Nation has engaged in a nearly continuous process of reclaiming, expanding, and fortifying its land base. Along the way, the Red Earth People repeatedly and strategically leveraged their collective land ownership in political contests of all kinds, navigating the many changes to local, state, and federal Indian policy over the course of the nineteenth and twentieth centuries. Meanwhile, tribal members experimented with variations of a land-based tribal economy, seeking a way to sustain their community while adapting to major changes occurring on and around the Settlement. Taken as a whole, all of these strategies supported the core objectives of supporting the Meskwaki community and protecting and affirming the tribe's control over its affairs. Throughout these processes, the Meskwaki Settlement has served as a mooring for cultural identity and community cohesion, as well as an anchor for environmental, economic, and political restoration.

The second goal of *Red Earth Nation* is to explore the Meskwaki Settlement's history as one of the best available case studies of direct-purchase Indigenous land reclamation in United States history. It offers a hybrid political and environmental history of the Meskwaki Settlement, showing how the Meskwaki Nation reframed its conceptions of the Settlement and its legal and political status to meet an evolving set of challenges and opportunities, all while the Red Earth People experimented with their

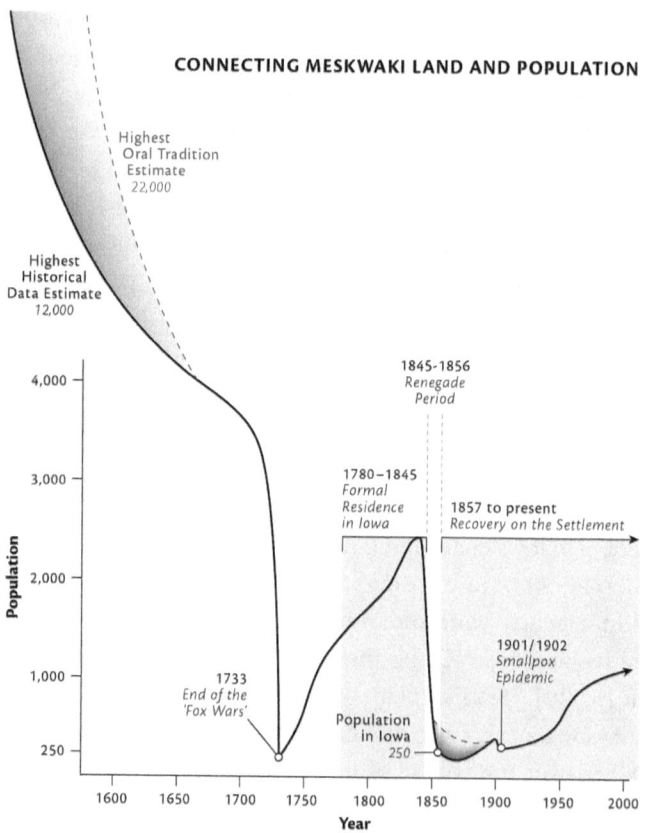

The number of Red Earth People has grown during two periods in the last four hundred years. In each case, the recovery of the Meskwaki population occurred while the tribe had a foothold on the geography in and around what we now call Iowa. The shading at the far left reflects the discrepancy between Meskwaki oral traditions, which suggest there may have been as many as 22,000 Red Earth People around 1600, and non-Native scholars, who place the number somewhere between 1,000 and 12,000 individuals. The shading around 1850 reflects the challenge of providing an accurate count of Meskwaki people at that time, given that roughly 250 returned to the Settlement after its creation, while others remained in Kansas with their Sauk relatives. All population figures are estimates based on archival documents; the Annual Reports of the Office of Indian Affairs, available from the University of Wisconsin–Madison Digital Collections; Barbara Alice Mann, *President by Massacre: Indian-Killing for Political Gain* (Santa Barbara, CA: ABC-CLIO, 2019), 261; and Jeffrey Ostler, *Surviving Genocide: Native Nations and the United States from the American Revolution to Bleeding Kansas* (New Haven: Yale University Press, 2019), 352–53. Created by Erin Greb Cartography, 2023.

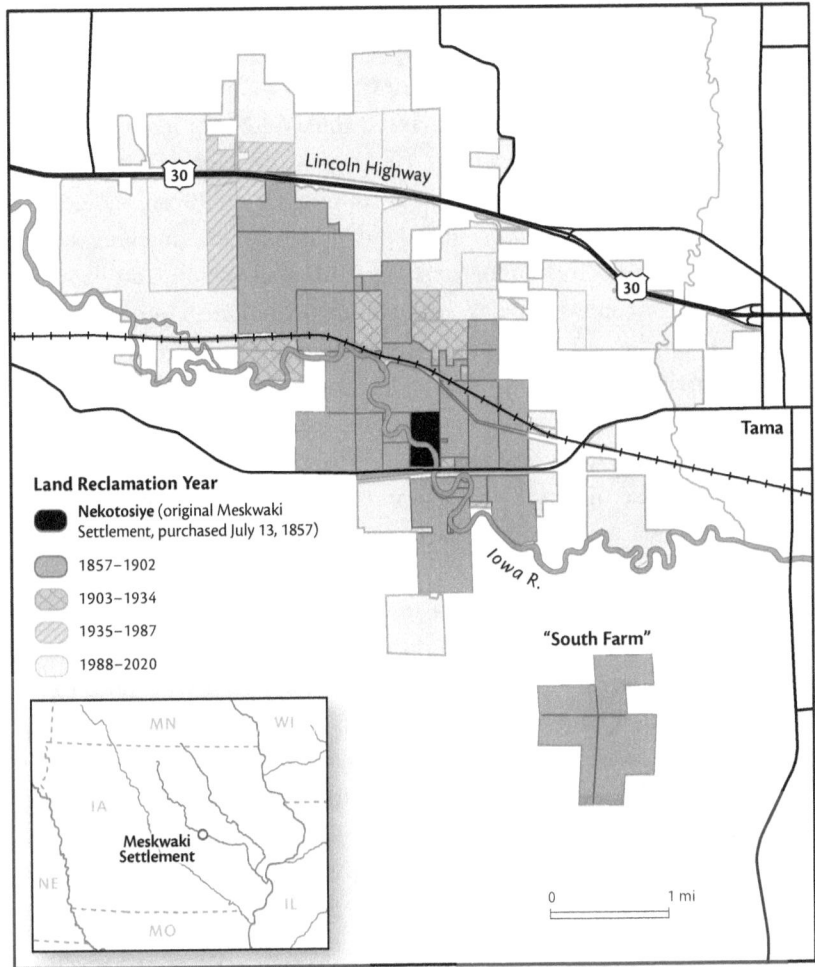

Meskwaki Land Reclamation, 1857–2020
Viewed in the context of ever-diminishing Indigenous landholdings in the United States, the growth of the Meskwaki Settlement since 1857 offers an example of "Native history in reverse." The original purchase totaled 80 acres. Today, the tribe owns more than 8,000 acres, including a 775-acre parcel in Palo Alto County not shown here. Map by Erin Greb Cartography, 2023. Redrawn with permission from a base map and GIS data provided by Joshua Sales, Meskwaki Nation GIS.

property and considered how its ecology and resources could sustain their community over the long term.

Upon graciously reading an early draft of my manuscript, the Oneida scholar Douglas Metoxen Kiel remarked that Meskwaki history felt like "reading Native history in reverse."[53] Geographically speaking, it is hard to disagree: as land across North America continued to fall from Indigenous control in the late nineteenth century, the Meskwaki Settlement expanded outward from a tiny, rectangular acreage into a sprawling land base. Yet Meskwaki history aligns in many ways with the experiences of other Native Nations. The tribe and its people were subject to the same broad policies—assimilation, boarding schools, the undercutting of tribal governance, and more—that affected Indigenous communities everywhere. In that sense, the Meskwaki Nation's story resembles a more conventional telling of Native American political history. These alignments, however, are what make the story of the Meskwaki Settlement such a compelling case study. If it diverged more radically from the rest of Native American history, the Meskwaki story might be interesting to tell, but a "one-off" limited in its utility to speak to the opportunities of the present. Adding a wrinkle to the story of Native land—one of an Indigenous geography in reverse—affords a chance to see exactly where, how, and under what political circumstances the Meskwaki Nation was able to use its land to act with a sense of creative autonomy—that is, to challenge dominant policy paradigms to meet the needs of its people. In that way, Meskwaki history cuts against entrenched narratives that frame Indigenous land and experience exclusively as stories of decline.

With the Landback movement and its antecedents in mind, a close examination of Meskwaki history reveals land as a critical asset in the slow recovery of the Red Earth People and their Meskwaki Nation. Land ownership has not solved all of the tribe's problems. Like any community, the Meskwaki Nation continues to grapple with hard questions and faces deep challenges. But the place we now call Iowa has been a vital resource for the Meskwaki people for over three centuries, and the Settlement has been an important source of political leverage and economic opportunity since 1857.

More broadly, the story of how the prairies, rivers, and forests of the Upper Mississippi became a Meskwaki homeland resonates across Planet Earth. Since at least the 1970s, international bodies like the United Nations have struggled to define the concept of Indigeneity itself.[54] In these debates, questions of land, place, and history—who was where, when, and especially "first"—have mattered very much. There are regions of this world that have been inhabited by more or less the same group of people since the deep past. There are also many Native communities whose cultural and spiritual connections are directly linked to a specific geography. Yet there are also many Indigenous peoples who moved, and often out of necessity. Meskwaki history demonstrates that Indigenous homelands recreated in crisis—and relied upon, in many cases, for bare survival—are no less valid than those culturally rooted, long established, or historically undisrupted. It reminds allies and policymakers to look to Indigenous peoples for guidance as to which lands are most relevant to their experiences and to support the reclamation of those places as a way to support Indigenous recovery.

As readers engage with this history, it is imperative to recognize that for all the opportunities land has created for the Meskwaki Nation, it is secondary to the people themselves. The Meskwaki community has maintained an astounding tradition of resilience over many centuries. It emanates from their clans and ceremonies and has taken many forms. This spiritual dimension of the Meskwaki story is not something I understand or have tried to understand. I believe Meskwaki people and those closest to them when they say that the Red Earth People are inspired to action by their clans, ceremonies, and community. But the available evidence clearly shows that however Meskwaki people viewed their personal or collective connections to the natural world, their commitment to the Settlement has certainly replenished the well of energy that drives Meskwaki people to advocate for their community.

In that sense, *Red Earth Nation* emphasizes the outcomes of the Meskwaki Nation's collective decision-making about its land, both as an environment that offers distinct ecological and economic resources and as a piece of property used as political leverage. Whether or not they believed in American concepts of land and property ownership, the Red Earth People devised ways to work pragmatically within the systems before them to secure, expand, and protect their land and, along the way, to affirm their tribe's sovereignty and create opportunities for self-determination.

This is perhaps best demonstrated in the slow evolution of Meskwaki people's strategic framing of their Settlement and the political authority it has afforded them over time. Examining some four centuries of Meskwaki history reveals gradual changes in the Red Earth People's utilization of environmental resources on and around their Settlement as well as the evolution of how the Meskwaki Nation conceived of the social and political utility of its land.[55] To that end, *Red Earth Nation* also argues that between their arrival on the Upper Mississippi hundreds of years ago and the late twentieth century, Meskwaki people went from articulating Iowa as one in a series of homelands that offered security and sustenance to their tribe to asserting, after 1857, that the unique status and history of their land had exempted them from the meddling of outside governments. Seeking to affirm its authority as a sovereign entity, fully appreciate its people's rights as American citizens, and realize the benefits of the federal trust responsibility, by the latter years of the twentieth century the Meskwaki Nation had reframed the Settlement once again, this time describing it as both a remarkably independent, privately owned Settlement *and* an Indian reservation with a legal status that resembled those across the United States. Constantly reframing the Settlement's political utility in these ways has informed numerous assertions of Meskwaki sovereignty and helped keep the tribe firmly at the boundary of American state and federal authority.[56]

Like every other Native community alive in the twenty-first century, the Meskwaki Nation has endured terrible things and overcome enormous odds. Tribal members have done so much more, placing their community on firm ground and using the relatively anomalous reclamation of their chosen homeland as an anchor for that plodding and tortuous, yet ultimately restorative, work.

The Meskwaki Nation's story stands as a sign of the many ways in which Native peoples have continued to rebuild. If the goal of Indigenous reclamation is about "getting indigenous lands back in indigenous hands," it is also about the long-term recovery of Native Nations. Depending on a tribe's geography, land and water can provide critical footholds for the maintenance and expansion of Indigenous ceremonies and languages and the creation of new opportunities for economic development and capacity building. Along with other reclamation histories, the story of the Meskwaki Settlement allows us to not only see that which was lost but to better understand why and how it is returning.

To tell this story, *Red Earth Nation* proceeds in four parts. The first, "The Red Earth People on the Emerald Horizon," synthesizes oral traditions, oral histories, archaeological evidence, and existing scholarship to offer a new interpretation of the long migration that led Meskwaki people from their creation place on the East Coast to the Upper Mississippi River and its tributaries. All reclamation histories are born in dispossession. To show how Iowa became a Meskwaki homeland, Part 1 explores how, after being nearly annihilated by the Fox Wars that ended in the 1730s, the Red Earth People allied with the Sauk Nation and developed an intricate economy in and near the region we now know as Iowa. This enabled the Red Earth People to stabilize their population and recover, only for the US government to usurp all Sauk and Meskwaki land between 1804 and 1842 while pushing both tribes to the edge of extinction, and then attempting to remove both tribes to a reservation in Kansas.

Part 2, "Settlement Sovereignty," explores how the Red Earth People refused to leave Iowa and began a decade-long effort to remain in their chosen homeland. Removal attempted to sever a deep connection between people and place and, for the first time in a century, slowed the growth of the Meskwaki Nation. In the 1850s, the Meskwaki Nation selected and purchased a small plot of land. From that point forward, the tribe cultivated political relationships and a layered, Settlement-based subsistence economy that enabled them to exist in a state of relative autonomy for four decades. Remarkably, the Meskwaki Settlement continued to grow and maintain a notable degree of political strength throughout the late nineteenth century—an era notorious for the rapid dispossession of Native land and myriad assaults on Indigenous lives and sovereignty.

Part 3, "Erosion," describes major transitions in Meskwaki life in the early twentieth century alongside the steady diminishment of Meskwaki political power. Between 1890 and 1910, federal Indian agents and local Indian reformers inflamed a Meskwaki leadership dispute and transferred the Meskwaki Settlement from its original state-tribal trust into federal trust. Afterward, the United States claimed it could manage the Meskwaki Settlement like any other reservation. Meskwaki people challenged this notion on the grounds that their historic Settlement purchase insulated the tribe and its land from outside interference. In 1902, a federal court decision left the question of jurisdiction and authority over the Meskwaki Settlement ambiguous, and it remained an open question for decades. Nevertheless, by the 1920s, Meskwaki political power had diminished to its historic nadir.

Part 4, "Rebuilding," details the Red Earth People's efforts to restore the economic and political health of their community from the 1930s to the 1970s, emphasizing how land-based strategies proved crucial to those projects. Land ownership was no panacea. But it did offer a vital point of political leverage as the Red Earth People constantly readjusted to fundamental oscillations in federal Indian policy. Since 1857, Meskwaki people had been arguing that their collective ownership of the Settlement should prevent outside incursions into tribal affairs. When the federal government targeted the tribe for termination in the 1950s, however, the tribe selectively embraced the federal trust responsibility to avoid being cut off from federal programs and services that the Red Earth People found helpful. Meanwhile, the Meskwaki economy struggled. Tribal members took advantage of everything from New Deal programs to military service, off-Settlement wage work, and Great Society initiatives as they attempted to provide for their families. Facing entrenched challenges, by the 1970s the Meskwaki Nation developed an economic development plan that aimed to restore the Meskwaki economy on tribal land.

The epilogue, titled "Recovery," examines the gradual and uneven restoration of the Meskwaki Nation's economic and political fortunes. The tribe implemented an on-Settlement bingo, casino, and hospitality venture in the 1980s and 1990s. In the era that followed, the Meskwaki Nation became the largest employer in the county and made enormous investments in education, infrastructure, its land, and its people. This included language and cultural programs, a robust food sovereignty initiative, and an expansive, diversified economic development strategy that supported the tribal and regional economy. These initiatives have improved the standard of living for the Red Earth People and restored the Meskwaki Nation's political position vis-à-vis the local, state, and federal governments around it. But the recovery of the Meskwaki Nation has been neither simple nor linear, and *Red Earth Nation* ends by situating a 2003 controversy over control of the tribe's gaming industry within the broader historical context of the Red Earth People's ongoing conversations about land ownership and what it means for tribal sovereignty and self-determination in the twenty-first century.

The history of the Meskwaki Nation reveals that land reclamation is a vital first step in a long, strategic process that can create a wide array of political and economic opportunities for Native Nations. Yet Meskwaki history also suggests that reclaiming Indigenous land in and of itself will not solve the many challenges tribes face today. It reminds us that across space, place, and time, Native peoples in the United States have been forced to battle—stream by stream, prairie by prairie, and sacred site by sacred site—to reclaim and affirm their authority over their land. It demonstrates that through thoughtful and patient negotiation of their land and an awareness of what land reclamation does and does not offer, tribes can continue to carve paths toward restoration.

The story of the Meskwaki Settlement offers one possible solution to a problem stated by the Meskwaki leader Wapello, who sat at a treaty table in 1841 and saw what was bearing down on his people. "This land is all we have. It is our only fortune," he said. "When it is gone, we shall have nothing left."[57]

He might have been speaking for Native peoples everywhere.

The next year, 1842, Wapello died and the Red Earth People lost their land. Fifteen years after that, a Meskwaki man rode his horse to a farmhouse along the Iowa River. His people bought a small piece of that farm and, on it, rebuilt the Meskwaki Nation.

PART I

The Red Earth People on the Emerald Horizon

"We govern by the appointment of the Great Spirit, and by the will of the nation. This land was given to us to do with as we please. After the Great Spirit made this vast island, he placed the chiefs upon it, he gave us the sun and moon and stars and all the great lights; he gave us the beasts of the field and the birds that fly for our meat and for our dresses. He made the trees and gave names to them for our benefit, and he not only gave us these but he gave us the great medicine bag and everything you see to make us a great people."

—Poweshiek, 1842

CHAPTER 1

Wisaka's Arrow

An arrow soared through the open sky, hundreds, maybe thousands, of feet above the ground. It bent in a long, slow arc toward the lush tallgrass prairies of the American Midwest. Moments earlier, it had been nocked into the sinewy draw of a handmade bow and pulled back with an otherworldly force. Upon its release the arrow shot westward, charting a path from somewhere in present-day Quebec that the Red Earth People would follow over the next several centuries.

This arrow belonged to a son of Gisha Manitou—the chief manitou, or spirit being—named Wisaka. He was the same being who had sometime before dug deep into the red earth of North America's Eastern Seaboard and from it made the Meskwaki people.

According to longtime Meskwaki Tribal Historian Johnathan Buffalo, Wisaka taught the Red Earth People "how to speak, how to behave, how to treat each other, and how to treat other people." He also imparted to them knowledge about "the universe, the history of the world, and gave [them] feelings of good and bad." He instructed his people how to hunt, fight, and live. When the arrow began its climb, Wisaka told his people to watch. He told them that they would soon have to follow the projectile to a distant and unknown land. The people protested, arguing that their rightful home remained in the East, near the sea. But Wisaka persisted, affirming that they must go west. One day, he said, the Red Earth People could return to their homeland.[1]

Over the course of several hundred years, the search for Wisaka's legendary dart led the Red Earth People on a winding path from Canada and through the Great Lakes. It brought them into a region that included all

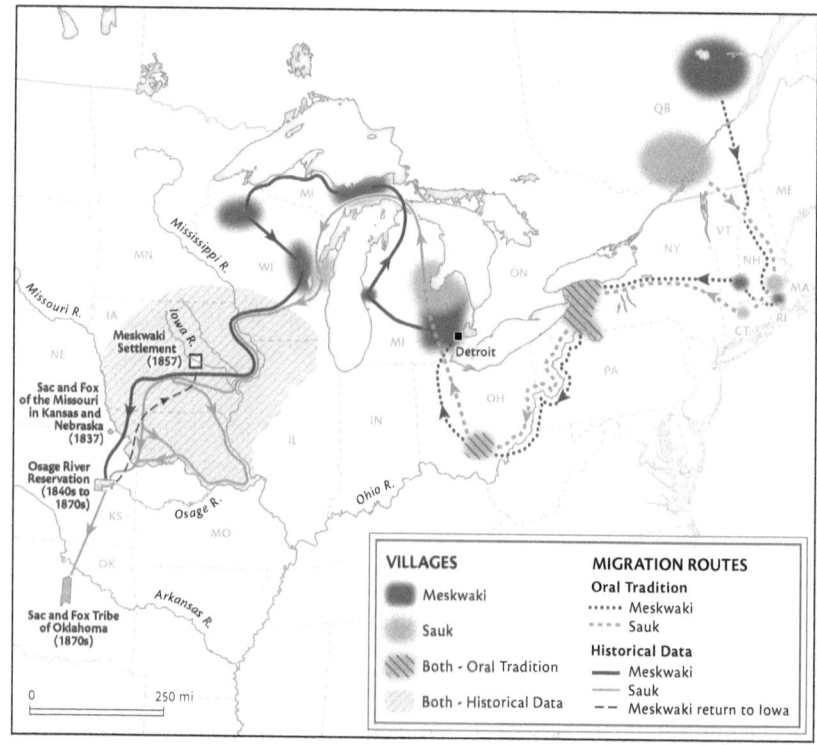

Meskwaki and Sauk Migrations, 1600–1870s
Overlaying historical and archaeological evidence with oral traditions sketches the migration of the Meskwaki and Sauk Nations. Over the course of nearly three centuries, both tribes made their way from their respective creation places in the Northeast, moving west along the Great Lakes, eventually reaching the Midwest. Map by Erin Greb Cartography, 2023. Redrawn with permission from a reference map by Meskwaki Nation GIS and EarthView Environmental, Inc.

the land and water from present-day northeastern Minnesota south along the east bank of the Mississippi River to Missouri, then eastward across the Great Lakes to the border between what are now Ohio and Pennsylvania. For centuries, this immense expanse was home to sprawling networks of Indigenous commerce and diplomacy. It probably had many Native names, but Euro-Americans who entered the Great Lakes area likely called it Anishinaabewaki, or "Indian Country."[2] The area became known to French fur traders as the *pays d'en haut* ("Upper Country") and later "New France."

The British considered it part of the province of Quebec. As the United States expanded deeper into the continent, settlers started referring to the area as the Northwest Territory. Today, most historians just call it the Old Northwest.[3]

The European quest for North American resources led to a long, brutal migration for the Red Earth People, beginning around the year 1600. Over the next 250 years, successive generations of Meskwaki people faced constant pressures to move, fight, and adapt in a world destabilized by disease, warfare, and ever-shifting alliances. Reflecting on the challenges his ancestors endured, Meskwaki elder Donald Wanatee noted, "As far as I know, each time they moved, their economy, political life, and social life [were] damaged beyond repair."[4]

Eventually, Wisaka's arrow landed more than a thousand miles away, in the heart of what would become Iowa. Johnathan Buffalo underscores Wisaka's promise that the Meskwaki people will one day return to their home by the sea. "We are in the process of going back home," he said, "Iowa has been our home for more than a hundred years. . . . [and] has become a place of safety." When the Red Earth People acquired their land in 1857, they selected a parcel of rich, hilly forests and wetlands bifurcated by the Iowa River. They have "been there ever since, in our home, in our Settlement."[5] This small, verdant parcel was a slice of a vast Meskwaki homeland the people remade out of colonial necessity.

THE TIME OF OUR SURROUNDED

The details of the Red Earth People's long westward trek are opaque. Generations of scholars and Meskwaki people have worked together, setting oral traditions alongside the archaeological and documentary records. This work sketches contours, however imprecise. Scholars, for example, estimate that by the 1600s the Meskwaki population was somewhere between 1,000 and 12,000 people. Oral traditions go even higher, suggesting that before contact, the tribe numbered as many as 22,000.[6] These stories place the Red Earth People by the North Atlantic, living along the St. Lawrence River around Quebec, Canada. "One day the enemy came," Buffalo explained, and "we think they were the Iroquois." These enemies pushed the Red Earth People south into Ohio, and that was "the first memory we have, traditional memories of living in Ohio. We were moving with the other Algonquin [language speakers]—our cousins in the Sauk, Kickapoo, Shawnee; that bunch."[7]

Meskwaki families spent a significant amount of time in Ohio and Michigan and ventured into the British colonies in New England. There, the Red Earth People may have visited the Massachusetts Bay Colony, which had been chartered in 1629 and settled in 1630. "But the English never recorded that meeting," Buffalo said, relaying oral histories passed down over many generations. Because French trappers documented an encounter with Meskwaki travelers around 1640, "that is more or less our contact date, when we became a tribe, because when anthropologists pronounce you a tribe," he continued sardonically, "that is when you become a tribe. Before that you are a conflict."[8]

These stories align with movements detailed by historians and archaeologists. Pushed along by European expansion, Meskwaki people made their way to what is now the border between Michigan and northwestern Ohio.[9] By the 1640s, warfare with other Native Nations pushed the Meskwaki Nation into eastern Wisconsin. At various times, Meskwaki rivals included members of the Haudenosaunee (Iroquois), Anishinaabe (Ojibwe), Dakota, and Illini Nations. By 1667, the Red Earth People had moved north to Lake Superior's Chequamegon Bay.[10] Over subsequent decades, Meskwaki bands established villages along riparian corridors, and they controlled trade in central Wisconsin into the 1700s.[11] These Red Earth People were, as Buffalo put it, "the last Meskwaki who could see, when they looked at the sky, that it was still a Meskwaki world. It was not a Frenchman's yet."[12]

In Wisconsin, the Red Earth People were one of several Indigenous groups who vied for control of territory, waterways, and resources. One predominately Meskwaki hub near present-day Oshkosh, Wisconsin, was known as the "Grand Village of the Meskwaki." The Red Earth People occupied the town, founded around 1680, with some Sauk, Illini, and Potawatomi relatives for about fifty years.[13]

Relationships, exchange, and camaraderie characterized Indigenous life in Anishinaabewaki. The region was also shaped by delicate diplomacy, expansive commerce, ever-shifting alliances, and deep rivalries between members of myriad Native tribes, including the Meskwaki, Sauk, Myaamiaki (Miami), Potawatomi, Kickapoo, Ho-Chunk, Anishinaabe, Dakota, and Mascouten Nations. Archaeological evidence speaks to Indigenous relationships at Prairie du Chien—the French name for the place where the Wisconsin River flows into the Mississippi—and hints at a form of diplomatic balance in the region. No early permanent settlement appears to have existed at this otherwise ideal location, leading one archaeologist to posit that Indigenous groups utilized the area as a neutral trading zone long before European arrival.[14]

Yet Europeans had already influenced this Indigenous world. French traders established themselves along the northern reaches of the Atlantic coast. British colonies cropped up farther south. In the Old Northwest, French and Spanish explorers traveled and traded between the Great Lakes and the Mississippi River. To do so, they cultivated delicate relationships with Native communities, many of which were reeling from diseases that had extended west long before whites. Populations collapsed as sickness and migration reconfigured the North American interior. French traders and a few Catholic missionaries came to Anishinaabewaki in the 1630s. There, they solidified alliances with many tribes, often by offering gifts and goods, mutual political support, and promises of military defense to those pushed west and weakened by violence.[15] By the 1680s, the French had established prominent trading posts near Prairie du Chien.[16]

Within about twenty years, the success of these French outposts had stressed the ecosystems Indigenous peoples relied upon in Wisconsin. Traveling farther west to hunt, the Red Earth People crossed the Mississippi River for the first time around the year 1700. This was their first expansion into what we now call Iowa—a swirling green ocean of tallgrass prairies, deciduous woodlands, and snaking streams that Cornelia Mutel called "the emerald horizon."[17] These hunting trips solidified Iowa as a significant place for the Red Earth People.[18]

These early Meskwaki forays into Iowa did not last long. Between 1712 and 1733, the Meskwaki Nation nearly disintegrated amid a long, bloody conflict. "History calls it the Fox Wars," said Tribal Historian Johnathan Buffalo, before clarifying that his people call the conflict by a Meskwaki name translating roughly to "the time of our surrounded" because every tribe in a hundred-mile radius had aligned itself with the French—and against the Meskwaki Nation.[19]

Times were certainly tense. Around the turn of the eighteenth century, French trade policy and the fallout from earlier violence and migrations had left central Wisconsin in a state of constant recalibration. The Meskwaki

Nation maintained a strong position and challenged the ability of France and its Indigenous allies to access riverine trade lines between Green Bay and the Mississippi River. Meskwaki people also resented the work of Catholic missionaries and chafed at the French Crown's expectation that they camp near French trade outposts and adhere to the new regional order.[20]

Over time, these disagreements fomented a deep animosity between France and the Meskwaki Nation. It led to two decades of terrible violence. Throughout the "time of our surrounded," the Red Earth People fought French invaders and their Native allies over territorial control and access to trade routes. A bloody three-week siege ensued at Detroit in 1712, as Meskwaki people battled French, Ottawa, Potawatomi, Huron, Peoria, and Anishinaabe fighters. Battered and starving, the residents of the Meskwaki villages attempted an escape. Their enemies followed. The fighting continued for several more days and quickly turned to slaughter. Around a thousand Meskwaki people and their Kickapoo and Mascouten allies perished.[21]

The Meskwaki survivors rejoined their relatives in Wisconsin. For the next twenty years, the Red Earth People continued to challenge the growing French influence in the region. They repeatedly raided forts and disrupted the goods and movements of the French and their allies.[22] Over time, the Red Earth People negotiated a loose alliance with the British, who had expanded farther west and saw the interior as another theater in an old colonial rivalry with France. These new British interlocutors encouraged the Meskwaki Nation to disrupt French expansion into Anishinaabewaki.[23]

The French, meanwhile, undertook a series of aggressive military campaigns between 1716 and the early 1730s, with the aim of eliminating the Red Earth People entirely. They nearly succeeded, and a series of French victories left most Meskwaki people either dead or enslaved by a rival tribe in 1733.[24] By then, only about 200 Red Earth People remained alive. As few as half that number walked free.[25]

RELATIVES

Faced with the total annihilation of their people in 1733, Meskwaki leaders sought security. The Red Earth People allied themselves with the Asakiwakis, or Sauk Nation. Like the Meskwaki Nation, the Sauk people's name for themselves was a reference to their homeland along the Saginaw River, where Sauk families resided around 1600. It translates to "People of the Yellow Earth."[26] Despite their many similarities and the deep bonds of kinship that would develop in the 1730s, the Meskwaki and Sauk Nations maintained degrees of clear separation, with separate councils and villages usually set a short distance apart. Nonetheless, after the Fox Wars, the two nations became close allies who would travel together for more than a century.[27]

The Meskwaki and Sauk Nations resembled one another in several ways. Some of these were cultural and linguistic. Members of both tribes spoke very similar dialects from the Algonquin language family.[28] Clan bundles, which passed down through the generations, offered spiritual nourishment. Tribal members were born into these clans, and each tribe had complex rules that imbued clan members with ceremonial and communal roles and responsibilities. These systems promoted balance and stability within each tribe. The connections between their villages, meanwhile, facilitated intermarriages between Meskwaki and Sauk people. This further solidified the kinship bonds and political confederacy between the two nations.[29]

Politically speaking, the Sauk and Meskwaki tribes were united in other ways. First, they both maintained an enduring suspicion of Europeans. Indeed, the two nations stood out among the Indigenous tribes of the Old Northwest for their exceedingly cautious approach to colonial alliances. Both staunchly rejected religious conversion and assimilation. In contrast to tribes that more wholly allied with French and British interests, the Sauk and Meskwaki Nations embraced European interests only when doing so met tribal needs, and they more freely rejected colonial authority.[30]

These tribes had similar systems of governance. Each was led by a "chief's council." These bodies met to make decisions about the welfare of their respective communities. Sauk and Meskwaki war chiefs were called upon to lead hunts, engage in raids, or defend their villages. In times of peace, however, authority rested with civil chiefs (often called "village chiefs" or "peace chiefs"). Meskwaki and Sauk men inherited these positions from their fathers and transferred them to descendants along specific clan lines.[31]

For the Red Earth People, the chief's council was composed of men representing about eight tribal clans. In later years, anthropologists would count twice as many clans; these groups disappeared or grew alongside fluctuations in the Meskwaki population. The peace chiefs usually descended from the "Mucqua, or Bear, clan," while members of the "Wahgohagi, or Fox clan" served as war chiefs. But these rules were not rigid. Another group, the "Neneemekee, or Thunder people," for example, could be either village or war chiefs. But Thunder people, along with members of several other clan groups, did not normally fill powerful leadership roles.[32]

The Meskwaki and Sauk councils adhered to decentralized, consensus-based decision-making systems. According to Johnathan Buffalo, no single leader governed as an absolute ruler of the Meskwaki Nation. Instead, leaders gained and wielded influence by cultivating respect within their community. Although clan membership was hereditary, power did not flow directly from the chieftainship. Instead, Meskwaki clan and political leaders guided tribal members by exemplifying strong leadership and a commitment to the entire tribe.[33]

Nevertheless, only council members were involved in producing final decisions, which they encouraged tribal members to follow. Most of the time, Meskwaki people adhered to the council's guidance, and this system allowed the tribe to exist in a state of relative order and cohesion.[34] Yet the decentralized nature of Sauk and Meskwaki governance also had its limits. Even the most senior leaders lacked the power to force individuals—much less groups of people—to follow the guidance of the chiefs.[35] As more and more settlers arrived in Anishinaabewaki, this lack of central authority would prove a catalyst of dispossession.

STABILITY ON THE UPPER MISSISSIPPI

In the decades after "the time of our surrounded," Meskwaki people scattered by bloodshed and enslavement found an opportunity for healing. Some married traders or other Native peoples. Most returned to the Mississippi River valley and the surrounding territory. There, they reestablished villages near their Sauk relatives. By the middle of the eighteenth century, Sauk and Meskwaki people had found refuge on the western outskirts of Anishinaabewaki, along the Des Moines and Wapsipinicon Rivers. They traveled back into Wisconsin but had returned to the northeastern corner of what would become Iowa by the 1780s. There, they established towns along the Mississippi River. The Red Earth People set up on the western bank, while their Sauk relatives camped on the opposite side.[36]

If joining with their Sauk relatives created an opportunity for Meskwaki people to enjoy a period of relative social and political safety, life on the emerald horizon offered a chance to recuperate. Resources available on the Iowa landscape supported an annual economic cycle that could rejuvenate their community. From their villages on the Iowa side of the Mississippi, Meskwaki families lived off a seasonal round of hunting and agriculture enriched by participation in the fur and mineral trades. They spent the spring and summer in small towns composed of large, rectangular homes. In early spring, the Red Earth People tapped maple trees for sap, and women began planting gardens in the rich Iowa soil. Men hunted birds and fished the streams. Families departed the village for a short summer hunt, harvesting elk and bison as the crops grew, and returned for the autumn harvest. Then the Meskwaki community divided into family groups and left for winter hunts, where they focused on deer. For months, they would occupy mobile camps, resting in smaller dome-shaped homes called wicki-ups. During the day, they searched for deer and other game along the rambling Mississippi tributaries.[37]

Consolidating in Iowa and relying on its gardens and hunts enabled the Meskwaki Nation to steadily increase its population. The Red Earth People and the Yellow Earth People relied on one another for mutual support and camaraderie. Each focused on their seasonal round, deepened their participation in the regional trade economy, and continued to grow.[38] Indeed, by about 1800, around 5,300 Sauk people were living on the Illinois side of the Mississippi. By then, the Meskwaki Nation had rebounded from only 200 survivors of the Fox Wars to a population of around 1,600 people.[39]

This achievement lent credence to the defiant words of a Meskwaki war chief named Pemoussa, who had warned the French attackers during the siege at Detroit generations earlier: "Know ye, that the Foxes are immortal."[40]

RIVALRIES

For the Meskwaki and Sauk Nations, the century after the Fox Wars was a time of growth and rehabilitation. It deepened the Red Earth People's sense of rootedness in eastern Iowa. But it was not an era of tranquility. Members of both tribes farmed, hunted, and traded with a cautious eye on the unpredictable and ever-changing set of European and Indigenous influences that kept the alliances of Anishinaabewaki in a state of flux.

From 1754 to 1763, France and Great Britain were embroiled in the Seven Years' War. The immediate origins of this conflict reached back to the 1740s, when territorial wars in Europe expanded as France and Great Britain battled for control of colonial outposts across the world. The Seven Years' War saw violence in Europe, India, Africa, the Philippines, and the Caribbean. In the North American interior, it focused on New France, which included all the French-claimed territory from Nova Scotia to New Orleans. Great Britain maintained its hold on its Atlantic coast colonies and around the Hudson Bay, while Spain claimed sovereignty over what are now Florida and Mexico.[41] Each of these assertions of dominion had its genesis in the "Discovery Doctrine," which had articulated the European rationale for taking Indigenous land.[42]

During the Seven Years' War, France relied on the strength of its army, which was bolstered by its network of alliances with Indigenous tribes throughout North America. These tribes, of course, maintained their own systems of territorial control. Their alliances with colonial powers only loosely regarded foreigners' concepts of, and claims to, European dominion. Nevertheless, the strong ties between France and various Native Nations who fought alongside them led many British colonists to label the conflict the "French and Indian War." Despite the ferocity of these French and Indigenous fighters, British naval superiority eventually pushed France to negotiate for peace. In the 1763 Treaty of Paris, France ceded nearly all its holdings in North America to the British. The agreement also solidified British control over Florida, while Spain received Louisiana, a huge territory west of the Mississippi River and south toward Mexico.[43]

On the ground, the evolution of political boundaries had a limited immediate impact on the Sauk and Meskwaki Nations. Battles occurred hundreds of miles from their villages. The Red Earth People tacitly embraced the Spanish and British presence on the Upper Mississippi. Meskwaki people, after all, had little regard for the French Crown, which had attempted their extermination barely a generation before. "We still think highly of the British," Meskwaki Tribal Historian Johnathan Buffalo said, "because they treated us better," and the Meskwaki Nation had few qualms with the Spanish.[44]

The Red Earth People's support for Great Britain, however, had waned after the Crown implemented new policies in 1763. Despite its deep rivalry with the Meskwaki Nation, the French government had cemented its relationships across Anishinaabewaki through patient diplomacy. Among other things, it demonstrated reciprocal partnership and regularly bestowed extravagant gifts upon Indigenous leaders. When France lost the Seven Years' War and ceded its claims in the region, many tribes sought to restart this process with the British. Initially, however, the British Crown refused to see Native Nations as partners and allies, viewing them instead as vanquished enemies.[45] This sparked conflict almost immediately, and the British spent two years fighting a coalition of Indigenous people guided by the Ottawa leader Pontiac, who rejected British policies in the eastern Great Lakes. After Pontiac's War ended in 1765, the British began to emulate the French strategy, restoring a tenuous order in the region.[46]

CONTINUITY

For all the changes underway in the Old Northwest after 1763, some elements of life endured. The French Crown no longer claimed Anishinaabewaki. But European title and actual territorial control were two different things. In the decades after 1763, even as they struck diplomatic and trade alliances with British administrators, Native Nations forced the redcoats to abandon much of the region. French fur traders, who had a century's worth of relationships and political experience working with Indigenous tribes, reestablished more than fifty trading posts in the western Great Lakes in the latter half of the eighteenth century. These encampments served as centers of exchange frequented by representatives from nearly a dozen Native communities, including the Sauk and Meskwaki Nations. Many of the outposts and villages were also home to families of mixed French and Indigenous heritage, which maintained French influence in the region and helped stabilize some Indigenous family lines.[47]

Indigenous warfare marked another continuity. These were not campaigns fought by ships and armies on a global scale. Nor was the violence aimed at colonizing far-flung properties or eradicating entire peoples. Instead, as Meskwaki and Sauk families worked to restore their populations in their villages, their men reengaged in raids against other Native Nations.

Conflicts settled disputes to control trade routes and hunting grounds. Sauk and Meskwaki bands tussled with other tribes into the 1820s.[48]

In the last decades of the eighteenth century, Sauk and Meskwaki people fought against Niutachi (Missouria) peoples for control over access to southern hunting grounds along the waterways west of St. Louis. Passing through the region in the summer of 1804, the American explorer, and later Indian agent, William Clark recounted in his diary a tale of Sauk ferocity. According to the story, Sauk fighters killed three hundred Niutachi people in a single battle. By the time of his writing, Clark claimed, only about eighty Niutachi people survived after an era of protracted warfare with various Mississippi River tribes.[49] Clark later wrote that Sauk and Meskwaki bands fought regularly with members of the Ioway and Dakota Nations and tribes farther west of the Mississippi, like the Osage Nation. He described Sauk and Meskwaki people as "extremely friendly to the whites, and seldom injure their traders; but they are the most implacable enemies to the Indian nations with whom they are at war." Clark also claimed that the Sauk and Meskwaki Nations were responsible for "the almost entire destruction" of several Native Nations in the region.[50]

Along the Mississippi River, as in much of the American West, rivalries and alliances within and between tribes reflected pragmatic responses to a fluid geopolitical landscape. Clark's observations overemphasized the violent nature of Indigenous competition for land and resources. He overlooked the role that diseases like smallpox played in the devastation heaped upon Indigenous peoples. That virus, for example, had killed many Niutachi people during the era Clark described. This, not just raids by Meskwaki and Sauk fighters, led them to ally with Jiwere (Otoe) peoples.[51] Clark also ignored important differences between the goals and forms of Indigenous and Euro-American violence and obscured the regularity with which tribes sought alliance and peace. Upon establishing their villages on the Upper Mississippi, for example, the Sauk and Meskwaki tribes negotiated a three-way agreement of mutual support with regional Ioways. All three Nations felt the stresses of overhunting, which were exacerbated by successive Indigenous migrations and the increasing number of settlers in their region. Scarcity bred competition and war. Out of necessity, the three tribes agreed to share hunting grounds and to work together to protect this common territory from enemy Nations.[52]

Warfare between tribes reverberated across the generations. By the 1830s, old rivalries would bring devastating consequences to the Sauk and Meskwaki Nations. Yet Native Nations were not the only people fighting in North America. In the 1770s, another British war brought a new actor to the Old Northwest.

LONG KNIVES

Just a few months after finalizing the Treaty of Paris with France, the British Crown issued the Royal Proclamation of 1763. This decree formally absorbed North American land won during the Seven Years' War. It also recognized that Indigenous tribes retained title to their lands in North America until they chose to cede it to the British government. The document established the rule of preemption, which reserved the right to acquire Native land to the Crown. Importantly, the proclamation also officially prohibited British subjects from settling west of the Appalachian Mountains. All of this aimed to prevent violence between British settlers and the many Native Nations who, along with French traders, still occupied the lands between the mountains and the Mississippi. Colonists, many of whom were squatting on Native land past the western "Proclamation Line," viewed this as a tyrannical restriction on westward expansion.[53]

The Crown's approach to Indian affairs was among many policies that grated on the American colonists in the lead up to the War for Independence.[54] During that conflict, most Native tribes supported the British. Existing trade relationships and favorable land policies likely contributed to their decisions. Nonetheless, some Native Nations either aligned themselves with the Americans or attempted to avoid the conflict altogether.[55]

Meskwaki leaders preferred neutrality. For one thing, the action of the American Revolution was far away and relatively inconsequential to the day-to-day lives of the Red Earth People. At the time, the Meskwaki Nation was engaged in territorial conflicts with bands of Dakota, Missouri, Jiwere, and Osage peoples along the Mississippi. Then, as Johnathan Buffalo put it, "a new type of white people was born. They were called Americans," and the tribe referred to them with a word that meant "long knife." The British asked for support from the Meskwaki Nation, but "even though" some members of both tribes "fought in the Revolutionary War as individuals, it was tribal policy to keep out." In the eyes of the chief's council, the best approach would be to simply "let them fight."[56]

Other historians have argued that the Meskwaki and Sauk Nations, like many tribes in Anishinaabewaki, allied with the British.[57] Even when they did, the two tribes' participation in the war was limited and unenthusiastic. The British, for example, pressured the Sauk and Meskwaki tribes to send fighters to help them attack St. Louis in the spring of 1780, in one of the far-flung battles of the War for Independence. Spanish and American forces had allied against the British along the Mississippi. Because the Meskwaki and Sauk Nations each had strong Spanish ties that reached back two decades, however, neither tribe was particularly aggressive in the assault, and the British lost. This nuance was lost on French, Spanish, and American residents of St. Louis, however, who launched a retaliatory assault on a Sauk village on the Upper Mississippi in June 1780.[58]

In Buffalo's account, the Meskwaki Nation's perspective on the War for Independence was straightforward: "Unfortunately," he told an interviewer, "the Americans won."[59]

INDIGENOUS POWER

When the War for Independence ended in 1783, many Indigenous tribes across Anishinaabewaki likely agreed with the Red Earth People's assessment. Most already observed the Americans with a wary and distrustful eye. They also waited to see how the outcome of the conflict, and the creation of a new colonial power, might affect the status quo.[60] Across the interior, Native Nations had chosen sides between the British and Americans as they navigated the disruption brought by war. Their decisions spun an intricate web of competing interests and alliances. Indeed, the American Revolution was both devastating and destabilizing for many Native Nations, especially those closest to the front.[61]

But the war did not eliminate Indigenous influence in the East—to say nothing of the West, where Native peoples controlled expansive territories and trade networks.[62] Indeed, in the Old Northwest, both the war and its aftermath felt familiar to tribes who had experienced the Seven Years' War. The Americans defeated the British and, on paper, claimed all the land west toward the Mississippi. But Indigenous tribes usually won the skirmishes on their western homelands, retaining their influence and territory in the region. Meanwhile, British interests remained in the area well into the 1790s, as the United States lacked the money, might, or political will to force them out. This fed the friction that would lead to another war by 1812.[63]

Despite these realities, the Americans attempted to assert unilateral authority over Indigenous peoples. The United States claimed that, as victors and conquerors, it could take Native land at will.[64] Violence continued well after the war ended in 1783. Under the Articles of Confederation—the legal framework that preceded the US Constitution—the United States forced a few dispossessive treaties upon Haudenosaunees (Iroquois), Shawnees, Ottawas, Lenape (Delawares), Cherokees, Chickasaws, and several other tribes in the mid-1780s.[65]

But the young nation was racked with debt and experimenting with a new, decentralized government. It faced the threat of rebellion from some dissatisfied citizens, and federal authority had been neither fully defined nor demonstrated. American leaders quickly recognized their weaknesses, and diplomatic relations grew strained between the United States and an Indigenous coalition including the Shawnee, Lenape, Myaamiaki, and other Native Nations in the Ohio Territory, just as the US government was attempting to raise money by selling land to speculators. Recognizing that his country could not afford a war with a group of confederated Native Nations, the secretary of war convinced Congress to acquiesce to tribal demands for a large meeting along the Detroit River in late 1786, where governmental officials and tribal leaders could negotiate.[66] This meeting did not bring peace, and a protracted series of conflicts known as the Northwest Indian War raged through Ohio between 1786 and 1795.[67]

These disagreements festered as the United States developed the Northwest Ordinance of 1787. In that document, the Continental Congress expressed, at least rhetorically, a general respect for tribes and their territory in the western reaches of the United States, declaring that "the utmost good faith shall always be observed towards the Indians; their land and property shall never be taken from them without their consent." It also promised that the Americans would neither invade nor disturb tribal land unless Congress had authorized a war.[68] The Ordinance, however, also articulated a plan for organizing the Northwest Territory into American states, effectively announcing the United States' intentions to settle on tribal lands just a few lines below affirming its respect for Indigenous sovereignty.[69]

The same year it adopted the Northwest Ordinance, the United States drafted its new Constitution, which the states ratified in 1789. In that document, the US government once again affirmed its recognition of tribal sovereignty. "The Congress," reads Article I, Section 8, "shall have Power.... To regulate Commerce with foreign Nations, and among the several States, and with the Indian Tribes."[70] Together, these documents provided the legal framework that would facilitate federal Indian policy for the next several decades. The Constitution affirmed tribal sovereignty and empowered the federal government to treat—and war—with Native Nations. The Northwest Ordinance, meanwhile, articulated the Americans' plan to buy up and settle Indigenous lands. Going forward, the United States could try to convince tribes to cede land. When that failed, it used dishonesty and pressure to acquire Native property. From the perspective of American officials, these land cessions were final and legal, and if tribes violated these agreements, the United States could justifiably deploy violence to enforce them.[71]

Like the British, the Americans learned the hard way that European conceptions of conquest and spoils did not align with the realities of Indigenous strength in the West. In the first years of the new republic, funding Indian wars proved a major federal spending priority.[72] These skirmishes produced mixed results. In some cases, Native Nations handily beat the American army; in others, the United States acquired Native land. By the middle of the 1790s, however, the Americans had won key contests along the Great Lakes. This secured vital geographical footholds for the United States. The federal government, meanwhile, struggled to constrain and control the steady advance of non-Natives flooding west to settle and speculate along the western frontier.[73]

Against this broader backdrop of American encroachment into the Northwest Territory, the Meskwaki and Sauk Nations joined the Indigenous coalition in Ohio to fight against the United States. Their reasons for doing so remain murky. After all, both tribes were comparatively small and had long ago moved far west of the Ohio Territory. Indeed, from a European perspective, the Meskwaki villages on the western bank of the Mississippi sat under Spanish domain and would not become an American claim until the Louisiana Purchase in 1803. One historian postulates that the Red Earth People and Yellow Earth People had a general distaste for the US government that had festered in Sauk and Meskwaki villages since the War for Independence.[74] Whatever their motivations, some Sauk and Meskwaki people would continue to stoke resentment toward the United States for years to come.[75]

Meanwhile, the American effort to free up Native land for sale to speculators had hardly subsided. American settlers sought to acquire land more aggressively than their European predecessors.[76] Congress, however, had also recognized that despite the early American hubris in the Old Northwest, Native Nations could not be easily defeated. By the late 1790s, the United States saw that it would be cheaper to negotiate for Native land than to fight for it. The Americans continued to observe a policy that, however imperfectly, recognized Indigenous authority and influence throughout the interior.[77] But, as it grew stronger, the United States developed and refined a system that used law and policy to chip away at Native land holdings.

LAND THAT PROVIDES

Meskwaki life during the first half century of the United States' existence was characterized by the use and exchange of natural resources in and near what became Iowa. The seasonal planting, hunting, and fishing round supplied calories, furs, and skins. According to a description penned by William Clark during the winter of 1804–1805, the Sauk and Meskwaki Nations "raise[d] an abundance of corn, beans and melons: they sometimes hunted in the country west of them, towards the Missouri, but their principal hunting [was] on both sides of the Mississippi, from the mouth of the [W]isconsin to the mouth of the Illinois river."[78]

Around that time, Sauk and Meskwaki families spread out in a series of villages. Sauk people generally lived on the east side of the Mississippi and south of Rock Island, from the Rock River south toward the mouth of the Des Moines River. Their main village, Saukenauk, had over two hundred summer lodges, each of which could be occupied by as many as twenty relatives at a time. Meskwaki people lived in about eight smaller villages from the Turkey River, in the area around Dubuque, across northeastern Iowa toward the Wapsipinicon. Together, these locations had about eighty-two lodges.[79]

Members of both tribes also continued to engage in the fur trade, as operators like the St. Louis-based Spanish Commercial Company, the Canadian North West Company, and, later, the dominant American Fur Company relied on Indigenous labor and networks to produce and move trade goods, pelts, and cash throughout the Upper Mississippi and beyond.[80] Indeed, the Red Earth People traveled along extensive trading lines. Upon visiting sáhniš (Arikara) villages along the Missouri River near what is now the border of North Dakota and South Dakota in the fall of 1804, Clark included a band of "Fox Indians"—likely Meskwaki people—among a list of ten tribes who had traveled hundreds of miles, bringing "Horses & robes" to trade.[81]

Lead mining was another critical component of this resource-based Meskwaki economy. Early Indigenous peoples' archaeological footprint suggests that they had been pulling galena, or lead sulfide, from the dirt near Catfish Creek in northeastern Iowa for around 8,000 years.[82] Early on, lead ore was a valued trade item because it could be mixed with other ingredients to produce dark paint. Native peoples from a wide region also bartered for Upper Mississippi ore to use in ceremonies.[83]

As their migration brought them farther west toward the Mississippi River, Sauk and Meskwaki families—alongside bands of Ho-Chunks—were arriving in the Upper Mississippi lead fields by the mid-1700s. One French traveler who visited a Sauk band in the 1760s, for example, claimed to have seen sizable amounts of the ore lying in the village streets.[84] By then, French traders had known about the galena deposits for more than a century. They first heard about the mines from members of a Dakota band in the 1650s. By then, archaeologists argue, Native peoples were already mining and smelting the ore.[85]

By the 1770s, the Red Earth People controlled most of the mines on the Iowa side of the river. Lead mining was exhausting, and Meskwaki women did most of the work, occasionally assisted by boys or elder men. The women's first task was to find a potential seam, for which they relied on their knowledge of the local landscape and ecology. They searched, for example, for prairie shoestring (or "lead weed"), a small bush with protruding violet blossoms, which sometimes foretold the presence of lead. Other methods included surveying the ground for subtle telltale depressions in the tallgrass and following minerals upstream.[86]

Once they found a promising site, Meskwaki workers dug deep. They systemically scraped their way down into square-shaped mines using shovels, pickaxes, and crowbars acquired at French trading houses. In some cases, they extracted ore buried 50 feet deep then processed it into black paint. Others superheated the element in smelting pits, with as many as twenty in operation at a time. As the lead cooled, Meskwaki workers hammered it into 70-pound plates that the women carried on their heads. They hauled or floated these plates to trade forts, where they exchanged the lead for cash and wares. From there, traders passed the lead further along the supply chain or bent and twisted it into tools for trade across the continent.[87]

As smelting techniques became more efficient and made their way to the Midwest, the mines became even more valuable. This was due, in part, to increasing demand for the lead balls that filled the chambers of muskets and cannons, as well as its uses in other tools.[88] Higher demand inspired Meskwaki and Ho-Chunk villagers to devote more energy to mining.[89] Demand spiked in the first decades of the nineteenth century. One estimate asserts that a Meskwaki village was buying around $5,000 worth of trade goods each year, covering half of their bill with lead alone.[90]

When lead's value grew, it attracted settlers to the Meskwaki homeland. In 1771, a Meskwaki woman—records only note that she was the wife of Meskwaki leader Peosta—discovered a major ore seam that ran along the western bank of the Upper Mississippi, about 65 miles downriver from Prairie du Chien. Seven years later, the tribe granted a French Canadian fur trapper and prospector, Julien Dubuque, permission to mine their territory, in part, according to some accounts, because his wife, Potosa, was Meskwaki. This arrangement was not as unusual as it initially seems. The Meskwaki Nation had been sharing territory with other parties, Indigenous and otherwise, for decades. Dubuque, moreover, was not the first Euro-American to mine in what is now Iowa. But he did leave the biggest mark on its memory. Dubuque was an able politician who capitalized on his French ancestry and Indigenous marriage to secure a 189-square-mile land grant from Spanish officials, which he strategically dubbed the "Mines of Spain." Dubuque worked that parcel alongside Meskwaki miners for over twenty years and established a trade outpost and farms on the property. Today, the largest city in the area—Dubuque, Iowa—still bears his name.[91]

The Red Earth People's extensive participation in the lead exchange shows how trade and commerce were deeply interwoven with the tribe's connection to Iowa and the resource economy that enabled their growth and success around the turn of the nineteenth century. In purely economic terms, these were fat times: By the 1820s, the lead trade was booming. By one estimate, in 1826, Indigenous women hauled some 800,000 pounds of lead to market on the Upper Mississippi.[92] Another suggests that, depending on its market price, that amount of lead would have been worth somewhere between $2.9 and $8.7 million today.[93]

All told, Meskwaki economic and commercial success in this era continued the Red Earth People's earlier pattern of demographic recovery: the number of Red Earth People had grown to a population of more than 2,000 by 1820.[94]

In political terms, however, the lead boom compounded a disaster that had already begun to destabilize the Meskwaki and Sauk world. Lead was lucrative, and as word of the mineral boom made its way east, eager settlers flooded in to tap into the trade. Unlike Native women, whose families passed down knowledge about the location of lead deposits, non-Native miners had only perception and blind luck to drive their search for ore. Prospecting was a frustrating, high-risk endeavor. Those lucky enough to find metal endured long days of backbreaking work as they scraped, shoveled, chipped, and hauled the dense mineral from the ground. Compared to this, the process for acquiring the land in which the lead lay was straightforward. The US government, after all, had spent the previous thirty years becoming a reliable ally for non-Natives seeking access to tribal land.[95]

TAKING

At the turn of the nineteenth century, Indigenous and European nations faced a tenuous balance in the West. Spanish, French, and British interests still claimed enormous swaths of the continent. If the United States was to grow, its government needed to find inroads to the heart of the continent. Treaties and purchases were one way to achieve this, although these documents did not actually transfer land from one European nation to another or to the United States. They merely reflected the purchase of the right of preemption and, therefore, the ability to acquire land from

Native Nations. This meant that the initial sale price of a massive chunk of North American land usually amounted to a fraction of the actual cost of obtaining Indigenous land, whether through peaceful negotiations, war, duplicity, or some combination thereof.[96]

Under this system, Spain had acquired 830,000 square miles of land, known as the Louisiana Territory, at the end of the Seven Years' War in 1763. The Spanish government sold its rights of preemption over this expanse to Napoleon's France in 1800, which held it for about three years before selling its claim to dominion to the United States. This Louisiana Purchase extended the boundary of the United States as far west as the Continental Divide in 1803.[97] The document that solidified the agreement also required the United States to uphold any existing treaties "between Spain and the tribes and nations of Indians" as of its signing on the last day of April that year.[98]

About a year after the Louisiana Purchase was complete, President Thomas Jefferson sent a small contingent of men on an expedition from St. Louis to the Pacific Ocean and back. Along their three-year journey, the so-called Corps of Discovery mapped western landscapes and waterways; documented flora, fauna, and other natural resources; and attempted to establish diplomatic and trade relationships with the many Native Nations it encountered along the way. This reconnaissance helped lay the groundwork for westward expansion.

Meriwether Lewis and William Clark's mission served myriad American goals. Although the United States claimed the trans-Mississippi West after the War for Independence, British and Indigenous people maintained a strong footing on the ground. A 1795 agreement with Great Britain known as Jay's Treaty firmed up the Canadian boundary. The much weaker United States also submitted to British demands to continue trading on the American side of the line. A series of conflicts with British interests and Native tribes in Michigan and Illinois kept American influence at bay. The United States did not move to secure its position on the Upper Mississippi until it also held the Louisiana Territory. Only then did it establish a military presence to help control the region.[99]

Neither the Meskwaki nor the Sauk Nation figures prominently in accounts of Lewis and Clark's trek. This is largely because the excursion began in St. Louis, which at the time was a trade outpost with a population of barely more than a thousand people. Until March 1804, it had been controlled by Spanish officials. The town sat on a stretch of the Mississippi River and the surrounding hinterlands where the presence of Sauk and Meskwaki people, along with Europeans and members of many other tribes, was common. Lewis and Clark spent the spring of 1804 in St. Louis planning their travels and gearing up for departure. On March 25, William Clark made a passing note about seeing around two dozen Sauk people in the vicinity. This was not uncommon, and Clark left no indication that the two parties interacted.[100]

As the expedition prepared for its mid-April launch, Lewis began outlining messages that he and other Americans would present to Native Nations along the trek. He crafted these speeches to strike a diplomatic tone. He wrote one to the allied Sauk and Meskwaki Nations. It informed members of the two tribes that the United States had acquired Louisiana and, wanting to preserve peace and stability in the West, that the "Great Father," Jefferson, had agreed to adopt them.[101]

The metaphor perfectly captured the paternalism of Euro-Americans, who believed themselves superior to Native peoples. For decades, American officials and Indigenous peoples used it to reflect bonds of fictive kinship modeled on earlier statements in the French language, which had promoted a version of mutual obligation between tribes and the Crown.[102] At first, this appeared to be an American concession to Indigenous power: The mistakes of the 1780s and 1790s had convinced federal officials to emulate the previous order. Kinship and camaraderie—not conquest— had enabled French and British governments to create alliances in the Old Northwest. Over the course of the nineteenth century, United States officials would reframe the "Great Father" to rationalize false promises and policy decisions that were devastating for Native peoples. At the time of Lewis's writing, however, the metaphor still implicitly recognized the strength of the Indigenous presence within the Louisiana Territory.[103]

The Americans stumbled through their first audience with the Sauk Nation in 1804. According to one account, a Sauk person delivered Meriwether Lewis's message from St. Louis to his tribe. There, the translator butchered Lewis's attempts to strike a benevolent tone. It is also possible that the Yellow Earth People, who presumably had not been looking to be adopted by Thomas Jefferson or anyone else, simply rejected the overture. In either case, the Americans had to send another interpreter to clarify the gaffe.[104]

Meanwhile, according to Meskwaki Tribal Historian Johnathan Buffalo, the Red Earth People were underwhelmed by Lewis and Clark's time in their territory. "For at least a hundred years, we had met white people in canoes coming down the river and going someplace. Lewis and Clark were not any different," he said. "We had our own thing going on. We were used to white people coming in—the French, English, and Spanish. So they went on and made history [for the Americans]. To us they were just a bunch of white guys, as long as they just passed our land."[105]

Lewis and Clark's expedition may not have felt especially consequential in the spring of 1804. But, as it was for Native Nations across the American West, the excursion was a harbinger of incredible changes to come. After acquiring the Louisiana Territory, the Jefferson administration laid the early groundwork for the removal policies that would dislocate thousands of Indigenous families. Barely six months after the Americans departed St. Louis, the United States would usurp a massive strip of Sauk and Meskwaki land.

THE TREATY OF 1804

Around the turn of the nineteenth century, the United States government erected policies that sought to acquire tribal land while controlling, as much as possible, the flow of settlers into Indian Country. First, the Trade and Intercourse Act of 1790 secured the British rule of preemption for the United States. This enabled the government to secure land cessions while regulating settlement. The Intercourse Act would be updated and expanded several times in decades to come, reifying a policy framework that sought a persistent, paced westward migration.[106]

Next, in 1795, the US government implemented the "factory system." This established a far-flung network of "factories," or American trade outposts, that served as regional headquarters for federal Indian policy. Over the course of about twenty-five years, this system grew to include more than two dozen factories that provided moorings for existing trade networks and positions from which the United States could monitor Indigenous movements and conduct policy in the West. Factories also offered an early blueprint for the agency offices from which government officials would administer Indian reservations later in the nineteenth century.[107]

Meanwhile, treaties continued to serve as the primary means through which the United States dispossessed Native peoples of their land and cleared the path for its own expansion. In two terms, for example, the Jefferson administration oversaw some fifteen agreements with Great Lakes tribes.[108] And, in the three years immediately following the Louisiana Purchase, the United States extracted massive land cessions from the Shawnee, Myaamiaki, Lenape, Potawatomi, and other tribes.[109]

Another negotiation took place in St. Louis in the late autumn of 1804. It was a watershed moment in Meskwaki and Sauk history, and it was born of crisis. That September, a group of Sauk men had killed a group of encroaching settlers in tribal territory just northwest of St. Louis. This violence occurred in a period of high tension between settlers and bands of Sauk and Meskwaki people. As area settlers panicked at the prospect of war, Sauk leaders sent a contingent to St. Louis to discuss the matter with William Henry Harrison, the future American general and president who, in addition to serving as governor of the Indiana Territory, had recently become governor of the Louisiana Territory.[110]

That summer, tensions between the Meskwaki and Sauk Nations and the United States ran high. In addition to their awkward introduction to the "Great Father" that spring, Sauk and Meskwaki people likely eyed the prospect of Americans replacing their longtime Spanish trading partners at St. Louis with deep skepticism. A fateful sequence of events followed. Sauk and Meskwaki peoples' distrust of the American government deepened as the United States appeared to be fortifying an association with the Osage Nation, an old rival of both tribes. In August 1804, American soldiers blocked a large contingent of Sauk and Meskwaki men on their way to fight with the Osages. A month later, some Sauk men attacked a group of settlers just outside St. Louis. Although historians have debated the precise cause of the attack, which left three settlers dead, this much is clear: settlers throughout the region believed an Indian war was coming. The Sauk chief's council, meanwhile, anticipated an American revenge campaign and quickly sent two diplomats to calm the situation in St.

Louis. There, American officials demanded that the Sauk assailants turn themselves in for trial. Although the chief's council could not force the men to surrender, by October at least one of the accused had arrived in St. Louis, escorted by a group of Sauk and Meskwaki diplomats, who tried to settle the case in their way—by exchanging cash and goods for the man's freedom. The Americans, however, sought execution. This brought the Sauk and Meskwaki delegation into negotiations with William Henry Harrison.[111]

By November 3, Harrison and his staff had convinced four Sauk men and one Meskwaki man to press their "x-marks" to a treaty that sold more than 50 million acres of tribal land to the United States. This included a strip of territory running from southwestern Wisconsin, along the east bank of the Mississippi, about halfway down Illinois, and then across the river and into Missouri. In exchange for this land, the tribes received a down payment of $2,234.50 followed by annual perpetual payments of $1,000 split 60–40 between the Sauk and Meskwaki people, respectively.[112]

The details of what transpired next remain opaque.[113] For one thing, the Sauk and Meskwaki chiefs' councils had empowered the delegates to negotiate only on behalf of the Sauk men responsible for killing the white settlers. Also, the single Meskwaki diplomat was likely there to represent the interests of his tribe and to demonstrate the Meskwaki chief's council's solidarity with their Sauk relatives. The small group had no power to cede land—much less a massive swath of land that included most of the key villages of the Sauk Nation.[114]

Even if the group had wielded such authority, it would not have ceded the ground beneath their villages—a claim Quashquame, a Sauk leader present at the negotiations, repeated throughout his life. He maintained that the group had agreed only to sell hunting lands on the periphery of Sauk territory.[115] Harrison and his aides also deviated in several ways from standard American treaty practice: they did not keep detailed notes of the negotiations, and their initial request for a meeting spoke only of peace talks, not land deals. All this confusion meant that, well after the ink had dried on the 1804 treaty, members of the Sauk and Meskwaki Nations remained unclear about the full scope of the taking.[116] This ambiguity did not dissuade the Americans, who stripped a massive swath of land from Native hands.

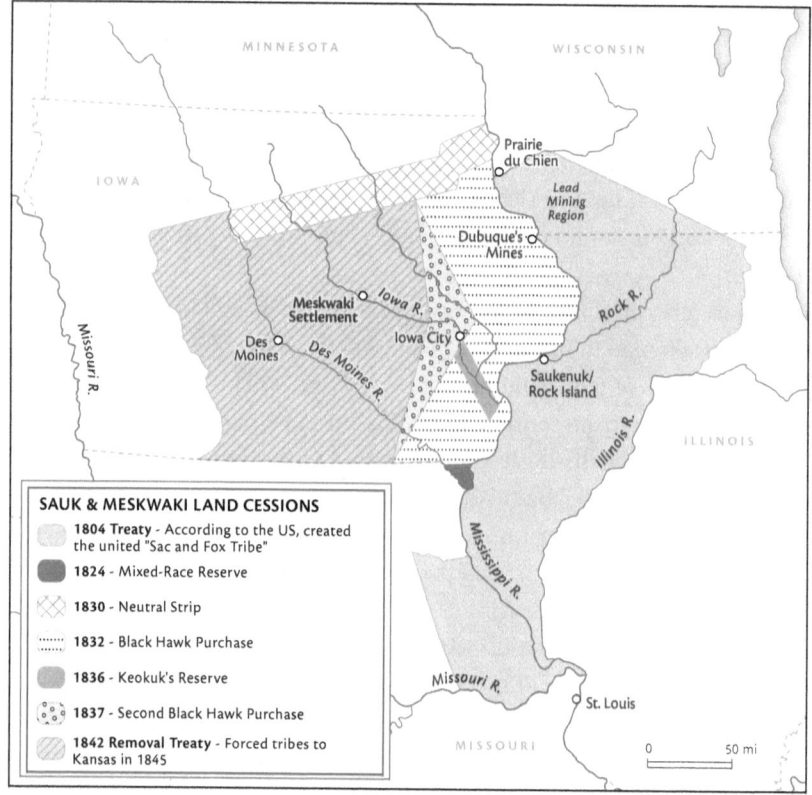

Map of the Dispossession of the Meskwaki and Sauk Nations
Under incredible economic, ecological, demographic, and political duress, the Sauk and Meskwaki Nations saw all of their land in what became Iowa, Illinois, and Missouri chipped away between 1804 and 1842. Map by Erin Greb Cartography, 2023. Based on a reference map in Patrick J. Jung, *The Black Hawk War of 1832* (Norman: University of Oklahoma Press, 2007), 32, used with permission.

CREATING THE "SAC AND FOX TRIBE"

In the decades after 1804, the treaty would prove a firm legal footing for the continued dispossession of Sauk and Meskwaki land. This process was facilitated by the fact that the 1804 document contained an insidious error: Harrison and his staff drafted the treaty as a binding agreement between the United States and the "united Tribes of Sac and Fox

Indians," *not* between the United States, the Sauk Nation, and the Meskwaki Nation.[117]

Historians have offered several explanations for this language. For Johnathan Buffalo, the creation of the "Sac and Fox Tribe" was about money. "With two tribes occupying the same land, [the United States] couldn't buy it from one tribe and not the other and they didn't want to pay double," he told an interviewer. "So to solve that problem, the US government made the Sac and Fox Tribe so they could make one treaty for the same lands."[118] For historian Anthony F. C. Wallace, the 1804 treaty "exemplifies perfectly the process of obtaining land by the pragmatic procedure of allowing whites to encroach, as hunters and settlers, on unceded Indian land." When tension begot violence, the US government would then negotiate a dispossessive treaty "as the price of peace."[119] It was also not unusual for American treatymakers to use negotiations with Native leaders to create what Bethel Saler calls "treaty polities," or new tribal governments that made it easier to identify and cede Indigenous lands. Along the way, American officials often recognized certain Native leaders as the rightful signatories to make these decisions, whether or not that aligned with the realities of tribal governance.[120]

Because no minutes of the treaty negotiations survive, it is impossible to know whether the precise language of the 1804 treaty was shaped by mistake or intentional deceit. The phrase "united tribes" at once underscored unification and pluralized "tribes." This suggests that the treaty's American authors knew they were dealing with two distinct nations, as does the 60–40 split between the treaty annuities. Given the odd circumstances surrounding the negotiations—the violence and tension that created a power imbalance favoring the American over tribal delegates, the lack of documentation of the treaty proceedings themselves, and the allegations of opacity and duplicity about the intentions of the negotiations—it seems likely that the American officials deliberately chose to consolidate the two tribes' land cessions into a single document. In so doing, the United States refused to acknowledge the Sauk Nation and the Meskwaki Nation as two separate, if closely confederated, peoples.[121]

This has had wide-ranging, long-term consequences for both tribes. The 1804 treaty sparked a feedback loop that would, over the course of about forty years, facilitate the total dispossession and ultimate removal of the

Sauk and Meskwaki Nations from their respective homelands.[122] At first, the Red Earth People may not have noticed or been bothered by the treaty language. However, their dissatisfaction grew as their people's land base diminished, more and more settlers moved into their territory, and the 1804 unification of the two tribes slowly drove a wedge of division between the old relatives.[123] The treaty was, after all, only the first of many agreements that would be written between the "Sac and Fox Tribe" and the United States of America.[124] Many subsequent treaties would lean on this legal fiction to systematically decouple Sauk and Meskwaki people from their land without burdening American officials with the messy details of which tribe actually owned it—a strategy that would echo deeply into the nineteenth century, when the United States made mass treaties with multiple tribes and often placed several tribes on a single reservation.[125]

Still, to the Sauk leader Makataimeshekiakiak (Black Sparrow Hawk or, more commonly, Black Hawk), who led a violent resistance movement against the United States in 1832, the precise intentions of the treaty language were less significant than the consequences the document had for his people. To him, the 1804 treaty was simply "the origin of all our difficulties with the whites."[126]

CHAPTER 2

Reconfiguration

The War of 1812 played out in many theaters but was in many ways a contest for control over the Old Northwest.[1] Old resentments, unresolved disputes, and deep economic competition pushed the United States and Great Britain to war. These conflicts were sparked by Indigenous resistance and revival movements along the eastern stretch of the Ohio River valley. There, two Shawnee brothers named Tecumseh and Tenskwatawa (the "Shawnee Prophet") drew upon anti-American sentiments and a broad desire for the restoration of Indigenous authority to build a coalition of followers from various Native Nations. American officials assumed that the British were encouraging Indigenous recalcitrance, a vantage that failed to see the alliance between British and Indigenous peoples as based in mutual concerns about American expansionism. Recent treaties had eroded Native landholdings in the Ohio River Valley, just as they were doing to the Sauk, Meskwaki, and other Nations farther south and west. The British, the Shawnees, and their partners formed a coalition. By the autumn of 1811, the Americans had marched toward Tecumseh and Tenskwatawa's village, Prophetstown, in what is now northwestern Indiana. A group of Ho-Chunk men fired upon the Americans, igniting the Battle of Tippecanoe, which ended in an American victory. More pressingly, it helped inspire an American declaration of war against Great Britain and its Native allies in the summer of 1812.[2]

In the years leading up to the War of 1812, the Red Earth People and the Yellow Earth People grew ever more skeptical of the American presence on the Mississippi River. On one hand, the American presence on Sauk and Meskwaki land, including the ceded territory, lagged behind the signing of the 1804 treaty. Under its terms, the tribes retained the area until the United States needed the land.[3] The trickle of settlers nonetheless led to occasional confrontations. Members of various tribes stole livestock and killed settlers who entered tribal hunting lands. Sauk and Meskwaki people were involved in around fifty such skirmishes. Meanwhile, remaking Native people in the mold of an idealized, yeoman farmer was a fantasy of Jeffersonian Indian policy. To enact it, the US government built an "instructional farm" in Sauk territory in 1805—one in a long series of federal attempts to use American conceptions of land use to further the goals of Indigenous assimilation. As with earlier French missionaries, Sauk and Meskwaki people did not appreciate these overtures. They communicated this in no uncertain terms: in 1806, Sauk and Meskwaki men destroyed all the government's livestock.[4] Relations did not improve thereafter, and both tribes' resentment of the Americans deepened as they monitored the Indigenous revival and resistance movements that began to swell to the northeast. Several large groups of Sauk and Meskwaki people traveled the Rock River into what is now Indiana to hear Tenskwatawa's message toward the end of the decade.[5]

Perhaps unsurprisingly, these factors led to an increase of Meskwaki and Sauk peoples' general support for Great Britain in the lead up to the war.[6] After Tippecanoe, the Americans tried to keep Native Nations neutral.[7] Although relations had improved between British, Sauk, and Meskwaki people since the 1760s, neither tribe emphatically supported Great Britain, and relatively few Sauk and Meskwaki men actually fought in the war.[8] Those that did supported the British in several attacks on American trade factories and military forts, and a large Indigenous coalition defended a large Sauk village from an American assault.[9]

When the Treaty of Ghent officially ended the war in February 1815, violence and uncertainty dragged on for months. Tribes had won often in the Old Northwest, and many had aligned themselves with the British, in part because they believed that, win or lose, Great Britain would retain some influence in the interior, as it had after the War for Independence. Britain, however, negotiated away its claims to the region, effectively selling out its Indigenous allies. The United States, meanwhile, set about negotiating more than a dozen peace treaties with individual tribes. Meskwaki and Sauk bands continued to skirmish with the Americans, leading the United

States to consider engaging them directly. This did not come to pass, and the Sauk and Meskwaki Nations eventually negotiated a series of separate peace treaties with the United States, in 1815 and 1816.[10]

FALLOUT

The treaties that ended the War of 1812 were significant to the Sauk and Meskwaki Nations for several reasons. First, and most obviously, they ended the immediate violence between the tribes and the United States. They also marked a turning point for the American role in the Old Northwest. With many other priorities, the United States' presence in the Sauk and Meskwaki homeland had thus far been relatively light. The War of 1812, however, brought a reconfiguration of the geopolitical landscape and power dynamics in the region. The Americans expelled British interests and slowly strengthened US control over Anishinaabewaki. This process entailed a full-scale re-evaluation of federal Indian policy. It began as a delicate accommodation between tribes and the United States. It steadily bent toward a strong American emphasis on assimilation, dispossession, and removal.[11]

The 1815 and 1816 treaties also confirmed the boundaries, and therefore the extent of the cession, outlined in the 1804 treaty. This was, and would remain, a point of contention for members of both tribes, who maintained that the five-man delegation in St. Louis never had the power to make the agreement in the first place. It is also possible that it took until after the War of 1812 for members of the Sauk and Meskwaki chiefs' councils to fully envision the extent of the taking.[12] In any case, even after 1816, members of both tribes remained adamantly opposed to such a large cession. During a meeting in 1817, a Meskwaki representative told an American official that the Red Earth People, who still crossed the Mississippi to hunt, trade, and mine, "would do without food and live on roots rather than part with their lands."[13] Ardent rhetoric like this, however, did not keep the people east of the river: by 1825, the Red Earth People had extended their hunting grounds west to what became the border between Iowa and Nebraska, and deeper south into Missouri.[14]

The peace treaties also reflected the spurious nature of the United States' approach to treaty-making with the Sauk and Meskwaki Nations. Less than a decade earlier, American officials had seized on unusual circumstances to force a massive land cession from both tribes, in part by legally uniting them as one "Sac and Fox Tribe." Fresh off their victory in the War of 1812, American officials once again found themselves in an advantageous position, although some members of the Sauk and Meskwaki Nations did not want to finalize the peace treaty.[15] Recognizing this challenge, the Americans targeted coalitions of people from both tribes who were favorable to peace then decided against creating another singular treaty with the "Sac and Fox Tribe." Instead, the US government entered into separate agreements that achieved the short-term goal of peace *and* confirmed the boundaries of the 1804 taking.

In short, when doing so eased the process of taking Sauk and Meskwaki land, the United States viewed both tribes as one nation. But when it made peace on terms desirable to the United States—and reified an earlier cession—the federal government treated each tribe as a distinct legal entity.[16]

American officials' bad-faith negotiations are further evidenced by the postwar actions of the former explorer William Clark. The historian Robert Lee recently exposed a scheme by which Clark sought to "graft a tract of Sauk, Meskwaki, and Iowa territory the size of Switzerland onto the United States after the War of 1812."[17] In 1815, Clark was serving as territorial governor of Missouri and the regional superintendent of Indian affairs. According to Lee, Clark attempted to buy millions of acres of land from the Sauk, Meskwaki, and Ioway Nations shortly after the war. When this fell through, Clark personally redrew a map that claimed a large tract of land in northwestern Missouri for the United States. This violated both the Treaty of Ghent and an earlier agreement between the United States and the Osage Nation. It manipulated the normal treaty process in a "thinly-veiled effort to dispossess Sauks, Meskwakis, and Iowas by writing their possession out of the recent past." His decision fueled a surge of settlers into Missouri.[18]

Even amid these losses, lines of Indigenous diplomacy connected the Native Nations of the Old Northwest to those farther down the Mississippi River and throughout the surrounding region. Several years after the War of 1812, a small group of primarily Sauk and a few Meskwaki people separated from their relatives and moved to the Missouri River valley near what is now the border between northeastern Kansas and southeastern Nebraska. They later signed a treaty with the US government that established them as the "Sac and Fox Nation of Missouri in Kansas and Nebraska."[19] Although legally distinct from their relatives on the Upper Mississippi after 1824, these families likely remained in touch with other Sauk and Meskwaki people as they moved throughout the region.

Members of the Sauk and Meskwaki Nations, meanwhile, continued to interact with other tribes in the region. This marked the continuation of Indigenous lines of diplomacy that operated amid broader concerns about the expansion of non-Native influence in the region. In 1819, for example, a group of Sauk and Meskwaki delegates had traveled to the Arkansas River valley at the invitation of Osage leaders. There, the Osages asked the Yellow Earth People and the Red Earth People to join them as allies in a bloody war against the Cherokees who, along with dozens of other tribes, had been dislocated in the fallout from the War of 1812. The Sauk and Meskwaki leaders whose villages remained on the Upper Mississippi declined to embroil their people in a brutal contest over southern land.[20] They had enough to worry about at home.

FLOOD

The first wave of Europeans came to what are now Illinois and Iowa looking for furs. The next came for the lead. In the five years after the Sauk Nation signed its peace treaty in 1816, the United States added five new states including Illinois and Missouri.[21] Yet until the early 1820s, Native peoples still outnumbered the handful of French, British, and American traders inhabiting the broad expanses used by the Red Earth People, Yellow Earth People, and other Indigenous Nations as hunting grounds. Within a few years, the trickle turned to a torrent.[22] One set of estimates placed the settler population in Illinois at just over 12,000 in 1810. Illinois became a state in 1818, and within two years that number had spiked to over 55,000. By 1840, it approached half a million.[23] To the south, Missouri jumped from about 66,500 people in 1820 to nearly 384,000 by 1840.[24] Between 1820 and 1840 the populations of the Sauk and Meskwaki Nations—which totaled about 6,800 people around 1818—began a steady decline for the first time in a century.[25]

Waves of settler migration were driven by the American demand for new western property and shaped by two fundamental US concerns. First, would western territories enter the union as free or slave states? Efforts to answer that question played out in Congress, which in 1820 admitted Maine to the union as a free state and allowed Missouri to become the last slave state north of the so-called Mason-Dixon Line. This proved to be one in a long series of compromises that attempted to salve antebellum anxieties and hold the union together. The second question also proved precarious: How would the United States deal with the Native Nations already inhabiting desirable land? Over time, the United States had evolved frontier policies and practices that continued to dislocate and dispossess Indigenous lands. As successive waves of settlers pushed into tribal territory, their presence—sometimes legal and sometimes not—sparked conflicts with Native Nations. Those skirmishes often ended in the federal expulsion of Indigenous peoples from ceded land.[26]

Meanwhile, Meskwaki and Sauk lead miners continued their work. Well into the second decade of the nineteenth century, they preferred to trade and interact with French partners who had been digging nearby for decades. As settlers filled Illinois, the state became a key supply hub for eager prospectors. The first illegal lead mine had popped up along the Fever River, east of Dubuque, shortly after Illinois achieved statehood.[27] Americans remained in the minority in lead country for a few years. The federal government tried meekly to keep the squatters out. By 1825, however, it was clear that the United States could not stem the tide, and settlers cascaded into the region. Some of them brought Black slaves to carry out the grueling work formerly undertaken by Indigenous women. The settlers pushed for more treaties and displaced established Native groups. First went the Ho-Chunk mining grounds to the north and east. They were soon followed by Sauk mines and, finally, Meskwaki territory on the west bank of the Mississippi, whose location had bought the Red Earth People a little more time. By 1830, lead production was growing alongside the presence of non-Native miners.[28]

The influx of new settlers strained the ecosystem along the Upper Mississippi and pushed tribes into conflict. Over the course of the 1820s, Indigenous land bases shrank just as demand for game that could provide calories and trade pelts was exploding. Prey became scarce, pushing Native groups into competition as they ventured farther into each other's territory. Meanwhile, most tribes fell into debt to traders like the American Fur Company, which steadily consolidated its control over regional commerce.[29] This occurred through an unscrupulous practice in which trade outfits maintained long ledgers of goods traded for or purchased on credit by individual Native people. Within a short period of time, Indigenous families fell so far behind they could no longer pay off the debt. Then companies transferred the debt to the tribe as a whole and notified Indian agents of the tribe's delinquency.[30] In the short term, this increased pressure on Native traders to find more pelts. Over time, it contributed to financial pressures that placed tribes at a steep disadvantage in treaty negotiations.

European and American traders shaped life in the Old Northwest in another way. Over the years, many had married and had families with Native women. On the Upper Mississippi, this meant that a significant number of mixed-race families were living independently from white society and the Sauk and Meskwaki villages. They sought a separate place to raise their families, and, after a series of negotiations in Washington, DC, an 1825 treaty ceded 119,000 acres of Meskwaki and Sauk land in the far southeast corner of Iowa. That property became a special reserve for mixed-race descendants of white traders and Indigenous peoples. They could live on that land, but—due to preemption—they could neither own nor sell the property. The treaty, meanwhile, also formally ceded all remaining Sauk and Meskwaki claims to land in Missouri.[31]

The area surrounding this "Mixed-Race Reserve" was also embroiled in violence. By the middle of the 1820s, groups of Dakota people were engaged in periodic wars with bands from the Anishinaabe (Ojibwe), Sauk, and Meskwaki Nations. Pushed downriver, by the influx of settlers into the lead mining territory, the Meskwaki and Sauk Nations soon engaged members of the Menominee and Ho-Chunk Nations. The fighting became so intense that the Menominee and Ho-Chunk tribes, along with a group of Dakotas, asked the United States for help negotiating a ceasefire.[32]

This brought representatives from nearly a dozen tribes to a large council at Prairie du Chien in 1825. In general, these negotiations divided disputed lands well enough to separate the tribes and stabilize their access to hunting grounds. This delivered a tenuous peace that lasted around three years. But by 1828 Sauk and Meskwaki fighters were once again at war with Dakota bands, which brought about another American intervention. At another treaty council in 1830, the parties agreed to another land cession that established the "Neutral Ground"—a long strip of land between the Mississippi and Des Moines Rivers that acted as a physical buffer between the Dakota bands to the north, and the Sauk, Meskwaki, and Ioway Nations to the south.[33]

Although the Mixed-Race Reserve and the Neutral Ground had been created to resolve separate issues, each reflected policies that contributed to the dispossession of Meskwaki and Sauk lands in Iowa. The Mixed-Race Reserve, for example, lasted only a few years before the federal government transferred the titles to mixed-race occupants, which enabled it to be sold outright, in 1834. This led to a sequence of events that would become familiar across Indian Country over the following century as eager land speculators flooded in and acquired most of the land in the reserve. This process was swift but rife with malfeasance and litigation, and legal battles over the rightful ownership of plots within the Mixed-Race Reserve dragged through the courts for years. The end result, however, was clear: by the early 1840s, neither the Mixed-Race Reserve nor the Neutral Ground would belong to people of Indigenous descent.[34]

RETRIBUTION

Vengeance arose in the Meskwaki and Sauk homeland in the summer of 1832. That year, a fervent Sauk leader named Makataimeshekiakiak (Black Hawk) led a group of primarily Sauk, Meskwaki, and Kickapoo people in a resistance movement against the US government. At the time, the Americans were in the process of enforcing earlier treaties and banishing the tribes west of the Mississippi River for good. The violence culminated in the US-Sauk War, which is better known as the Black Hawk War.

The conflict is well documented. By the end of the 1820s, settlers had made their way to the Sauk villages on the east side of the Mississippi. Whites soon called on their government to expel Native peoples from the area. Officials acquiesced and, by early 1829, advised Meskwaki and Sauk leaders to abandon Illinois.[35] In the months that followed, Sauk leaders like Keokuk and Pashipaho agreed with Wapello, an influential Meskwaki chief. Their councils hoped to avoid conflict. They, along with a large majority of both tribes, agreed to follow the terms of the 1804 treaty and move west.[36]

Others, like Makataimeshekiakiak, rejected the treaty and built a coalition of more than a thousand followers from several tribes. Because they resisted American expansion and hoped to resurrect the British presence in the region, the group became known as the "British Band." As tensions mounted over the course of 1830 and 1831, the US military increased its presence and recruited Indigenous allies to quell Makataimeshekiakiak's movement. Meanwhile, Wapello, Keokuk, and others tried unsuccessfully to convince the British Band to rejoin the Sauk and Meskwaki communities and pursue peace through accommodation.[37]

After the winter hunts ended in 1831, Makataimeshekiakiak and his supporters rejected an American order to keep clear of Illinois. Shortly after they crossed the Mississippi River, an American force tried and failed to oust the British Band. In response, the Americans sent around 2,500 state and federal troops to complete the campaign. A cholera outbreak slowed their progress, forcing the army to chase the resistors throughout Illinois and part of Wisconsin throughout the summer. By August, the British Band's fortunes had turned. The American military and its Indigenous allies brutally cut Makataimeshekiakiak's group, which included many women and children, in half. They captured and imprisoned Makataimeshekiakiak along with several other leaders and brought a swift end to the war.[38]

The US-Sauk War was one outcome of myriad overlapping historical processes that were playing out in the Old Northwest and across the eastern half of the United States. For Makataimeshekiakiak and his followers, the war had begun as a protest against American expansionism and escalated into violence. In that sense, it was a defense of the Sauk, Meskwaki, and Kickapoo people and revenge for the unauthorized diminishment of their land. After all, Makataimeshekiakiak had sternly rejected the validity of the 1804 treaty. It was also fueled by their hopes of resurrecting the British presence in the Old Northwest.[39] For the bands of Dakota, Menominee, Ho-Chunk, and Potawatomie peoples who allied with the United States during the conflict, the Black Hawk War was another fight in a long trajectory of violence with the Sauk and Meskwaki Nations. Historical and visceral memories of bloodshed fueled their allegiances, and Makataimeshekiakiak's unwillingness to comply with American policy created an arena for revenge. In that sense, the confrontation was as much an "Indian War"—that is, a war between Native peoples for reasons only partially related to American settlement—as it was a fight between Makataimeshekiakiak's followers and the United States.[40]

For the Americans, the conflict had different causes. Locally, the war underscored the failure of American efforts to treat for peace, as it had tried to do with the meetings at Prairie du Chien and the creation of the Neutral Ground. The Upper Mississippi was contested territory, and the American government could not salve the abrasions among various groups of Native and non-Indigenous people.[41] As their efforts to maintain peace were devolving toward violence, US officials worried that Makataimeshekiakiak could build a coalition reminiscent of Tecumseh's. They also grew paranoid that the British were scheming on the western frontier, prodding the British Band along. Despite the resistors' collective nickname, the British government did not materially support Makataimeshekiakiak's movement. Nonetheless, the US government launched its 1832 offensive, in part, to quell any Indigenous and British momentum brewing on the Upper Mississippi.[42] American aggression was also fueled by deep undercurrents of federal policy that authorized devastating violence against Native Americans who resisted the settler advance into the interior.[43]

The US-Sauk War, however, also occurred within a national context of rapidly changing Indian policy. By the late 1820s, the United States strengthened its moorings east of the Mississippi River and plainly stated its desire for western expansion. The United States reneged on its recognition of nation-to-nation status with tribes, which had been articulated in the Constitution. In a series of three Supreme Court cases decided between 1823 and 1832 known as the Marshall Trilogy, the United States created a convoluted legal and political quagmire that would hamper Indigenous sovereignty for the next two centuries. Where they had previously held a status coequal with other foreign governments, tribes were now considered "domestic dependent nations" by the federal government. Going forward, tribes occupied a nebulous legal space somewhere between the federal government and the states. This reality trapped tribes in a convoluted jurisprudence that both promised and limited their sovereignty.[44]

During that era, the US government shifted toward explicit policies that sought the forced permanent deportation of most Indigenous Americans west of the Mississippi; the confinement of Native Nations on federally assigned reservations; and outspoken support for religious, educational, and social programs that sought to "civilize" Native people through Christian conversion and assimilation.[45] Of the many Indian removals enforced by the US government, the southern "Trail of Tears" is most notorious. In the two decades that followed the passage of the Indian Removal Act of 1830, the United States government forced thousands of Indigenous families from the southeast to the "Indian Territory" of present-day Oklahoma. Thousands perished from disease, malnutrition, and mistreatment along the way.[46]

The Trail of Tears was just one of many forced removals that spanned time and geography. Across the eastern half of the continent, removals fractured Native Nations. Family lines disappeared. With them vanished untold millennia worth of songs, stories, ceremonies, and other forms of cultural knowledge. In the Old Northwest, the Sauk and Meskwaki Nations and dozens of other Native tribes struggled as the United States dispossessed their people and pushed them away.[47] Due to its notoriety, the US-Sauk War is sometimes equated with the Trail of Tears. This is an oversimplification, as the two removals occurred in different places and under separate circumstances and were shaped by different historical actors.[48] Yet it is difficult to ignore core commonalities in their results: each brought terrible death to the Indigenous communities involved and ended in their official removal to the Indian Territory within just a few years.

CRISIS AND CESSION

Finally, the settlers came for the soil. On the Iowa side of the Mississippi River, 30 million acres of biologically diverse, nutrient-rich prairie covered about four-fifths of the landscape.[49] Thick forests thrived on the edges of the lakes, rivers, and streams that churned life through the massive Meskwaki and Sauk territory. It was a vast, verdant ocean filled with flora and fauna ranging from grasses and wildflowers to insects, elk, bison, and deer. Native people had known this landscape and its fruits for millennia.[50] It was ripped from Meskwaki and Sauk ownership in a cascade of removal treaties inked in 1832, 1836, 1837, and 1842.

The first was the "Black Hawk Purchase," an eponym that deliberately belied the context in which it was negotiated. The US-Sauk War had solidified

American dominance in Illinois and Iowa. The massive land cession that followed amounted to stern punishment for the Sauk and Meskwaki Nations, even though most members of both tribes had not participated in the campaign. A relatively small number of Meskwaki people fought with Makataimeshekiakiak. Nonetheless, returning to its earlier reasoning, the United States ignored Meskwaki leaders who argued that any Sauk land taken after the war should not include Meskwaki lead mines on the west bank of the Mississippi. The United States insisted on negotiating with the unified "Sac and Fox Tribe," and the new treaty charged the entire Sauk and Meskwaki Nations with staggering restitution for the actions of a few. This included the American acquisition of the Meskwaki mines outside Dubuque.[51]

Finalized just weeks after the conclusion of the US-Sauk War, the 1832 treaty ceded nearly the entire eastern border of present-day Iowa to the United States. It encompassed six million acres, extending westward to where Iowa City now sits, and legalized white settlement in Iowa. There was one exception: the US government set aside a comparatively modest strip of land known as "Keokuk's Reserve," which was ten miles wide and jutted forty miles southeast of Iowa City. The creation of the reserve feigned American goodwill and served as consolation for the Sauk and Meskwaki majorities who had not followed Makataimeshekiakiak into Illinois.[52]

The Black Hawk Purchase went into effect on the first of June in 1833. After that, as one reporter wrote, "settlers began to pour into the Black Hawk purchase from all parts of the union."[53] By 1836, 10,500 had arrived. Some followed the law onto ceded land. Others settled illegally within Keokuk's Reserve. By 1836, these squatters had squeezed out whatever space and utility the reserve and surrounding area offered the Sauk and Meskwaki communities, so the tribes sold it in another treaty. The very next year, representatives of both tribes met with federal officials in Washington, DC, where they ceded a wedge of land that extended the original taking west by 1.25 million acres. The year after this "Second Purchase" was complete, the number of settlers jumped to over 23,000, and the United States established the Sac and Fox Agency in what became Wapello County in southeastern Iowa. From this office, officials monitored interactions between a variety of Native peoples still living and moving through the region and the more than 43,000 non-Native people who had moved in by

1840. By the end of that year, the federal government was pondering the total removal of the Sauk and Meskwaki Nations from Iowa forever.[54]

Overlapping catastrophes facilitated territorial loss. First was an ecological crisis that was spreading throughout the Sauk and Meskwaki homeland. Pushed farther and farther west, north, and south in the years after the War of 1812, tribes throughout the Upper Mississippi region struggled to hunt for sustenance and trade. Indeed, these stresses, combined with the fact that Indigenous efforts to relieve them pressed tribes deeper and deeper into each other's territories, helped foment intertribal violence in the 1820s. This steadily depleted game populations. Immediately after settling near the Iowa River after the US-Sauk War, Meskwaki and Sauk families found the once-fertile area thin on vital resources like bison, elk, ducks, geese, muskrat, deer, and turkeys.[55]

Hunters searched farther and wider to supply their communities. They rode to what is now eastern South Dakota to harvest buffalo and swept as far as 300 miles in a western radius to procure other animals. Trade ledgers maintained by the American Fur Company and Chouteau and Company between the early 1820s and the early 1840s reveal key indicators of the ecological stress facing Indigenous hunters. The number of deer hide shipments varied greatly from year to year during that period. More tellingly, however, the average weight of those shipments declined steadily, demonstrating that as ungulate populations fell, Sauk and Meskwaki hunters were forced to harvest immature specimens to survive.[56]

In addition to having fewer animals to catch, the Red Earth People and the Yellow Earth People also had less land on which to hunt. By 1825, members of both tribes were using nearly the entire expanse of what is now Iowa, except the Neutral Ground, as well as a sliver of northwestern Missouri. By the early 1840s, they were constrained to a much smaller territory. Where the tribes had previously spanned from the Missouri River to the Mississippi, they were now roughly bounded by the North Raccoon River and the Wapsipinicon River in central Iowa. The issue this presented had less to do with total landmass than the kinds of land needed to maintain the health of each community. Meskwaki and Sauk families required a combination of woodlands and rivers to hunt and fish, as well as prairies and wetlands in which to plant. They consolidated in central Iowa, in part because these areas offered crucial corridors with a sustainable

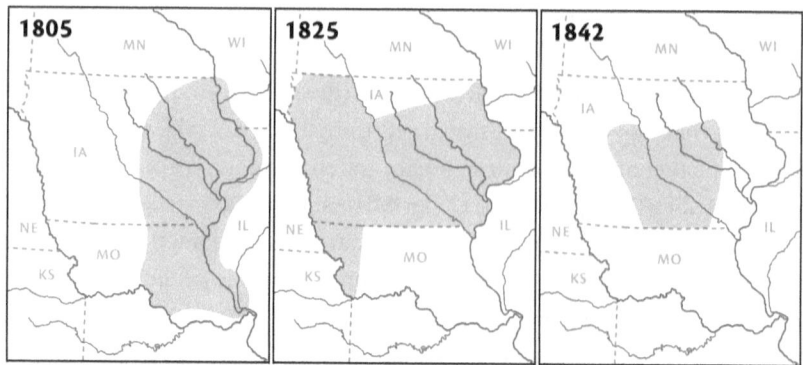

The Red Earth People's Presence in Iowa, 1805–1842
By 1842, the Red Earth People had concentrated their activities along the river corridors in central and southern Iowa. This is the area to which they would return and purchase land fifteen years after the treaty that facilitated their removal. Maps by Erin Greb Cartography, 2023. Redrawn from a reference map in Royce Kurtz, "Timber and Treaties," *Forest & Conservation History* 35, no. 2 (April 1991): 59, used with permission.

combination of all three environments. But access to these resources was steadily diminishing: one historian used the journals of explorer Zebulon Pike, who traveled through Iowa in 1805, to show how Sauk and Meskwaki people each had about 3.3 square miles of forest land per person. Forests were the best kind of property, inhabited by the highest number of game animals. By 1842, the tribes' access to forests had decreased to 1.5 square miles per capita.[57]

Declining animal stocks and acreages contributed to economic calamity. By the 1830s, it was becoming harder and harder for Sauk and Meskwaki families to pay debts owed to fur traders. For generations, members of the Sauk and Meskwaki Nations, like those of many other tribes, had been eager participants in an expansive trade system. It afforded them cash, food, and finished goods like tools. It also offered home implements, novelties like playing cards and umbrellas, and clothing, which they acquired by bartering minerals, animal pelts, Indigenous crafts and artwork, medical treatments, and manual labor.[58]

As the fur trade slowed in the 1840s, companies continued to allow Indigenous traders to run up high debts; then these companies held entire tribes accountable when families could not settle up. This problem worsened as fewer and fewer animals were available to be sold and Sauk and Meskwaki people were forced, through cessions, from the lead markets. Lacking sufficient pelts or other goods, land was one of the few remaining assets tribes could use to pay their bills. The federal government authorized its officials to settle Native debts with treaty annuities in 1825. Rather than stemming the tide, the backing of the federal government merely fed traders' willingness to extend Indigenous credit lines even further.[59]

By the time of the Black Hawk Purchase, using annuities to settle debts had become commonplace, and by 1842 traders across the United States were recovering more than $2 million a year from tribal annuities alone. In Iowa, debt pressure on the Sauk and Meskwaki Nations constituted a major incentive for land cessions. The Black Hawk Purchase, for example, included a provision that would relieve $40,000 of tribal debt. But these payments came with exploitative costs. One group of historical archaeologists estimates that the government paid ten cents per acre for the Black Hawk Purchase then flipped the land to settlers for more than twelve times that amount shortly thereafter.[60] By 1842, the Sauk and Meskwaki Nation's need for cash was apparent: together, they carried more than $250,000 in trade debt.[61]

As these conditions worsened, animosities festered within the Sauk and Meskwaki communities. Scholars have emphasized internal divisions as a primary driver of the land cessions that defined the years preceding the Sauk and Meskwaki removal. They highlight deep divisions between "pro-conciliation" tribal leaders, who embraced accommodation, and those who preferred resistance after the War of 1812. They also point to internal disagreements about which leaders had the appropriate cultural and hereditary rights to lead their councils. Historians have also unveiled lingering discontentment at the appointment of so-called "money chiefs," like Keokuk, Appanoose, Poweshiek, and Wapello, to whom the United States paid salaries and whom it recognized as the main treaty negotiators and managers of annuities. Some tribal members alleged that their leaders hoarded money, spent lavishly on themselves, or, in some cases, took government bribes. Historians have also pointed out that, after the US-Sauk War, the United States had named Keokuk, a Sauk, as the "head chief" of both tribes. This fed long-festering discontentment about the Sac and Fox unification forged in the 1804 treaty, especially since Meskwaki people had the strongest historical ties to the west side of the Mississippi and felt they should be consulted first about that land.[62]

All of these factors were certainly at play. Yet the emphasis on interpersonal conflicts and intertribal disputes—the kinds of issues that pop up in the letters and reports of American officials—has tended to overshadow two overarching facts that every Sauk and Meskwaki person, as well as the leaders who represented them, had to have been keenly aware of. First, the environmental, economic, landed, and political crises they faced were dire. Second, however, all of these concerns paled in comparison to the combined outcome of the tribes' misfortune: for the first time in a century, the populations of both tribes were on the decline.

Although estimates are imprecise, Sauk and Meskwaki populations appear to have grown steadily from the Fox Wars until about the late 1820s, when the combined forces of violence, malnutrition, poverty, and disease forced them into a downward spiral.[63] Zebulon Pike counted about 4,600 people in both tribes in 1805. This number may have topped out at around 7,000 by the late 1820s, 5,000 of whom were Sauk and about 2,000 were Meskwaki. At least 600 Sauk and Meskwaki people died during the US-Sauk War. By 1836, one estimate suggests there were around 4,100 Sauk and Meskwaki people left. That figure continued to fall, and censuses taken in the early 1840s put the total population of both tribes at as little as between 2,300 and 2,500 people.[64] A later estimate suggests that by 1846, the Meskwaki Nation on its own numbered just 1,271 people.[65] In this era, federal officials pondered whether the Sauk and Meskwaki Nations were on the verge of extinction, and one historian has argued that the overall effect of successive removals had left both tribes in a state of "virtual homelessness," which, compounded by violence, disease, and starvation in the years since 1832, had left them on the brink of annihilation.[66]

With the myriad crises of the 1830s and 1840s in mind, the discord of that era can be read as a symptom of forces much broader and more profound than the oft-cited instances of intertribal squabbling. By the time they sat down with American negotiators in 1841 and 1842, Sauk and Meskwaki leaders, and the communities they represented, viewed the prospect of removal not only as one of diminishing land, but as a question of mere existence.

SYMBOLS OF SOVEREIGNTY

The most potent symbols of Meskwaki political power hung from the necks of a select few tribal members. Bear claw necklaces harnessed clan leaders' esteem and represented the responsibility bestowed upon their wearers. A long fur tail extended from the center of the holder's back up to their shoulders. From there, the necklace drooped around the upper chest while small beads alternated with grizzly bear claws. Uniformly curving toward the chest, these talons appeared to grip the wearer as an eagle clasps its prey. Donned by respected warriors, ceremonial leaders, and members of the chief's council, these adornments served for centuries as a "badge of office" that "embodied the authority and strength of the Meskwaki people."[67]

The Meskwaki leaders who guided their people through the difficult years after Wisaka sent them west wore such necklaces. In the seventeenth and eighteenth centuries, they led the Red Earth People as they moved, fought, and built and recast alliances. In the early 1840s, these leaders were in a difficult position. Indeed, the Meskwaki and Sauk Nations were deeply in debt, running out of resources to eat or earn, cognizant of the increasingly efficient treaty-making machine of the American government, and dying in historic numbers. They were haunted by the bad-faith actions of American treaty negotiators, who had since 1804 used everything from opportunistic legal interpretations to half-truths and outright bribery to press for repeated cessions.

The Sauk and Meskwaki people had three choices. They could fight for their land, knowing that the outcome would likely resemble the terrible fallout of the US-Sauk War. Alternatively, they could refuse to treat and hold out as long as possible. Each day would increase the risk of once again losing enormous amounts of land, probably for pennies on the dollar. Or they could negotiate a cession for the best possible price and under the most preferable terms, and then use that money to pay off debts and stockpile cash. From there, they could confront the challenging questions of where and how to stay alive.[68]

As they pondered these options, Meskwaki leaders listened to their people. Local journalists and visitors, like the folklorist Mary Alecia Owen, occasionally visited the Meskwaki community in the late nineteenth century. Their writings include descriptions of how meetings of the chief's council operated. Projecting backward a generation offers an imperfect sketch of how this system might have worked. Tribal leaders acted only after all the people of their tribe had a chance to make their voices heard. In regular times, the chief's council held about four formal meetings each year. These events coincided with the major annual turning points. The men first gathered after the corn planting each spring. They gathered again as the stalks grew tall and green under the summer sun, then when the first frost came, and once more in the dead of winter. These meetings could last four days. They offered opportunities to address outstanding issues and to plan for the coming season.[69]

Outside the formal discussions and ceremonies associated with collective decision-making, Meskwaki adults shared their opinions and desires with clan leaders, who brought these perspectives to the meeting. As Owen put it, Meskwaki women did not directly "engage men in public debate," and decorum precluded them from speaking during council. But Meskwaki women held significant political power. They met regularly outside the council, developed a group opinion, and pressed the men in their homes to share their positions in public. This practice earned Meskwaki women a reputation for "turning public opinion this way or that." Through these channels, the decisions of tribal leaders, under ideal circumstances, reflected the consensus of the whole.[70]

The chief's council could also call special meetings when pressing issues arose—such as, perhaps, the receipt of an invitation to a treaty council.[71] The negotiations that ended in the Sauk and Meskwaki Nations' formal removal from Iowa occurred in two rounds: first in October 1841 and again, a year later, in the autumn of 1842. American secretaries captured minutes from those discussions. Although the details of the exclusively Indigenous meetings on this subject are lost to history, it is likely that the chief's council for each tribe met before these sessions, and it is clear from the dockets that tribal leaders met between formal councils with the Americans to build consensus among themselves. History has tended to frame Sauk and Meskwaki leadership—and, by extension, the ultimate outcomes of the negotiations—as primarily influenced by fecklessness, infighting, greed, or disagreement. Another read reframes Indigenous decisions during these negotiations as acts of pragmatism and strategy in the face of overwhelming challenges.

RECONFIGURATION

PREFERRED LAND

In the fall of 1841, a contingent of federal and territorial officials led by the territorial governor, John Chambers, met with leaders from the Sauk and Meskwaki Nations to discuss the sale of their remaining Iowa lands. An interpreter passed messages between the diplomats, while a young secretary named James Grimes took down the minutes. The meeting began on Friday, October 15. Chambers opened the meeting at eleven o'clock in the morning at the Sac and Fox Agency in Wapello County. Then he introduced Commissioner of Indian Affairs Hartley Crawford, who had traveled from Washington, to make what the Americans believed was a beneficial agreement.[72]

In exchange for their remaining territory in Iowa, the United States government would pay $1 million to the confederated Sauk and Meskwaki Nations, from which tribal members would receive annuity payments, and would pay off the tribes' trade debts entirely. The government would also lay and staff infrastructure for what would have amounted to a small Sauk and Meskwaki city: The government offered to build a house for each family and provide six acres for gardens. (Chiefs would get twelve acres.) The tribes would also receive "farms & farmers, mills and millers, blacksmiths, gunsmiths, school houses, and a fine Council House," and the government would pay for teachers to teach tribal children "to read & write." Crawford promised that this deal would make all tribal members "contented and happy." After some supporting remarks by Chambers, the group disbanded so tribal leaders could discuss the offer.[73]

The tribes then took two days to confer and deliberate. When they met again on Sunday, October 17, the Sauk and Meskwaki leaders made it clear that the deal was fatally flawed: The United States wanted the tribes to move to the wrong place. The proposal would have relocated them to a new territory "on the head waters of the Des Moines and west of the Blue Earth River," in what is now southwestern Minnesota. This was unacceptable. That location was squarely within Dakota land, and members of both tribes knew that violence would result from the old enemies being forced into proximity. Anticipating this concern, the United States had offered to build three military forts to keep the peace and promised to punish any Dakota band that raided the Sauk and Meskwaki village. This did not satisfy the tribes.[74]

Most importantly, the Red Earth People and the Yellow Earth People knew the landscape and did not want to relocate to northern prairies, which according to them were ill-suited to Sauk and Meskwaki needs. A Sauk leader named Wishecomacquet told the officials, "It is impossible for us to accept your proposals. We can't subsist in the country where you wish us to go."[75] In the ensuing conversation, two younger Meskwaki men, named Kishkekosh and Wishewahka, pointed out that what remained of their territory in Iowa was vital because it contained timber. They feared that the proposed removal site lacked the woodlands—and, by implication, game and other critical resources—to survive.[76]

Wapello and Poweshiek recognized these problems but harbored larger concerns. Poweshiek began, "We have thought of the condition of our families. We hold this country from our fathers. We have an hereditary right to it, and we think we have a right to judge whether we will sell it or not. According to our custom, our chiefs own all the trees and the earth and they are used for the benefit of our people." He pointed out that leaving Iowa for Minnesota would be to abandon necessary woodlands for "prairie country." He ended by calling "the great spirit, earth, sky and weather to witness that we choose what is best for our people."[77]

Poweshiek's phrasing reflected the evolution of his people's understanding of the context in which they were operating. His emphasis on the welfare of Meskwaki families echoed the tribal leaders' commitments to and respect for consensus-based decision-making. He reinforced spiritual and physical connections to place. Perhaps most revealing was Poweshiek's emphasis on ownership. Meskwaki, Sauk, and other Indigenous peoples had long negotiated systems of territorial control. These were different from Euro-American land ethics—specifically, land as an asset that could be bought and sold through individual markets.[78] Historians have long suggested that the dissonance between these conceptions of territorial control factored into the Sauk and Meskwaki communities' confusion about the terms and scale of the 1804 land cession. Nearly four decades later, Poweshiek, his people, and their Sauk relatives plainly understood what the Americans gained from land cessions. Framing his opposition to the 1841 treaty proposal by establishing the Meskwaki Nation's authority to decide whether to sell—what we today would call sovereignty—reflected

Poweshiek's effort to avoid terms that would be unsatisfactory to his people.

Wapello was adamantly opposed to removal. When he addressed the council, he invoked history and discussed the consequences of land sales. He also described the Red Earth People's connection to the land and water on the Upper Mississippi, which had saved them from oblivion and offered respite and enjoyment during a tumultuous epoch. "We were once a powerful, but now a small nation," he said. "When the white people first crossed the big water and landed on this Island, they were then small as we now are. I remember when Wiskonsin [sic] was ours and it now has our name. We sold it to you. Rock River & Rock Island was once ours. We sold them to you. Dubuque was once ours. We sold that to you and they are now occupied by white men who live happy. Rock River was the only place where we lived happily & we sold that to you." Then he turned to the consequences of the deal. "This land is all we have. It is our only fortune. When it is gone, we shall have nothing left."[79]

By the end of the conversation, the Sauk leaders Keokuk and Appanoose had also spoken. The men declared their agreement with the Red Earth People. There would be no sale. At that, a flustered Chambers expressed dismay. He chastised the Sauk and Meskwaki leaders for their decision and accused them of squandering government money on whiskey and other unnecessary goods. He warned them that creditors would soon refuse to trade with the tribes. If the Meskwaki and Sauk leaders left the Americans with a retort, Grimes did not record it. The conversation ended with no agreement struck.[80]

ONE THOUSAND BOXES OF MONEY

Just days shy of one year later, on October 4, 1842, tribal leaders once again sat across from American negotiators at the Sac and Fox Agency. Around 2,000 Meskwaki and Sauk people camped in wickiups near the agency office, anticipating news about the fate of their lands.[81] Governor Chambers was the primary representative for the Americans—Commissioner Crawford had not made the trip. Instead, his subordinate, the Indian agent John Beach, took notes. Poweshiek and Keokuk were both present, but tribal leadership had a notable absence: the fifty-five-year-old Wapello had passed away earlier in the year.[82]

Prospects had not improved for either the Meskwaki or Sauk tribes since the previous fall. If anything, pressure to cede land had increased. Some tribal leaders were leaning that way. Chambers privately reported to Crawford that in "confidential communications" with Keokuk, the Sauk leader had said that his people were "disposed to sell *all* their lands," but made it clear "that there would be difficulty in bringing the Fox Chiefs and Braves into their views."[83] Going into the meeting, the Meskwaki Nation was still unconvinced that a land sale was the correct path.

Chambers opened the 1842 session by reminding the group of the previous year's negotiations, and the United States' continued interest in acquiring "the whole of your country." He did not hide his government's frustration, noting that the president wished to make a single treaty. He alluded to the settlers filling the periphery of Sauk and Meskwaki land and framed the government's position in paternalistic tones. The United States had stationed military units "to protect you" from settlers, he told the Sauk and Meskwaki leaders, and wanted to "give you a home where they can no longer molest you." He also leaned heavily on the debts, noting that "The Whites will follow you as buzzards do a carcass to get your money and everything of value you have." If the tribes continued selling land in piecemeal fashion, they would eventually run out of property and would have no other way to get in the black.[84]

If Chambers's statements fell short of threats, they certainly articulated the growing pressure on the tribes, which placed the Americans in an advantageous position. Indeed, the 1842 offer was considerably lower than that from the previous year. That agreement had been for $1 million *and* the two tribes' accumulated trade debt. In 1842, the offer had been reduced to "one million dollars (one thousand boxes of money)," from which the tribes would pay their debts and draw annuities on whatever remained.[85]

After hearing this proposal, the group disbanded so the tribes could confer. They met again on Thursday morning, and a junior Meskwaki leader named Kawkawke introduced Poweshiek. Notably, this was the first time the Meskwaki delegates had opened the negotiations—a point they reinforced verbally to remind the audience of their firm belief that the land in question, west of the Mississippi, was primarily theirs. He reminded Chambers of the spiritual and communal authority of his council. "We govern by the appointment of the Great Spirit, and by the will of the nation," he began. Then he spoke of the Red Earth People's connection to place. "This land was given to us to do with as we please. After the Great Spirit made this vast island, he placed the chiefs upon it, he gave us the sun and moon and stars and all the great lights; he gave us the beasts of the field and the birds that fly for our meat and for our dresses. He made the trees and gave names to them for our benefit, and he not only gave us these but he gave us the great medicine bag and everything you see to make us a great people."[86]

Poweshiek then noted that the two tribes had spent considerable time weighing several separate counterproposals. The Sauk diplomat Wishecomacquet described the fourth and final of these ideas, to which both tribes had agreed. "The country we now have left upon which to support our women and children is small," he said, but they would make a substantial land sale "to pay our traders and to place our friends and relations by giving something to them." The tribes, however, wanted to retain the western portion of their Iowa homeland. They proposed parting with a large tract of land that would run from the northern border of Missouri to a place on the Des Moines River called Painted Rocks, then north along part of the Iowa River toward the Neutral Ground.[87] Although its precise boundaries were never detailed, this was an attempt to retain land in the same area to which the Meskwaki Nation would eventually return.

Chambers did not budge, and for several days Sauk and Meskwaki leaders haggled with him, breaking each day for separate councils and returning with clarifying questions and counteroffers. They asked Chambers to restore the $1 million plus debt offer from the year before and persuaded him to compromise: In the end, the United States would acquire all of the Sauk and Meskwaki lands in Iowa for $800,000, from which the tribes would receive a 5 percent annuity, plus full debt relief. This totaled $1,058,566.34.[88]

Meskwaki and Sauk leaders made the best of an impossible situation. Chambers had considerable leverage to compel a cession and even had a $10,000 budget for bribes. The treaty council that took the last 11 million acres of Sauk and Meskwaki land occurred amid deep stresses, entrenched distrust, and the threats of economic and demographic collapse. Many Meskwaki people opposed the outcome.[89] The stakes, of course, were high and the outcome devastating. Yet, given all the challenges surrounding their people and the disagreements they sparked, the deal finalized on October 11 included several important concessions to the tribes.

First, by rejecting the 1841 offer, the Sauk and Meskwaki Nations avoided being deported to undesirable and potentially dangerous land to the north. Instead, the 1842 treaty promised to create a "permanent and perpetual residence" for both tribes, a "tract of land suitable and convenient for Indian purposes." Although the exact location was not yet determined, the treaty stipulated that it would be "upon the Missouri River, or some of its waters."[90] Meskwaki and Sauk people had spent a substantial amount of time on the southern reaches of the Missouri watershed. Nearly forty years earlier, Meriwether Lewis had noted that the "Saukes, Foxes, and Ayauways usually pass[ed]" Murrow Creek, "a distance of five miles above the mouth of the Osage River," as they traveled the Kansas and Missouri plains to raid against the Osage Nation. Lewis described the area as "a tolerable country, well timbered and waterd," and Sauk and Meskwaki leaders saw this as a more acceptable site, at least, than southern Minnesota.[91]

Tribal leaders also arranged for the removal process to be staggered. Sauk and Meskwaki people would move from a portion of the territory beyond what was known as the "Red Rock Line" as soon as the treaty went into effect, but they would complete the final removal only after a transition period. This, as Keokuk put it, gave his people time "to look at our new home and prepare to move their women and children there." The tribes also rejected federal advances that would have required them to spend their money on assimilatory education. And, having heard that the government "sometimes altered treaties . . . after they were signed," the tribes secured a clause confirming that if the US Senate changed the terms of their treaty, it would be sent back to the tribes for their review and approval.[92]

Finally came the issue of price. Although lower than the 1841 offer, the final treaty was higher than the $1 million figure his superiors had hoped Chambers could talk the Meskwaki and Sauk leaders down to.[93] It included infrastructure like blacksmiths and other federal support—but no compulsory education—as well as a clause enabling the tribes to use "any portion of the annuities payable to them, under this or any former treaty, to the purchase of goods or provisions, *or to agricultural purposes,* or any other object tending to their improvement, *or calculated to increase the comfort and happiness of their people.*"[94] Unbeknownst to them at the time, this provision would open the door to land acquisitions decades down the road. Most important in 1842, however, was the fact that the Sauk and Meskwaki Nations parted from their Iowa lands for between about 10 and 11 dollars an acre, a much higher price than the ten cents the tribes received for each acre lost to the Black Hawk Purchase. In short, the tribes let go of $200,000 on their annuity principle and accepted just over one thousand boxes of money in exchange for preferable land, total debt relief, a periodic infusion of cash, and a few other benefits, like a quality headstone and burial plot for the recently deceased leader Wapello.[95]

Taking the long view of their history, Meskwaki and Sauk leaders saw that Iowa offered the resources necessary to stabilize in a time of crisis—just as it had after "the time of our surrounded," a century earlier. They hesitated to treat and tried bargaining to keep a portion of their homeland. But, flanked by crises, facing no better options, and with cession seeming inevitable, they agreed on paper to removal. One witness to the negotiations wrote that "the conviction that there was little or no game in their present country, and that the one to which they were invited abounded in every species," was the factor that drove the most hesitant leaders to affirm the treaty.[96] This decision did not mark surrender; it was a means to an end. It bought time, and it would ultimately reveal itself as creating, rather paradoxically, the best chance the Red Earth People had to remain in Iowa for good.

None of these considerations, of course, outweighed the devastating loss experienced by the Red Earth People and the Yellow Earth People, who had spent a century reconstituting a homeland after a long, devastating migration. The pain they felt from the 1842 taking and the high possibility that they might never return to the villages was real. One white witness to the treaty council would later recall Poweshiek's grief as the reality of the pending deportation sunk in. He understood that the tribes had made the best decision, given the circumstances, but saw that there "will be crying in the bottoms" when he delivered the news to his people.[97] Another observer recalled "the silent and systematic action" of the Sauk and Meskwaki families as they broke camp and departed the treaty grounds.[98]

A half year later, the removal of the Sauk and Meskwaki Nations began on schedule. In an episode that presaged the land runs that would make

Oklahoma "Sooners" famous later in the century, "thousands of land seekers . . . gathered on the border" of a tract in central Iowa. They waited until the treaty went into effect on May 1, 1843, then flooded in to claim land. Reflecting back on the era following these land runs, one Iowa reporter noted that, "slowly but surely the Indians were crowded out and the hills and valleys that used to be the home of deer and wild turkeys began to produce wheat and corn and oats."[99] The process repeated in 1845, and, with that, the deportation of the Sauk and Meskwaki Nations from Iowa was complete.

Or at least it would have been. The Red Earth People never really left.

PART II

Settlement Sovereignty

"We have reason to be satisfied with [Iowa], the place where we now dwell. There is not too much prairie; wood is plentiful, of which there are many kinds, and enough for all our needs. Water is always good to drink. Winters are never too cold, and the summers are always pleasant. It is our wish to dwell here always."

—Meskwaki person, as quoted by anthropologist William Jones

CHAPTER 3

Renegades

October 1845 came and went. Under the terms of the removal treaty signed three years before, that was the month by which the Red Earth People should have abandoned Iowa, a land that, according to the Indian agent John Beach, "from long possession, they [had] naturally become much attached."[1] Most Meskwaki families did not leave, instead moving west to camp for a time with Potawatomi families near the Missouri River on the western edge of Iowa.[2] These Red Earth People spent the next several years hunting and living on the fringes of burgeoning settler towns in Iowa, all while evading American dragoons tasked with forcing them south. By then, the federal government had assigned the Sauk and Meskwaki Nations a reservation in what was known as the "Indian Territory," which the federal government had slated to become the final holding place for the myriad Indigenous communities it forcibly deported across the Mississippi River.[3]

The Osage River reservation sat along the western stretch of a Missouri tributary, about forty miles south of what is now Topeka, Kansas. Those Red Earth People who accompanied their Sauk relatives there despised the place. Members of both tribes knew the Osage River territory well, but whatever optimism Meskwaki families had during the treaty negotiations about the condition of their new homeland evaporated once the tribes actually visited their federal assignment. Although one soil survey describes most of the land around the reservation as being covered with fine earth, it was also prone to intense summer heat that, coupled with prolonged dry periods, could severely hamper the growing season. In the 1840s and 1850s, the place suffered periodic droughts and had rocky soil that, at least to Meskwaki families, did not compare to the fertile land

81

further north. Making matters worse, the water was undrinkable and fresh springs few.[4]

Historians and other scholars have highlighted the important role relationality plays in Indigenous conceptions of land and place.[5] Meskwaki people's reflections on Kansas, which emphasize the failures of the Osage River reservation, reveal another dimension: the capacity of a land base to fail to care for its people, and a people's ability to willfully avoid places that could not sustain them. Recalling his community's experience in Kansas, one Meskwaki man complained to an anthropologist about Kansas around 1900: "The country toward the south is too warm in summer," he said, "the water there is not good to drink, and the hot winds parch the soil and the plants that try to grow."[6] Summarizing the sentiments of his ancestors more than a century later, Meskwaki Tribal Historian Johnathan Buffalo put it this way: "Kansas [was] out of our environment. Iowa was at the edge of our environment, but Kansas was a different type of environment, a different grass. Even the buffalo behaved differently, because we were used to the woodland buffalo. We were used to our rattlesnakes or swamp rattlesnakes. Prairie rattlesnakes are different. So everything was different."[7]

Meskwaki and Sauk families faced additional challenges in Kansas. With a firmer grip on the Indian Territory, the federal Office of Indian Affairs pushed assimilationist policies. Despite the tone and terms of the 1842 treaty, Meskwaki people found that on the Osage River reservation, their people were closely monitored by federal agents, who subjected them to relentless pressure to convert to Christianity and take up commercial farming.[8] Epidemic diseases ran rampant through the Indian Territory. Several hundred Sauk and Meskwaki people had died from outbreaks of cholera, diphtheria, pneumonia, and smallpox in Kansas by 1852. Outbreaks of violence with Osage and Comanche enemies compounded the difficulties of life on the new reservation.[9] And no visitor to "bleeding Kansas" would have been unaware of the violence over Indigenous lands and the expansion of slavery that raged across that place in the 1850s.[10]

For all these reasons, Meskwaki people preferred to remain in Iowa. When the 1845 deadline went into effect, the tribe dispersed into smaller bands and left for the river valleys. As summer 1846 approached, only about one out of five Meskwaki people had reported to the Osage River reservation. Around 900 Red Earth People remained scattered throughout the Iowa countryside.[11] They traveled widely, with some spending the winters with Kickapoo relatives on their Kansas reservation.[12] According to one member of the Meskwaki tribe who had been born in 1854 and whose father was among those who would organize the Iowa land purchase three years later, the decision to leave Kansas was straightforward. Those tribal members who stayed near Tama "didn't like the idea of moving, and they didn't like the country in Kansas. They liked Iowa."[13] These challenges led many to prefer the tallgrass prairies and wooded river landings of Iowa.[14] Such was their people's disdain for the reservation that, some years after purchasing their Iowa settlement, several Meskwaki leaders informed an Indian agent that they would "suffer death rather than go" back to Kansas.[15]

As Meskwaki leaders like Poweshiek planned this return, they sought to dissolve the Meskwaki Nation's formal relationship with the Sauk Nation, which was a step toward gaining a separate home. Beginning in 1846, the Meskwaki Nation made repeated overtures to the Indian Service, asking that the federal government recognize the "Sac and Fox Tribe" as separate Sauk and Meskwaki tribes. The Meskwaki leaders wanted to live, negotiate, and be paid separately from their old allies. Claiming that a dissolution of the "Sac and Fox Tribe" would violate old treaties and set a bad precedent for other tribes, the agents repeatedly refused these requests. They also denied Poweshiek and his council an invitation to meet in Washington.[16]

Amid these setbacks, the Red Earth People continued to live in Iowa. Archaeologists have sketched the movements of these Meskwaki renegades. Prior to 1842, the Meskwaki and Sauk communities generally lived separately in a few key villages, which had been pushed west after the US-Sauk War. Poweshiek led a major Meskwaki village on the banks of the Iowa River. Before his death, Wapello and others located farther away on the Des Moines River, close to the Sauk families who had congregated there. In several cases, these villages had substantial gardens and agricultural fields and were within a reasonable proximity to trade forts that provided access to goods.[17] After the removal period, these villages are harder to pinpoint, but around 600 Meskwaki people were living along the Iowa River in 1847. Iowa had achieved statehood the year before and, with that designation, named ninety-nine mostly rectangular counties. Settlers reported that the

Red Earth People had returned to Tama County, the eventual site of the Meskwaki Settlement, to harvest corn and maple sap for sugar the next year. Shortly thereafter, small villages had also popped up in nearby Linn and Iowa Counties.[18]

Throughout the 1840s and early 1850s, many members of the Meskwaki tribe spent their summers in Iowa's river valleys, in defiance of the 1842 treaty. They lived alongside communities of people from the Potawatomie and Ho-Chunk Nations—considered "renegades" from their assigned reservations—who also camped and hunted in Iowa during this time. This is not to say that Meskwaki people never went to the Osage River reservation. Quite the opposite: many commuted to and from Kansas each year as they waited out bitter winters, collected their annuity payments, and visited relatives. Sometimes, American dragoons would catch up with a Meskwaki band and escort them to Kansas, but this never lasted long. Despite considerable effort, the army never removed all the Red Earth People from Iowa.[19]

The decision to remain in Iowa was shaped by the Meskwaki Nation's connection to place and historical appreciation for the space and resources it offered. The same Meskwaki informant who detailed why the Red Earth People did not like Kansas articulated the tribe's preference for Iowa: "We have reason to be satisfied with the place where we now dwell," the informant said. "There is not too much prairie; wood is plentiful, of which there are many kinds, and enough for all our needs. Water is always good to drink. Winters are never too cold, and the summers are always pleasant. It is our wish to dwell here always."[20]

Many generations earlier, in the fallout from the Fox Wars, the Sauk and Meskwaki Nations decided their best chance for survival lay in alliance, camaraderie, and restoration along the Upper Mississippi. Facing terrible options in the 1842 treaty negotiations, moving to a new homeland along the Missouri River watershed had seemed viable. When Meskwaki families decided the Osage River reservation was unacceptable, their path diverged from their old Sauk relatives and those Meskwaki people who chose to remain in Kansas. In the 1840s and 1850s, new challenges presented an array of potential solutions. Even as they attempted to break the legal unification imposed upon them by the federal government, the two nations never abandoned their bonds of kinship. They just undertook different strategies. Many Meskwaki people, their prospects growing dim as the nineteenth century reached its midpoint, believed that only a permanent return to the emerald horizon could restore their community.

MAKING NICE

Evading the American military required a deft awareness of the land and how to move on it. But it also demanded patience, restraint, and diplomacy. Tension and intermittent violence between tribes and settlers raged across Iowa. Across the expanding United States, the US Army and Native tribes engaged in more than 520 violent encounters between 1850 and 1865. Several were terrible slaughters of Native men, women, and children by army soldiers, who hauled increasingly lethal weapons west to "pacify" the continent. In addition to the tensions in western Iowa, violence scarred neighboring Nebraska, Kansas, and Minnesota.[21]

As blood seeped into Western land, settler communities became very adept at pressing state and federal officials for protection from nearby Native Americans. They sometimes exaggerated this threat, knowing that federal intervention would deliver the double benefit of clearing Indigenous peoples from their land and boosting the local economy by bringing soldiers—and the federal contracts that fed, sheltered, and equipped them—to the region.[22]

The Meskwaki Nation countered by trying to avoid conflict. Meskwaki leaders sought to make nice with their white neighbors throughout the early 1850s. The chief's council, led by Poweshiek until his death in 1854, traveled to communities across central Iowa. As one agent wrote, tribal leaders visited "with every [white] settlement within their reach" and strictly prohibited any "disturbances or depredations by reckless members of the band."[23] They sought to craft an image of peace and goodwill and to avoid inflaming tensions with the residents of the new farming towns that had begun to dot the Iowa countryside.[24]

To do so, the tribe did several things. In 1848, some Meskwaki families offered supplies and help to a group of American land surveyors who had been raided by a Dakota band along the Des Moines River.[25] In the early summer of 1850, around seventy Meskwaki people held a grand parade into Des Moines and performed for the public or, as one observer put it, "displayed the light fantastic toe for about an hour on the greensward."[26]

Meskwaki leaders also refused to retaliate after two groups of settlers in Linn and Marshall Counties, angry at Meskwaki families for hunting and cutting down trees, destroyed Meskwaki camps around 1850.[27] Tribal members maintained good relations with inhabitants of the Community of True Inspirationists, a Christian sect of German immigrants that had also settled in east-central Iowa and began building the 26,000-acre "Amana Colonies" in the 1850s.[28]

These efforts were not always successful. In 1852, settlers asked government officials to chase the Red Earth People out of Iowa; when it did, Meskwaki families returned.[29] Complaints against Indigenous peoples continued for years. In January 1855, James Grimes wrote to Iowa's four congressional delegates. He was the same man that had served as secretary during the 1841 treaty negotiations. In the decade that followed, Grimes had become a star in Iowa politics and was now a worried governor. He told his state's federal representatives that he was "constantly receiving petitions and letters from the people on the frontier, asking for protection" from Indigenous peoples. Grimes believed that the bands of Dakota, Nakota, Potawatomi, and Omaha peoples mentioned in these petitions were simply camping in Iowa over the winter "with no apparent hostile intent." He nonetheless asked an officer from Fort Dodge to "protect both the settlers and the Indians, and particularly to preserve the peace." But, concerned that he lacked the legal authority or funds for any military action, and hearing reports that another group of Dakotas, near the newly founded Sioux City, might present an actual threat, Grimes requested federal assistance.[30]

Eleven months later, Grimes wrote another, more impassioned, letter, this time to President Franklin Pierce. The governor stated that Iowa's northwestern counties were "greatly disturbed by the intrusion of wandering bands of Winnebagoes, Sioux, Pottawattamies, Omahas, and Sacs and Foxes." He claimed that these tribes "were a constant annoyance to the citizens of those counties—destroying their stock—stealing their grain and provisions—threatening their lives, and in some instances committing robbery and murder."[31] Yet, with the exception of asking the sheriff of one county to push a group of Potawatomis west of the Missouri River after an incident left a settler dead, he declined to "call out the militia and expel [the tribes] by force."[32]

Grimes feared that without a military fort in the West, either paranoid settlers or desperate Natives would instigate serious violence in the region. He asked the president to establish an army outpost to assuage the tensions. Grimes was right. Facing starvation over the harsh winter of 1857–1858, a Wahpekute Dakota band killed thirty-eight settlers in a raid at Spirit Lake along the state's northwestern border with Minnesota.[33] That area would remain embroiled in the ongoing territorial conflict between regional Dakota groups and the US government into the 1860s.[34]

SECURING RESIDENCY

The Meskwaki Nation did more than avoid violence. In the early 1850s, it launched into a years-long lobbying effort aimed at convincing the State of Iowa to support the tribe's permanent return to Iowa, despite the terms of the 1842 treaty. The details of how this idea came to be and how the process played out are surprisingly thin. No records tell of the chief's council meetings on this subject, or the extent to which tribal leaders relied on settler allies for advice about navigating the Iowa political system. It is clear, however, that as early as February 1852, two groups of settlers had petitioned the Iowa General Assembly, asking the state government to authorize the tribe's efforts to buy a parcel of land in the state and stay forever.[35]

We are left with only fragments of evidence of how the Meskwaki chief's council realized that state support could restore their people's residency and, in addition to making nice with the locals, how they decided to find a way to make it happen. According to the historian Duran Ward, who wrote extensively about Meskwaki history in the early twentieth century, the idea could be traced to a group of Meskwaki leaders. One was Mamiwanige, who led the chief's council in the early 1860s, and the other was a Meskwaki man named Patagoto. Neither of these men signed the 1842 treaty, but they were growing into leadership positions by the early 1850s.[36]

One petition from the citizens of Marion County, for example, revealed some of the arguments Meskwaki leaders were making at that time. "Many of the Indians," the petitioners wrote, "have returned to their old hunting grounds among us." Meskwaki people told the settlers that they were "fast wasting away" and "that their children die off rapidly." The tribe made it clear that they were not there to fight and, indeed, lacked "sufficient force to sustain themselves against their more powerful neighbors" even if violence erupted. Finally, the tribe "represent[ed] also that they are disposed to turn their attention to agriculture, and are particularly anxious to be allowed a grant of land sufficient for that purpose somewhere on the waters of the Red Cedar."[37] By the next year Meskwaki leaders had tasked a small group of tribal members with making plans to buy property.[38]

Why would Iowa support this unusual request? Several historians have documented how, although some settlers continued to demand the tribe's removal into the 1850s, most of those living closest to the Red Earth People grew to support the tribe's bid for residency.[39] Scholars have postulated that settlers petitioned on behalf of the Meskwaki Nation out of a sense of benevolent pragmatism. Some were genuinely convinced of the need and intentions of the Red Earth People, and, framing their support in the assimilationist logic of the era, "recommend[ed] them as Good Civil Indians," noting that "the majority of the citizens in this County have no objection to their remaining in this country and are willing to assist them all they can."[40] Others recognized that tribal members had annuities to spend and were good customers for local mercantilists. Regardless of settlers' motivations, these petitions highlighted the overall effectiveness of Meskwaki diplomacy.[41]

Meanwhile, as the Red Earth People worked to secure their official return to Iowa, a new political coalition was forming at the state capital, Iowa City. By the 1850s, the issues of the day had driven Iowa party politics into chaos. The debate over free and slave states lingered alongside new questions. How many immigrants would be allowed into western states? How much influence should Catholics and Mormons have in state government? By the mid-1850s, a half dozen political parties had organized around different answers to these questions.[42]

The Meskwaki Nation found an ally in James Grimes, the man who had taken notes during the 1841 treaty negotiations where Poweshiek and Wapello made impassioned statements about the importance of Iowa to their people. More than a decade later, Grimes was among a group of Iowa politicians who were coalescing around major political changes. Elected governor as a Whig in 1854, Grimes helped found the state's Republican Party two years later, when he and others united abolitionist Protestants.[43] Their new, staunchly anti-slavery party stitched together a winning coalition of Iowans from across the state's busy political spectrum. Along with delivering Grimes another two-year term of office (this time as a Republican) in 1856, Iowa voters elected Republican legislators like Josiah Grinnell, who won a seat in the state senate that year.[44]

These Republicans supported the Red Earth People. This was partly ideological. As Grinnell argued, a party fighting for the rights of African American slaves should, by extension, also help Native people.[45] Yet Republican support for the Meskwaki Nation also stood to solve part of the state's brewing problem with the many groups of Indigenous peoples still living within its boundaries. At the same moment that the Red Earth People lobbied the state legislature for a return bill, Governor Grimes was desperately trying to avoid serious violence between tribes and settlers in the western reaches of the state.

Sometime in 1856, another group of white Iowans sent a petition supporting the Meskwaki Nation to Grinnell during his campaign for state senate.[46] Grinnell looked into the issue, and although details of their meetings are scarce, it seems that Meskwaki leaders made a convincing case. Following these discussions, Grimes chose to support the Red Earth People and used his influence in the new Republican Party to push a bill asking that "the Indians now residing in Tama county [sic] known as a portion of the Sacs and Foxes, be permitted to remain and reside in the State." The bill also asked the federal government to continue paying the tribe its treaty annuities despite its outlaw status. The bill passed on July 15, 1856.[47]

After a long and difficult epoch, the Red Earth People had followed Wisaka's arrow back to central Iowa, carefully negotiating and winning their formal, legal return to the state—at least as far as Iowa was concerned. Their next challenge was locating and acquiring a parcel of land the Meskwaki Nation could reclaim.

VISION

In the old story, Wisaka sent the Red Earth People west. Their migration followed a circuitous path along the prairie peninsula and into the emerald horizon. Over hundreds of years and untold trips into and around the Old Northwest, their journey was shaped by nearly constant conflict and dislocation, punctuated by periods of relative stability and growth. In the 1840s, however, a devastating array of challenges led to their formal removal from Iowa forever. Another story, passed down through the generations and recounted by Meskwaki elder Donald Wanatee, explains how the Meskwaki Nation selected the small riparian plot upon which its people would heal and grow.

Sometime in the early 1850s, the story goes, the Red Earth People were camped along the Iowa River when several Meskwaki clan leaders held a ceremony. It required them to build a boat, fast for several days, and journey up the river. After the men turned around a sharp bend, a woman appeared before them. She stood waist deep in the water and said they had found the right place. The woman said to return to that spot, where the river bends sharply, forming a long, backward "S." This curve was situated on marshy lowlands at the base of a ridge just west of the towns of Tama and Toledo. There, she said, the people should settle. Then the woman disappeared.[48]

Soon afterward, the Red Earth People began searching for property in that vicinity. Their search continued throughout the 1850s and overlapped with—and likely informed—Meskwaki leaders' efforts to gain the bill that reinstated their Iowa residency in 1856. Within a year of that law's passage, tribal leaders sent a Meskwaki man to visit a pair of white Iowa settlers named Isaac and Susan Butler, the settlers who would make the fateful sale to the Red Earth People.

Isaac Butler had been born in the American South early in the century. He was a veteran of the Mexican American War, and he and Susan had moved to Wisconsin and then Linn County, Iowa, before settling along the Iowa River in 1852. An influential member of the local community, Butler served as postmaster and justice of the peace. Over time, he acquired a great deal of land in an area called the Indian Village Township. The Butler family was so prominent, in fact, that locals simply referred to the area as "Butlerville."[49]

Of the millions of Midwestern acres they had lived on and used, the Red Earth People focused their attention on a small riparian region in central Iowa. They had several reasons. Wanatee's story offers one. Another was the area's sparse population. It was located away from burgeoning urban centers like Des Moines, which was about 70 miles southwest of Butlerville. The first white settlers had arrived in the area in 1849. Tama County was formed in 1853 and quickly became home to about 200 settlers. The local population grew slowly from there, and by 1870 the town of Tama had increased to just over 1,000 residents.[50]

This remoteness served an important purpose. Seeing the potential for violence, the Meskwaki Nation sought a place with relatively few neighbors and continued to carefully cultivate cordial relationships with them. As long as commerce and casual diplomacy kept the peace, settling in the southwestern corner of Tama County would allow the Red Earth People to live quietly on the woods and prairies.

Meskwaki people knew that the Butler property possessed several crucial attributes that would allow them to reestablish the subsistence economy that had served their people for generations. One possible site was located at an Iowa River campsite that tribal members had used often while skirting the federal dragoons until at least 1855. Fixed near the water's edge, the site included first-rate soil and promised ample game, fish, and crops, not to mention the maple, elm, black walnut, and other trees that provided fuel for fires and timber for shelter and tools. The site also included an "old Indian sugar camp," where Meskwaki families made maple syrup, and a 3.5-acre garden. Four trails spiraled outward in each direction from the village, suggesting that it was a central hub for Meskwaki travelers who made trading trips through central Iowa. A short walk southwest led to a small cabin that belonged to a settler who had set up a post to facilitate trade with the Red Earth People.[51]

This site, called "Indiantown," should have been perfect. But it was not where, in the old story, the woman from the river told the people to settle. That place was five miles downriver.[52] Not coincidentally, the acreage she recommended offered a near duplicate of the Indiantown environment. Although most of the property between the Indiantown village site and the Settlement's eventual location contained mostly "broken and second-rate land," surveyors reported that the eighty Settlement acres consisted of "level [and] first rate land with oak, ash, sycamore, cottonwood, and maple timbers."[53]

The Iowa River snaked its way from the northwestern to southeastern corners of the plot, bringing fresh water and fish through Meskwaki land, along with deer and small mammals. Flat ground, rich soil, heavy tree cover teeming with game, and a constant source of food and water made the Settlement an ideal location to replicate the Indiantown village that had previously served the Red Earth People well. Meskwaki leaders knew this was the prime location upon which to rebuild their community.

STRIKING A DEAL

By the fall of 1856, the Meskwaki Nation was ready to move forward. According to a Meskwaki man named Hapayasha, he traveled to central Iowa that autumn with Mamiwanige and around eighty Red Earth People. They traveled in three small groups, assembling wickiups along the Iowa River, on the Cedar River, and near the town of Marengo. Mamiwanige had $735 in his saddle, money the tribe had raised from annuities and crafts sales. They came to buy land.[54]

In February, the chief's council sent around a dozen delegates to Iowa City, where they met at the Old Capitol building, now the iconic heart of the University of Iowa's campus. According to newspaper accounts, the Meskwaki men arrived "bedizened with paint, and arrayed in the grandiest style." Presumably, some wore bear claw necklaces. There, they held a dance performance in the Senate chamber and met with Governor Grimes. "They prefer their old hunting grounds to their present location in Kansas," one reporter wrote, and came "to get the Governor's aid in locating lands" for the purpose of returning to Iowa forever.[55] Meskwaki delegates returned to Iowa City at least once more, about two weeks later.[56] According to one Meskwaki oral history, during one of these meetings Governor Grimes told the Meskwaki Nation's chief's council that although he could not compel any settler to sell property to the tribe, if they could find someone to do it, his office would support the transaction.[57]

A few months later, in the spring of 1857, Mamiwanige and the chief's council sent a representative to the Butler Farm. Some sources suggest this was Patagoto.[58] Whoever it was, the delegate arrived on horseback and offered to purchase a portion of the family's land. Isaac Butler expressed interest, and, after some discussion, the Meskwaki man returned to the chief's council to share the farmer's terms of sale. In the months that followed, he returned at least twice more. On his final visit, the diplomat informed Butler that the Meskwaki Nation had agreed to pay $1,000—which was slightly over the average market price—for 80 acres of Butler's property.[59]

Although the deal was struck, finalizing it required an extension of the Meskwaki Nation's political strategy. The tribe had secured permission from the state legislature in 1856 to inhabit the Iowa countryside, but, under the terms of the 1842 treaty, they were formally banished from Iowa.[60] With the Butlers in agreement, the chief's council sent five diplomats, men named Mathanuh, Waukano, Chalkkalamah, Matauaquah, and Patagoto, to secure the deal. They gathered in the Old Capitol and established the process through which their community could acquire 80 acres along the Iowa River.[61] They appealed to Grimes, who agreed to purchase the land with the tribe's money and hold it in trust.[62] The Red Earth People had raised the necessary $1,000 by selling handmade crafts and stockpiling their treaty annuities.[63]

The terms of their agreement were straightforward. The governor would use the Meskwaki money to buy the land, hold it in trust, and then arrange for this unique agreement to continue through his successors in office. Although Iowa's governors would technically hold title to the Settlement, the state's agreement with the Meskwaki Nation preserved the tribe's control over its land. In exchange for this promise, the Meskwaki Nation agreed to pay Iowa property taxes and ensure that its members would follow Iowa's laws.[64]

On July 13, 1857—just two days shy of the one-year anniversary of the 1856 residency act—Isaac Butler and his two sons, Philip and David, traveled to Toledo. There, they asked a county officer to draft the final deed that sold 80 acres of Butler family property to "James W. Grimes Governor of the State of Iowa and his successors in office in trust" for the Meskwaki Nation. With the document prepared, the five Meskwaki representatives traveled to Iowa City, where they delivered it and their people's money to Governor Grimes. To fulfill his part of the transaction, Grimes gave the payment—$1,000 in gold—to a Tama County farmer who appears to have been in Iowa City on business but had agreed to act as a courier. The man loaded the gold into his lumber wagon and delivered it to the Butlers. When they received the money, the purchase of the Meskwaki Settlement was complete.[65]

There was one small problem. Just like the 1804 treaty with the "Sac and Fox Nation," the 1857 deed had been cast in the language and form of American real estate transactions. Instead of the entire Meskwaki Nation, the deed mistakenly named Mathanuh, Waukano, Chalkkalamah, Matauaquah, and Patagoto "and their heirs forever" as the trustees to the tribe's new land.[66] Decades down the road, this wording would sow disagreement within the Meskwaki Nation. In the summer of 1857, however, the details were not important. All that mattered was that the Red Earth People were coming home.

REGENERATION

Using a long, curved needle made from the ribcage of bison or deer, Meskwaki women handwove cattail reeds into thick mats. They layered them over a dome-shaped wooden frame. These structures were called "wickiups," and they offered shelter and portability when the Red Earth People left the village to hunt, skirted a swelling river, or moved their homes to be near the season's fields and gardens.[67] As the weather warmed, the Red Earth People built larger bark-covered summer houses that could accommodate families of various sizes or even several families at once—"usually about four," as one observer noted.[68] According to the anthropologist Erik Gooding, these summer homes could be as large as 60 feet long and 20 feet wide, accompanied by large shade arbors that offered space for everything from meal preparation to storage and recreational space. Located on the river bottom and organized around a rectangular plaza, a summer village could last twenty years or longer. In these villages, the original one of which was known as Nekotosiye, residences were laid out according to clan and ceremonial relationships.[69]

Heavy hardwood smoke filled the air. Depending on the size, one or two central fires provided indoor heat and a cooking space. Pots of soup, boiling potatoes, or frying grease hung over an open flame, suspended by long chains and hooks arranged near ventilation holes in the ceiling. Arranged around the outer walls, beadwork and other crafts, tools, blankets, clothes, or produce filled handmade baskets. At each end of a home, a platform offered beds for residents and guests.[70]

By summer's end in 1857, the Red Earth People had established a central village called *Nekotosiye* on the lowlands near the Iowa River.[71] Over the next few years, tribal members who had been living in Kansas or camped somewhere in between slowly rejoined their relatives on the Settlement. Some Red Earth People married Sauks and chose to remain in the Indian

Territory.[72] Those who came to Iowa arrived in groups, usually led by a Meskwaki man. A history provided by the Meskwaki elder Young Bear around 1905, for example, notes that Patagoto escorted 188 Red Earth People to Iowa in the 1850s. In 1862, Mamiwanige arrived at the village with 76 people. The next year, Wapanuka brought 36 more, Paquesheka came with 13 in 1864, and Makaka brought 10 people up from Kansas in 1865. Within a few short years, the Settlement village was home to about 250 people.[73]

Beginning with the passage of the Homestead Act in 1862, the United States would provide quarter sections of land to settlers willing to head west to claim and break formerly Indigenous land. Compared to that amount of property—160 acres for a single family—the 80 Settlement acres seem hardly large enough for the growing Meskwaki community. To yeomen farm families that sought to prove up their land, gain title, and sell the commodities they raised at market, the land was an asset necessary for production. It was bounded by the next person's property line.

For the Red Earth People, however, the Settlement offered a gathering space and an anchor. It was a relative upon whom the community could rely for sustenance and security. Everything there took place in the Meskwaki language and according to the worldview and customs of the Red Earth People. It was a haven upon which Meskwaki people could live, govern, pray, and—perhaps most importantly, at least in the short term—work and survive on their own terms.

The Settlement enabled the Red Earth People to resume a version of the seasonal hunting, foraging, and gardening-based economy that had sustained them for generations. The rest of Iowa's rural areas slowly shifted toward mass agricultural production. Its urban centers industrialized in the late nineteenth century.[74] But, out on the rural riverine prairie of Tama County, the Red Earth People did what they knew best: they made a living through seasonal work.

Meskwaki women grew, gathered, and processed their people's food. They cultivated gardens along the bottomlands, including corn, beans, squash, and pumpkins. They also foraged for wild plums, potatoes, nuts, and berries on higher ground.[75] They scoured the forest for edible and medicinal herbs or flora that provided raw materials for crafts and goods. Wild ginger, for example, was a popular catfish seasoning and a remedy for a sore throat. Skunk cabbage was said to cure toothaches and relieve swelling. The bark of black ash trees, meanwhile, was sought after for baskets.[76] Women also cleaned game, tanned skins, prepared meals, supervised children, gathered firewood and water, made clothing, and carried out other vital daily tasks.[77]

According to one Meskwaki woman, who grew up on the Settlement in the 1860s and 1870s, Meskwaki girls began learning the roles and responsibilities that would characterize their adult lives early on. It began with play: the girls made dolls from corn husks, observing their mothers and aunts as they cared for infants. They slowly learned how to sew and make moccasins by preparing clothes for their dolls. By age nine, a Meskwaki girl would be expected to help older women with their springtime planting. She also began cooking and washing clothes in the river.[78]

As girls learned these skills, older women imbued community values like being good to elders and generous and kind to others. By age ten, Meskwaki girls were gathering wood for fires and learning how to braid bags and rush mats that covered their wickiups. Meskwaki girls could make life-size moccasins by age twelve, and by age seventeen they would be paid for the skilled beadwork and crafting that produced a variety of goods traded to other tribes and local whites.[79]

In winter, families ventured off the Settlement, and Meskwaki men hunted deer and small game, bringing home venison to eat and hides for tools, saddles, and other goods. On these trips, they hunted as much as possible, storing surplus meat and furs for trade. Hunting taught young men strategy and leadership. It tested their skills. When the summer heat drove animals deeper into the lush forests, men fished the creeks and rivers. During the autumn harvest, young men worked as day laborers on local farms. Between these tasks, they also honed artisanal talents like saddle making, canoe carving, or horsemanship. They trained ponies for transportation and the plow. Leading men conducted business with government officials.[80]

The Red Earth People wove these skills, roles, responsibilities, and resources into a supportive network that could care for their families and their community over the long term. When game was scarce, gardens sustained them. If crops failed, meat, foraging, and trade provided sustenance. In times of plenty, tribal members traded for delicacies with visiting Menominees and Ho-Chunks, offering handmade Meskwaki goods and maple syrup in exchange for wild rice knocked from stalks in distant lakes.[81]

They maintained relationships with area merchants and purchased or bartered for items like "pan-cakes and coffee . . . cups and saucers, plates and other kinds of table-ware," as well as "kettle[s], ovens, pots and pans."[82]

Although this system allowed the Red Earth People to stabilize and grow, life was filled with uncertainty. Whites continued to press into the region, and reports of faraway violence must have left tribal members wondering how long their unique arrangement with Iowa would last. The threat of racial retribution also made safe passage uncertain. During the 1862 US-Dakota War in Minnesota, for example, Meskwaki people feared that they would be mistaken for hostiles if they left the Settlement. They stayed close to home and reassured locals of their peaceful intentions. Drawing from the well of goodwill they had been filling for a decade or longer, this paid off: as Meskwaki supplies dwindled that year, some local settlers donated extra venison to help the Meskwaki Nation through the winter.[83]

Rebuilding these systems sustained the Red Earth People for generations. White observers, of course, took an ungenerous view of Meskwaki life. Reviewing the early era of the Meskwaki Settlement, one historian described the place as "terribly crowded" and the Red Earth People as impoverished because they had "no regular income, and even the necessities of life were exceedingly precarious."[84] Shaded by his own expectations of material wealth and well-being, this observer failed to see that, relative to tribes forced to live off reservation rations or witness the rapid depletion of vital resources like bison, the Red Earth People had all they needed to live.

RECLAMATION

Purchasing the Meskwaki Settlement was a crucial, strategic move for the Red Earth People. This act of reclamation carved a space from which the Meskwaki Nation could regroup and separate itself from its white neighbors, who were close enough for trade but distant enough to minimize tensions. As far as the State of Iowa and the Meskwaki chief's council were concerned, the tribe collectively owned the 80 Settlement acres. It was a small but definitively Meskwaki space from which the Red Earth People could stabilize their community. Reclaiming their land was not enough, however, to defend their people from political assaults. That required the same patient political planning that had brought the Meskwaki Nation back to Iowa.

While the Red Earth People were regrouping on their Settlement, a bloody insurrection swelled in the East. After the first cannons fired on Fort Sumter in April 1861, the Civil War consumed much of the federal government's attention—although warfare against Indigenous peoples continued.[85] Keeping with its general strategy of non-belligerence, the Meskwaki Nation generally avoided the fray.

By the time the war started, the United States had added layers to the removal policies of the 1830s. In addition to forcing Indigenous people from their homelands, confining them to reservations, and steadily eroding the political power of Native Nations, policymakers increased their focus on assimilating Native people. Christian missionaries, educators, and the federal government assured equal footing for any Native person willing to "civilize" into American society. These promises would prove false.[86]

In the meantime, Native peoples faced corrosive pressures from state governments. Despite the Constitution, the treaties, and the legal quagmire created by the Marshall Trilogy—which limited state authority in tribal affairs—states exploited legal ambiguities to increase their power over the tribes that shared their geography.[87] This had been going on since the earliest days of the republic, when states began finding ways—usually through local court rulings and law enforcement actions—to incrementally extend their jurisdiction over Indian Country. This work almost always led to the disempowerment or outright deprivation of tribes and their people.[88]

In the context of these broader developments, the reclamation of the Meskwaki Settlement was not just a necessary step for regenerating the Meskwaki community. Reclaiming their land and using it to leverage the tribe's authority was an act of political defiance. Meskwaki leaders had rejected federal orders and orchestrated a formal return to Iowa. In so doing, the Red Earth People set the terms of their confinement in a way that few, if any, other Indigenous peoples could.

TRUST IN IOWA

In the 1850s, the State of Iowa played a remarkable role in enabling, facilitating, and supporting the Meskwaki Nation's efforts to craft their own fate. Iowa's stance toward Native peoples was expectedly paternalistic. After all, holding Meskwaki land in the trust of a series of white men, however useful to the tribe at the time, rang of the "Great Father" rhetoric of the day. But, compared to many other states, Iowa's relationship with the lone Native Nation planning on long-term residency within its borders was relatively benign.

Iowa did not have an office, a staff, or even a single state bureaucrat dedicated to managing affairs between tribes and the state government. In fact, the state's only discernible Indian policy seems to have centered upon members of the executive branch—often governors themselves—engaging with tribes on a case-by-case basis. The state legislature, meanwhile, continued to support Native residency. In March 1858, for example, lawmakers granted a group of Potawatomi people permission to reside in Iowa. They lived for a time in Marshall County, which borders Tama County to the west, but, unlike the Meskwaki Nation, the Potawatomi people did not stay.[89]

For four decades, beginning in 1856, Iowa attempted to neither amend its agreement with the Meskwaki Nation nor interfere in tribal affairs.[90] Successive Iowa governors honored and upheld the 1857 agreement by holding the Settlement in trust and otherwise generally staying out of tribal issues. Governors, it seems, viewed themselves as caretakers for the tribe and even worked as supportive interlocutors whom Meskwaki leaders called on in disputes with the federal government.[91]

RECOGNITION AND COERCION

The United States government stridently opposed the Meskwaki Nation's return to Iowa. Even after the state endorsed the tribe's residency and facilitated the Settlement purchase, the federal government refused to recognize the Meskwaki Nation as separate from the "Sac and Fox Tribe." Instead, the Indian Office considered the Red Earth People fugitives from the Kansas reservation and maintained that, by living in Iowa, tribal members were in violation of the 1842 removal treaty. In an effort to cajole the Red Earth People back to the Osage River, the federal government—which had thus far failed to clear the Meskwaki Nation from Iowa via either force or diplomacy—revoked the Meskwaki Nation's federal status in 1856.[92]

"Federal recognition" refers to the official acknowledgment of the nation-to-nation relationships between tribes and the United States. Recognized tribes have explicit legal and political bonds with the federal government that, at best, honor tribal sovereignty and support treaty-based rights and privileges for tribes, their people, and their land and water. So-called unrecognized tribes—including some that are recognized by states but not the federal government—lack these formal relationships.[93] So, in the eyes of the United States government, as of 1856 the Meskwaki Nation was no longer a tribe at all.

Revoking the Meskwaki Nation's status was not just a broadside attack on Meskwaki political power. It was a starvation tactic. Withholding payments—and, in many cases, rations—was a key implement in the federal toolkit for coercing tribal compliance.[94] After severing the tribe's relationship with the federal government, Indian Office administrators declared the Meskwaki Nation ineligible for the treaty annuities that had supplemented their coffers for decades. Without government money, agents believed, the Red Earth People would be unable to survive on the Iowa countryside. Eventually, they would return to Kansas, where they could be confined and controlled.[95] Federal agents also tried to diminish Mamiwanige's power in 1861 by attempting to recognize another Meskwaki man as head of the chief's council.[96]

The government was wrong on both counts. Because of the carefully structured economy they were rebuilding on the Settlement, the Red Earth People lived comfortably without their treaty annuities. Although cash poor by white standards, tribal members never became desperate enough to abandon the Settlement. And Mamiwanige continued to lead the Meskwaki Nation until his death in the 1880s.

The Indian Office tried to strain tribal finances. But the Meskwaki Nation found ways to pay its state property taxes. This could not have been easy and likely required tribal members to pass up creature comforts, and sometimes necessities, to scrape together enough cash from stockpiled annuities, trade, and wage work to clear these expenses. When times were tough, the Red Earth People prioritized their Settlement and paid their collective taxes before reaching out to state officials or locals for other assistance.[97]

For ten years, the Office of Indian Affairs continued to squeeze the Meskwaki Nation by denying their federal status and treaty payments. As the decade wore on, federal officials recognized their failure. The Red Earth People could live without the annuities and were not leaving Iowa—a position strengthened by continued advocacy from their state allies.[98]

Most importantly, however, the Indian agents saw the administrative trap they had laid for themselves: by refusing to recognize the Meskwaki Nation, the Indian Office could hardly support a budget request for an agent to oversee a non-tribe of Meskwaki people. By 1865, this issue became even more pronounced. When the Civil War ended that year, the newly re-United States returned its attention to the West. Escalating violence with other tribes—some three hundred skirmishes occurred in the first three years of Reconstruction alone—led to a resumption of the federal government's practice of proctoring massive multi-tribe treaties to keep peace in Indian Country.[99]

Amid this violence, and intent on focusing farther west, where larger tribes posed a military threat, the United States saw that its attempt to coerce the Red Earth People to Kansas had failed. In November 1865, six members of the Meskwaki chief's council traveled to Washington, DC, where they met with the commissioner of Indian affairs and President Andrew Johnson. Demonstrating their sovereignty in this way—participating in two days' worth of meetings in the US capital—tribal leaders expressed their deep desire not to return to Kansas.[100] Their diplomacy worked. Rather than staging a forced removal, the Indian Office restored the tribe's federal status in 1866. It allocated $5,588 to the Meskwaki Nation the following spring.[101]

This decision marked a victory for the Meskwaki Nation. Yet it came at a price. Federal recognition enabled the Indian Office to return to treating the tribe like all others: as a government ward to be monitored and managed by federal bureaucrats. Shortly after re-recognizing the tribe, the agency assigned a man named Leander Clark to oversee the "Tama Agency," as it called the Settlement, from an office in the nearby town of Toledo. His primary responsibility was to pay the Red Earth People's annuities, to serve as a federal watchdog, and to push the agency's goals.[102] The Meskwaki Nation found in Clark a bureaucrat willing and able to help serve an important mission.

EXPANSION

Amid the recognition contest that frustrated the Indian Office, the Meskwaki chief's council had developed a new goal: getting more land for their people.[103] An early opportunity arose in 1865, just eight years after the original Settlement purchase and one year before the tribe won re-recognition. That year, Mamiwanige and his council negotiated with a farmer named James Burge. They struck a deal. The tribe agreed to trade 130 trees for 40 acres next to the Settlement. The governor of Iowa approved the swap and folded the land into the existing trust.[104]

From that moment forward, the chief's council prioritized the acquisition of additional land. Immediately after the United States reinstated the tribe's federal recognition in 1866, Mamiwanige and his council asked Clark to set aside $2,000 of the tribe's annuities for purchasing additional land.[105] During his tenure at the Tama Agency, Clark had been a useful ally for the Meskwaki Nation. He did not advocate for the forced removal of the Meskwaki Nation—an idea that had percolated behind federal desks for years. And when tribal members asked Clark to allow Sauk and Meskwaki relatives from Kansas to join the Settlement community, he obliged, even when his superiors in Washington disapproved.[106]

The 1842 removal treaty had contained a provision empowering the Meskwaki Nation to use their annuities for "agricultural purposes [or to] increase the comfort and happiness of their people."[107] Clark agreed that land purchases fit within these terms and, recognizing that the growing Meskwaki community would need more property, authorized the expenditures. For him, adding land would enable Meskwaki families to fit more comfortably on their property and inch toward individualized farming—a keystone goal of the assimilation movement.

Over the following two years, the chief's council convinced Clark to facilitate three more land transactions, spending $7,100 on 280 acres, all adjacent to the Settlement.[108] The agent reported that tribal leaders had selected this land because it was "situated on the River bottom adjoining some timber land they had owned for a long time."[109] As the Meskwaki Nation grew in acreage and population, the tribe moved its original central village north, perhaps to get upstream and out of the floodplain. Meanwhile at least two other communities popped up on Meskwaki land but outside the central village. One was called Bear City, to which a group of tribal members moved in the fallout from a political spat. The other village was composed of visitors, like a group of Potawatomi people who spent time near the Settlement, as more and more Red Earth People married partners from tribes throughout the region.[110]

This growth occurred just as other parts of Native America were shrinking. In October 1867, the United States finalized a series of agreements with the Kiowa, Comanche, Kiowa-Apache (or Plains Apache), Southern Cheyenne, and Arapaho tribes during councils near Medicine Lodge, Kansas. Collectively known as the Treaty of Medicine Lodge, these documents facilitated the clearing of vast swaths of Native territory on the southern plains for white settlement. Just six months later, on a prairie in what is now the southeastern corner of Wyoming, representatives from several Oceti Sakowin ("Great Sioux Nation") tribes, as well as dignitaries from the Arapaho Nation, signed the Treaty of Fort Laramie. It reduced earlier territory and created a new "Great Sioux Reservation," which encompassed the western half of what is now South Dakota.[111]

But, back in Iowa, the Meskwaki chief's council arranged nineteen more transactions after 1867. This cost the tribe around $83,600 ($1.4 million today), and successive Iowa governors added each new parcel into the state trust. Remarkably, in the forty years following their formal return to Iowa in 1856, the Red Earth People went from not owning a single inch of their former homeland to controlling some 2,900 acres by 1896.[112]

The growth of the Meskwaki Settlement was unusual but not entirely unique. In other parts of the United States, a handful of Native American communities acquired property or otherwise expanded their land bases in this era. For example, some families in the Southwest acquired homesteads or inhabited small colonies outside reservations. Tribes like the Navajo Nation gained property under executive orders in the late 1870s and early 1880s. In the early 1900s, the Office of Indian Affairs established several dozen rancherias in California in an effort to restore property to "landless" Indigenous communities the federal government had neglected to support after a series of treaties had gone unratified in the nineteenth century.[113] By incrementally increasing its Settlement, the Meskwaki Nation contributed to this deeper legacy of what we now call Landback.

CHAPTER 4

Pressure

At midyear, cattail flowers begin to thicken until they resemble cigars balanced at the ends of long stems. When temperatures cool, wispy seeds burst from these cylinders. Birds and the autumn breeze spread them widely, allowing the species to grow anew in the spring marshes. Under the summer sun, the plants release heavy pollen and restart their reproductive cycles. As the cattails along the Iowa River launched into this cycle in the summer of 1874, violence came to the Meskwaki Settlement.

The bullets were not exchanged in a volley between army soldiers and Meskwaki men. Instead, they traveled from the barrel of a Meskwaki man's gun. His name was recorded in a Tama County history only as "Black Wolf," and his unnamed victim was Pawnee. The latter man had come to Meskwaki territory with three others, presumably to trade. By the 1870s, people from Ho-Chunk, Sauk, and other Indigenous communities stopped often at the Settlement to conduct business and visit friends and relatives. Sometime during his trip, the Pawnee man stole some Meskwaki ponies. In response, Black Wolf fired three times. One bullet pierced the back of the Pawnee's head, killing him instantly.[1]

A barrage of county officials, including a deputy and a coroner, along with the Indian agent, swarmed the scene. They hauled Black Wolf and the corpse to Tama. After a brief investigation, the deputy arrested Black Wolf and charged him with murder. The Meskwaki defendant remained incarcerated for eight months but was released in 1875 after no witnesses appeared to testify against him.[2]

At the moment of Black Wolf's release, the Meskwaki Settlement had existed for eighteen years. It had been a successful period, marked by the founding and expansion of the Meskwaki Settlement, the stabilization of the Meskwaki community, and political victories shored up by the tribe's land ownership and savvy management of its relationship with the Iowa government.

The Black Wolf shooting could have ended this delicate arrangement. It had been the only serious crime committed by a Meskwaki person or on the Settlement since its founding. Iowa remained a loose political ally and the trustee of Meskwaki property, but it rarely tried to exercise any authority over the Red Earth People. The Meskwaki community handled internal disagreements privately, paid its property taxes, and mitigated conflicts with off-Settlement residents. By and large, according to one Meskwaki author, the Red Earth People had governed themselves from a position of "substantial political equality with their White neighbors" throughout these early years. As a result, the extent of Iowa's jurisdiction over Meskwaki land had gone untested.[3]

Yet the Black Wolf case raised the kinds of questions that were brewing across Indian Country. If, as scholar Shiri Pasternak argues, "jurisdiction is not a technicality of sovereignty," but "the apparatus through which sovereignty is rendered meaningful," questions like this one—who had the authority to try crimes on tribal land—reflected ongoing concerns about the status of Meskwaki sovereignty itself.[4] Ultimately, Tama County had released Black Wolf because prosecutors could not align enough evidence for trial. Had they secured a witness, would Black Wolf have been convicted? If he had appealed, would a higher court have upheld the county's jurisdiction over the Meskwaki Settlement?

Nearly a decade after Black Wolf's release, a similar, faraway murder pushed the US Supreme Court and Congress to resolve these ambiguities. When a Lakota leader killed another on the Rosebud Reservation in 1883, he was sentenced to death by the territorial court. The Supreme Court, however, found that Dakota Territory lacked jurisdiction and ordered the perpetrator released. In response, Congress passed the Major Crimes Act of 1885, which established federal jurisdiction over seven serious offenses, including kidnapping and murder, in Indian Country. Had Black Wolf's incident occurred eleven years after it did, the federal government would have held him, tried his case, and carried out his sentencing under that law.[5]

REFINING COLONIALISM

During the last half of the nineteenth century, settlers made their way to the Pacific Ocean then worked inward, slowly filling the rural interior of North America. As the nation confronted its anxieties over the closing "frontier" in the 1890s, American leaders looked to Asia and the Caribbean, extending American influence across the globe. Back home, federal power over Native lives and nations increased incrementally throughout the Gilded Age.[6]

Shaped by competing ideological and political visions, as well as the personalities of white leaders and Native activists and officials alike, the process of defining and implementing coherent Indian policies was complicated and tortuous. The growing pressure on Indian Country was neither linear nor predetermined, but the federal government had gotten good at colonization. Gatling guns and withheld rations slayed and starved any tribe that opposed federal decree. Land law focused on diminishment and dispossession. Culture itself became corrosive as Native peoples were pushed to leave their language, songs, and ceremonies behind. Meanwhile, the pressure to enroll in federal censuses, send one's children to boarding school, or sign a document reducing tribal land sowed discord within tribes.[7]

The treaty process had fostered friction between earlier generations of Sauk and Meskwaki leaders. The new hallmarks of federal Indian policy—confinement, allotment, assimilation, and political reform—were becoming clear by the 1890s. Sometimes by design and sometimes through convenience, they created divisions within tribes everywhere. This advanced federal objectives while weakening Indigenous peoples' ability to coalesce around unified visions of opposition and empowerment.[8]

As the United States tightened its grip on Indian Country, jurisdictional and administrative questions became more and more significant to the daily lives of Native people. For the Meskwaki Nation, Black Wolf's 1874 crime marked the first of several events showing the cracks in the delicate political framework that had thus far kept the Meskwaki Nation independent in an era infamous for the subjugation of Native peoples.

ENROLLMENT AND REMOVAL

In the 1870s and 1880s, the federal government began to find traction in its efforts to compel the Red Earth People to cooperate with federal priorities.

A battle over federal census policies, shortly after the Black Wolf murder, signaled the shifting status quo. Counting tribal members enabled government officials to shape administrative budgets and determine the distribution of annuity payments. It enhanced the agency's ability to monitor tribal members and their movements. Making sure that tribal members signed off on these "annuity rolls," as they were called, was a high priority. Even Iowa's 1856 Meskwaki residency statute had included a provision ordering the county sheriff to immediately "take the census" of the Red Earth People, "giving their names, and sex, which said list shall be filed and recorded" in the Tama County courthouse.[9]

In 1876, the Tama Agency asked for a full count of the Meskwaki Nation, arguing that it needed precise numbers to accurately divide up the tribe's treaty payments.[10] But, with the agency's earlier effort to coerce the tribe to Kansas still fresh in their minds, tribal members cast a wary eye. When Meskwaki families signaled that they would not sign the annuity rolls in 1876, the Indian Office threatened to hold their money ransom.[11]

Meskwaki leaders argued that the Indian Service had no business counting their people or withholding their tribe's annuities. For them, this was about the tribe's inherent right to manage its own affairs—an opportunity to affirm tribal sovereignty by once again swimming against the tide of federal decree.[12] The agents, however, summed up Meskwaki resistance in terms of cultural superiority, calling the chief's council "intensely Indian" and maintaining that the Red Earth People had rejected the census because they were "opposed to any advancement in the ways of civilization."[13]

As federal frustration mounted, the acting commissioner of Indian affairs, E. S. Stevens, ordered the Tama Agency's superintendent—now a man named George L'oste Davenport—to "use every means at your command to obtain a full and complete census of these Indians."[14] Davenport, who was married to a Sauk woman, spoke fluent Meskwaki, and had a constructive working relationship with the tribe in other matters, was nonetheless a judicious adherent to agency protocols.[15] Upon receiving Stevens's correspondence, Davenport immediately revoked the tribe's annuity payments.[16]

This time, the Red Earth People were in a bind. Unlike during the Indian Service's previous attempt to force their hand by holding cash hostage, the tribe needed the money—but not for survival. By withholding the funds, Davenport was pitting the tribe's desire for more land against its interest in challenging the federal enrollment order. Informed by its previous victories in tribal-federal gamesmanship, the tribe chose the latter. Led by the chief's council, the Red Earth People refused to sign the rolls.[17]

A six-year stalemate ensued. As it dragged on, the Meskwaki Nation faced a deepening disadvantage. Since the early 1860s, when it had only 80 acres to worry about, the tribe's land base had grown substantially. So had its taxes. In 1878—two years after the controversy began—the tribe finally defaulted on its state property taxes. This violated the state-tribal trust, and Tama County temporarily claimed the Settlement's title, though neither it nor the state made any effort to force the tribe off its land. Instead, the state offered the tribe an extension, agreeing not to change the Settlement's status if the Red Earth People cleared their debt by October 1882.[18]

The tribe had another problem. Although it had built a strong rapport with most of its neighbors, some locals proved persistently unwelcoming. A few years earlier, for example, a small group of settlers—led, a little too appropriately, by an Iowan named Andrew Jackson—had formed a committee to create petitions demanding the tribe's removal. Jackson and his followers complained that the Red Earth People allowed their ponies to graze on settlers' land and, in the bigoted language of the day, chastised tribal members for drinking, accused them of having "filthy habits of life," and bemoaned the tribe's unwillingness to cultivate its land according to Euro-American norms.[19]

The state ignored the first round of petitions. In 1878, emboldened by the tribe's tax issue, Jackson's crowd took another shot. This time, Meskwaki people had reason to worry. For years, the Indian Office had hoped that returning the Red Earth People to the Indian Territory might expedite their assimilation. A growing chorus of voices toward that end undoubtedly piqued the agency's interest.[20]

The Meskwaki Nation had a supportive group of white petitioners. One appealed to the commissioner of Indian affairs directly, arguing "that it would be an act of great injustice . . . and a breach of faith on our part, to remove [the tribe] without their consent, from their own lands which they have purchased." These allies supported the Red Earth People as "peaceable, quiet, honest and law abiding people [who] compare[d] favorably in their obedience to the laws with the . . . whites surrounding them."[21]

On the state side, Iowa legislators did nothing to undo its agreement with the Meskwaki Nation. Federal politics were a different story. A resolution for the tribe's removal made it through the US House of Representatives. Fortunately for the Red Earth People, who were "unanimously and utterly adverse [*sic*]" to leaving their Settlement, the resolution failed to pass the Senate, and the issue was not reconsidered.[22]

Frustrated by the annuity stalemate and concerned about the removal attempt, the Meskwaki chief's council turned to their old agent, Leander Clark, for help. He had left the Tama Agency for a judgeship in nearby Toledo. Clark referred the Meskwaki delegates to Iowa governor Buren R. Sherman. When the chief's council dispatched a group to Des Moines to explain the situation, Sherman encouraged tribal members to sign the rolls so the tribe could pay its state taxes and regain title to its homeland.[23] He also agreed to reach out to the Office of Indian Affairs on the tribe's behalf.[24]

In January 1882, a group of Meskwaki men donned their bear claw necklaces and headed east to Washington. There, they met with Commissioner of Indian Affairs Hiram Price and signaled that their people might be willing to sign the rolls, but only if their annuities were reinstated and the tribe received their back payment—six years' worth of withheld annuities—*before* the census began. Under these terms, the Meskwaki Nation would have the cash to square up with Iowa. With the Settlement secure, the diplomats reasoned, the Indian Office would be unable to force the tribe from its land.[25]

But the federal government countered, this time with Secretary of the Interior Henry M. Teller personally asserting "that the government could do nothing" about returning annuities "until [the tribe] signed the new rolls," listing their names on the census.

The Meskwaki diplomats shared Teller's terms with the chief's council. As they discussed the issue, Commissioner Price authorized $20,000 worth of annuities—the maximum allowed at one time—for the tribe, to be paid after it upheld its end of the agreement.[26] With this signal of good faith in place, Meskwaki leaders decided to access these funds and pay their property taxes. Reinstating the state-tribal trust was more important than continuing the fight against federal enrollment. In the end, most Red Earth People signed the rolls, although a few dozen still refused.[27] When the Indian agents completed the census in 1888, it listed 381 Red Earth People.[28] The agreement had saved the Meskwaki Settlement.

FRACTURE

Just as the tribe was preparing its challenge to the Indian Office's enrollment policy, tragedy struck the Meskwaki Settlement. Mamiwanige, who had led the chief's council for more than two decades, passed away in the summer of 1881. Per Meskwaki custom, his eldest son, Wakumo, ascended to the head of the council. But Wakumo, too, died unexpectedly just a few weeks later. Facing an unusual leadership vacuum and with the fate of the Settlement hinging on the enrollment issue, the chief's council acted quickly. Their decisions—and the sequence they followed—are subject to myriad versions and interpretations. By his own account, the group first offered the chieftainship to James Poweshiek, who was a biological descendant of Poweshiek. He declined, and the chief's council eventually selected the forty-year-old Pushetonequa, another relative of Poweshiek's. They had based this decision, in part, on the strong recommendation of Matauaquah, a widely respected elder who had signed the Meskwaki land deed in 1857 and served on Mamiwanige's council (and then Pushetonequa's) for years.[29]

Although most Red Earth People initially accepted this decision, controversy quickly set in. The issue focused on whether the chief's council should have followed a hereditary line of succession after Mamiwanige and Wakumo died. By selecting Pushetonequa, the council had bypassed two of Mamiwanige's younger sons. Apparently, the council viewed these descendants as unready to assume the heavy responsibility of communal leadership—especially at this critical moment in Meskwaki history.[30] This debate raged for years, and as it did, Mamiwanige's son, Moquibushito, or "Old Bear," matured and claimed a hereditary right to his father's position at the head of the council.[31]

For generations, members of the Meskwaki community, anthropologists, historians, and other observers have weighed in on this controversy. They have found that the chief's council probably had the prerogative to elevate Pushetonequa as they did. Yet, still today, some Meskwaki people maintain that certain families hold proof that Moquibushito and his descendants were the rightful leaders of the Meskwaki Nation. This evidence, however, has never been made publicly available.[32] This has long perplexed outsiders. If these families hold evidence proving a right to leadership, why not produce it? Taken in the broader context of Indigenous history—namely,

Pushetonequa, who led the Meskwaki chief's council from the early 1880s until his death in 1919, was the last Meskwaki person recognized as a "head chief" by the US government. His service in tribal leadership was marked by intense disagreements over hereditary governance and numerous conflicts over tribal sovereignty with local, state, federal, and corporate interests. Photo courtesy of the John Henry Hauberg papers, Image 27.I-ME.gp.2.27, Special Collections, Augustana College, Rock Island, Illinois.

that Native people have endured generations of outside meddling in their affairs—this refusal to engage with demands for sensitive community information stands as a boundary to be respected, even if not fully understood.[33]

Much has been made of this disagreement in the century and a half since Mamiwanige died. Yet the fine details of tribal politics paled in significance to the two main threads of history that were playing out during this era: the US government's sustained effort to drive division within the Meskwaki community and break up the Meskwaki Settlement (or, at the very least, assume control of it), and the Meskwaki Nation's efforts to deflect incursions into tribal affairs.

The Indian Office continued to consolidate its power. In the 1890s, Congress authorized the creation of "tribal business councils," which would supersede entities like the chief's council. Bypassing the slow work of communal consensus building, after all, was easier than trying to understand and navigate nuanced Indigenous governance structures. Fortunately for the Meskwaki Nation, the Indian Office did not mandate this change. Instead, it encouraged tribes to hold elections over whether to replace their government with a tribal business council.[34]

The Red Earth People refused this option, choosing instead to keep their chief's council. Pushetonequa remained the tribe's primary leader but took intense criticism from all sides. The employees of the Tama Agency begrudgingly supported him, and even the famed anthropologist George Bird Grinnell—who visited the Meskwaki Nation during the era of Pushetonequa's leadership—opined that the chief's frequent resistance to federal demands "h[eld] the tribe back."[35] On the other side of the ledger—as they would in any small community—his and his council's decisions invited biting critiques and robust opposition from other tribal members.

Pushetonequa nonetheless led the Red Earth People—recognized by the US government, empowered by his council, and with his position symbolized, like generations of Meskwaki leaders before him, by his bear claw necklace—until 1919.[36] He would be the last Meskwaki leader to hold this title.

AVOIDING ALLOTMENT

As the Red Earth People dealt with the fallout from Mamiwanige's death in the 1880s, the United States passed the most consequential piece of Indian affairs legislation since the Indian Removal Act in 1830. It was known as the Dawes Allotment Act after its primary congressional sponsor, Senator Henry Dawes. The Dawes Act became law in February 1887 and launched a nationwide assault on Indigenous lands. Building on the model of the Homestead Act, the plan was to divide up communally held tribal land and give it to individual Native families. Indian reformers and federal agents believed that if they could push Native people to assume individualized, commercially oriented farming, they would see the light of settler society and assimilate. The government incentivized allotment by promising land titles and US citizenship for Indigenous people who took their plot of allotted land.[37]

The logic underpinning the Dawes Act, of course, ignored the fact that for millennia Native peoples across North America had been farming and refining complex economic, social, and political systems in response to their ecosystems. But the rhetoric of assimilation and reform thinly masked the new law's other key goal: after allotting all the land inside a reservation's boundaries, the government could sell the remaining property—called surplus lands—to white settlers. Rampant corruption and maladministration of the allotment program not only failed to improve Native people's lives and positions in American society. It also stripped about 90 million acres from Indigenous hands by 1934.[38]

The Indian Office desperately wanted to break up the Meskwaki Settlement. Like many pieces of national legislation, the Dawes Act was not the beginning of allotment—the practice had been tested and refined in different Indian agencies for years before it became national policy. The Tama Agency knew this and wanted to use the Meskwaki Nation as a test case. A full decade before the Dawes Act's passage, a superintendent wrote that Meskwaki "lands being held in common ... works to their decided disadvantage in the way of agriculture." Because the tribe shared the Settlement, he continued, it could not "advance successfully." He advised the Indian Office that "some means [be] adopted to give each head of a family all the land necessary" to support themselves, "and make them depend primarily upon this."[39]

The Meskwaki Nation, however, was one of the few tribes to avoid allotment—a fact that it owed to its unique ownership of the 2,900-acre Meskwaki Settlement. Although the tribe did not own its land in "fee simple," the legal term for outright private ownership, its trust arrangement with Iowa meant that the Indian Service could not unilaterally disperse Meskwaki property as it could other federally assigned reservation lands. Early in the Settlement's life, agents referred to it as a "reservation," a "settlement," and sometimes "reservation lands" in correspondence—indicating a lack of clarity about what, exactly, the land was and the extent of federal authority over it.[40]

This confusion over the Settlement's status had even played a role in the tribe's decision to sign the annuity rolls in 1882. After hearing that tribal trust land—the term for most of the tribally owned land on federal reservations—was not subject to state property taxes, a few Meskwaki leaders inquired about the Settlement's tax status. Calculating whether they could use the Indian Service's own phrasing of "reservation lands" to undo their state tax burden, these Meskwaki leaders were trying to save their Settlement *and* win the annuity battle. But Commissioner Price told the tribe's agent that, because Meskwaki land was "outside of a reservation" and had been purchased directly from whites, the Indian Service considered the Settlement "in the same tenure as land owned by white people." He noted that it was "subject to taxation as [were] other lands."[41]

Price's determination in 1882 kept the pressure on Meskwaki leaders to assent to the census of the Red Earth People. But five years later it worked to the tribe's advantage. The same logic provided the vital obstacle that prevented the Indian Office from using the Dawes Act to allot the Meskwaki Settlement, which was by then a checkerboard of a different sort. Rather than being a patchwork of reservation parcels owned by Native and non-Native peoples, the Meskwaki Settlement was a mosaic of parcels incrementally tacked onto the original Settlement and held in trust by Iowa governors.[42]

QUAGMIRE

The complicated status of the Meskwaki Settlement had its drawbacks. For one thing, several decades after acquiring the Settlement, the Meskwaki Nation still needed an intermediary to buy land. Federal preemption rules combined with lingering questions over the Red Earth People's citizenship that had persisted since the creation of the fictive "Sac and Fox Tribe" a century before. One account of the 1857 Settlement purchase, as relayed by an Iowa City resident named Peter Dey, speaks to Meskwaki people's frustration with this arrangement. After a Meskwaki delegate presented Governor Grimes with the money to buy the Settlement, at the Old Capitol building in Iowa City, according to Dey, the governor asked why the tribe wanted to buy land in the first place. Dey claimed that "the chief replied, 'White Man buy land, White man business. Indian buy land, Indian business.'"[43]

Land acquisitions were not the only arena in which frustrations over the complexities of Meskwaki land and the tribe's legal status played out. Several disputes in the 1890s showed mounting disagreements among everyone involved. In 1891, Congress amended the Dawes Act to allow Native allottees to lease their land. The idea was to assist those who, due to age or infirmity, might not be able to conduct intensive farm labor. Initially, the law required the secretary of the interior to approve these leases. This measure offered a layer of oversight intended to protect tribal members from the unscrupulous tactics deployed by settlers seeking Indigenous land. Yet within a decade, the leasing authority had been delegated down the administrative ladder. With local Indian agents able to authorize leases, many colluded with greedy settlers. Across the country, these grifters teamed up to rent tribal land for a song, enabling settlers to reap high returns on farming and ranching operations.[44]

Although this predatory practice does not appear to have affected the Red Earth People, the Meskwaki Nation faced a different problem. Property taxes continued to trouble tribal leaders long after the annuity disagreement in 1882. Their sizable Settlement required significant property taxes. Covering them required regular cash flow. When Pushetonequa raised this issue with a white friend in 1892, the individual suggested leasing some tribal land. Shortly thereafter, the Meskwaki Nation bought a section of land known as the South Farm. Unlike the other Settlement purchases, it was not connected to the rest of the Settlement. Instead, this parcel sat a half mile southeast of the Settlement's southeast corner. Its location indicated its purpose: the tribe had secured the parcel solely for creating revenues to cover tribal property taxes.[45]

For most other tribes, whose land was in federal trust, these leases would have required only a petition to the secretary of the interior. The unique status of the Meskwaki Settlement, however, required additional work. Tribal leaders turned to the Indian agent, Wallace R. Lesser, with whom they had a tense relationship. He was still pushing the tribe to elect a tribal business council. But Lesser was the Meskwaki Nation's main point of contact, and, when they inquired, he supported the leasing idea because he believed that renting tribal land would improve the tribe's fiscal health. Lesser was no doubt attracted to the idea of having a couple of farmers on tribal land who could exemplify the virtues of Anglo-American agrarianism. By September, Lesser had received the necessary approvals, and two separate farmers signed leases for 707 acres of Meskwaki property.

This garnered over $1,100 in annual rent for the tribe. This was more than enough to cover the tribe's tax bill.[46]

This arrangement went swimmingly until 1895, when Governor Frank D. Jackson asked his attorney general, Milton Remley, for a legal opinion on the Meskwaki leases. Remley argued that, under the terms of the state-tribal trust, only contracts signed by the governor on the tribe's behalf could be enforced. This ruling, in the eyes of the Iowa government—which technically owned the land—invalidated the tribe's leases.[47]

Agent Lesser rejected this ruling. In a colorful change of pace from the usually dry administrative disagreements between the tribe, Iowa, and the Indian Office over Meskwaki policy, Remley and Lesser launched into a bitter debate. The agent eventually complained to Governor Jackson, attacking Remley's character and reminding the governor that his attorney general was a Democrat and "the same fellow that gave" Jackson, a Republican, "such a trouncing in the *Toledo Democrat* . . . when [he was] a candidate for governor."[48] Lesser further asserted that, as an agent of the federal government responsible for Meskwaki affairs, he had orchestrated the tribe's lease in good faith. He implored Jackson not to take seriously the "statements of a [D]emocrat of shady reputation for veracity," and to allow the leases to stand. Finally, the bureaucrat asked the governor to defer to the Office of Indian Affairs when it came to enforcing Meskwaki land agreements.[49]

Following this dustup, Jackson agreed to approve tribal leases. Thereafter, the leasing protocol mirrored Meskwaki land purchases: Tribal leaders would identify prospective lessees then ask the Tama Agency to help negotiate a reasonable price with the prospective tenant. When it was all said and done, the agent would pass the lease along to the governor, who would sign off. This system worked well—so well, in fact, that Meskwaki leaders sometimes asked the Indian Office to mediate disputes with their tenants. In 1895, for example, Pushetonequa contacted the tribe's agent, complaining that one of the lessees was subletting half of his parcel at a profit.[50] The Indian Office contacted the governor, who pressed the farmer to either stop subletting, renegotiate his lease, or vacate the Settlement. The tenant chose the former. While it ended in the tribe's best interests—it continued to lease lands to pay property taxes until the 1970s—the whole ordeal brought the cumbersome process for managing Meskwaki land into sharp relief.[51]

RAILROADED

Until 1894, questions about Meskwaki property involved only public offices—tribal, state, and federal. That year, however, a private party rumbled into the mix. A train owned by the Chicago & Northwestern Railway Company sparked a brushfire as it passed through the Meskwaki Settlement that summer. Whether from errant embers of coal or sparks from the iron tracks, the flames consumed nearly forty acres of Meskwaki timber. They also destroyed a shed filled with some of the tribe's farm equipment. Chicago & Northwestern initially agreed to compensate the tribe for the damages. But when the Indian Office followed up, "the [railroad's] claim agent denied all responsibility for the damage." The Indian agent forwarded the matter to the Office of Indian Affairs headquarters in Washington, DC, which found that, because Meskwaki land was in trust with Iowa, the matter would have to be settled in state court.[52]

The case inched along while the state government transitioned from Governor Jackson to his successor, Francis M. Drake. After taking office, Drake secured damages in the amount of $2,000 for the tribe. According to a Tama Agency report, "Delay followed delay until another governor," Leslie M. Shaw, who took office in 1898, had his attorney general reach a new agreement with Chicago & Northwestern's attorneys. They reduced the claim to only $750, which "was not enough" to "pay for the [lost] warehouse and tools." Frustrated with the delays and lackluster support from state authorities, Meskwaki leaders begrudgingly agreed to this lower payment.[53]

EMINENT DOMAIN

Barely two years after the railroad fire, Tama County decided to build a road. Since the most direct route transgressed the Meskwaki Settlement, and because they knew the Red Earth People might oppose this project, the county leapfrogged over the tribe and went to the governor's office for approval. Many Meskwaki tribal members did not want the road to cross tribal land because, as one wrote to the governor, they feared that the one-and-a-half-mile stretch slated to cross the Settlement would cut through the tribe's village and fields.[54]

The tribe sent a delegation to Des Moines on March 12, 1896, for a meeting with the general assembly. The delegation included Pushetonequa and several other Meskwaki men, Netwatwytuk, Matauaquah, and Meskwapuswa, the latter of whom served as the tribe's interpreter and went by the name Joseph Tesson. The men gave speeches to the legislators, opposing the road and making it clear that they viewed its construction as an unwarranted incursion onto sovereign land.[55]

The elder Matauaquah spoke first. He declared that "the young men and women and children are not satisfied with the way [Tama County has] laid out the road. They have cut the land right in two." The Red Earth People, he said, wanted the road to run along the Settlement's border rather than through its middle. And, because the tribe held its land in common, he argued, "outsiders ... [e]ven the [federal] government can not have any control of it, the way it is situated." Matauaquah complained that the county "didn't ask where the road should be," and that, rather than listening to the tribe, the planners mapped the road through Meskwaki land.[56]

When he rose, Pushetonequa echoed these concerns. He cordially asked the legislators "to help us out and change the road to somewhere else." Not cutting through tribal land, he and the rest of the Meskwaki delegation believed, was where "it ought to be."[57]

Governor Drake, however, agreed with Tama County, which argued that the road would make the Meskwaki land more valuable and provide easier access to nearby towns.[58] He told Pushetonequa and his delegation that, although the state believed the Meskwaki Nation was entitled to a hearing over the issue, the state retained the right to take land for infrastructural development. He tried to reassure the Meskwaki leaders that their people had not been discriminated against, noting that both Chicago & Northwestern and the Tama Water Power Company had also given up land to make way for the road. Drake went on, reminding the tribe that because it owned its Settlement "in fee simple, the same as my own farm belongs to me," its land was subject to the same power of eminent domain as any other landowner.[59] With that, the state authorized Tama County to move forward with its plans. The Meskwaki Nation then asked for $1,000 in compensation. It received $325, which the Indian Service found satisfactory.[60]

Some Red Earth People were furious. Although Pushetonequa and the council begrudgingly accepted the meager payment and moved on,

PRESSURE   119

Moquibushito continued to protest. He wrote Governor Drake and claimed that the tribe "as a whole" was "bitterly opposed" to the road, demanded to know who had authorized it, and asked "what you can do . . . to prevent the road from going through [our] lands."[61] Moquibushito's discontent carried on for two more years. When construction delays pushed out the road's completion, he and others went to Des Moines to lobby the governor.

These meetings laid bare the deepening rift between the two Meskwaki leaders. As Moquibushito planned a capital visit in the summer of 1898, Pushetonequa asked the Tama Agency to relay a message to the governor's office. Pushetonequa reminded Governor Drake, "the delegation which is about to call upon you are not recognized as having any authority in this tribe and [are] composed of a few discontented spirits who oppose every movement that is made for the betterment of the tribe."[62]

UNRAVELING

In the end, the Meskwaki Nation got its leases, Chicago & Northwestern paid pennies for their damage to Meskwaki property, and Tama County built its road. These three disputes showed that by the 1890s, managing the Meskwaki Settlement had become, at best, administratively inconvenient. At worst, the land's status was downright perplexing. In earlier years, the Red Earth People had found ways to exploit this murkiness. But the tribe faced a nearly constant barrage of new questions over tribal land and who controlled it.

Together, these developments revealed the slow unraveling of the delicate political balance that had enabled the Red Earth People to carve a unique space within the broader regime of Indian policy. By 1896—while several of the disputes over Meskwaki property were still being sorted out—this would culminate in a devastating change for the Meskwaki Nation, its land, and its people. All it took was a nudge from some white reformers.

RED EARTH LOST?

Horace M. Rebok had had enough of the Red Earth People's resistance. An ardent assimilationist who became the superintendent of the Tama Agency in 1894, he arrived while the Red Earth People were working through internal discord over their leadership, arguing to protect the sovereignty of their Settlement, and fighting in ways large and small to reject the intense pressures of assimilation. For decades, Meskwaki people had been refusing to send their children to day schools established by churches and the Indian Office and living by hunting, gardening, trading, and laboring, rather than commercial farming.[63] Rebok resented these positions and complained that the Red Earth People's aversion to federal policy was "the worst problem to deal with ... among any of the Indians" across the United States. He strongly advocated "break[ing]" tribal leaders' "power and influence" so the Indian Service could force the tribe to conform.[64]

Rebok saw what Meskwaki leaders before him had known: the Meskwaki Settlement's unique state-tribal trust provided a firm footing for the tribe whenever it wanted to challenge federal authority. He saw the dissolution of that trust as the key to eroding Meskwaki power.

To see this through, Rebok organized a local branch of the Indian Rights Association, a group of Christian reformers with branches across the country.[65] Rebok's chapter quickly swelled to more than 140 members, mostly prominent men from Tama and Toledo and surrounding towns like Marshalltown and Cedar Rapids. A few even came up from Des Moines, as did a handful of women and some Presbyterian clergymen. By 1895, they were gathering for regular lectures and discussions about the righteous salvation of Native Americans via forced assimilation.[66]

The Indian Rights Association had a singular goal: to "take such steps as were necessary to determine and fix, as far as possible, the legal status of the Indians and to promote education and civilization among them."[67] By January 1896, the Indian Rights Association had drafted a federal bill toward that end. It would transfer the state's trust ownership of the Meskwaki Settlement to the federal government. Rebok and his colleagues argued that such a transfer would be a good thing for the Red Earth People because it would decrease their property taxes, which amounted to nearly $270 a year. The clear motivation, however, was to remove the state government as an obstacle to federal authority and, by converting the Settlement to federal trust land, provide the Indian Office with the power to build a boarding school on Meskwaki land.[68]

Over the next several months, association members lobbied Iowa's congressional delegation and the Indian Office in Washington, DC, hoping to secure support for an appropriation of $35,000 to build the school. Although they never involved the Red Earth People in their meetings or consulted them about the plan, the reformers lobbied hard with influential Iowa politicians like Senator William B. Allison. They even offered to name the school after him.[69] Within a few months, the Indian Rights Association had secured the backing of both Commissioner of Indian Affairs Daniel Browning and Senator Allison and began pushing their bill through Congress.[70]

Meanwhile, back in Iowa, the reformers lobbied state politicians. The transfer, after all, required the consent of the governor of Iowa, who still held the title to the Meskwaki Settlement. For nearly forty years, the State of Iowa had avoided interfering in Meskwaki affairs except when acting on the tribe's behalf. By the middle of the 1890s, however, the mounting number of confrontations over Meskwaki land rights—including the lingering questions about taxes, leases, roads, and jurisdiction—had begun to wear on state government. As one member of the general assembly told the governor, something had to be done to "relieve the legal difficulty" surrounding the Meskwaki Settlement's status and to ensure that "the Indians may not suffer by reason of the undefined question of jurisdiction over them."[71]

As the pressure mounted from the Indian Rights Association and Iowa's congressional delegation, the state government slowly began to support the idea of a trust transfer.[72] Although the governor could have signed away the trust on his own, the general assembly wanted a state bill outlining the exact terms of the transfer. They worried that turning over full jurisdiction to the federal government would stem the flow of Meskwaki property taxes and limit local law enforcement's reach on the Settlement.

To meet these concerns, the Indian Rights Association sweetened their bill. The document would consolidate responsibility for the Red Earth People in the hands of the federal government, thereby stripping it from either tribal or state hands. They retained, however, Iowa's ability to tax the Meskwaki Nation "for State, county, road, and bridge purposes" and extended Iowa's criminal jurisdiction and the power of eminent domain over the Settlement. But the state would no longer collect Meskwaki tax dollars for schools and universities that tribal members did not attend.[73]

In short, for only a nominal decrease in their annual tax revenues, the State of Iowa would maintain its control over the aspects of Meskwaki affairs that concerned its white citizens while relinquishing the obligations to the Meskwaki Nation it had promised to uphold in 1857. In an apologetic statement to the Red Earth People, Governor Drake acknowledged this dramatic turn in state policy. After all thirteen of his predecessors had supported the tribe in its efforts to maintain control of the sliver of homeland they had managed to acquire decades before, he told the Red Earth People that the transfer would smooth their assimilation and promised that adopting American culture was "the better way" to live.[74]

On June 10, 1896, the Indian Rights Association, the Office of Indian Affairs, and the Iowa General Assembly dealt a devastating blow to the Meskwaki Nation. Iowa transferred around 2,900 acres of Meskwaki land to the federal government. A thousand miles to the east, Congress formally accepted the transfer that same day. This change permanently altered the legal status of the land upon which the Red Earth People had rebuilt their community, converting it to the federal trust status shared by Indian reservations elsewhere.[75]

The trust transfer shattered the delicate balance that had afforded the Meskwaki Nation strong political leverage since 1857. Stripped of its unique land ownership, the tribe was vulnerable to Horace Rebok's Tama Agency, which sat poised to execute its authority over the Red Earth People. The fight was not over. Two years later, a long legal battle that cracked the Indian Office's control over the Meskwaki Settlement began when two little Meskwaki girls ran away from school.

PART III

Erosion

"We do not want our lands divided."
—Chakotakosee, 1909

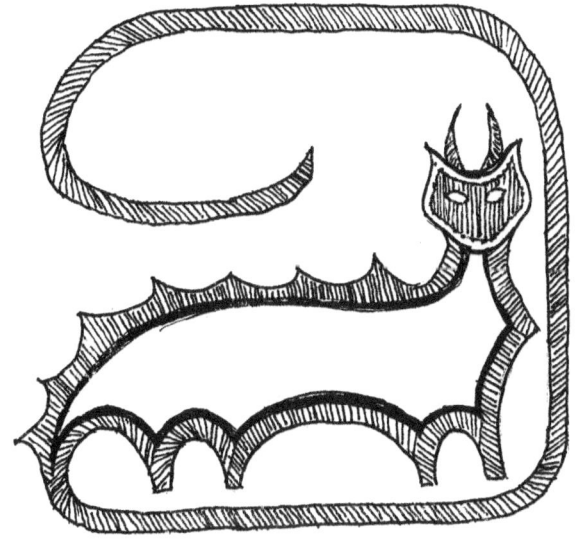

CHAPTER 5

Peters v. Malin

Masqasee tiptoed into the icy darkness. She hated the boarding school in Toledo and missed the warmth of her relatives' wickiups. It was January 1899, and Masqasee's mother had encouraged her escape. But she knew the child could not simply sneak home, at least not right away. The Indian Service was watching, ready and willing to drag the truant back to school. Knowing this, Masqasee's mother asked another tribal member, Pyepaha—who also went by the name Jim Peters—to help hide her daughter.[1]

Under the cover of a black Iowa night, Masqasee made her way out of the building and into her mother's arms. The pair rendezvoused with Peters, who drove mother and child thirty-five miles southeast of the Meskwaki Settlement, where they were "secreted [away] . . . with a white family in an obscure locality."[2]

In time, Masqasee would find herself back at school. Jim Peters languished in the county jail. When he sued for freedom, Peters's case established a complicated legal precedent that both reaffirmed and disempowered the Meskwaki Nation. His freedom hinged on the fallout from the Meskwaki Settlement trust transfer a few years earlier.

When Masqasee reconnected with her mother, Native America faced dire challenges. Four centuries after European contact, the Indigenous population had collapsed. In early October 1492, as many as 18 million Indigenous people lived north of the Rio Grande. Disease, warfare, and unscrupulous policies annihilated tribal populations, and, by 1890, the number of Indigenous people in the United States had dipped to its historic nadir of just under 240,000.[3] Around 250 Meskwaki survivors had moved to the Settlement in its early years. The tribe's population grew incrementally from there and reached around 400 people by 1890.[4]

At that time, a visitor to the Settlement would have also encountered anywhere from ten to fifty other Indigenous people, usually Sauk and Meskwaki relatives who traveled north from their reservation or members of the Ho-Chunk communities in Nebraska or Minnesota. These people had many reasons to visit the Settlement: some were there to trade, and others were visiting friends and family. Many did both. Occasionally, an outsider fell in love with a Meskwaki person and married into the community.[5] During their first four decades on the Settlement, the Red Earth People did more than stem their losses. They fostered growth. As a result, at the turn of the century, the Meskwaki Nation was one of the few Native Nations that was, in terms of both its land base and its population, growing.

PLENARY POWER

The forced removals and bloody battles of late nineteenth-century America devastated Indigenous populations. By the turn of the century, the US government had confined most tribes to reservations. According to historian Fred Hoxie, assimilation policies, which promised full and equal participation in American society for any Native American willing to adopt the social, cultural, and economic norms of white citizens, began to shift around 1900. Within a few years, it became clear that Indigenous Americans would be forced to exist on the periphery of American society.[6] Allotment, furthermore, steadily chipped away at Indigenous land holdings, fragmenting entire communities. Emboldened by these century-old policy achievements, the Office of Indian Affairs steadily undercut Indigenous systems of governance. The United States wielded unprecedented control over Native communities, and federal officials, it seemed, seized every opportunity to insert themselves into communal decision-making.[7]

Meanwhile, the laws and decisions flowing from Congress and the Supreme Court bolstered federal authority over virtually every aspect of Indigenous life. Boarding schools pushed assimilation. Land speculators and Indian agents whittled away at tribes' land and natural resources. In 1903, the Supreme Court unanimously decided that Congress wielded an absolute "plenary power" to abrogate treaties with Native Nations in a

The Indian Industrial School (Meskwaki Boarding School) at Toledo, Iowa, around 1906. Like other Indigenous boarding schools across the United States and elsewhere, the staff at this facility viewed education as a mechanism for assimilation. The school became the source of significant tension between the Red Earth People and federal officials around the turn of the twentieth century, as Meskwaki families rejected incursions into tribal affairs. Photo courtesy of Special Collections and Archives, Grinnell College Libraries, Grinnell, Iowa.

case called *Lone Wolf v. Hitchcock*. Other decisions similarly pruned tribal sovereignty over the course of several decades. The nation-to-nation status between tribes and the United States thinned so much in this period that, until Congress established the Indian Claims Commission in 1946, tribes seeking reparations for federal misdeeds had to get federal approval for their cases to even be heard.[8]

THE BOARDING SCHOOL

The same legislation that the Indian Rights Association had used to push the Meskwaki Settlement into federal trust in 1896 also authorized $35,000 to build a large government boarding school a few miles from the Settlement, near the agency office in Toledo. Banzhof & Reimer, a construction company based out of nearby Marshalltown, erected the Indian Training School the next fall. It boasted living quarters and classrooms for about 110 students in its two above-ground stories and basement. Along with a barn, warehouse, workshop, and laundry facility, the campus spread over some seventy acres.[9]

Many Meskwaki families resented the school and had been resisting efforts to assimilate their children for decades. A group of Quakers, for example, tried and failed to establish a school for Meskwaki children shortly after the Settlement purchase. In the early 1870s, some Lutherans from Ohio set up a small office on the Settlement, but they failed to recruit the Red Earth People to attend Sabbath services. In 1875, the Indian Office built a government school, but three frustrated instructors came and went before the facility closed in 1890.[10] Meskwaki families' recalcitrance maddened their non-Native instructors. One called the tribe "the most difficult of any to reach in the matter of education, or progression of any kind, which they steadily oppose, if not in outward manifestation, with a sullen, passive resistance."[11] Indeed, the only facility tribal members seemed to tolerate was a Presbyterian mission established by a married couple near the Settlement in 1883. Even there, however, participation remained sparse for many years.[12]

The Tama Agency never wearied. Five years after the school closed in 1890, while the Indian Rights Association was still lobbying Congress for the Settlement trust transfer, the group had reached out to Dr. Charles A. Eastman for help. Known in his Santee Dakota community as Ohiyesha, Eastman had taken his medical degree from Boston University and became a well-known proponent of Indigenous rights. He was also an outspoken believer in the benefits of "industrial education." He shared these views with a group of local whites and a few members of the Meskwaki community in Toledo on July 1, 1895. Although Eastman felt he had given a persuasive talk, he later recounted hearing "one of the strongest rebukes I ever received from an Indian for my acceptance of these ideals."[13]

During the meeting, Meskwaki families continued to reject the government schools. They already devoted enormous time and energy to teaching, they reasoned. Meskwaki children spent years learning the hunting, gardening, and other skills that would ensure their survival. They also taught the stories and ceremonies that formed the bedrock of their community. During the session, a Meskwaki elder told Eastman that while industrial education may have worked for some, his tribe would continue to "follow the old trail. If you should live long," he said, "and some day the Great Spirit shall permit you to visit us again, you will find us still Indians, eating with wooden spoons out of bowls of wood." The metaphor referred to an enduring vision of Meskwaki cultural and material sovereignty that the elder linked to ceremonial bowls.[14]

Given this history, the Indian Service should not have been surprised when, in 1898, Meskwaki families refused to comply with an order to send their children to the new school. Angered by this mandate, the Red Earth People sent Pushetonequa and several members of the chief's council to Washington, DC. There, in an expression of sovereignty rooted in the tribe's nation-to-nation relationship with the United States, the group of Meskwaki leaders shared these concerns with federal officials. The agents attempted to buy Pushetonequa's support by offering him a designation as "head chief" and a $500 annual salary.[15]

The chief initially refused, reportedly telling the Indian Office that "you may come and kill us, but we will not give you our children."[16] Foreseeing another fight over annuity payments, the tribe briefly refused to accept them. This protest was intended to show the Indian Office that the Red Earth People would not tolerate any attempts to leverage the payments to force the children's attendance.[17]

The agents chose a different weapon. They threatened to send students from other tribes to the school. That, agents warned, would lead to increased intermarriage, an issue they knew concerned many Red Earth People, who worried that diluting their annuities across a more diverse population could threaten the careful economic strategy that kept the Settlement going and the community healthy.[18]

After the chief's council returned from Washington, DC, Horace Rebok teamed up with George Nellis, the superintendent of the new school in Toledo. Nellis had previously served as superintendent of a reservation boarding school in western South Dakota. At his new post, Nellis became an active member of the Indian Rights Association of Iowa.[19] He and Rebok traversed the Settlement attempting to convince Meskwaki families to enroll their children.

Although the pair were not well received in most Meskwaki homes, Rebok and Nellis kept pressure on tribal leaders and slowly made headway. In December, Pushetonequa and several council members agreed to send their kids to the school. This was an unpopular decision made worse by the leader's eventual acceptance of the federal title and salary. Nonetheless, some families followed suit, and, by 1899, about fifty students sporadically attended classes at the school. Nellis saw this as progress but believed it would be "some time before the school [could] be filled by voluntary attendance."[20] Although Rebek and Nellis believed they were making progress, most Meskwaki families continued to reject the school.[21]

Whether to send their children to government schools proved a difficult choice for Meskwaki parents. Native families across the nation shared in this conundrum, and more than one Indigenous community split over the issue.[22] On the Settlement, underlying political disagreements added strain, with some tribal members deriding Pushetonequa as a corrupt "government chief" who had agreed to send his children to the school out of greed and against the interests of the Meskwaki Nation.[23]

ARRESTS

As the school and the agency worked to compel attendance, Horace Rebok used his position as Indian agent to secure legal guardianship of the students at the Toledo school. Under this arrangement, as far as the county district court was concerned, Rebok had the authority to keep the children in school and round up truants. As historian Angela Keysor has shown, this effectively eliminated Meskwaki parents' rights to make decisions about their children's well-being.[24]

Rebok also went on the offensive, arresting Meskwaki adults who opposed the school.[25] Several years earlier, Rebok had formed a squad of Meskwaki policemen, whom he tasked with tracking down accused rabblerousers.[26] Often, Rebok's charges were spurious, and Meskwaki defendants turned to people such as E. I. Wilcox, a former city official and school administrator from nearby Montour, or local attorneys like the Toledo-based J. W. Lamb for representation.[27]

In one such case, Rebok had a Meskwaki critic named Makatawahquahtwa charged with defrauding the federal annuity process. The man spent two years in the state penitentiary at Anamosa, although one historian asserts that his only misdeed had been speaking out against the Indian Service. Upon his release in 1899, Makatawahquahtwa sued Rebok, only to have his suit dismissed for procedural reasons. Another case stemmed from an incident between Rebok and an eighty-four-year-old Meskwaki healer named Ytatahwah, another critic of the government school. When Ytatahwah used Meskwaki remedies to treat an ailing tribal member, Rebok had him arrested for practicing medicine without a license, which was a state offense. Ytatahwah sued Rebok upon his release, arguing that the agent had impinged on his rights. This time, the courts agreed: the charges against Ytatahwah were thrown out. Rebok left the Tama Agency at the end of January 1899.[28]

If anyone at the Indian Office or on the Settlement thought Rebok's ouster might improve the relationship between the Red Earth People and the Tama Agency, they were wrong. A longtime Tama County resident succeeded Horace Rebok. William Malin was a staunch assimilationist who hated E. I. Wilcox. Malin once called the Meskwaki ally a "populist demagogue" and asked the district attorney about a way to ban Wilcox from working with Meskwaki people. Malin criticized Wilcox, Lamb, and other "bad advisers" bent on orchestrating "nefarious schemes" to subvert the Indian Service.[29] He even accused Wilcox of meddling in agency affairs simply to bilk tribal members out of legal fees.[30]

Malin also held a deep disdain for people like Makatawahquahtwa and Ytatahwah. Referring to them as "retrogressives" or the "reactionary faction," Malin viewed Meskwaki disagreements with federal policy as emblems of cultural inferiority and greed.[31]

Yet of all the Meskwaki people who opposed the Indian Service during these years, it was Jim Peters, who had helped Masqasee escape the school, who struck the most lasting blow. When Malin came to the Tama Agency in 1899, he continued Rebok's practice of claiming guardianship over Meskwaki students like Masqasee.[32] So when Jim Peters helped Masqasee flee the boarding school, Malin—overlooking the role of Masqasee's mother in the escape—declared the case a kidnapping and dispatched three Meskwaki policemen to apprehend Peters.[33]

Kidnapping fell under the Major Crimes Act, so the Meskwaki police complied. When they cornered Peters, a group of his friends prepared to mount a defense. The situation grew tense, but the county sheriff showed up and, apparently, convinced Peters to surrender and let the courts sort it out.[34]

Peters spent nine days in custody. During the trial, his lawyers challenged the validity of his arrest. Even if Malin was authorized to prosecute kidnappings, they argued, his insistence that he was the state guardian of

Meskwaki schoolchildren was both illegal and rife with conflicts of interest. Malin, they said, could not be both the guardian who claimed that Peters had enticed Masqasee away from school *and* the agent responsible for charging him under federal law. The county court agreed, and Jim Peters walked free.[35]

A RESERVATION LIKE ANY OTHER

Shortly after his acquittal, Jim Peters's attorneys filed a false imprisonment suit against the Tama Agency.[36] Heard in federal court in Dubuque, the case was called *Peters v. Malin*. The judge upheld the district court's ruling that "the state had exceeded its jurisdiction in appointing Mr. Malin as [the children's] guardian."[37]

These findings had wide-ranging and paradoxical consequences for the Meskwaki Nation. In one sense, it was a major win for the tribe—especially those Red Earth People who staunchly opposed the Toledo school. Jim Peters remained free, and, under the judge's orders, agents like Malin could neither compel Meskwaki enrollment at the school nor use the threat of withheld annuity payments as leverage. After *Peters v. Malin*, the Tama Agency never sustained attendance. The Indian Service closed the school and converted it to a tuberculosis sanatorium in the early 1910s.[38] A few years later, tribal members convinced the Indian Service to open day schools on the Settlement so their children could learn closer to home.

The case strengthened the tribe's hand in other ways. The decision put an end to the Tama Agency's habit of commanding Meskwaki police to enforce state laws. Indeed, *Peters v. Malin* held that the State of Iowa lacked jurisdiction on the Meskwaki Settlement. The Major Crimes Act applied only to specific infractions committed by Native people against other Native people on tribal land. So, after *Peters v. Malin*, neither the state nor the federal government had any jurisdiction over a wide range of Meskwaki criminal and civil issues. In one sense, this was a major affirmation of Meskwaki sovereignty, since it established that, in most cases, the Meskwaki Nation held the ultimate authority on its land.[39]

The case also handed the Red Earth People a long-sought victory. As Keysor notes, ninety-seven years after the 1804 treaty falsely unified the "Sac and Fox Tribe," the federal judge's willingness to hear a Meskwaki man's case in Iowa implicitly recognized the Meskwaki Nation as a distinct legal entity, separate from their relatives in Kansas.[40]

The case, however, was not a total victory for the Meskwaki Nation. For years, white activists had slowly eroded the relationship between the chief's council and state politicians. As the Indian Service and the Indian Rights Association gained supporters in the 1890s, fewer and fewer state leaders took seriously the Red Earth People's insistence that because they had purchased their land, it was not subject to incessant federal meddling.

During the arguments in *Peters v. Malin*, Agent Malin's defense team had tried to turn the Meskwaki Nation's long-held belief about its land's unique status against the tribe. Jim Peters should have been susceptible to state law, Malin's lawyers claimed, because the Meskwaki Settlement could "not be deemed a reservation" since it had been purchased via a state-tribal trust.[41]

The judge rejected this claim, holding that the unique tenure of the Meskwaki Settlement did not negate the federal-tribal trust relationship. He drew from *US v. Kagama*, an 1886 Supreme Court case that had declared Native peoples "weak," "helpless," and reliant on Congress.[42] According to *Kagama*, the judge wrote, the relationship between Native Americans and the United States "does not grow out of the ownership of the land," but is rooted in Indigenous people's wardship to the federal government. The Meskwaki Settlement had to be dealt with "in fact and in law" like any other reservation. The fact that the United States had become the trustee for Meskwaki land in 1896, the judge maintained, simply reinforced this argument.[43]

Peters v. Malin reflected a central theme in the long history of state and federal Indian law. Attempting to balance the individual facts of Jim Peters's case and William Malin's actions with overarching policy goals, all layered over existing legal precedents, the judge created a new, convoluted precedent that affirmed Meskwaki sovereignty in some ways while eroding it in others. It took several years for the day-to-day consequences of this major legal determination to reveal themselves. In the short run, the Meskwaki Nation had little time to digest the victory or mull the legal precarities of its shared land base. Within months of the case's completion, the Meskwaki Nation had another, much larger problem to deal with. The Red Earth People were dying.

THE WINTER OF DEATH

As the Iowa River ran cold in the autumn of 1901, catastrophe tore across Meskwaki land. Death and suffering traveled from home to home over the course of five frigid months. The episode ended in a torrent of chemicals and flame that brought about a fundamental restructuring of Meskwaki life and landscape.

When the first cases appeared in late September, the Settlement housed 394 Red Earth People and 8 visiting Ho-Chunks. It arrived with either some of these visitors or a returning Meskwaki traveler.[44] In either case, *Variola major*—which is better known as smallpox—bore a brutal curse. According to author Jonathan B. Tucker, roughly two weeks after exposure, the disease brought fever, aches, and nausea then covered its victims with terrible pustules.[45] These blisters emitted a repulsive scent, second in its horror only to the burning agony the afflicted had to endure over the course of about ten days. Nearly one in three patients died. Survivors healed slowly and incompletely. Pocked skin was a tragic reminder worn by many for the rest of their lives. Smallpox was also viciously contagious. Although rudimentary vaccines dated back to the late 1700s, it continued to kill two million of the ten to fifteen million people infected each year until the late 1960s.[46]

At the turn of the twentieth century, smallpox was not unique to the Meskwaki Settlement. In fact, it had passed through the Upper Mississippi and made its way west several times, notably as part of large-scale epidemics in the 1780s and 1830s, ravaging Indigenous communities across North America. Neither of these outbreaks seems to have significantly affected the Red Earth People, in the latter case, perhaps, due to federal vaccination efforts in the region.[47] More immediately, in the fall of 1901, the disease swept through the towns of Traer, just twenty-five miles northeast of the Settlement, and Grinnell, which sits roughly the same distance to the south—as well as more than twenty other Iowa communities.[48] This was part of a broader bout that lasted several years. St. Paul, Minnesota, saw 104 cases between May 1899 and 1901, 300 hit Philadelphia in 1901, and in Illinois the boils ravaged more than 5,000 people between October 1901 and March 1902—the same stretch of time as the Iowa outbreak.[49]

Given the horrific virality of this disease, it is not difficult to see why, in mid-October, the Iowa State Board of Health developed a response to halt the spread. The board hastily appointed Dr. A. M. Linn of Des Moines to handle smallpox after its appearance in Tama County.[50] Linn worked in almost constant correspondence with William Malin, the Indian agent who had only recently read a judge's decision stripping him of most of his legal authority on Meskwaki land.

By mid-October, Malin, Linn, and the chief's council had begun a localized quarantine of smallpox patients on the Settlement. The agent assured the commissioner of Indian affairs that there was "absolutely no cause for panic" because only a few full-fledged cases had yet occurred. He also happily reported that the Indian school, which had been constructed in Toledo in 1898, was locked down and that not a single case of smallpox had reared its head among the institution's thirty-five students.[51] When the majority of the Red Earth People left the central village—which still rested on the Settlement's lowlands, near the river—for their winter hunt late that October, Malin even hoped the lower concentration of people could stem the virus's spread.[52]

This was not to be. In just days, *Variola major* swept through Meskwaki land with all the speed, scorching, and scarring of a prairie wildfire. Malin recruited three physicians from nearby towns to help inspect the community on November 4. The foursome started in the Settlement's northwest corner and made their way through tribal land, recording twenty-eight full-blown smallpox cases. They found eight people who had already survived its wrath. Heavy rain and snow had forced the Red Earth People into their wickiups, where the virus spread quickly through close quarters. The disease was heavily concentrated on the Settlement's south side, between the Chicago & Northwestern rail line and the Iowa River, in the village where most community activity took place.[53]

The Red Earth People, of course, had attempted to control the outbreak on their own. Families separated infected persons from others inside their wickiups, and Meskwaki healers relieved symptoms using customary combinations of ceremony and herbal remedies. Even then, the Meskwaki casualties crept to seventeen.[54] Upon receipt of this news, the board of health quickly placed the entire Meskwaki Settlement under quarantine.

Paranoid residents from surrounding communities worried that the Meskwaki people would bring death to their towns. These concerns were fueled by racist assumptions that people of color were predisposed to infection.⁵⁵ As Settlement cases dropped to about a dozen in mid-November, locals claimed that more than a hundred Red Earth People had the disease.⁵⁶ No non-Natives had contracted it, but Tama County residents still complained to Governor L. M. Shaw, worried that the Red Earth People were sure to bring smallpox to their doorstep. At the end of November, Shaw wrote to Secretary of the Interior Ethan A. Hitchcock, requesting authorization to enforce a strict quarantine. Hitchcock reassured the governor that the federal government would "be glad to cooperate with the state authorities in protecting the people of Tama against smallpox among the Indians." He authorized the state to "take any necessary action," including force, to keep the Red Earth People on the Settlement.⁵⁷

Although a few Meskwaki people slipped out during quarantine, Malin reported that the vast majority of Settlement residents "commanded the respect, and even admiration of the law abiding citizens of Tama and Toledo, by quietly staying on their own lands, and their scrupulous regard for the quarantine laws of the state."⁵⁸ Moreover, no one tried to connect the Red Earth People, at least in print, to the concurrent outbreaks in Grinnell and Traer. And despite the intensity of local fears, the virus ultimately did not make it to Tama or Toledo.

By the middle of November, the health board had administered smallpox vaccinations to almost everyone on the Settlement. A handful of residents refused the treatment, presumably due to a distrust of Western medicine and government officials.⁵⁹ When cases surged later that month, even the most oppositional members of the tribe did not push back against the construction of a medical tent on the Settlement.⁶⁰ Fortunately, by the time the structure had been raised, the worst of the epidemic had passed.⁶¹

All told, half the people on the Settlement contracted smallpox. Forty-two members of the Meskwaki community lost their lives between late September and December 1901.⁶² Conservatively, this bestowed a crushing 10 percent decrease in the Settlement's population.⁶³ By comparison, the global influenza pandemic in 1918 killed as much as 6 percent of the human race, including some 675,000 Americans, amounting to less than 1 percent of the US population at the time.⁶⁴ According to one estimate, as of late 2023 the COVID-19 pandemic had killed over 6.7 million people

To halt the spread of smallpox, government officials burned Meskwaki wickiups in early 1902. Within a few years, most families moved from these dwellings into framed houses, although many still used summer houses and wickiups at different times of year. Photo courtesy of the Jacob Breid Photograph Album on the Meskwaki Settlement, Image PH8410.49.1, State Historical Society of Iowa, Des Moines.

worldwide and hospitalized many more. For all the tragedy and disruption it caused, this total approaches barely a fraction of a percent of the global population.[65]

Variola major was under control by the first day of 1902. But the winter and the crisis facing the Meskwaki community were not over.

CLEANUP BY FIRE

On a crisp March morning in 1902, a man stepped forward and touched a flame to a cattail mat wrapped around a sturdy dome of entwined oak and maple sprigs. The long Iowa winter had left the structure cold and damp, so the heat lingered for a moment before igniting the fuel that had doused the dwelling. The man stepped back just as his conflagration consumed the wickiup. Acting on orders from his superiors at the Office of Indian Affairs and the Iowa Department of Health, the man and his team repeated this process until the entire Meskwaki village—the single shared space that had comprised the center of the tribe's economic and political life for forty-five years—had been reduced to ashes. Perhaps the only materials that survived the fire were a few sacred bundles. According to oral history, some Red Earth People had buried them under the floors of their wickiups and recovered them several months later. With them lived the stories and ceremonies that had sustained the Meskwaki Nation since time immemorial.[66]

The fire had been planned for months. In early November, agent Malin and Dr. Linn, per common procedure, had recommended that everything in the village be disinfected as soon as the epidemic subsided.[67] *Variola major's* ability to cling to clothes and surfaces demanded that most material goods in an infected area be incinerated. Rare or irreplaceable items could be doused in a caustic concoction of corrosive sublimate—a deadly poison liable to eat through metal containers or piping.[68]

Disinfecting the Settlement posed a series of problems. Lighting a fire was easy. Housing and clothing the displaced Meskwaki and Ho-Chunk residents in the dead of a numbing Iowa winter was a different matter altogether. Poor weather had delayed the "cleaning up," as Malin called it, until late March.[69] Meanwhile, the state and federal governments had to fund the quarantine, including rations and medical supplies and care, during the five-month isolation, as well as the cleanup itself. Weakened by illness and unable to hunt, the Red Earth People relied on credit to buy goods. One Meskwaki policeman kept track of individual families' debts while the tribe negotiated with the Indian Office about paying them.[70]

Last came the challenge of convincing tribal members to allow the charring of their homes and effects. The Indian Office did not go to great lengths to consult with Meskwaki leaders, choosing instead to let white officials issue the order. In late February and early March, agent Malin held several meetings with white physicians and the mayors of Tama and Toledo. He also traveled to Des Moines for a conference with Dr. Linn and Governor A. B. Cummins, who had succeeded James Shaw that January, to map out the destruction.[71] No member of the Meskwaki community attended either meeting, and only once did Malin mention that Pushetonequa's council and most tribal members were "willing that the work of disinfection shall be complete, even though it [will] involve the destruction of their wickiups and clothing, under the promise" that they would be reimbursed for lost property.[72]

Some Red Earth People, of course, ardently opposed the burning of their homes and possessions. Fresh from his legal battle with Malin's office, Jim Peters claimed that sleeping in a wood-floored tent or framed house—the two structures being contemplated by the Indian Office as replacements for the torched wickiups—was against Meskwaki religion.[73] Others tried to convince officials that tribal custom dictated any item slated for burning had to first sit outside for four days. Whether or not this was a genuine cultural consideration, it also bought time for Meskwaki people who wished to sneak into the village and save items from the flames.[74]

The fire went forward. On the morning of March 24, state and federal officials looked on as their subordinates ignited the wickiups. They reduced the Meskwaki village to ashes and, in the aftermath of the blaze, lifted the quarantine.[75] In late February, the state legislature approved a $7,000 appropriation for the purchase of forty wood-framed homes and a set of clothes and a blanket for every man, woman, and child on the Settlement, expenses for which Congress reimbursed the state.[76]

Everyone on the Settlement also received a pair of stockings and shoes. Men got suits. Meskwaki women received dresses, but many refused to don them as they were "made as white women wear them." Instead of the bustles, bonnets, and frills that were fashionable among white women of the era, most Meskwaki women preferred simpler wraps that they complemented by shawling fabric or a blanket over their shoulders. Agent Malin grumbled but ultimately conceded to the women's wishes. It was a small Meskwaki victory in the almost exclusively non-Indigenous cleanup that concluded the Red Earth People's winter of death.[77]

A MIGHTY PULVERIZING ENGINE

On April 1, 1902, the Indian Office declared the smallpox epidemic on the Meskwaki Settlement "happily over."[78] Members of the Meskwaki community, still reeling from the loss of over forty friends and relatives, not to mention most of their worldly possessions, probably shared in this relief. But as the cattails grew that spring, tribal members could not have predicted the long-term change the torching of their village would have on the physical and economic makeup of their community.

In his second address to Congress in 1901, President Theodore Roosevelt—a man not widely remembered for his support of "squalid savages," as he once called Native Americans, or for their rights to collective landownership—described the Dawes Act as "a mighty pulverizing engine, to break up the tribal mass" and touted its usefulness for speeding assimilation.[79]

In the years leading up to the smallpox epidemic of 1901-1902, the Red Earth People had deftly avoided this piston. Despite continuous pressure from the Indian Service, allotment failed time and again to rupture the Meskwaki land base. Throughout the smallpox outbreak, Malin and his correspondents in Washington, DC, and Des Moines wrote almost exclusively about safety and disease prevention. They did not expound, at least in writing, on the ways in which the destruction of the Meskwaki village supported broader policy goals. Yet the crisis posed a long-awaited opportunity to take a critical step toward allotment.

The Indian Service believed that the smallpox epidemic had left the Red Earth People, as Malin put it, "with a higher and better conception of the white man's civilization."[80] This assessment was not surprising, given the bureaucrats' predilection toward using assimilation as the yardstick for measuring every change in Meskwaki life. In the early years of the twentieth century, several academics came to Meskwaki country. This included William Jones, who had been born on the Sac and Fox reservation in Oklahoma. Educated at Harvard and then under the influential scholar Franz Boaz at Columbia University, Jones became the first Native American to earn a PhD in anthropology.[81] Jones echoed a common refrain expressed by many outsiders after visiting the Meskwaki Nation. He wrote in 1904 that the Red Earth People "still cling to the life of the past with all that firm tenacity which has been their predominating trait ever since the day they were first known to the French."[82]

This was a curious observation. At the time of Jones's visits, Meskwaki families were in the process of reimagining the relationship between their community and its landscape. Concerned that the close quarters of the central village could hasten another outbreak, families spaced out their wickiups after 1902. They never returned to the central village and deliberately adjusted their annual movements.[83] Families still migrated seasonally, but the distance slowly shrank. As one Meskwaki man put it, "it was the custom to move" into the "timber [or to the] back of a hill out of the wind," during frosty winter months. In the summer, families "would move to open places for more breeze and where their garden spots were."[84]

The countryside, after all, had grown crowded. Just two years before the Settlement purchase in 1857, iron tracks for the first time connected the sixty-mile distance between Iowa City and Davenport, a rough river town of 22,000 that thrived at the confluence of various rail lines and the Mississippi River on the state's eastern edge. Within twenty years, rail cars ousted stagecoaches and steamboats as Iowans' preferred mode of transit. By 1900, some 9,000 miles of railroad tracks crisscrossed the state. Trains brought people, livestock, and crops to and from eastern markets. That same year, 97 percent of the land in the state was devoted to farming. Yields moved freely from farms to national markets alongside pork and oats processed in Iowa's burgeoning cities.[85]

The state's population reflected its growing economy, even in rural towns like Tama. The community expanded from just over 5,000 residents in 1860 to some 25,000 in 1900.[86] Over the next few decades, more settlers cleared forests and tallgrass prairies. They dug irrigation channels that snaked toward flattened fields. There, farmers' tills and plows ravaged the prairie ecosystems that had long offered produce and supported ample populations of small game.[87]

Due to these changes, having a readily transportable home became less of a priority for Meskwaki families. Many began to replace their wickiups with framed houses. In 1905, wickiups constituted about three-fourths of the dwellings on Meskwaki land, and there stood only about fifteen framed houses.[88] By 1927, Meskwaki families had reversed this trend, choosing instead to take a lump-sum payment of several years' worth of annuities to purchase a house. By then, only three families lived full time in wickiups, although many still moved wickiups into the trees and riverbanks at midyear or built stick-frame structures called "summer shades" that relieved oppressive heat and humidity.[89]

None of these developments brought the predictions of men like Theodore Roosevelt and William Jones to bear. Tenacious, yes—the Red Earth People were as devoted to persisting in the face of terrible circumstances as they had been during the Fox Wars. But the Meskwaki Nation was hardly stuck in the past. Where visitors and federal officials waited impatiently to record cracks in the wall of Meskwaki cultural resistance, Meskwaki families lived, adjusting on their own terms to meet everyday needs.

WHOSE LAND?

Meskwaki families moved their homes following the destruction of the central village in 1902. Rather than dividing the Settlement into regular-sized individual plots that tribal members owned outright, the Red Earth People offered a twist on allotment. The tribe observed an informal use-rights system in which a family chose a plot of Settlement land, built a house, and planted a garden. As their children grew up, many built their own homes near their relatives. Over time, these informal land claims were passed between the generations and began to resemble family neighborhoods.[90] Meanwhile, the broader community recognized common areas for collecting resources or conducting ceremonies. Importantly, the division of Settlement land was done by the tribe, and the property continued to be owned by the Meskwaki Nation as a whole. And, unlike tribal lands vulnerable to the most pernicious detail of the allotment policy, the Meskwaki Settlement contained no gaps of "surplus land" that could be sold off to non-Natives.

The Meskwaki Nation's land tenure model was not perfect. Most tribal members supported the collective ownership of the Meskwaki Settlement. Some challenged this notion. In the late 1890s, for example, a few Red Earth People raised concerns about a potential error in the language of the original 1857 deed to the Meskwaki Settlement. That document had named five members of the chief's council as the owners of the original 80 acres. Some of those men's descendants argued that the land belonged to them, not the tribe as a whole.[91]

County, state, and federal authorities rejected this claim. Since the 1857 sale had been made under state law, the matter ended up in county court. The court found that the original deed had been negotiated between the governor of Iowa, the Butler family, and the Meskwaki chief's council on behalf of the whole tribe. The original acreage and all the Settlement land added to it over the years—which around 1900 totaled just over 2,900 acres—belonged to the entire Meskwaki Nation.[92]

Legally speaking, this decision resolved the issue, and the Red Earth People's collective ownership of their Settlement remained intact. But the debate over land and power raged on, deepening the rift over tribal leadership. By 1905, one of Mamiwanige's grandsons, a thirty-three-year-old named John Tataposh, had formed a separate leadership group that claimed to be the real tribal council, basing his claim to power on a hereditary right to both the chieftainship and the Settlement itself.[93] As one man put it, Mamiwanige "bought this land. He was the head, the main Chief. This is the reason why [Mamiwanige's] grandson is now the controller of this land."[94]

Fueled by this belief in the rightful ownership of the Meskwaki Settlement, a group of a dozen or so Meskwaki activists challenged the Indian Office and Pushetonequa's council at every turn. At least once, they traveled to Des Moines in an attempt to convince the governor to support their claims to the Settlement and the authority to govern it.[95] They also tried to use *Peters v. Malin* to prevent the agent from paying the state property taxes on the tribe's behalf. If state criminal laws did not apply on Meskwaki land, they asserted, neither should taxes. Malin consulted with the governor's office. State officials agreed that if the tribe defaulted on its property taxes, the Meskwaki Nation could lose its Settlement. But, since the land was in trust with the federal government, questions remained.[96]

Attempting to clear up the ambiguities surrounding the legal status of the Meskwaki Settlement, the Indian Service enlisted Pushetonequa's support for a formal request that the state investigate the status and taxation of the Meskwaki Settlement.[97] The question bounced around between state and federal offices for nearly two years. Finally, in July 1907, Acting Secretary of the Interior Jesse E. Wilson submitted a detailed report to Governor A. B. Cummins. Its findings surprised everyone involved.[98]

Wilson found that although the Settlement trust transfer had been authorized by the state and federal governments in 1896, officials had forgotten to sign over many of the deeds to Meskwaki land. Between 1857 and 1896, the trust responsibility for all the Meskwaki Nation's purchases of additional property technically resided with the state. The Department of the Interior affirmed that the Meskwaki Nation had made these purchases and that the federal government had intended to absorb them into trust but noted that no Iowa governor had actually formalized the change.[99]

In short, due to a series of bureaucratic errors, the transfer of the Meskwaki Settlement into federal trust had been authorized in 1896 but the actual, legal transition of the Meskwaki Settlement had never taken place. Acting Secretary Wilson asked Governor Cummins to sign the deeds straight away. That process took until July 1908. When it was complete, the ownership of the Meskwaki Settlement was clear: it was tribal land, bought with Meskwaki money and owned communally by the Red Earth People, but vested in a federal trust that resembled Native American reservations across the United States.[100] In all the confusion, however, the question that had sparked this investigation—what would happen if the tribe did not pay its state property taxes?—fell to the wayside. Unwilling to risk losing the Settlement, the Meskwaki Nation continued to pay property taxes for more than seventy years.

AVOIDING ALLOTMENT—AGAIN

As the tribe, the state, and the federal government ironed out disputes over title and ownership between 1896 and 1908, another problem faced the Red Earth People: there was not enough land to go around. This was not only a matter of size, but of quality and distribution. If it had been divided equally among the Meskwaki population, every Meskwaki man, woman, and child would have received a little more than nine acres, worth about $125 apiece near the turn of the century. A family of five, then, would have less than fifty acres between them, worth a total of about $6,000. For the sake of comparison, the quarter tracts owned by many white farmers would have been worth about $20,000.[101]

All of this assumes that each Settlement acre was as good as the next. It was not. In fact, because of terrain, forests, and flooding, less than half of the Settlement offered quality farmland.[102] In earlier eras, the Red Earth People had designed their seasonal rounds in part to skirt the Iowa River, which regularly swelled beyond its banks. As more families moved into permanent wood-framed homes, many of which were located along the lowlands, floodwaters periodically destroyed homes and crops. The issue became so serious that, in 1917, tribal members convinced the Indian Service to hire an engineer to develop a drainage plan for a 100-acre section of the Settlement known as Whiskey Bottom.[103]

This problem compounded over time. Although the use-rights system had worked immediately after the village fire in 1902, within a few years, some Meskwaki families had dozens of acres while others had only a sliver.[104] The issue grew contentious. In a few cases, younger tribal members had tried to farm land tacitly belonging to other, usually older, tribal members, only to have "their crops . . . destroyed and their fences torn down."[105]

Meanwhile, leadership of the Tama Agency changed hands. In September 1908, William Malin resigned after eight tempestuous years as superintendent.[106] He was replaced by Orville J. Green on October 1.[107] Like Malin, Green would try and fail to force Meskwaki parents to enroll their children at the agency school. He, too, would arrest Jim Peters and other Red Earth People when they challenged his authority. Green would be taken to court by Meskwaki people who had been arrested and lose. Although none of these cases had the lasting impact of *Peters v. Malin*, they illustrated the continuation of political tension on and about Meskwaki land.[108]

Even more than his predecessor, Green focused heavily on land tenure. His time at the Tama Agency was punctuated by a revival of federal interest in allotting the Settlement. His appointment had come just as Iowa and the United States were finalizing the deed transfers and as the inequities in the tribe's land distribution system were becoming apparent. With these developments in mind, Green sought to align the administration of the Meskwaki Settlement with the management of most reservation lands across the country. Commissioner of Indian Affairs Robert G. Valentine articulated the conclusion at which he, Green, and their colleagues had arrived in 1910: the "first step" in any new plan for the management of the Meskwaki Settlement, Valentine wrote, "should unquestionably be the allotment of their lands."[109]

Although committed to this idea, Valentine saw two problems. The Meskwaki Nation had purchased the Settlement with its own money. He believed that allotment could not be done without tribal consent, and that, he knew, would be a tough sell.[110] Even if the Indian Service could build enough support, Valentine remained unsure of its ability to enforce the policy on the Settlement. This, he wrote, boiled down to a basic fact: "They own their lands."[111]

Valentine also remained uneasy about a contradiction in the Indian Service's logic. On one hand, the inequality of Settlement land distribution was driving the disagreement between members of the tribe. Drawing attention to the issue may have even allowed the agency to court the favor of some tribal members. But, Valentine knew, allotment could not solve a basic problem: There simply was not enough land to go around. Divvying up the Meskwaki Settlement would create small plots insufficient to support the Red Earth People.[112]

Cognizant of these drawbacks, the Indian Service remained committed to allotment. It repeatedly pressed the Red Earth People to break up the Settlement, taking formal steps toward that end in 1910, 1916, and 1923.[113] Each of these efforts failed because the Red Earth People refused to give up their communal hold on the Settlement and because they knew that, given the nature of the tribe's property, allotment would not solve their problems. The tribal secretary, a man named Chakotakosee, summed this up in 1909, when Green and his colleagues began to raise the issue: "We do not want our lands divided. There is not enough land. And how could you do it[?] Some of our land is very hilly and some is just low land often covered with water, and some of it is very good land. Who will have the water land and who will have the hills and who will have the best land[?] And perhaps some of us would have no timber on our land and how would we get wood to burn? You better leave the land like it is now."[114]

CHAPTER 6

Living on the Land

The Red Earth People sought diverse and creative ways to make a living in the first decades of the twentieth century. Despite the challenges associated with its limited acreage, the Meskwaki Settlement remained the foundation upon which the Red Earth People defined their success. Investing in the people on their land reflected a commitment to developing the homeland the Red Earth People had been remaking since 1857.

Agriculture remained a cornerstone of Meskwaki life. Tribal members had been raising crops in community and individual subsistence gardens for generations. Herbs gathered in the forest and along the riverbed never disappeared from Meskwaki menus or medicine chests. One agent called "agriculture ... the chief industrial pursuit in which these Indians engage," noting that in the year 1901, one Meskwaki man had "planted 47 acres, another 36, and others [cultivated] areas ranging from 10 to 25 acres each."[1] Two years later, another report noted that Meskwaki families had cultivated some 375 total acres of corn, 65 acres of beans, and another 75 acres of potatoes, squash, and millets. They also owned a significant number of livestock—about 450 horses and ponies, 109 hogs, 10 head of cattle, and more than 700 chickens.[2]

New tools and agricultural strategies increased yields and access to local markets, allowing Meskwaki families to sell even more produce.[3] Some of this success was owed to extension programs. As it had done on reservations across the country, the Indian Service had hired several part-time "government farmers," who lived near the Settlement and were tasked with agricultural education. They had struggled to find a foothold in the Meskwaki community for years. By the mid-1890s, community members

147

were calling on these instructors for guidance on new technologies and approaches that added to Meskwaki agricultural knowledge often enough that the agency made the position permanent.[4]

Dwindling game populations threatened a vital source of protein for Meskwaki families. A writer for the *Meskwaki Booster*, which was sponsored and often written by the Indian Service, opined in 1915 that "if the game and fur bearing animals are not protected for at least a part of the year they will become exterminated."[5] This troubled the Red Earth People for decades. By midcentury, an agent would report that "the competition for furs and other wildlife [was] quite heavy" on the small, densely populated Meskwaki Settlement. Without some conservation program in place, he wrote, "all forms of wildlife either now or are rapidly becoming depleted from" tribal land.[6]

Facing limited resources, Meskwaki hunters looked off Settlement. Sometimes, this irritated white farmers, whose complaints about trespassing seemed to grow in tandem with the decline of available game. Others took a symbiotic approach, inviting Meskwaki hunters into their fields to dig out muskrat, skunk, and other dens, which protected crops. For their efforts, the Red Earth People took home a little extra meat and a few furs that they could use or sell. Even then, some farmers complained when Meskwaki hunters forgot to refill the holes they had dug, leaving perilous obstacles for wandering livestock.[7]

By the mid-1930s, nine out of every ten Meskwaki people lived on the Settlement, but many traveled for work in surrounding farms and communities.[8] Despite early and ardent resistance, the majority of families began to enroll their children in a Settlement day school after the closure of the Toledo boarding school.[9] Around ninety Meskwaki students enrolled at federal boarding schools in Kansas, Oklahoma, Nebraska, Minnesota, and South Dakota in this era.[10] Education at these facilities enabled Meskwaki students to find jobs as railroad or construction workers, as laborers in local industrial plants, and in a variety of other blue-collar positions. Most returned to the Settlement, where they combined agricultural and wage work with the production of crafts like baskets, beadwork, jewelry, and souvenirs, which they sold to tourists passing the Settlement on the nearby Lincoln Highway.[11]

The Red Earth People had been capitalizing on non-Native interest in their art and culture for decades.[12] In 1870 a group of Meskwaki dancers earned $20 performing at the Independence Day celebration in Tama.[13] A few years later, several Meskwaki people met Isaac C. Millard, a local choir director and Sunday school teacher who co-owned and operated a mercantile store with his wife, Lydia, in the town of Montour. Isaac had become fluent in Meskwaki through his dealings with tribal members, and by 1887 he was coordinating performances that harnessed for the Red Earth People some of the pop-culture attention that made Buffalo Bill's Wild West Show such a success. Mr. Millard traveled with Meskwaki dancers to celebrations across Iowa, and in 1887, for example, twenty-five Meskwaki performers danced at Seni-Om-Sed ("Des Moines" spelled backward), a large street party held in the state capital to promote the Iowa State Fair each year.[14]

A quarter century later, the Meskwaki Nation organized an on-Settlement powwow. For generations, the Red Earth People had been holding a gathering each August to celebrate the coming harvest. These events slowly attracted local attention. This was partially due to the booming popularity of Indian pageants in the era before film, which was itself part of an enduring and well-documented fascination with Indigenous peoples and their cultures. This interest was as alive in central Iowa as in other parts of the country.[15]

Capitalizing on this energy, around 1912, a few Meskwaki men had the idea to formalize the event and advertise it to outsiders. They pitched the idea to the chief's council and moved forward from there.[16] The following year, the Meskwaki Nation established its annual powwow, which has continued every year since, save for a brief hiatus during World War II. By the mid-1930s, the event brought about 7,000 visitors to the Settlement each year. At the height of its popularity, powwow revenues provided each performer roughly an extra $20, vital cash for families making less than $500 annually.[17] Over the years, the powwow also provided opportunities for the Red Earth People to use popular interest in their community as a way to reject assimilation and keep Meskwaki culture and traditions alive.[18]

The Meskwaki Nation also sought to shore up the tribe's finances by reclaiming lost payments owed to the tribe from federal treaties. By 1918, the tribe was receiving roughly $13,300 each year, which amounted to a mere $37—just under $600 today—per tribal member.[19] From this sum, each Meskwaki person gave $5 to a collective account for road and fence

The Meskwaki Nation created a Powwow Association to manage the annual powwow, which had become a major week-long event by the time this photograph was taken in the mid-1920s. It shows members of the Meskwaki band, who performed during the powwow. Pictured are Tom Scott, Kenneth Kapayou, Kenneth Young Bear, Robert Young Bear, George Young Bear, Albert Davenport, George Mitchell, Dan Young Bear, John Young Bear, George Buffalo, Moses Slick, John Jones, John Roberts, John Bear Jr., and Edward Davenport. Photo courtesy of the Josephine Wallace Photograph Collection, Image PH1139, State Historical Society of Iowa, Des Moines.

maintenance on the Settlement, the property taxes for which continued to be paid by leasing revenues from the South Farm.[20]

The tribe, however, also sought to resolve some outstanding treaty concerns. Since at least 1888, the Red Earth People had been arguing that they were entitled to a portion of the $11,500 in treaty annuities still being paid to the combined "Sac & Fox Tribe." The Meskwaki Nation had been cut out of these payments since leaving the reservation along the Osage River in the 1850s.[21] The tribe initiated an inquiry in the 1890s, which led to a decade-long lawsuit with the Sac and Fox Tribe of Oklahoma. Finally settled in 1907, the case awarded the Meskwaki Nation nearly $39,000 in restitution, which many tribal members wanted dispersed on a per capita basis.[22]

Agent Green refused to pay. "It would be as well to throw nine-tenths of the money into the Iowa River," he wrote, "as to give it to the Indians to spend."[23] Based on his advice, Congress placed the funds in an account in Washington, DC, from which tribal members would receive semiannual installments drawn from 5 percent interest. True to form, the Red Earth People pushed back and demanded that some of the money be invested in their Settlement. Congress acquiesced and agreed to appropriate $5,000 for infrastructural improvements and set aside an additional $24,000 to purchase additional acres for the Meskwaki community. This and other purchases helped the tribe increase the size of the Settlement to around 3,000 acres by 1910.[24]

A PORTRAIT OF MESKWAKI LIFE

For Meskwaki families, these economic strategies created a comfortable, but not opulent, life on their Settlement. The family of James and Mary Poweshiek, among many other examples, illustrates these experiences. Mary was a Potawatomi woman born with the name Nahnowah. She became a member of the Meskwaki community following a fateful trip in 1882. That year, she and some relatives made a delivery to the Meskwaki Nation.[25] There, Mary met James Poweshiek, a Meskwaki man in his late twenties who had been born with the name Bawashika, or "Shedding Bear." James was the son of Medenea, one of the five Meskwaki emissaries who had purchased the original Settlement on the tribe's behalf. Mary and James married and she bore twelve children, five of whom survived to adulthood.[26]

Mary and Jim made a life on the Settlement. He worked as an Indian Service policeman and became well known around the area as "Old Jim" Poweshiek. He retired in 1913, the same year Mary passed away. For decades, Old Jim continued to live in the modest white-washed home he and Mary had built. He stayed for most of the rest of his life, moving into a nursing home in nearby Boone in his nineties, and died in 1950.[27]

Old Jim and his family lived like many Red Earth People of their era. With the help of his adult sons Horace and Willie, Old Jim raised corn, oats, and a handful of other crops on a 60-acre parcel of Settlement land.[28]

By the 1920s, Old Jim's otherwise austere home was "furnished well with [a] range, table, chairs, beds, [and a] lounge [chair]." It boasted a linoleum-floored kitchen and carpeted living room. He also had a barn and granary, which stored his produce and the "plow, harrow, disk, corn planter, cultivator, mower, and rake" he used to coax food from the earth.[29]

The leasing of the South Farm by the tribe reduced the Poweshieks' tax burden. This helped since cash was sparse. Although the Indian Office offered some funds for seed and tools, annual yields reflected the disadvantages faced by Meskwaki families. In a good year, Meskwaki farmers harvested about 35 bushels of corn and 30 bushels of oats per acre. Old Jim also kept a pony, 6 pigs, and about 75 chickens, enough for him and his family to exist in relative comfort.[30] Yet the Poweshiek property was much smaller than the average Iowa family farm. Estimates from the early 1920s, for example, revealed that while Tama County farms varied from 80 to 640 acres, most filled 160-acre plots known as "quarter sections." These estimates also reveal that the average farmer owned 138 chickens, 16 head of cattle, 8 horses, 28 hogs, and 4 sheep.[31]

Old Jim's children provided for their families by mixing farming and hunting with wage work. His middle son, Jonas, was a bit of an outlier. As a boy, Jonas had run away from the boarding school in Toledo "two or three times." Each time, Jonas would later write, Old Jim would catch his son and haul him "right back because it was his duty, being a government police."[32]

Jonas grew interested in tribal history and culture. From Toledo, he went to the Chilocco Indian Agricultural School in Oklahoma, next to the Haskell Institute in Lawrence, Kansas, and then on to the Carlisle Indian Industrial School in Pennsylvania. Along the way, he earned an industrial certificate in painting but also became a skilled tailor. He enlisted in the army during World War I. One of four Meskwaki men who served in that conflict, Jonas was a quartermaster based out of Oklahoma and then Texas. After the war, he made his way home, working briefly at the Indian Office in Toledo before he and his wife, Ruth, moved to Des Moines in 1924. There, Jonas worked at the State Historical Society of Iowa. Although employed and paid as a custodian, he served as the state's unofficial translator and a consultant on Meskwaki affairs for years.[33]

The careers of Jonas's brothers, Horace and Willie, aligned more closely with most Red Earth People. Married with two stepchildren, Horace was a

Jonas Poweshiek, at left, poses in Meskwaki regalia with his wife, Ruth, and their infant child. The family lived in Des Moines, where Jonas worked at the State Historical Society of Iowa and facilitated the relationship between his tribe and that institution. Photo courtesy of the Josephine Wallace Photograph Collection, Image PH8428.37, State Historical Society of Iowa, Des Moines.

house painter and carpenter who had studied at Carlisle, where he was a schoolmate of famed athlete Jim Thorpe.[34] He was also active in the Native American Church and tribal politics and government.[35] Willie also went to Chilocco then returned to the Settlement, where he lived with his wife, Alice, their one-year-old daughter, Harlan, and their flock of chickens and sizable garden.[36] Willie, too, was immersed in tribal politics. Later in life, he spent the winters working as a deliveryman for a laundry service in Tama and a meat-packing company in Waterloo.[37]

As a young girl, Alice spent three years at the boarding school at Flandreau, South Dakota.[38] There, she received formal training in domestic labor and the equivalent of a ninth-grade education. This supplemented her lifetime of instruction from elder Meskwaki women. They taught her and other young Meskwaki women—like her sisters-in-law, Ida and Mary—how to cook, garden, gather wood and water, and make clothes. Many also made basketry, crafts, and beadwork, which they sold to tourists and locals. Alice was a skilled seamstress and canner who stockpiled fruits and vegetables from the

Ida Snowball Poweshiek, who, like many Meskwaki women of her generation, was a skilled artist and craftsperson. She likely earned extra income by selling items like these at the annual powwow. Photo courtesy of the Josephine Wallace Photograph Collection, Image PH8428.10, State Historical Society of Iowa, Des Moines.

family garden for winter use.[39] Like generations of Meskwaki women before her, she passed her knowledge and skills to her six daughters.[40]

Emblematic of Meskwaki families living on the Settlement and off, the Poweshieks made their livings by layering the new expectations and opportunities of the twentieth-century economy over the staples of Meskwaki life. These decisions reflected the conscious maintenance of a multilayered on-Settlement economy that brought success to the Red Earth People in the first decades of the 1900s.

Despite these achievements, this work occurred against a backdrop of continued political discord and constant assaults on tribal land and governance.

PUSHETONEQUA'S DEATH

The first years of the twentieth century proved a devastating epoch for the autonomy of Indigenous people. As the Salish-Kootenai intellectual and activist D'Arcy McNickle wrote, "The bureaucratic apparatus" of the federal government "had penetrated the entire fabric of Indian life" by that time, "usurping tribal decision-making, intruding into the family, and demeaning local leadership."[41] He was not wrong. Federal talons bore deep into the flesh of the Meskwaki Nation.

The boarding school in Toledo closed, more than a decade after *Peters v. Malin* had stymied the Indian Service's ability to compel attendance. In the spring of 1914, the converted campus reopened as the Sac and Fox Tuberculosis Sanatorium. By then, Dr. Robert L. Russell had been serving as its superintendent for a few months. A physician by training, he assumed the suite of administrative responsibilities as well as the role of director of the clinic. There, Russell loosened some of the strictures enforced by earlier superintendents. He led the Tama Agency from 1913 to 1919, and where his immediate predecessors had tried to coerce the Red Earth People into bending to federal will, Russell took a more ameliorative tack. He generally avoided meddling in cultural matters unless directed by policy and, according to historian Lisa Dianne Lykins, developed a friendly rapport with many members of the Meskwaki community.[42] His term of service initially seemed to offer a respite from the constant bitter contests that had hamstrung tribal-federal relations for years.

Indeed, Russell's popularity might have created an opportunity for the Red Earth People to leverage their relationship with him to regain some political traction. This was not to be. Instead, the old dispute over the chieftainship flared up. In early 1914, some two hundred tribal members signed a petition demanding Pushetonequa's removal. Rather than deposing the leader, who was now well into his seventies, Russell asked the Washington office for the authority to hand select the tribal council. This move would consolidate federal power over tribal affairs and erase one of the few remaining responsibilities of the chieftainship.[43]

The damage was done. By the fall, the Indian Office had empowered Russell to unilaterally select the council. This undercut the chief's ability, as council member Charles Davenport said, "to watch over, take care of *everything* that happened to the tribe—*everything*."[44] The results of Russell's actions were staggering. The Meskwaki historian Johnathan Buffalo has argued that after losing his power to select council members, Pushetonequa's "potency to act" as a tribal leader "was broken."[45]

The last five years of Pushetonequa's leadership of the Meskwaki Nation were characterized by the stark diminishment of his and his council's authority. His nearly four decades in leadership had been characterized by persistent challenges to his legitimacy, enormous changes to the social and economic fabric of the Meskwaki Nation and the Midwest, constant external pressures, and changing political realities. And his passing in 1919 marked more than the end of his tenure. Since the Indian Service refused to name his successor, Pushetonequa's death also marked the end of the Meskwaki chieftainship as it had been known for generations.[46]

The government's decision devastated the Red Earth People. In May 1920, several tribal members inquired why the agency would not endorse a successor. Assistant Commissioner of Indian Affairs E. B. Merritt replied that "the policy of the Department at this time is to encourage Indian tribes and bands to break up their tribal relations," and therefore it "declined to appoint successors to Chiefs who die, or to fill such vacancies in the tribe." If the community wanted to designate a symbolic leader, Merritt continued, they could do so. But he was adamant that such an individual would carry no force of law.[47]

So for about a decade after Pushetonequa's death, the Meskwaki government was made up of an agency-appointed business council. Meskwaki leaders struggled to maintain any semblance of power, in part because the Indian Office reduced the council's membership from twelve members to five. With no one left to establish order, and still grappling with internal partisanship, this small council went an entire year without so much as a meeting, and the Indian Service replaced the entire group. Devoid of any meaningful power, this council acted as little more than a liaison between the Red Earth People and government officers.[48] Meskwaki self-governance, for all practical purposes, was broken.

A PECULIAR CONDITION

The reforms forced upon the chief's council between 1914 and 1920 obliterated the governing capacity of the Meskwaki Nation. But, like Indigenous peoples across the United States, the Red Earth People searched for ways to work within and beyond the normal channels of the American political system. They explored legal vagaries and policy loopholes in a constant search for creative ways to push back against state and federal pressure, to affirm tribal sovereignty, and to assert Meskwaki control over Meskwaki lives.

Although the Meskwaki Nation stood at a firm political disadvantage in opposing the United States, its members retained some ammunition in the fight for self-governance. Most importantly, tribal members wielded the anomalous history of the Meskwaki Settlement as a strong rhetorical and legal weapon. This was due, in part, to the jurisdictional quagmire created by *Peters v. Malin*. Even that, however, offered little solace to Meskwaki people who were watching their long-revered council wither. As a possible remedy, in the early 1920s, some tribal members suggested launching an effort to return jurisdiction over the Settlement to the state government—a process that they hoped might restore some version of the autonomy their tribe had once enjoyed.[49] These conversations even prompted a short-lived discussion of the prospect of converting the Settlement into a state park.[50] In 1925, nine tribal members went so far as to ask the commissioner of Indian affairs whether it would be possible to remove the Meskwaki Settlement from federal trusteeship. It was possible, he explained, but to do so, the tribe would have to allot the Settlement. This was a nonstarter, and the Red Earth People dropped the issue.[51]

Throughout this period, government officials from Iowa and the United States remained confused about the status of the Meskwaki Settlement. In 1928, for instance, Congressman Cyrenus Cole described the Red Earth People as "differently situated from nearly all other Indians" because "they live on a tract of land which they own in fee simple. They are taxed on these lands." As a result, he said, they operated within a "peculiar condition" deserving of special policy considerations.[52] Cole, of course, had erred. The tribe had never owned the Settlement fee simple; it was held in trust, first by Iowa and then by the United States. His argument nonetheless reflected the efforts of the Red Earth People to shape policymakers' understanding of Meskwaki history and to articulate the ways in which they believed the "peculiar condition" of tribal land offered them greater opportunities for self-determination. The Meskwaki Nation, after all, had been funding its own land acquisitions and paying state property taxes for generations. Tribal members often reminded outsiders of these facts, using them as leverage in a series of controversies that, absent an impactful tribal government, constituted opportunities to defend Meskwaki sovereignty.

ONE STATE ALLY

With the Meskwaki Settlement formally in federal trust after 1908, the State of Iowa abandoned almost any interest in Meskwaki affairs. Tribal members still secured the occasional audience with state leaders, to be sure, but gone were the days when delegates from the chief's council would stride into a packed legislative chamber and make an impassioned address. When tribal members did engage with Des Moines, responses were slow and anemic, and the state usually deferred to the Indian Service on tribal matters. In this sense, the state government had implicitly endorsed the dismantling of the Meskwaki chief's council.

There was one exception to Iowa's policy of inaction. In 1914, a young curator named Edgar Harlan visited the Meskwaki Settlement through what he called a "singular accident."[53] Edgar's great-uncle, Aaron W. Harlan, had been stationed with the American dragoons along the west bank of the Mississippi River around the time of the 1832 US-Sauk War. Aaron lived to a hundred and, before passing, told Edgar stories about a romance with one of Makataimeshekiakiak's (Black Hawk's) daughters. He had wintered in a Sauk wickiup after the conflict and claimed to have befriended many Sauk and Meskwaki people during that time. Curious about his ancestor's tale, Edgar Harlan took a trip to Tama in 1914. There, he met a man named Joseph Svacina, who was friendly with many tribal members and assisted with the annual powwow.[54]

Harlan had come looking for "Indian lore." Svacina put him in touch with a Meskwaki man named Young Bear.[55] Approaching age fifty, Young Bear did not speak English. He and Harlan nonetheless struck up a friendship. It was a fortuitous arrangement. Harlan, after all, was in the first act of a three-decade career at the State Historical Society of Iowa. Under his tenure, Harlan would lead an effort to document Iowans' service in World War I, help establish Iowa's first state park (not coincidentally, he was among those who believed the Settlement might benefit from such a status), and develop a popular radio program on regional history.[56]

Young Bear, on the other hand, was Pushetonequa's son. Widowered in the early 1920s and again just before his own death in 1944, Young Bear had six daughters and five sons. They in turn produced fifty-one grand- and great-grandchildren.[57] After his father's death, Young Bear became the patriarch of a sprawling Meskwaki family. He was well known on and around the Settlement, and, as an Indian agent put it, was "one of the best reservation politicians. He can adapt himself to any kind of circumstances." He always emerged from political disputes, to the agent's chagrin, in a favorable position.[58]

Shortly after their meeting, Young Bear asked Harlan to scour state records for evidence of unpaid treaty annuities owed to the Meskwaki Nation. For years, Young Bear had relentlessly pursued a belief that the federal government owed his people almost $200,000.[59] Although he would not live to see a resolution to the case, the project allowed Harlan to connect with several Meskwaki families.[60]

Like many non-Native interlocutors of his time, Harlan was paternalistic toward his Meskwaki associates and expanded the state's artifact collections by purchasing items from tribal members.[61] The curator also had a genuine interest in helping tribal members where he could. He hired Jonas Poweshiek to work in the historical society's office in Des Moines, and it was Jonas who translated Harlan's correspondences with Young Bear. Harlan joined Svacina and the tribe as they planned the annual powwow. He arranged for Meskwaki performers who gave cultural shows in faraway states like Wyoming and Nevada.[62] He also sponsored the young Frank Wanatee's attendance at Drake University and helped one of Jonas's sisters sort out a messy divorce.[63]

Tribal members also relied on Harlan to run interference with outsiders. The same interest that drove powwow attendance attracted regular correspondence.[64] Scholars and interested citizens from all over sent a steady flow of inquiries to Meskwaki people, asking for information about the tribe's history, culture, and spirituality. In these cases, it was useful to have a prominent non-Native to deflect probing questions. In early 1924, for example, Grace Boston, the curator of the Iowa Masonic Library in Cedar Rapids, asked Robert Young Bear about ceremonial dances. Confronting this inquest into his religious life, Robert referred Boston to Harlan, telling her that the curator "knows more about us than we know about ourselves."[65] Answering Boston's follow-up questions, Harlan clarified: "Robert Young Bear intended to pay me a compliment of course, but more than anything else to keep to himself the information he possesses."[66]

Young Bear, one of several Meskwaki men who attempted to reform the chief's council following the death of his father, Pushetonequa. Young Bear also developed a cordial relationship with Edgar Harlan, the curator at the State Historical Society of Iowa, who became a confidant of and ally to several Meskwaki people around the mid-1920s, when this photograph was taken. Photo courtesy of the Josephine Wallace Photograph Collection, Image PH8428.2, State Historical Society of Iowa, Des Moines.

Through this work, Harlan gained meaningful friendships on the Settlement. When his health began to fail in the 1930s, Young Bear invited him over for "good medicine" and "old fashioned sweat baths."[67] The Meskwaki Nation ceremonially adopted Harlan in 1923, giving him the name Mesheka, or "Snapping Turtle." This honor recognized Harlan's commitment to the community as well as the mutual respect between him and many tribal members.[68]

These relationships mattered. As a prominent white professional and a representative of an otherwise disinterested state government, the curator became a key interlocutor as tribal members countervailed the cascade of federal incursions into their lives. This earned Harlan the ire of the Indian Service. In 1919, the agency superintendent, Dr. Robert Russell, was replaced by Dr. Jacob Breid. The new superintendent was a brusque technocrat who viewed agency policies and protocols as firm imperatives and quickly reverted away from Russell's efforts to build a strong rapport with tribal members. Although his commitment to federal policy earned him shining reviews from the higher ups in Washington, Breid's tactlessness incited deep animosity among Meskwaki people and patients, as well as from Edgar Harlan.[69]

At one point, Harlan complained to the Washington office that Breid had been rude and dismissive when he reached out with tribal members' concerns.[70] Burke pointed out that by "offering cooperation with the Superintendent through the Indian committee instead of with the Indians through the Superintendent," Harlan had hardly invited Breid's goodwill. Harlan, it seems, had ruffled feathers by doing the unthinkable: consulting members of the Meskwaki community about their own affairs, rather than asking the agency what he should do to further its goals.[71] Breid's time on the Settlement was turbulent. Young Bear put it simply in 1926: Breid "says he helps," the influential Meskwaki observed, "but he doesn't."[72]

CREATIVE AUTONOMY

Over the course of the 1920s, members of the Meskwaki Nation, aware that their council had been stripped of much of its authority, found inventive ways to oppose federal meddling. Control over Meskwaki land remained a central concern. In October 1920, for instance, a Meskwaki man named Katwaya, or Jack Old Bear, wrote the Indian Office in Washington.[73] By then, the agency had swapped the boarding school for a more widely accepted day school. Old Bear and others viewed the construction of federal facilities as unwanted intrusions on tribal land. He opposed the construction of a physical plant near one of the schools, framing his concerns as a matter of sovereign jurisdiction. "The Indians of Tama County," Old Bear wrote, "find that some of our land is being taken for some purpose to us unknown, and several buildings are being erected thereon, without our consent or knowledge, and we want it stopped."[74]

The agency dismissed Old Bear's criticism, mostly because it considered him a cultural conservative (he lived in a wickiup) and because, as a descendant of Mamiwanige, he was a combatant in the leadership dispute. Indian agents believed that his "real objection was not the loss of the land to the tribe" but to the operation of the school.[75] Old Bear's argument, however, illustrated more about the interplay between land and politics on the Meskwaki Settlement. Well after the Settlement had been fully ensconced in federal trust, and even as their own council and chieftainship had withered under the weight of federal authority, the Red Earth People recognized the anomalous history of their land as a key asset in arguments for Meskwaki control over tribal affairs.

MATRIMONY

Not every issue was focused on the land. Some were more personal. Influenced by Christian Indian reformers, the Indian Service became rather obsessed with Native marriage. The agency promoted legal—and usually religious—marriage between one man and one woman, thereby using the most intimate parts of Indigenous families' lives to advance the goals of assimilation by socializing them to mainstream American expectations.[76]

Many Meskwaki marriages did not conform to American standards. Meskwaki family life, after all, centered upon a wider net of mutually supportive relatives.[77] It was not uncommon for a Meskwaki home to house a couple, their children, and others. Often, children from former marriages lived with a parent, and unwed couples, widowers, or even divorced couples lived together. Love was not necessarily constrained to a single lifelong partner. In the 1930s, one anthropologist pointed out that many Red Earth People had been married several times by their mid twenties. A few did so at the Presbyterian mission or a local courthouse. Others chose private tribal ceremonies. And some couples simply chose to "live together openly."[78]

The Red Earth People's marital practices had concerned the Tama Agency for years. Dr. Russell raised the issue in his annual report in 1916, for example, and searched for ways to bring Meskwaki relationships in line with federal policy. He could not find any state or federal law allowing him to do so.[79] Unlike non-Native matrimony, which required legal documentation for both the commencement and termination of a marriage, many Red Earth People preferred to wed in ceremonies that reflected community customs and traditions, but did not require paperwork.

Enter Edgar Harlan. By 1920, marriage had become a hot-button issue on the Settlement. Probably at the request of a tribal member, Harlan wrote to B. L. Wick at the Linn County Historical Society in Cedar Rapids to inquire about the applicability of state marriage laws to the Settlement. According to a 1919 state law, Wick replied, Meskwaki marriages that took place on the

LIVING ON THE LAND

Settlement and between Indigenous people (Meskwaki or not) required no state license.[80] Iowa, it seems, had added a provision to the state code that year to clear up this very ambiguity over Meskwaki marriages. The law authorized the "superintendent of any Indian agency" to "solemnize" a marriage between two Indigenous people and record it within fifteen days.[81] But based on the findings in a federal case out of Minnesota, Wick added, the state could not punish Native people for adultery if they had "married in accordance with Indian custom."[82]

Harlan, it seems, shared Wick's findings with the Red Earth People, who continued to marry according to their preferences. In the mid-1930s, four of the seven Meskwaki marriages registered one year occurred by "tribal custom"; the remainder followed "legal procedure."[83]

These laws did not prevent the Indian Service from attempting to meddle in Meskwaki marriages. In 1926, for example, an official noticed that a Meskwaki couple was cohabitating. The office pressured the couple to get married and even persuaded the man to sign a document promising that he and his partner would stop living together unless they got "legally married." The couple lived separately for a time. By the next summer, however, the agent reported that the couple was once again "conduct[ing] themselves as man and wife," although no state-sanctioned wedding had occurred.[84] If the pair wed in a private ceremony, they did so far from prying federal eyes, choosing instead to love on Meskwaki terms.

THE POWWOW ASSOCIATION

The Meskwaki Nation also launched a new business venture in this era. By the early 1920s, the annual powwow celebration had grown to span a full week. It was filled with dances and musical performances, exhibits by Meskwaki artists, and displays of tribal history and culture. It attracted hundreds of non-Native visitors and guests from tribes across the country and the region, benefiting many tribal members along the way. For the first decade of its operation, a fifteen-member ad hoc committee governed the event.[85]

In 1920, however, seven Meskwaki men filed a federal lawsuit, alleging that the powwow committee had unfairly paid more than $17,000 in revenues to the community between 1916 and 1920.[86] The suit failed, but the issue did not die. In 1923, the ad hoc powwow committee had failed to notify tribal members that it would keep half the revenues to pay operating expenses. As a result, some participants boycotted the powwow the next year.[87]

The controversy inspired the tribe to organize the Meskwaki Indian Powwow Association in 1924. This body formalized accounting and recordkeeping. It was governed by a written constitution that empowered the association to plan the event and maintain the powwow grounds and related facilities. In its statement of purpose, the association declared that it hoped "to help some of the Indians that are unemployed," and to ensure a "clean moral Pow Wow." It banned gambling and tried to deter promiscuity during the celebration. The document declared that the committee would work closely with the local police and assist in "stamping out all the evils that may arise during the Pow Wow."[88]

The constitution also attempted to assuage the concerns that had fueled the earlier lawsuit. It limited membership in the association to tribal members but allowed the council to authorize exceptions. It required that members be elected by the tribe and be "of good character, conservative and to some degree possess knowledge of the tribal affairs." It also created a "National fund . . . for the benefit of the entire tribe," drawn from the event's proceeds.[89] Through the powwow, the Meskwaki Nation launched one of its earliest efforts to develop a collective, on-Settlement business venture that could support the Red Earth People over the long term.

The creation of the Powwow Association also occurred just as the Indian Service produced the "No Dancing Letter," which the Meskwaki Historic Preservation Office uses to educate twenty-first century powwow audiences and museum visitors about the endurance of Meskwaki culture in the face of corrosive policies. Dated February 23, 1923, the document is an announcement of a pair of Indian Service orders known as "Circular 1665," which had been issued in 1921 and updated in early 1923. The document tasked superintendents across Indian Country with limiting the length of ceremonial "dances, celebrations, [and] powwows" that lasted several days, viewing them as counterproductive distractions that encouraged the wasting of time, energy, and property. The Indian Service, as several historians have shown, struggled into the 1920s as it tried to encourage Indigenous innovation and market participation, cultural activities, and the objectives of assimilation.[90]

Read alongside the complexity of the moment, the Meskwaki powwow and the association that governed it reveal the Red Earth People's efforts to weave together local commerce, act in a spirit of self-governance, and continue to keep Meskwaki culture alive. In this sense, the Powwow Association was a harbinger of strategies to come.

THE MERIAM REPORT

During the 1920s, conflicts between the Indian Service's ever-tightening control over Meskwaki life and the Red Earth People's efforts to reclaim control over their land and lives occurred amid a slow realization on the part of the US government: Indian policy was not working. The experiences of Indigenous veterans brought these problems into sharp relief. Some 10,000 Native Americans had served in World War I. When they returned, many found their communities still straining to endure severe poverty, improve stagnant tribal economies, and navigate continued state and federal efforts to dismantle tribal sovereignty, cultures, and communities.[91] Meanwhile, Indigenous intellectuals and advocates from organizations like the Society of American Indians (SAI), founded in 1911, were raising awareness of the failures of Indian policy and debating policy solutions.[92]

In 1924, President Calvin Coolidge signed the Indian Citizenship Act. The law conferred federal citizenship upon every Native person, marking a departure from earlier policies, which had paid citizenship only to those Indigenous people who, for example, fulfilled the requirements of the allotment program or obtained citizenship through treaties or other mechanisms. Leading figures at the SAI had been discussing the citizenship question for years, and some Native people rejected the Citizenship Act, seeing it as yet another intrusion into their sovereignty. Many had neither requested citizenship nor wanted to be US citizens. Some states, meanwhile, still controlled the conditions under which Indigenous citizens could fully participate in civic life and had restricted Native people's basic rights—like voting—for decades.[93] Most Meskwaki people appeared to embrace their newfound franchise, and in 1924 seventy-seven cast ballots in their first presidential election.[94]

Shortly after the passage of the Indian Citizenship Act, an Institute for Government Research (now the Brookings Institution) team undertook a national study of Native issues. Although coauthored by Ho-Chunk intellectual Henry Roe Cloud, the "Meriam Report" was named after the project's director, Lewis Meriam. It rendered a withering portrait of federal policy. Published in 1928, it detailed the gross inadequacies of federal efforts in Indian Country and reviewed the failures of the allotment program. After the report became public, the Tama Agency stopped advocating the allotment of the Meskwaki Settlement.[95] In addition to broad critiques of education policy and other criticisms, the document found that "an overwhelming majority of the Indians are poor, even extremely poor, and they are not adjusted to the economic and social system of the dominant white civilization."[96]

The Meriam Report affirmed the need for major policy revisions. It upheld the basic assumption that sound federal Indian policy would inevitably promote assimilation. But the document also opened the door to new proposals, including strengthening the US government's recognition of Indigenous peoples' capacity for self-governance.[97] The report also called for the abolishment of government boarding schools, the expansion of federal loans to Native people, a curtailment of allotment, and administrative decentralization at the Office of Indian Affairs. It promised programs to help tribes maximize the potential of their natural resources.[98]

It took several years for these ideas to become actionable in the halls of Washington. In the meantime, the Red Earth People continued to try to wrest control over their government. Following a series of meetings, a group of Meskwaki leaders nominated Jack Old Bear as chief in 1928. He selected a council, and the tribe asked the agency to recognize his new government. The officials, however, insisted that the council be democratically elected. The Red Earth People tried again, this time organizing a Settlement-wide election in May 1929. This produced a seven-member council occupied by leading men from all sides of the old leadership dispute.[99] As one reporter wrote, the election brought "great expectations" for a new era of political cooperation on the Settlement.[100]

But the council soon found itself deadlocked on a number of issues and met only sporadically. Between 1928 and 1934, the tribe held several such elections. Each was an attempt to jump-start an effective council. All failed and, eventually, five elders formed an acting council.[101] None of these bodies had much authority, and the Indian Service refused to recognize any council "without a written constitution and without full tribal consent."[102] Assisted by internal disagreements, the agency had killed the Meskwaki Nation's government in the 1910s and stifled Meskwaki efforts to resuscitate it in the 1920s. By the 1930s, the acting council knew its limitations. When an agent asked them to settle a domestic dispute between two tribal members, the council said it "did not consider [its] authority sufficient to act as arbitrators ... or even to make a recommendation."[103]

NATAQUATUK'S NECKLACE

On a crisp September evening in 1932, Democratic congressman Albert C. Willford sat cross-legged in a small Meskwaki cottage that belonged to Mary Davenport and her husband Charles. Accompanying him were Edgar Harlan, several prominent whites, and a reporter for the *Waterloo Daily Courier*, who took detailed notes as the evening transpired. Each shifted awkwardly, their suits and manners unaccustomed to the Meskwaki family's floor. Before them sat a stark linen tablecloth topped by steaming plates of fry bread, stewed veal, and corn.[104]

Alongside the men were twelve Meskwaki people, including the sixty-seven-year-old Young Bear; his son George Young Bear, who served as the group's interpreter; their cohost, Charles Davenport; William Poweshiek; and Sam Slick. Over the course of the dinner, Willford presented Young Bear with a gold watch as a mark of respect. Young Bear thanked Willford and the other guests for traveling to his people's Settlement.

This scene encapsulated the diminishment of Meskwaki political power. Bolstered by their land's "peculiar condition," leaders like Mamiwanige and Pushetonequa had once spoken with a unified voice—at least outside council. When they did the Meskwaki Nation's business, it often took place in Des Moines or Washington, DC. But by the time Willford dined with Young Bear, no such leader existed and Meskwaki land sat firmly in the federal government's control. Indeed, Young Bear probably had to ask his friend Harlan—the tribe's only real ally in state government—to secure the congressman's visit. With no friendly governor willing to lobby the congressman, Young Bear and his allies spoke with Willford directly. They made their cases only as respected elders and members of the interim tribal council, speaking on Meskwaki land but in a tribal member's home.

As the party dined on their dessert—cinnamon rolls dripping with Meskwaki maple syrup that Charles and Mary had made the previous winter—Young Bear outlined a series of grievances ranging from his long-running claim for unpaid annuities, to the tribe's objection to the proposed site of a new government hospital, to dissatisfaction with the agency's educational policies. Finally, Young Bear spoke about his concerns over the slow erosion of Meskwaki political power and his community's turgid relationship with the Indian Office. According to the reporter's account, the elder expressed a general "complaint that the government authorities do not consent with the chief or his tribesmen over matters of policy for the conduct of the 3,200 acres that constitute a project in communal labor and living" on the Meskwaki Settlement.[105]

Willford, of course, could make few promises. In the three or four decades preceding his visit, the Red Earth People had adapted their lives and labor to meet the demands of the twentieth-century world. A few had battled within the American federal system, winning lawsuits that insulated the tribe from state and federal authority in some cases. And, despite decades of tension within the community, the tribe maintained collective ownership of its land and, notably, managed to expand tribal landholdings in the process. All the congressman and his colleagues could really do, at least for the moment, was listen.[106]

Two absences left a notable void at the dinner. The first was a person. Superintendent Breid was nowhere to be seen. Perhaps he was not invited, or perhaps by 1932 an audience with tribal elders—even with a congressman and a state official in tow—would have been low on Breid's priority list. His nonattendance bespoke the desiccated relationship between tribal leaders and the Indian Service. The agency's decades-long efforts to debilitate the authority of the Meskwaki chief's council had come to slow fruition. In 1896, the federal government had successfully stripped the Red Earth People of their state-tribal trust, and it had burned the Meskwaki village a few years later. In the years that followed, the Indian Office finalized the transfer of the land deeds, pushed allotment, and replaced the chief's council. Despite the challenges wrought by the curious tenure of the Meskwaki Settlement and the vexing jurisdictional situation created by *Peters v. Malin*, the Indian Service was almost unilaterally controlling the administrative affairs of the Meskwaki Nation.

Sam Slick outside his home on the Meskwaki Settlement in the early 1920s. Part of a federal program called the "Surveys of Indian Industry," this photograph accompanied detailed descriptions of the work and daily lives of tribal members. The image shows the kinds of frame houses to which most Meskwaki families had moved in the decades after the smallpox epidemic. A few years after posing for this picture, Slick sold his family's bear claw necklace, which is shown on page 238. Photo courtesy of The National Archives at Chicago.

The other absentee was not a human. It was the bear claw necklace that otherwise might have hung around the neck of a fifty-six-year-old Meskwaki farmer named Sam Slick.[107] More than a year before the dinner in the Davenports' house, Slick had written to Edgar Harlan, mentioning that he would be willing to sell his family's prized item. Slick's father, Nataquatuk, had made the clawed pendant himself and was one of the Red Earth People who had trekked from the Osage River Reservation to Iowa in the 1850s. Despite its importance, Slick wrote in April 1931, he was willing to "sell it cheap" for a meager twenty dollars, along with some of his aged mother's belongings, "because we are having [a] hard time to get our food."[108]

Slick's sale underscored the desperation of a family struggling to make ends meet. The Great Depression had descended upon central Iowa, straining the livelihoods of many Red Earth People. Yet Slick's willingness to sell such a powerful artifact suggests that something more valuable than money had been lost.

Facing tight times and the historic nadir of their tribe's authority vis-à-vis the United States government, Sam Slick would have been justified in wondering whether Meskwaki sovereignty was dead.

PART IV

Rebuilding

"This tract of land, upon which my tribe dwells, is communally owned by the [Meskwaki] Indians, purchased with their ancestors' own money. Therefore, we have the right to, through the right of ownership, decide how our affairs should be handled. Every member of my tribe has a right, a right of ownership of the land on which we live, to the disposal of our affairs as he sees fit."

—John Tataposh

CHAPTER 7

Testing Ground

Preston Duncan's grandmother delivered him inside a wickiup in 1938. Although many Meskwaki women of her generation decided to labor in nearby hospitals, Duncan's mother chose an older way. The shelter had been built specifically for a birth in the quiet forest. It had two doors—one to the east and one to the west. According to tribal custom, Duncan's mother would have gone to the dome alone after feeling her first contraction. The child's father, meanwhile, informed close relatives. Elder women gathered to tend to Duncan's mother's needs. They knew the herbs and medicine that would ease her delivery.[1]

"I was born out here in the timbers," Duncan recalled, sharing details he learned later in life. Just before he emerged, the women dug a rectangle in the still-thawing spring sod. It was barely large enough for his tiny body. "My grandma took me out, then put me on that fresh dirt. There was fresh, black earth there. And she talked to the earth. And she told the earth to take good care of me." When she did that, he continued, she was speaking to "Grandmother Earth," who was "the first one to cradle me." After praying over the newborn baby, the elder women bathed Duncan inside the wickiup and swaddled him in blankets. His mother also bathed while the women cut and buried the child's umbilical cord. After telling this story, Duncan added that, when his life is over, his "physical form" will return to Grandmother Earth. "That's where it goes, in the end," he said. "That's the way we believe."[2]

Preston Duncan was one of a surge of Meskwaki children born between 1930 and 1960. The tribe's population grew dramatically during this period, preceding and contributing to the nationwide postwar baby boom. By the early 1960s, some 60 percent of Red Earth People were under twenty-one years of age.³ Each of them grew up watching their parents and grandparents wrestle over how to restore the Meskwaki political authority that had waned in previous decades, how best to manage their shared land base, and how to adjust to major developments that threatened to reshape how Meskwaki people viewed their Settlement. In that historical moment, seemingly small decisions—like Duncan's mother's choice to deliver him in a Meskwaki way—reflected the Red Earth People's commitment to acting with a sense of autonomy over their lives.⁴

THE INDIAN NEW DEAL

The thirty-first president of the United States, Herbert Hoover, spent his early childhood less than 90 miles from the Meskwaki Settlement. He went on to a long career in public service and had occupied the Oval Office for just under eight months when the stock market crashed on October 29, 1929. This event signaled the collapse of the American economy. Hoover attempted to stem the panic but nonetheless shouldered the public's ire for what many deemed an anemic federal response. Three years after the crash, New York governor Franklin Delano Roosevelt routed Hoover in the 1932 elections. None of Hoover's electoral votes came from Iowa.⁵

Roosevelt assumed office in March 1933. His administration assembled an unprecedented suite of federal policies known as the New Deal, many of which sought to assuage the nation's staggering unemployment rate. Roosevelt's administration initiated massive work relief programs, like the Civilian Conservation Corps, which members of the Meskwaki Nation availed themselves of. Between his inauguration and 1939, a full two-thirds of federal relief spending funded these initiatives.⁶ The Roosevelt administration battled the Great Depression until World War II. Along the way, it undertook huge financial reforms and created a social safety net that would far outlive the early, temporary relief programs.⁷

The New Deal also extended to Indian Country. As Indigenous people struggled against worsening economies in the 1920s, a sociologist named John Collier cultivated a national reputation as a leading voice on Indian policy reform. Collier had spent much of the 1920s working in the American Southwest. His work with tribes and reformers there left him an outspoken critic of federal policy. Collier had supported the commissioning of the Meriam Report and, after Roosevelt named him commissioner of Indian affairs in 1933, began developing new policies that reflected many of the prescriptions set forth by the report.[8]

Collier's reforms came to be known as the "Indian New Deal." During his tenure at the Indian Service, which lasted from 1933 to 1945, the agency supported policies that ended allotment, tried to create jobs, and invested in efforts to better improve management of tribal resources. It also promoted Native artwork through the Indian Arts and Crafts Board, for example, funded states with grants for tribal education and health care, and supported tribal agricultural programs.[9]

Many Meskwaki families took advantage of these programs. By 1936, almost half of Settlement families were participating in at least one New Deal program.[10] Several, for example, took out home renovation loans made available through the Indian Relief and Rehabilitation Act.[11] Six elderly tribal members received direct payments from the newly founded Old Age Assistance program, while others made the most of the Agricultural Adjustment Act (AAA), which paid farmers to control production. Because of the tribe's collective ownership of the Meskwaki Settlement, federal administrators considered it one large, privately owned farm. This decision capped annual program payments to the tribe at about $1,000. In one small demonstration of Meskwaki people's political ingenuity, several tribal members discovered that they could double their AAA relief by registering their farming plots under individual accounts.[12]

The effectiveness of these relief programs, of course, varied from tribe to tribe, and the extent to which they made significant improvements to Indigenous peoples' lives remains an open question. In a 1980 *New York Times* opinion piece, the venerated Lakota scholar Vine Deloria Jr. wrote that, if nothing else, federal relief checks allowed his people to "climb from absolute deprivation to mere poverty."[13]

In addition to the material aid the Indian New Deal offered tribes, Collier's administration made a concerted effort to amplify Indigenous involvement in tribal affairs. He encouraged tribal members to participate in community decision-making and the management of local programs. In that sense, he shifted the momentum of the Indian Service substantially from the days when direct, full-bore federal dominance of Native tribes topped the agency's agenda.[14]

Critics, however, have long maintained that the Indian New Deal amounted to little more than a change in style, rather than form. Collier and his staff continued to cast a long, paternalistic shadow over tribes, and the policy reforms embedded in the Indian New Deal ultimately upheld the United States' ability to subvert tribal sovereignty and self-determination.[15] Despite these drawbacks, the Collier era was a critical turning point in the history of the Meskwaki Nation.

DEPRESSION AND DISCRIMINATION

The Red Earth People straddled a precarious line prior to the Great Depression. They had spent decades slowly adapting their age-old subsistence economy to the new challenges of the twentieth century. Most Meskwaki families had limited access to cash but nonetheless hunted and grew ample supplies of food. As one field matron wrote in 1916, most Meskwaki families were "able to provide for themselves" from the cash and goods gleaned in the Settlement economy built since the 1850s.[16] Had the Depression only wiped out the financial market and white-collar industries, the average Meskwaki family might have suffered minimally. But the disaster also glutted the agricultural markets and brought layoffs to blue-collar industries. So, from a cash and income perspective, many Red Earth People had been stripped of crucial opportunities to work as farm hands and day laborers, and many struggled to make ends meet during these years.[17]

Employment discrimination compounded these challenges. The Red Earth People had maintained relatively amicable relationships with their white neighbors over the years. The region, of course, was not immune to prejudice. The occasional dustup inflamed tensions between Meskwaki people and local whites, especially as the strain of the Depression exacerbated racial tensions in central Iowa and across early twentieth-century America.[18]

White workers had enjoyed hiring priority before the Depression. Iowa's farm economy had stumbled and staggered after the First World War.[19] In 1927, one congressman reported to the Indian Office that his Meskwaki constituents were struggling to find work, in some cases because they did not speak English, but primarily because "most employers prefer[red] white help."[20] By 1934, the Tama Agency reported that "it is not possible for the white people of the community to secure employment, and until that has been accomplished, the Indian does not have a fair chance to get a job."[21]

The Tama Agency tried to place Meskwaki workers in regional industry. It facilitated a contract with the Marshalltown Canning Factory, in 1929, for whom nearly three dozen Meskwaki families grew string beans. One agent declared that the program "furnished employment for everyone" and called it "very profitable," and each Meskwaki participant earned about $87 the first year.[22] Even with successful initiatives like this one, however, many members of the Meskwaki community squeaked by on homegrown vegetables during the Depression.[23] Like members of other Native communities in the Midwest, the Red Earth People used the Settlement as a kind of shelter to which they could return throughout the Depression, as the local subsistence economy and the support of their relatives served as a backstop against the instability of outside markets.[24]

The Indian Service also provided blue-collar jobs for a handful of Red Earth People. Superintendent Jacob Breid and his successor, Ira D. Nelson, stretched their budgets to hire Meskwaki workers at the tuberculosis sanatorium in Toledo. There, Meskwaki men and women worked as orderlies, custodians, and groundskeepers. The demand for sanatorium jobs proved so intense during the Depression that officials had to rotate work schedules to spread wages as evenly across the tribe as possible.[25]

These efforts could not sustain the tribe. Meskwaki incomes were perilously low, and most Meskwaki families scraped by through the 1930s on about a fourth of the average annual income of their white neighbors.[26] One particularly harsh winter, conditions grew so dire that the elder Young Bear, working through Edgar Harlan, contacted charities in Des Moines to ask for donations to support a starving Meskwaki widow.[27]

TOO LITTLE LAND

Although the Red Earth People ultimately staved off allotment—not to mention the loss of land that followed it into Indian Country—the flaws of the tribe's use-rights system became more and more apparent by the 1930s. Around that time, some Meskwaki families had large plots while others barely had space for their homes. While many Meskwaki families could combine wage work with hunting and gardening to keep themselves fed prior to the Great Depression, inequitable land distribution exacerbated the crisis for many of the community's most vulnerable members.[28]

Meanwhile, only about 1,300 of the Settlement's more than 3,200 acres consisted of cultivable land. This added to the tribe's predicament: even if the Meskwaki Nation had decided to break up its land equally among tribal members, such a distribution would have provided only three acres to each person. This was hardly enough—even if families lumped their three-acre parcels together—to turn a profit. Depression-era markets, moreover, offered little revenue for even those with the most land.[29] Only half managed enough land "to do more than raise gardens," and many grew just a bit more than they needed to get by.[30]

THE SETTLEMENT PROVIDES

The Settlement was small and times were tight. But abject poverty was not commonplace in the Meskwaki Nation during the Depression.[31] Land and employment issues aside, the Red Earth People remained committed to time-tested practices that had stabilized the Settlement economy for generations. By growing, gathering, trading, and making clothes and wares, Meskwaki families produced all they needed to weather the long, difficult Depression.

Meskwaki men fished the Iowa River and hunted "small fur-bearing animals such as skunk, possum, and [rac]coons" on and around tribal land. They cured meat, sold animal skins at market, and harvested as many as 150 pheasants each year. In addition to planting, harvesting, and cooking underneath outdoor shelters, women and girls canned vegetables to eat and barter—over 12,000 quarts one year—and helped raise chickens.[32]

Federal agricultural extension programs encouraged Meskwaki men to adopt the latest techniques and maximize their yields for the commercial market. The Indian Service provided seeds for carrots, cabbage, tomatoes, potatoes, and other produce. But Meskwaki farmers, one agent complained, preferred to plant the corn, beans, and squash their community had relied upon for generations.[33] Many families also raised chickens, while the Indian Office supplied the sanatorium and Settlement with milk from its two dozen dairy cows.[34] Each tribal member also received $20 in annuities every year, as long as they had not taken a lump-sum payment to finance a house or other major expense.[35]

The Red Earth People also continued to make maple syrup. A family could make up to 100 pounds of maple sugar in a single season, which they used during ceremonies and as a condiment. One Meskwaki man said his people had "a custom of using maple sugar in their own families, as well as [for] exchange with neighboring tribes." He maintained that it was reserved for intertribal barter or for ceremonial or personal use: it was "not for sale" to non-Natives.[36]

The process was grueling. In late winter, families would relocate to "sugar camps" near the maple stands along the river bottom. Amos Morgan, for example, waited in the cold air of 1937 while sap dripped from the metal spigots he had drilled into the tree trunks. The time it took to fill a bucket depended on the weather. A cold snap could grind production to a halt. Once he had two buckets ready, Amos would haul them into the wickiup he and his wife, Cora, had covered in rush mats and potato sacks. A fire roared at the center of the space, fed by hardwood kindling gathered nearby. Inside the sweltering dome, Amos hung the pails from iron chains, and Cora and her friend Mary Black Cloud stirred the sap for hours until it became maple syrup and brown sugar.[37]

Meskwaki children also helped their families make ends meet. A group of fifteen Meskwaki boys and girls formed the "Sac and Fox Indian Poultry Club" around 1931. Each member received about a dozen chicks from a hatchery in Traer. With the help of a government farmer, club members secured 100 pounds of feed, on which the children raised their chicks. Members also competed at regional fairs and learned valuable skills that would serve them throughout their lives.[38]

The next year, 1932, a group of young Meskwaki women established the "Ne-No-Tal Indian Girls 4-H Club," whose members ranged from their preteens to early twenties. They met once a week to make pillow slips, scarves, and clothes for themselves and their younger siblings and to learn new tailoring techniques and sewing patterns. By the following summer, the group had grown to nineteen members, who showed beadwork and sewing patterns at the state fair, had ice cream socials with their white peers, and attended lectures on topics like the "Health and Usefulness of Rural Girls." They coupled these lessons with community knowledge passed down from their aunts and mothers to assist their families as they could.[39]

In the 1930s, Meskwaki children and young adults formed a number of agricultural and service clubs, like the Meskwaki Children's Poultry Club. They learned vital skills and supported the on-Settlement subsistence economy that helped the community endure the Depression. Photo courtesy of the Jacob Breid Photograph Album on the Meskwaki Settlement, Image PH8410.23.4, State Historical Society of Iowa, Des Moines.

More than a sixth of the Settlement was open pasture. The Red Earth People did not have any cows on the Settlement, one woman reported, "because they eat everything—all the plants—and we use the herbs for medicine and the berries to eat."[40] Instead, Meskwaki families had several hundred horses, which roamed freely. Preston Duncan cared for the horses as a child and remembered that it "sound[ed] like thunder when the horses ran to their water tanks to drink." The tribe, he said, used the horses to pull plows and for transportation.[41] When the lowlands flooded, as Don Wanatee recalled, men harnessed the horses to large planks of wood and used them to push water back into the swollen Iowa River.[42] The animals were a fixture on the Meskwaki Settlement until the late 1940s, when technology changed. As one Meskwaki farmer put it, in 1949, "Horses aren't much good if you want to farm nowadays. What you need is power. I want to get a tractor."[43]

Selling crafts continued to generate vital revenues for Meskwaki artisans, who made baskets, beadwork, clothes, and leather goods and sold

TESTING GROUND 181

Capitalizing on the rise of automobile tourism in the 1920s and 1930s, Meskwaki artists and craftspeople established roadside stands like this one, where tourists could buy handmade jewelry, beadwork, and other wares. Photo courtesy of the Jacob Breid Photograph Album on the Meskwaki Settlement, Image PH8410.15.1, State Historical Society of Iowa, Des Moines.

them in town or during the annual celebration.[44] In the 1930s, Meskwaki women established small souvenir stands along the Lincoln Highway and pitched their wares to tourists and passersby. In 1939, this work brought in $490, or around $9,100 today.[45]

The powwow remained a popular and prosperous annual event. By the late 1930s, the event had grown to include hundreds of Meskwaki performers. It featured dance contests, sets by the Waterloo Drum and Bugle Corps, and speeches by Meskwaki leaders and politicians from neighboring towns, as well as lectures by historians from Iowa City.[46] The event, one reporter wrote, drew "thousands of persons from all corners of the United States."[47] In 1941, Iowa Governor George A. Wilson delivered the keynote address, drawing more than 5,000 spectators despite a hard rain.[48]

MAKING THE MESKWAKI CONSTITUTION

The 1930s offered more than relief programs and a conceptual turn for the Indian Service. The Indian Reorganization Act (IRA), the legislative centerpiece of the Indian New Deal, promised tribes a return to self-governance. The IRA presented tribes with the option to "reorganize" their governments and councils into constitutional democracies that would mirror the United States government and be developed in lockstep with federal officials. For these reasons, the law's critics—on the Meskwaki Settlement and throughout Indian Country—panned the IRA for empowering tribes only on the federal government's terms and thereby failing to respect tribal sovereignty.[49] Many members of the Meskwaki Nation, however, saw the IRA as an opportunity to restore their tribe's political authority.

While Congress debated the law in early 1934, John Collier and his staff set off on a tour of Indigenous communities and pitched the IRA to delegations of tribal leaders.[50] These meetings provided an opportunity for the Indian Office to describe its efforts to replace "administrative absolutism" with local, tribal self-governance to Native Nations across the country.[51] Nobody reacted to the law with the enthusiasm Collier had expected. After a long process of amendment and adjustment, the final draft of the IRA presented tribes with a chance to adopt tribal constitutions that, while restoring some semblance of Indigenous political independence, still subjected these powers to federal authority.[52]

The IRA became law on June 18, 1934, and outlined a series of steps that tribes would take toward reorganization.[53] First, they had to vote to accept the IRA then draft a constitution under the guidance of the Indian Office. Federal officials—many of whom were intent on pressuring Native people to integrate American-style democracy into their constitutions—then oversaw a long period of drafting and revision as tribes sorted out the issues most relevant to them. Finally, after the document was drafted, adjusted, and presented to tribal members, the secretary of the interior would call a ratification election. If ratification failed, tribal government would continue as it had before the IRA. If the constitution passed, however, an official from Interior would approve the election, and only then would the document take effect. Nationwide, 181 tribes reorganized while 77 did not.[54]

For the Red Earth People, this process began in April 1934. At a meeting on April 7, the tribe selected an eight-member committee to study the IRA. In a series of over twenty working sessions, this group parsed the law and explained it to community members.[55] Once again, Edgar Harlan acted as an intermediary. Many Red Earth People, he wrote to Collier in September, remained unclear about the changes between the draft legislation and the final IRA. They were deeply concerned about how the law would affect the Meskwaki Nation, given the unique status of the Settlement. Harlan observed that tribal members leaning against the IRA were mostly suspicious of parts of the bill that had nothing to do with their tribe. The Red Earth People, he wrote, tended to doubt new policies that appeared "manifestly intended for a different tribe or culture."[56]

Meskwaki voters also drew skepticism from the Indian Office's strong support for the law. Experience, after all, had shown that the policies Indian agents pushed the hardest usually brought serious consequences. Collier circulated informational documents that did not hide his intentions. He stopped short of threatening tribes with retribution for failing to accept the IRA but presented them with a harsh alternative. Without the IRA, he wrote, tribes would "merely drift to the rear of the great advance open to the Indian race," and he mentioned that this might cause them to "continue to lose [their] lands."[57]

This language resonated with many Red Earth People. Some saw reorganization as a new and effective tool for self-governance, which might empower them to stop the assaults on their land and council. Others rejected it outright, in part because they placed any shift in political power within the context of the long-running leadership dispute that, now in its third or fourth generation, still resonated with some tribal members. Still others supported a change but, rather than creating a new constitution, wanted to restore the chief's council that had led the tribe for so long. They wrote to Secretary of the Interior Harold Ickes, arguing that their tribe was "capable of self-government" without the law and raised concerns that reorganization would strip away their Settlement.[58] Collier responded on the secretary's behalf, reassuring the Meskwaki constituents that the IRA would not disrupt the status of their Settlement.[59] Still others simply weighed reorganization based on whether they believed it offered real solutions to the challenges their people faced.[60]

The IRA left little room for the texture and nuance of community debates. Meskwaki voters faced two choices: accept or reject the IRA. As opposition grew, Collier asked the agency superintendent, Ira D. Nelson, to gauge tribal members' inclinations toward the law and to uncover the causes of discontent.[61] Based on his observations, Nelson responded, only a few Red Earth People opposed the law. He admitted, however, to feeling that some would be "much better satisfied" by another visit from an agency official. The Indian Service sent two representatives straightaway.[62] Their efforts paid off, and 38 percent of eligible voters cast their ballots on June 15. The Meskwaki Nation had accepted the IRA 63 to 13.[63]

At first glance, this wide margin of victory seemed to show overwhelming support for reorganization. The reality was far more complicated. Nearly two-thirds of the tribe did not vote, and a substantial number had intentionally abstained.[64] The opposition, the Indian Service quickly realized, had boycotted the election in an attempt to shut it down. This episode has received a great deal of attention from historians. Some have argued that the anti-reorganization crowd did not understand how the elections worked. Others assert that because of the voting and discussion norms within the chief's council, in which an abstention counted as a "no," the abstainers intentionally avoided the election to kill the measure. Still others suggest that low turnout was due to the difficulty tribal members faced in reaching the ballot box. But the Red Earth People had been participating in democratic elections for over a decade. And the Settlement was, in the words of one agent, "small and [therefore] easy for the voters to get together," especially in nice June weather.[65]

Another possibility was that these abstentions reflected a faulty political strategy. A group of Meskwaki voters opposed reorganization. After reading the IRA, they thought they had found a loophole buried in Section 17.[66] If fewer than a third of tribal members voted, they believed, this low turnout would nullify the election. This was a mistake, as the provision in question applied only to the tribal corporate charters, which were distinct from constitutions.[67] The abstention vote, then, had been a calculated effort to prevent reorganization and maintain the tribe's customary system of governance. This effort failed, and the Meskwaki Nation moved on to the next phase of the IRA process. And this time, the opposition showed up.

THE CONSTITUTIONAL COMMITTEE

Several eager tribal members had elected a constitutional committee even before the IRA had become law. They quickly set about drafting the document. This group included George Young Bear, brothers William and Horace Poweshiek, and Ed Davenport. They worked closely with the Indian Office over the course of eighteen months. The men—all of whom had at least some higher education—used other tribes' constitutions as frameworks. Meanwhile, agents critiqued the document but left most of the decisions to the tribe.[68] The committee proceeded slowly, wary of making mistakes or drafting language their people would reject. Field agent Benjamin Reifel, a Lakota administrator who would later represent South Dakota in Congress, called the committee "one of the most exacting that I have ever worked with," while another administrator called them "extraordinarily painstaking in their deliberations."[69]

The distribution of Settlement land was a key issue as the Red Earth People debated and discussed the provisions that would be enshrined in their constitution. Some tribal members wanted to empower the council to reassign the use-rights tracts that had been in place, by that point, for over three decades. Meskwaki families that claimed larger tracts, some of whom rented their plots to others, staunchly opposed this idea.[70] The constitutional committee sought a compromise. The document ultimately recognized existing land assignments but empowered the tribal council, under certain circumstances, to reassign tribal property.[71]

Tribal citizenship was another major issue. It echoed community-wide concerns over land and tribal resources. By the mid-1930s, intermarriage between Meskwaki people and members of other Indigenous tribes had become more commonplace.[72] Some tribal members worried, as one wrote to the Indian Office, that if the tribe adopted "just anyone," there would develop "such a mix-up" that people would cease to respect "real" tribal members and the Settlement would fill up with outsiders. Tribal members of this opinion supported a constitutional provision under which "children should be enrolled with the father," an unofficial convention that had been followed on the Settlement for several years.[73] Attempting again to appease both sides, the committee preserved the patrilineal rule but allowed the council to adopt children of mixed Meskwaki lineage as it wished.[74]

Drafts of the constitution made the rounds at the Indian Office, throughout 1937, where officials suggested slight changes. Tribal members could see that the document would shift the power dynamics on the Settlement. It based tribal membership on the 1937 census, for example, meaning that anyone seeking membership in the future would need to be able to link their ancestry back to the families on the books that year. The constitution also broke from long-standing customs in other ways. It lowered the minimum age to hold a seat on the council to twenty-five and—for the first time—allowed women to hold seats on the tribal council.[75]

By November 1937, the time had come for the Red Earth People to cast their ballots. The committee approved its final draft in early autumn, and the agency called a vote and mailed two hundred copies to the tribe, giving members time to review the law.[76] On November 13, with more than double the 1934 turnout, the tribe ratified the document by a narrow vote of 80–78. The Department of the Interior certified the election five weeks later.[77] In January 1938, the Red Earth People had two more elections. This time, they were primaries and a general election to seat the seven-member council, which ended up being filled by a group of young men chaired by Horace Poweshiek.[78] With that, the Meskwaki Nation had reorganized its government.

CONTESTING THE CONSTITUTION

As the Iowa winter locked the Meskwaki Settlement in its characteristically Midwestern grip of gray skies and subzero temperatures, a group of Red Earth People led an intense campaign to repeal their new constitution. They peppered President Roosevelt and Iowa governor Nelson G. Kraschel with letters and petitions—one of them bearing a hundred signatures. The Meskwaki Nation, they insisted, should be left alone to handle its affairs according to ancient customs. They underscored the importance of keeping the Settlement under tribal control. John Tataposh, for example, wrote to FDR in February 1938. More than a hundred signatures were affixed to his letter, which argued: "This tract of land, upon which my tribe dwells, is communally owned by the [Meskwaki] Indians, purchased with their ancestors' own money. Therefore," he continued, "we have the right to, through the right of ownership, decide how our affairs should be handled. Every member of my tribe has a right, a right of ownership of the land on which we live, to the disposal of our affairs as he sees fit."[79]

Some tribal members claimed that the IRA's supporters had rigged the election. In one story, the constitutional committee counted the ballots and, seeing that ratification had failed, burned some ballots on the train tracks on the south end of the Settlement, thereby eking out the two-vote victory.[80] These stories persist on the Settlement, even though none of these efforts to undo the ratification worked.

In fact, dissatisfaction with the Meskwaki Constitution was so prevalent that efforts to amend the document would gain momentum every decade or so after its ratification. Each of these efforts has failed, and the document still governs the Meskwaki Nation in the 2020s. Meanwhile, charges of nepotism and corruption in tribal government have produced numerous electoral recalls and a nearly constant revolution of council membership over the course of many years.[81]

Tribal members and scholars alike have spilled untold barrels of ink trying to sort out these disagreements. For some, the split extends from the old dispute between Pushetonequa and Mamiwanige's heirs, which dates back to the 1880s. As Meskwaki politician and author Donald Wanatee put it, the "elected government did not provide any recognition for positions relating to the hereditary chieftainship." He considered this a critical misstep because these hereditary positions "formed the basis for the political and social integration and future" of the Meskwaki community.[82] For anthropologists, the disagreement reflected a split between young, well-educated, and "highly acculturated" tribal members and elderly, less well-educated, and unassimilated "traditionalists."[83] For some Meskwaki politicians and activists, these issues were deeply personal. One Meskwaki activist likened the constitution to an assault on the families and government of her nation. It was orchestrated, she wrote, by "half breeds, who had begun to seek a voice in tribal matters." She accused three specific families of wanting to break customary Meskwaki governance to enhance their own influence.[84]

Sometimes, these disagreements brought about a breakdown in tribal government. In the 1940s, for example, the tribal council authorized the sale of $5,000 worth of black walnut trees to the federal government. Some tribal members wanted the revenues deposited into the tribal treasury; others thought it should be distributed like an annuity. When the council chose the latter option, the tribe faced a political crisis. The tribal constitution contained no specific provision empowering the tribal council to distribute funds to tribal members. Sensing unrest over the controversy, federal administrators stepped in and stopped the payments. The agency maintained that the tribal council lacked the authority to make them. Angry at the Indian Service for meddling in tribal affairs and feeling disaffected about the weakness of their constitution and leadership, Meskwaki voters recalled the tribal chairman in 1945.[85]

The net result of these many stories about Meskwaki politics has created a perception that tribal politics are rowdy and deeply partisan.[86] As they do in most communities, personal disputes, political disagreements, and envies certainly shaped politics on the Settlement. At times, these tensions have hampered the tribe's capacity for collective decision-making, which frustrated the Red Earth People, and in the first decades under constitutional government, tribal members complained often about their community's inability to "get together."[87]

The obsession with Meskwaki political discord, however, has overlooked essential truths about the continuous efforts the Red Earth People and their leaders have undertaken to address the many challenges facing their people and their land. Politics on the Meskwaki Settlement, as in many communities, were at times contentious. But conflict derived as much from shared anxieties about the future of their community as it did from familial or ideological animosities.

LAND AND SOVEREIGNTY

The driving political question around the tribal government in the 1930s focused on the Meskwaki Settlement, who owned the land, and who had the authority to make decisions on and about it. In April 1938, Young Bear and Charles Davenport traveled to Des Moines for a meeting with Governor Kraschel. Jonas Poweshiek joined them as an interpreter.[88]

Young Bear and Davenport wrapped their rhetoric in the power of the hereditary lines, but a closer read reveals that their inquiry was fundamentally about the extent to which reorganization had jeopardized the unique status of the Meskwaki Settlement. The elders led off by challenging the authority of the United States to impose laws on land "bought . . . with their own money." Even if the United States held that power, Young Bear and Davenport said, they questioned whether the federal government could "approve an election at which new tribal rulers were elected, thus disposing [of] Chief Young Bear and stopping the hereditary line of chiefs." Finally, they asked, if the federal government wielded all these powers over Meskwaki land, why was the tribe still responsible for paying state property taxes?[89]

Governor Kraschel forwarded the elders' questions to the Indian Service, which followed up with an explanation of the 1896 trust transfer and how it had placed the Settlement under federal jurisdiction while preserving Iowa's powers of taxation. Following this exchange, the governor did not push the Indian Office any further on the elders' behalf. And the State of Iowa continued to recognize the elected tribal council as the official government of the Meskwaki Nation.[90]

This meeting underscored that, for all the bluster of Meskwaki politics, the fundamental concerns of the Red Earth People focused on land and sovereignty. The session also sheds light on the fact that, in the small Meskwaki community, apparently cantankerous political disputes took a back seat to personal ties. Young Bear and Davenport were elder men who sat on an unelected council that actively attempted to subvert the constitutionally elected council, and in that sense their meeting with Governor Kraschel was an attempt to lobby the state into restoring their power. Yet at the end of a long day of meetings, it was still George Young Bear, who helped write the constitution that threatened to dilute his father's birthright to political power, who drove the elder men home from their conference in the capital.[91]

Of all the federal programs that shaped Settlement life during the Depression, the Civilian Conservation Corps–Indian Division (CCC-ID) left perhaps the most visible imprint on the Meskwaki landscape and the people who depended on it. As importantly, the work of the CCC-ID, carried out from 1933 to 1941, ran parallel to the creation, ratification, and implementation of the Meskwaki Constitution. Although one historian has argued that "decidedly frenzied and much ballyhooed" programs like the CCC "were short lived and ultimately inconsequential," the Red Earth People's experience reveals how what began as a small field office for a New Deal program became a crucial testing ground for the authority of the new Meskwaki government.[92]

The CCC-ID was tasked with rebuilding the natural and built environments on reservations throughout Indian Country. The program began as a discrete part of the broader CCC, which sought to create jobs while improving the country's infrastructure by building hospitals, roads, and bridges; erecting dams; planting trees; and fighting erosion. It employed some 2.5 million men over the course of a decade.[93] In Iowa alone, thirty-six CCC camps (not including the single Indian Division on the Meskwaki Settlement), a variety of WPA projects, and other relief programs supported state residents.[94] The Indian Division, in comparison, employed 77,000 Native Americans nationwide by 1942. The income they earned benefited more than 100,000 of their families, friends, and community members.[95]

The Tama Agency had a budget for only twenty Meskwaki workers during the program's inaugural season, making it the smallest of the eighteen Indian Division programs launched in 1933.[96] Early the next year, that number increased to sixty-one, and administrators were staggering employment so the men could toggle between work at the agency and tending crops in their families' farms and gardens.[97] In most CCC-ID programs, the men lived in camps, separate from their families. The Settlement was small enough for the workers to stay at home, convene each morning for their daily assignments, then drive to their job sites.[98] Every Meskwaki enrollee earned about $30 per month, the same as regular Corps enrollees.[99]

The Indian Division provided the organizational, educational, technological, and financial means to improve Meskwaki land. By curbing problems like erosion and flooding and by developing their roads and buildings, tribal members enriched their land, positioning their community for more effective transportation, communication, and resource management in coming decades.[100] In this sense, "improving" the Settlement environment was less about managing the landscape as a healthy ecosystem, although some projects likely supported that, as it reflected the Red Earth People's efforts to utilize federal resources to make their land more suitable to the needs of the tribe.

According to the program's final summary in 1942, the CCC-ID employed a total of 112 Meskwaki men between 1933 and 1942, contributing to the cash-strapped community's efforts to weather the Great Depression.[101] The Indian Division's work fit into several major categories. Tribal members tended 565 acres of hardwood forest, which covered about a fifth of the Settlement's landmass. Workers pruned and shaped live trees while slashing and burning the dead and diseased. Continuing a timber production project begun in collaboration with Iowa State University in 1921, CCC-ID workers produced over eight million board feet of lumber and cordwood. Meskwaki enrollees also planted 116 acres of pine, black ash, and miscellaneous hardwood trees during the program's ten years—some 28,000 saplings in 1939 alone. Planting contributed to the dozens of erosion control projects designed to speed up drainage when the Iowa River encroached on farmlands and residential areas. Meskwaki laborers also developed three natural springs, dug seven wells, built drainage ditches and dams, and revegetated a 100-acre patch of pastureland at the heart of the Settlement.[102]

The CCC-ID also focused on the built environment. In 1933, workers laid over a mile of telephone line connecting an agency office to the day schools. They built a fence around the entire Settlement and laid a 1.5 mile road linking the middle of the Settlement to the South Farm. They landscaped around the day school and the Indian Office and sanatorium in Toledo. Meskwaki laborers also improved the Settlement's recreational areas by building toilets, fireplaces, tables, benches, a storage facility, and a baseball diamond near the powwow grounds.[103] In 1942, Meskwaki workers completed a 30 by 60 foot "stonehouse" and a park with tables and outdoor fireplaces. This complex served as an outdoor market for selling arts and crafts along the nearby Lincoln Highway.[104] In these ways, the Red Earth People utilized federal work relief programs to enhance the infrastructure on their shared Settlement.

RESTORING SELF-GOVERNANCE

The Meskwaki Nation also used federal programs to test the Indian Service's commitment to empowering tribal self-governance. This was no easy task. Federal bureaucracy had suppressed tribal governance for years. It took more than the stroke of a pen or the rhetoric of John Collier to transfer meaningful authority back to tribes. Some historians have suggested that, despite the high-minded rhetoric of the Indian New Deal, Native Nations had little real power in these programs. All CCC-ID projects, to be sure, had to conform to federal regulations, and when Native and non-Native officials disagreed, the white administrators almost always held sway.[105] Officials sometimes coerced Native employees into compliance with federal rules. At least twice, program supervisors withheld employment when

Meskwaki workers violated prohibitions on drinking or quarreled with supervisors.[106]

Yet Meskwaki leaders saw political opportunity in the rhetoric of the Indian New Deal. They seized on the momentum of the moment to influence decisions about everything from specific programs to the agency's personnel decisions. Some of these activities predated the ratification of the tribal constitution. In 1935, for example, the acting council led by the elder Young Bear delayed CCC-ID projects while they debated the best locations for timber planting. A few months later, they convinced the Indian Service to transfer a government forester away from the Settlement following an altercation with a Meskwaki worker.[107] Set against the nearly total disintegration of the council's authority the decade before, these small victories reflected the incremental strengthening of tribal political authority.

Empowered by its new constitution, the tribal council took this work a step further. The body reviewed and agreed to all of the agency's CCC-ID plans. In September 1938, the council requested surveys of various tracts of land so it could determine which sections to lease to outsiders and which to improve with available Indian Division work.[108] The council then spent six weeks negotiating a higher rental fee so the tribe could pay its state property taxes.[109] Similarly, in 1941, the council selected the location for the stonehouse and park along the Lincoln Highway and negotiated an agreement with tribal member Peter Morgan, who lived on that part of the Settlement, to use his portion of the Nation's property.[110]

Program participants also negotiated for better working conditions. As a general policy, the CCC withheld 60 percent of a worker's monthly wage. The government set this money aside for the employee's family. Rather than living in a remote CCC camp, Meskwaki workers went home every day, and they convinced CCC-ID managers to pay them in full so they could care for their families on their own.[111]

Like all New Deal work relief programs, the Indian Division wound down as the United States entered World War II. On behalf of their tribe, the council formally thanked the CCC-ID's leaders in 1941. As council president Edward Davenport wrote, the tribe wished to "express our most sincere appreciation" to the Indian Office and the CCC-ID for the "training and education in forestry, conservation, construction and surveying, as well as the many improvements made possible on our tribal property."[112]

WARTIME

After more than a decade of Depression, the US economy finally swelled as the nation prepared for and entered World War II. Economic growth was slow to reach Indian Country. Nevertheless, Native Americans served the war effort at home and abroad, and the booming wartime economy brought incomes for Indigenous peoples. More than 25,000 Native Americans from hundreds of tribes across the country served in the conflict. This constituted a higher percentage of service than any other group.[113] Countless other Indigenous people served in war industries, and for those who traveled to factories or the front lines, the war entailed exposure to new skills, perspectives, and ideas. Most brought these experiences home after the war.[114]

More Meskwaki people served in the American military during World War II than in any previous US conflict. Jonas Poweshiek, then assistant curator at the State Historical Society, explained this phenomenon in a 1945 essay. For one thing, he pointed out, the 1924 Indian Citizenship Act had made Meskwaki men eligible for the draft, which had not been the case during the Great War.[115] Motivated by a sense of patriotic duty and a desire to be well positioned in the draft, some Meskwaki men enlisted before Pearl Harbor. Eight young men, for example, joined the National Guard in February 1941 and began training as radio operators in nearby Marshalltown.[116]

This group included Dewey Young Bear, Frank and Willard Sanache, Judy and Mike Wayne, Dewey Roberts, Edward Benson, and Melvin Twin. During the war, these men vexed enemy codebreakers by transmitting intelligence and orders in the Meskwaki language.[117] They were the Meskwaki Nation's contribution to a group of soldiers from some eighteen Native Nations who served as "code talkers" during the war.[118] Around fifty Meskwaki men fought in the conflict, serving as everything from tank destroyers to submariners and infantrymen in the African, European, and Pacific theaters.[119] Several sustained combat wounds. The Nazis held Judy Wayne, Dewey Youngbear, and Frank Sanache prisoner for months. Robert Morgan and Clement Mauskemo died in combat on opposite ends of the world.[120] Only Sanache, who received several medals in 2002, lived to see public recognition for his service. All the Meskwaki code talkers received a posthumous Congressional Gold Medal in 2014.[121]

HOME AND AWAY

Back home on the Settlement, the Red Earth People farmed to meet wartime demands. In early 1942, the head of the tribal council told a reporter that the tribe would quadruple its corn crop; double its gardens, chickens, and pigs; and produce twice as many canned vegetables that year.[122] Some Meskwaki people found creative ways to contribute, joining a national movement of Native people who spent their spare time hauling metal to the local scrap center. According to one reporter, Native people collected more than 1,600 tons of junk metal nationwide. This was enough steel and iron for 6,000 aerial bombs, brass for 166,000 cartridges, lead for two million bullets, and enough aluminum "to build two pursuit planes."[123]

By October 1942, half of Settlement men had left for factory jobs. Some found work in nearby Des Moines or Cedar Rapids. Some went alone; others uprooted their entire families and left for Illinois, Washington, and elsewhere.[124] Many moved to Wisconsin, where, according to Willie Poweshiek, "some of the plants hesitate about hiring some of the whites [as] there are so many foreigners among them. But they know that they can be sure of an Indian's loyalty; he is a real American."[125]

The war also gave Meskwaki women unprecedented opportunities to work off the Settlement. Marie Jefferson and Ada Old Bear, for example, had spent their lives creating intricate beadwork. They applied this dexterity and attention to detail inspecting ammunition at an ordnance plant in Des Moines.[126] Nell G. Ward also worked in Iowa's capital. She became both the first Meskwaki woman to serve in the military and the tribe's first licensed nurse after enlisting in the Cadet Nurse Corps and working as an army nurse during the war.[127]

These activities bolstered the tribal economy and provided work experience and professional skills for Meskwaki people. All this movement also raised concerns about how Meskwaki values would survive the conflict, and whether the Settlement would continue to serve as a physical anchor for the Meskwaki community. As George Young Bear put it in 1942, "These families leaving us are being scattered throughout the country.... Their children are growing up where the ways of life and customs are different." "They won't," he feared, "want to come back here and live again."[128] He was partially correct. In 1937, only about 10 percent of tribal members lived off Settlement. By 1978, that number would rise to around 30 percent.[129]

During World War II, Ada Old Bear and Marie Jefferson left the Settlement for work in an ordnance plant in Des Moines. For many young Meskwaki men and women, the conflict promised unprecedented access to off-Settlement wage work. Photo courtesy of the *Des Moines Register*, August 30, 1942 © The Des Moines Register, USA Today Network.

GOING AWAY

Wartime opportunities slowly convinced many Red Earth People to abandon the on-Settlement economy that had sustained them since 1857. Full integration into the regional workforce had been a long-running implicit promise of the assimilation movement. The American Dream, successive officials had told Meskwaki people, awaited any Indigenous person willing to set aside their culture and ways of living and embrace the American economy. This was not to be.

Each paycheck reinforced an economic illusion. Even with more cash in their pockets, most Red Earth People left World War II less well off than before the conflict: Calculations based on the figures in Indian Service reports suggest that the average Meskwaki family's income may have actually declined by as much as 25 percent between 1940 and 1944.[130] With the Depression subsumed by war, the US government eliminated critical New Deal relief programs like the CCC-ID, and the tribe canceled the powwow in 1943 and 1944.[131]

The core problem, however, was employment discrimination. One Meskwaki man pointed out that close to home Meskwaki laborers were "not as sought after as in" nearby states.[132] In Tama County, some non-Natives harbored a paranoid suspicion of Native Americans. Late in 1938, for example, the *Tama News-Herald* reported that a man with a "thick German accent" had visited the Settlement, purchased some beadwork, and talked with several tribal members. The reporter linked this otherwise innocuous event to broader concerns that "Nazi agents" in the United States had "begun attempts to stir up unrest among Indians on some reservations." The *Herald* quoted a warning from the Indian Office that "Nazi agitators believe their best opportunity for implanting [the] seeds of totalitarianism are among discontented minority groups."[133]

Although overblown, this story reflects the continuation of the same racial anxieties that had fueled rumors about Meskwaki people spreading smallpox several decades before. Many Red Earth People, to be sure, found work near the Settlement during World War II. But they worked in a context of distrust. When the regional economy was strong, a Meskwaki applicant could find work. But wages remained low, educational attainment and career advancement were elusive, and whenever things slowed down, Meskwaki workers were the first to be let go. This pattern continued for years.[134]

THE POSTWAR PLAN

As early as 1943, the Indian Service knew that the wartime industrial boom that had created jobs for Native people would not last. Concerned that Indian Country's fortunes would cascade at the war's end, John Collier instructed Indian agents across the United States to study the economic trends at their agencies and submit postwar development plans.[135] The agent for the Meskwaki Nation, Peru Farver, completed this task while bringing the tribe under his purview at the Tomah Indian Agency in Wisconsin.[136] The Toledo sanatorium closed in 1942. The Indian Service then converted the Tama Agency into the "Sac and Fox Sub-Agency," where a handful of field staff reported to Farver.[137]

The Tomah Agency had big plans for the small Meskwaki Settlement. Agent Farver believed the best way to prepare the Red Earth People for the postwar economy would be to quintuple the size of the Settlement to more than 15,000 acres over the course of twenty years. By his calculation, this land base would leave each Meskwaki family with a property roughly equal to that of the average Iowa farmer.[138] The plan would have also drained 350 acres of bottomland and straightened and dammed the

Iowa River.[139] Flooding was a major problem on the Settlement's lowlands. Floods in 1944, 1946, and 1947 displaced dozens of families and overran the highway.[140] Farver's plan also called for maintaining the Settlement's fences and roads, improving the powwow grounds, digging wells, relocating the subagency's office, and engineering a more sophisticated sewage system for the Settlement day school. It would have used tribal funds to buy more land, new homes, trees, and better pastures. It had provisions for tribal collaboration with the county and the state for road maintenance and even outlined a revised tax system to cover these costs.[141]

If these elements of the postwar plan were appealing to the Red Earth People, others courted suspicion. Farver proposed that individual tribal members give up their private use-rights so the tribal council could work with agricultural experts at Iowa State University to develop a new land use plan.[142] This, Farver imagined, would focus on cash crops like corn and alfalfa and the creation of a tribal hog-raising operation. Farver tasked the field staff with presenting his draft plan to the tribal council while making it clear that the Indian Office was "interested in undertaking a type of program that will provide a wage economy for members of the community."[143]

OFF SETTLEMENT

Distance and timing did not work to Farver's advantage. The Red Earth People considered implementing his postwar plan several times during the 1940s. Had he pitched it a few years earlier, they might have enthusiastically embraced parts of the proposal. Expanding the Settlement and strengthening an on-Settlement agricultural economy, after all, fit perfectly with around eighty-five years of Meskwaki history. Farver's lack of experience on the Settlement, however, left him blind to the tribe's intense suspicion of any federal plan to reallocate tribal land.

The war, moreover, had changed things. A new economic paradigm was emerging, and more and more Meskwaki workers were preferring off-Settlement wage labor. By 1951, an agency report estimated that only four Meskwaki families made their living off commercial farming, which had been a staple of the tribal economy only twenty years before, even though family gardens still supplemented Meskwaki diets.[144] Nathan Bear grew up in this era and recalled how his family gardened. Some families hunted regularly, he said, but game was scarce. Speaking of the long tradition of Meskwaki families leaving for winter hunts, Bear recalled only that "[we] killed a squirrel every once in a while."[145]

In 1956, an anthropologist reported that "the Indians earn their livings by working as unskilled and skilled laborers and artisans in the [nearby] towns." Most "commut[ed] to the Settlement each day, or else liv[ed] in town and return[ed] to the Settlement on weekends or on special occasions." By 1962, only one Meskwaki family farmed commercially. Meanwhile, around 240 acres of good cropland sat unused on the Settlement. Otherwise, the only large farm on the Settlement was plowed by a white farmer, to whom the tribe still leased 520 acres to pay its property taxes.[146]

Some Meskwaki families took part in "relocation," a program that used federal funds to help Native families move to major cities like Chicago, Oakland, Dallas, and Minneapolis so they could seek out education or new job opportunities. In many cases, the federal government had overstated its promise to help relocated families get their feet on the ground. Many Native families faced hard times acclimating to their new communities.[147] Nevertheless, over time relocation contributed to a massive demographic shift across Native America: by the 1990s, more than half of all Indigenous Americans lived in urban areas rather than on reservations.[148]

Mary Young Bear recalled how her family moved to Denver, where her "father went to school to be a cabinet maker." He then "worked for a couple of different companies and made custom cabinets." Her mother "just worked wherever she could find work." Feeling isolated in the city, her parents brought Mary and her siblings back to the Settlement to visit family and attend the annual powwow whenever they could, and at age nineteen Mary moved to the Settlement, where she raised her family.[149]

Education and military service also drew Meskwaki people away from the Settlement. Scholarship programs helped a few dozen young Meskwaki people attend college or graduate school in the 1950s and 1960s. Many of these students permanently left the Settlement, although a few worked for the Indian Service or built careers in tribal government and economic development.[150] Others joined the armed forces, seeking employment and a chance to see the country and the world. Nathan Bear, for example, served in the Navy then moved to Des Moines in the 1960s. He spent three years laying concrete, and he occasionally "got a couple of factory jobs [but] didn't care for that too much" then retired on the Settlement.[151] More than a dozen tribal members served in Vietnam in the late 1960s, and three Meskwaki men—Dale Benson, Terry Roberts, and Richard Young Bear—died in combat. As in many communities, some veterans struggled with injuries and the ravages of posttraumatic stress disorder.[152]

SQUEEZED OUT

The Red Earth People's sudden, intense turn toward off-Settlement opportunities vexed observers. In 1948, a team of graduate students under the direction of the University of Chicago anthropologist Sol Tax came to the Meskwaki Settlement. They conducted an experiment in what Tax called "action anthropology," which combined academic field research with efforts to assist struggling communities. He and his team visited the Settlement off and on for a decade, and their work became known as the "Fox Project."[153]

One of Tax's students, Fred Gearing, drafted a series of short articles in the voice of a Meskwaki person. Gearing was interested in intercultural conflict, and his impersonation sought to make Meskwaki peoples' perspectives more palatable to the non-Native readers of local newspapers like the *Tama News-Herald*.[154] One was called "Why We'd Just as Soon Not Farm Much." In it, Gearing attempted to answer a common question: if the tribe had economic problems, why didn't the Red Earth People just devote more energy to agriculture? Gearing summarized what he had heard from some Meskwaki people. "OUR LAND," he blared, "WAS NOT BOUGHT TO BE USED." Rather, Gearing had been told, the Settlement was "a place of safety, a refuge, a permanent home," not "something from which to earn a living."[155]

Other Meskwaki people told the anthropologists that the issue had little to do with any tribal philosophy or environmental ethic. There was plenty of land, older tribal members argued, but the younger generations were plainly uninterested in agriculture.[156] Still others maintained that the shift away from farming had political motivations: even if everyone wanted to farm, they feared, the tribal council would not fairly divide the land. One

Meskwaki person chalked this up to bluster, claiming that it was "easy to get land from the council," if someone really wanted it.[157]

In the early 1960s, an economist from Iowa State University named Elizabeth E. Hoyt came to a different set of conclusions about the transformations underway in the Meskwaki economy. Focusing on big-picture changes to technology and infrastructure, for example, she described how affordable cars and better roads had made it easier for Meskwaki workers to commute. Now that the drive to work in Cedar Rapids, Marshalltown, or Waterloo took only a matter of hours, she pointed out, it was easier and more economical for Meskwaki people to work in those places.[158] This aligned with the perspective of one Meskwaki person, who said plainly that people "can get more money, and faster, on outside jobs."[159]

Hoyt also emphasized the expansion of mechanized farming and corporatized agriculture across Iowa. Meskwaki farmers, like other small single-family farms, were being squeezed out of the agricultural markets. At the time, Iowa was home to some 2.5 million people, and the Settlement had more than 600 residents. The Settlement remained at about 3,200 acres—only half of which were pasture or farmland.[160] Large commercial operations were beginning to dominate. Many small farmers sold out to huge operations that consolidated Iowa's landmass into fewer, larger farms. Increasing productivity created a vicious cycle. Crop surpluses lowered prices, so farmers planted more to recoup revenues. Overproduction restarted and deepened the problem while expensive new machines, seeds, and pesticides increased costs. These forces left small farms vulnerable to market instability and reinforced the Red Earth People's growing preference for wage work over agriculture.[161]

The Meskwaki Nation never adopted the Indian Service's postwar plan. By the time it would have been implemented, many Meskwaki people had committed themselves to searching for off-Settlement jobs, and try as he might, Agent Farver was unable to convince them otherwise. His proposal also got tangled in red tape. By the time it had been pared down by budget hawks in Washington, the plan suggested purchasing only 6,000 additional acres of Meskwaki land—just over a third of the expansion originally planned.[162]

Had the tribe adopted this pared-down proposal, redistributed Meskwaki farms would have remained too small to compete with non-Native farmers.

Even if the tribe "were to attain an optimum utilization of their natural resources," one agent admitted, the postwar plan would be unable to stimulate significant growth in the Meskwaki economy. The lack of land on the Settlement "has already oriented the [tribal] economy toward wage employment."[163] The shift off Settlement, he presumed, was complete. Time would prove otherwise.

CHAPTER 8

Strategic Embrace

Even if the Red Earth People had embraced the Indian Service's postwar plan, it likely never would have come to fruition. After World War II, federal policymakers steadily focused their attentions on a new policy known as "termination," or the complete elimination of tribal sovereignty. The idea had been percolating in policy circles since the early 1920s but was overtaken by the political inertia of the Indian New Deal. When John Collier left the Indian Office in 1945, he did so amid looming budget cuts and criticisms that his policies had not resolved entrenched challenges in Indian Country. Government officials and Native leaders argued for a fresh approach, and, within a few years, termination experienced a revival.[1] Its advocates believed the policy could reduce federal spending while incentivizing Indigenous people to pull themselves from poverty, all while fully and finally integrating them into the American economy.[2] Some proponents of termination also hoped that Native Americans would reject communal systems of land ownership—an idea particularly attractive amid Cold War suspicions that Indigenous social and economic systems resembled Communism.[3]

The policy proceeded in a phased approach. The federal government first "targeted" tribes that it believed "ready" for termination. Congress then passed a law unilaterally dissolving the nation-to-nation status between the United States and that tribe. This process included the dispersal of tribal trust lands and the end of federal support for tribal programs. The goal was to systematically terminate every tribe. Along the way, the Office of Indian Affairs, which changed its name to the Bureau of Indian Affairs (BIA) in 1947, would make itself obsolete.[4]

Termination began in earnest in 1953, and within about a decade the federal government had terminated 109 tribes, removing more than 1.3 million acres of Indigenous land from federal trust.[5] Termination received bipartisan support during the Truman and Eisenhower administrations. It even saw some initial interest among Native Americans who had grown tired of the patriarchy and inefficiency of the BIA. Most Native people quickly changed their view after hearing of its disastrous consequences: the policy stripped vital benefits from already fragile tribal economies and quickly devastated them.[6] For years, Native people across the country worried their tribe would be next.

By the late 1940s, the Red Earth People could feel the gradual reduction of federal support that characterized the termination era. In 1947, some tribal members, concerned that the BIA was not paying attention to their community, petitioned for the Settlement's part-time subagent to be replaced with a full-time agent. Instead, the BIA halved the tribe's budget and closed the agency office, transferring it to the BIA's Minneapolis Area Office, which oversaw more than two dozen tribes in Minnesota, Iowa, Michigan, and Wisconsin.[7] Thereafter, the Settlement day school was the BIA's most prominent foothold on Meskwaki land.[8] Otherwise, the agency paid for a part-time physician, who was on call for Meskwaki patients one hour per day, and a dentist who saw Meskwaki children once per year. The BIA offered minimal welfare assistance, kept tribal records, occasionally consulted with the tribal council, and funded some road work that was in the process of being transferred to the county. All in all, by the early 1950s the agency was spending between about $114 and $130 a year—or around $1,500 today—on each Meskwaki person.[9]

The tribe also received limited services from local and state government. The Meskwaki Nation paid eight of sixteen possible state taxes, which added up to about two-thirds of the overall tax burden of the average county property owner. Because of its trust status, the Settlement did not incur levies for services like the courts, poor relief, or county schools. The tribe did, however, pay general property taxes for road maintenance and weed eradication, which cut into the leasing revenue that funded tribal operations. Iowa assumed half the costs for several welfare programs that benefited Meskwaki people in need. The University of Iowa hospital offered obstetrical services to impoverished Meskwaki women. Transporting expectant mothers from the Settlement to the hospital in Iowa City was the only service Tama County provided to tribal members.[10]

Between the mid-1940s and the early 1960s—as its people were experimenting with major transitions in their economic lives—the Meskwaki Nation navigated a series of intense political struggles. These confrontations highlighted the growing complexity of local, state, federal, and tribal interactions. Each brought long-percolating concerns to the surface: questions of who had ultimate authority over the tribe, its land, and individual Meskwaki people. Along the way, the Red Earth People slowly articulated a remarkable new vision of the political utility the Meskwaki Settlement afforded their tribe. The first of these disputes began more than a year before two mushroom clouds signaled the end of World War II.

AID TO DEPENDENT CHILDREN

As the spring rains buffeted central Iowa in early 1944, Tama County officials decided to take a stand. Their concerns about Meskwaki marriages had resurfaced, but with a new emphasis that emerged when the county rejected the Aid to Dependent Children (ADC) applications of four unwed Meskwaki mothers. It claimed that paying for Meskwaki women's welfare would incentivize the birth of children of unwed parents on the Settlement. Local newspapers ran racialized rumors: one railed against an "Indian brave [who] became a father three times in a period of two weeks" and dredged up an old acknowledgment by a tribal councilman that some Meskwaki children had been born out of wedlock.[11] A *Des Moines Register* reporter distilled the controversy this way: "A matter of $25 a month has arrayed Indian against Indian, redman against white, and Tama county [*sic*] officials against the federal and state governments."[12]

Tama County's position was clear: it did not want to spend taxpayers' money on Meskwaki people. Letting Meskwaki mothers receive ADC, officials argued, would "set a precedent for making" the Red Earth People "eligible for all types of relief."[13] One official was less concerned with the meager costs at stake than the principle of the matter: Tama County should not be funding Meskwaki people's welfare at all, because Natives were a federal "burden." When asked if the county would commit to a cost-sharing agreement with the tribe, he deflected. The "responsibility" for Native families, he insisted, "does not rest with the county and the state."[14]

The Red Earth People rendered split opinions. One tribal councilman urged Tama County to fund the ADC program on the grounds that the county had abandoned its responsibility to his people. While his was a sovereign nation, its members were also woven into the fabric of the United States: Meskwaki people were state and federal citizens who paid taxes like everyone else. He referenced the wartime contributions of the Red Earth People and disparaged the county politicians who "make a habit of coming out to visit us the night before the election. They give us sandwiches and cigars and kiss our babies," then make promises. "But when the time comes that we need these promises to be fulfilled," he complained, the candidates suddenly developed "grave doubts about our citizenship."[15]

Another Meskwaki man, a former councilman whose daughter was one of the ADC mothers, had a different take. He believed that the Indian Office wanted to "dump us Indians onto the state where we will have to pay more taxes." He feared that the federal government was trying to abrogate its responsibility to the tribe. If Iowa could force Tama County to pay for Meskwaki relief, he reasoned, it might also creep into other Meskwaki affairs, and "state control" over the Settlement would bring an end to any federal assistance for his people.[16] The Meskwaki man told an Iowa congressman that most Red Earth People were "against state supervision of we Indians as a people and our property and future." They wanted to preserve "the present friendly relationship of our federal supervision."[17]

Meskwaki logic won the day. In separate reviews, the state and federal governments found that Tama County had to pay its share of ADC costs to every citizen, regardless of their race. Members of Iowa's social welfare board, meanwhile, feared that failing to support Native families would violate federal anti-discrimination regulations—a charge that could disqualify the state from as much as $3 million in funding. For these officials, the issue was not about tribal land or sovereignty, but federal citizenship.[18]

County residents did not give up. Throughout 1944 and 1945, locals engaged in what one local journalist called "very active campaigning" for a new state law to ensure that "the county would have nothing to pay" for the welfare of Native people.[19] They succeeded, and in March 1945, the governor "save[d] Tama county [*sic*] a lot of money and trouble," as one reporter wrote, by signing a state law that did just that.[20] Under the new system, Iowa would draw directly from state coffers (which were funded in part by federal dollars) to pay ADC benefits directly to Meskwaki mothers. This arrangement passed state and federal reviews, and a year and a half after they had initially applied, the Meskwaki women finally got their money. But Tama County did not pay a dime.[21]

LAW AND ORDER

The ADC controversy was only one in a series of developments that signaled growing local and state interest in Meskwaki affairs. Questions about everything from tribal hunting and fishing rights to local taxation and law enforcement had been percolating for years. Indigenous people's use of alcohol and peyote, the latter of which was used in Native American Church ceremonies, were of particular concern. Selling liquor on reservations had been illegal under federal law for more than a century, and alcohol was outlawed in much of Indian Country for more than twenty years after Prohibition ended in 1933. The Indian Office regularly requested federal support in apprehending "bootleggers or things of that sort" during the Meskwaki powwow.[22] And many Meskwaki veterans returned from World War II only to be denied service in area bars, including the local VFW.[23]

The State of Iowa pushed to extend criminal jurisdiction over the Meskwaki Settlement in 1948. This was part of a broader movement by states seeking more control over Indigenous lands. Shortly after the passage of the Major Crimes Act in 1885, federal administrators had established "Courts of Indian Offences," which provided law enforcement on some reservations, but, a few decades on, states had tired of this system. In Iowa, for example, the federal government had the authority to arrest and prosecute certain crimes on the Settlement but rarely did so. This issue was compounded by postwar budget cuts that left Wisconsin, Minnesota, and Iowa sharing only one law enforcement officer dedicated to Indian Country. That officer spent most of his time at the central office in Minneapolis. *Peters v. Malin*, meanwhile, had restricted state jurisdiction on the Settlement. The prevailing concern was that places like the Meskwaki Settlement had become, as Judith Daubenmier writes, a jurisdictionally nebulous "no man's land."[24]

By the end of the 1930s, people across Tama County were raising concerns about a state of "lawlessness" on the Meskwaki Settlement, and within a few years everyone from local judges to area news reporters was commenting on the issue.[25] Many Red Earth People had also grown frustrated with a rowdy group of tribal members who had a penchant for brawling, disrupting ceremonies, theft, and raising hell on and near tribal land. In 1941, the tribe had established its own court system to handle minor on-Settlement crimes between Native people. The Indian Office named three tribal judges and provided a basic penal code. Everyone spoke Meskwaki during this court's proceedings and, with few formally trained Meskwaki lawyers, friends and associates helped defendants plead their cases.[26] The experiment proved short-lived. The tribal council initially supported the court, but tribal members quickly began accusing the judges, who also served as law enforcement officers, of cutting breaks for friends and family.[27] Within a few months of its creation, the court stopped policing the Settlement, and by 1943 it had been dismantled.[28]

The problems persisted, leading a group of Red Earth People to complain to the BIA in 1947. They received disappointing news. One solution, wrote BIA representative Ben Reifel, would be to request that a white officer be assigned to patrol the Settlement. Another option would be for the Meskwaki Nation to ask Congress to place the tribe under Iowa's criminal jurisdiction.[29]

As Meskwaki people considered this issue, non-Natives went to work in nearby towns. An ambitious county attorney named Walter J. Willett, a self-described friend of the Red Earth People who grew up just two miles from the Settlement, had been concerned about law and order on Meskwaki land for some time.[30] Around 1947, Willett enlisted the help of W. G. MacMartin, the head of the Tama chapter of the Daughters of the American Revolution. The pair lobbied for the Settlement to be placed under Iowa's criminal jurisdiction. The BIA agreed to consider this if the tribe supported it. And there was precedent for the move: Congress had recently afforded both Kansas and North Dakota criminal jurisdiction over the Indigenous populations in those states.[31] As the issue moved forward, some Meskwaki people supported a jurisdictional change out of simple pragmatism. "We need protection," one Meskwaki woman said.[32]

Meetings between federal authorities and tribal leaders continued into the fall of 1947, but nobody could have guessed that the matter would be settled so quickly.[33] In October 1947, two Settlement youths assaulted a sixty-six-year-old Tama man who had been fishing on tribal land late at night. The incident sparked a public outcry that linked concerns over Meskwaki "lawlessness" to alcohol. As one story read, the angler's assailants had been "crazed with fire water" when the attack took place.[34] Within a matter of weeks, the Tama County Grand Jury launched an investigation into criminal jurisdiction on the Meskwaki Settlement and unanimously passed a resolution demanding that Congress place the tribe under the state's criminal jurisdiction.[35]

As locals pressured Iowa's congressional delegation into the fall of 1947, the Red Earth People debated jurisdiction, which quickly became a central issue in tribal elections. Several tribal councilmen believed state jurisdiction could help reduce crime on the Settlement, but they lost their seats to anti-transfer candidates.[36] With a bill before Congress by early 1948, a group of Meskwaki people testified before the Senate Subcommittee on Indian Affairs in Washington, DC. They characterized it as another effort to further non-Indian power that would "open a way for people to come into our land and do as they please."[37] These Meskwaki concerns aligned

Adeline Wanatee, who was inducted into The Iowa Women's Hall of Fame in 1993 in honor of her lifetime of service to the Meskwaki Nation. Shown here in 1960, she was a prolific educator and advocate for Meskwaki rights who served on the tribal school board and was the first woman elected to the tribal council. Photo courtesy of *The Courier*.

with the arguments of the recently founded National Congress of American Indians, which criticized state jurisdictional transfers for failing to uphold treaty promises, thereby diminishing tribal sovereignty.[38]

Despite these protests, the Meskwaki bill became law in the summer of 1948. Thereafter, the sheriff's office could patrol the Settlement, and state courts held jurisdiction on Meskwaki land.[39] Tama County, however, lacked the resources to adequately patrol rural communities, and within a few years only serious Meskwaki crimes were receiving police attention. Tama County rarely used its hard-won police powers, it seems, unless a tribal member was picked up for disorderly conduct or drinking and driving in town or near the Settlement.[40]

EDUCATION

When Adeline Wanatee addressed the Meskwaki tribal council in the spring of 1952, she described an issue that had plagued her people for decades: where, how, and by whom Meskwaki children would be educated.[41] The federal government, which had long administered the Settlement's day school, had recently informed the tribal council that it planned to close the facility, transfer tribal education to the State Board of Education, and send Meskwaki students to town. Adeline kept her remarks brief. She had been educated at the Flandreau and Haskell Indian schools and was concerned that area teachers would not understand Meskwaki children and their needs. The BIA was imperfect, she reasoned, but at least it hired teachers with an interest in Native issues. Adeline worried that students would drop out if they felt alienated at school.[42]

Decades before, Meskwaki parents had pushed to close the Toledo boarding school because they wanted their children educated on the Settlement. The Indian Service acquiesced but, as early as 1934, wanted to shutter the two on-Settlement day schools and bus Meskwaki children to the nearby town of Montour. When Meskwaki students complained of unfair treatment by white teachers and peers, their parents organized a "Student-Parents Association" and railed against the agency for making decisions "without consulting the tribe." Eventually, Meskwaki parents struck a compromise: One school closed, but the Indian Service built a new one in 1938. Meskwaki children attended this school through eighth grade then attended high school in Tama.[43]

A little over a decade later, federal officials were once again seeking to consolidate Meskwaki students in state schools. Over the winter of 1951 to 1952, Meskwaki leaders, supported by the anthropologist Sol Tax, convinced the BIA and the State Board of Education that the Red Earth People would reject this move.[44] Their victory proved short-lived, and in 1953 the BIA announced that it had canceled the tribe's kindergarten program and would be sending Meskwaki eighth graders to school in Tama. Many Meskwaki families pulled their children out of class, and the tribal council told the BIA that this protest "was based on their belief that the Indian Service would eventually move all the grades into Tama, and they would lose their school on the reservation."[45]

The BIA had two reasons for attempting to close the school. The move aligned with a broader postwar curtailment of federal services to the tribe. The Settlement school was also stuck in an administrative quagmire. It had 139 students, which BIA guidelines considered too many for employing just three teachers and a principal, yet enrollment was too low to justify adding a fifth employee. The BIA argued that it would have to make the principal teach, contract with Tama schools for an administrator, or reduce the student-to-teacher ratio by sending eighth graders to town.[46] Officials chose the latter.

As in the ADC fight, Meskwaki people criticized the BIA's efforts to dump federal commitments onto the state. One tribal leader asserted that the BIA should keep the day school open "in accordance with promises through agreements and treaties, instead of the Indian Office attempting to get out from under its obligations."[47] Under pressure from the tribe, the BIA revived the kindergarten program and convinced Meskwaki families that it would not shut down the Settlement school. Most Meskwaki eighth graders enrolled in Tama for the fall term in 1953. First through seventh graders stayed on the Settlement.[48]

Despite this compromise, the BIA slowly reduced its educational services to the Meskwaki Nation, and by 1961 the facility served only first through sixth graders. By then, Meskwaki parents seemed more comfortable with the Tama school. It provided some culturally relevant programming for adults, although many parents remained anxious about the lack of Meskwaki-specific curricula.[49] Over time, the rapport between the tribe and the Tama school improved, and, at one point, the Meskwaki Nation asked the BIA to help fund a campus expansion project. Even there, however, the tribal council clarified that its support of the plan should "*not* be interpreted or construed as approving, advocating, or requesting the discontinuance" of the Settlement school.[50]

AVOIDING TERMINATION

The BIA saw the Meskwaki Nation as a strong potential candidate for termination. This was in part, the agency argued, because the Meskwaki economy was "far better" than that of Native communities in "Northern Minnesota, Wisconsin, and Michigan." The agency dispatched a social scientist named John B. Keliiaa to the Settlement to explore the possibility in 1951.[51] True to form, Tama County claimed that county resources were overstretched and maintained that the federal government should pay for tribal programs. The county would support termination only if the Red Earth People were "able to assume the responsibilities of full citizenship"—meaning they would pay all county taxes—or if "the state would assume full financial responsibility" for the tribe.[52]

The Red Earth People strongly opposed termination. Some told Keliiaa that they would not be treated fairly by local whites. Others feared that neither individuals nor the tribe would be able to afford the increased tax burden that would accompany the change. Many expressed anger that the federal government had promised to provide services in treaties and had already broken them many times before. Some claimed that the tribe was "not now competent" and that the Red Earth People were "still closely tied to tribal customs and could not be able to make their way among the population at large." Their "only chance of tribal survival," they argued, was "under federal supervision."[53] A few tribal members worried that termination was inevitable and stressed that it should not be rushed and unduly troublesome. Many of the Meskwaki people who spoke to Keliiaa staunchly proclaimed that no matter what happened to their tribal status, the Settlement had to remain collectively owned.[54]

Despite all this local opposition, the State of Iowa—and, by extension, the Meskwaki Nation—appeared in an early draft of House Concurrent Resolution 108 (HCR-108), the 1953 law that targeted all the tribes in several states and a few other specific tribes for termination. According to historian Judith Daubenmier, it remains unclear exactly why Iowa was included in initial versions of HCR-108. One possibility is that this happened because the BIA was attempting to close the Settlement day school at that time, and termination would have aligned with that decision. It is similarly unclear how an Iowa congressman was able to remove the state from the final bill. As Daubenmier observes, Meskwaki people "seem to have succeeded in fending off termination through a combination of their own effective lobbying and the timely action of their representative in Congress," with whom some tribal members had built a strong rapport. Whatever happened behind closed doors, when HCR-108 became law, Iowa no longer appeared in its text.[55]

EVOLUTION

The Meskwaki Nation narrowly avoided termination in the summer of 1953, and the tribe and its Settlement remained intact. Despite searching for opportunities elsewhere around that time, the Red Earth People ardently protected the Settlement from dissolution. The Settlement, of course, had been a central concern and key asset in Meskwaki political strategies for decades. But as a general convention, before World War II tribal members had viewed the "peculiar condition" of their Settlement as a bulwark against outside interference.

This began to shift in the postwar years. Decades of wrangling between the county, state, and federal governments, each of whom wanted control over the Settlement in some respects but to deny responsibility in others, had stitched a confusing patchwork of jurisdictional coverage and political authority over the tribe and its members. In this context—although the Settlement's status did not guarantee victory in every dispute—the tribe's landed history provided crucial legal and rhetorical leverage that the Red Earth People could deploy strategically to meet their needs.

Meskwaki people understood this and, in the 1940s, began to describe the Settlement not just as a piece of property whose tenure protected it from control by outside governments, but as the physical anchor of a sovereign Meskwaki Nation whose members enjoyed rights to self-government and self-determination *as well as* the benefits available to any local, state, or federal citizen.[56] In a series of slow, piecemeal responses to the issues of the day, the Red Earth People asserted that when the federal government absorbed the Settlement into trust—an act from an earlier era designed to erode the tribe's political power—it had also, perhaps inadvertently, established a deep federal obligation to support the tribe and its interests. This built upon the nation-to-nation relationship supported by treaties, providing multiple points from which the Red Earth People could pursue political strategies that supported their needs.

Strategically embracing the federal trust responsibility and the American federal system in these ways, the Red Earth People had preserved their tribal sovereignty, ensured their community members' access to vital government programs, and successfully maintained the integrity of the Meskwaki Settlement through an era of incredible change and instability.

FALSE PROMISE

Leaving office in January 1957, Governor Leo A. Hoegh reflected on his time in Iowa's highest office. He boasted improvements to the state's educational system, soil conservation and irrigation projects, the construction of over 1,000 miles of new roads, bridge maintenance, and the re-engineering of dangerous curves across the state highway system. He reported that the state had added or expanded 183 industrial sites during his tenure, which he called "the greatest industrial growth in Iowa's history." This had created more than 10,000 jobs and injected some $150 million in investments into the state. He also touted his support for farmers and reported that, even after a couple of years of severe drought, the economy of Iowa—like much of the United States in the postwar period—was strong.[57]

Like most Indigenous Americans, the Red Earth People did not share in this postwar prosperity. The tribe's unemployment rate bounced between 30 and 50 percent throughout the 1950s. By contrast, Iowa's lingered around 4 percent.[58] By the early 1960s, the promise of full inclusion in the local wage economy—the very logic that underpinned policies like termination and relocation—had proven false. There were almost no jobs on the Settlement, so most Meskwaki workers labored off Settlement. All but a few were relegated to the shallowest waters of the labor pool. Most could not afford to live off Settlement and had to commute to cities like Waterloo, Des Moines or Cedar Rapids because prejudice in nearby towns made it difficult to get jobs closer to home.⁵⁹ Aware of these issues, in the mid-1950s, several faith communities and nonprofit organizations organized an "Iowa Committee on Indian Affairs," which offered various charitable services.⁶⁰ These organizations often did little to understand tribal preferences and cultural protocols, and no amount of private support broke the pattern of economic instability that plagued the Settlement.⁶¹ One Meskwaki family had seven counselors from various groups trying to offer aid. "We need help," one frustrated Meskwaki man told economist Elizabeth Hoyt, "but our helpers need it more."⁶²

By the late 1950s, the State of Iowa had created an "Indian Relief" program that earmarked state funds for general assistance, foster care, education, and other needs for Native people.⁶³ This decision had been inspired by the advocacy of Bonnie Buffalo, a middle-aged Meskwaki widow. Bonnie wrote to Tama County in 1958, asking for support from its general welfare program. Bonnie noted that she struggled to find work due to her "limited skills and work history," and that she and her daughter relied upon ADC support. Her daughter was about to turn eighteen, making them ineligible for the program, and Bonnie was afraid her daughter would drop out of school to support the family.⁶⁴ Rather than denying her outright, Tama County told Bonnie that it believed all counties should share the costs of Native people's welfare, not just that in which tribal members resided. Her request eventually made its way to the BIA. The agency recommended that Native people receive benefits "for which they are eligible on the same basis as non-Indians."⁶⁵

Shortly thereafter, state legislators created the Indian Relief program, which endured for several decades. Like all things, it was vulnerable to the vicissitudes of state politics. In 1961, the legislature slashed the state budget, forcing the BIA to temporarily contract for foster care.⁶⁶ Six years later, a bill funding the construction of a $250,000 Settlement road passed the legislature only to be recalled and killed by a state senator from a district far from Meskwaki land.⁶⁷ The BIA, meanwhile, used the creation of this state program as a reason to end its own general assistance program for the Meskwaki Nation. After that, bureau services were "mainly limited to operating an education program, handling various land transactions, maintaining tribal individual Indian accounts, and processing the tribe's annuity payments."⁶⁸

Facing these challenges, some Red Earth People began looking for on-Settlement economic development opportunities. Several Meskwaki people, for example, sought to capitalize on the long tradition of selling crafts and beadwork to tourists. They were building on a tradition exemplified by the annual powwow and several other efforts at collectivized entrepreneurialism. In the 1930s and 1940s, for example, some tribal members had used federal programs to buy tractors and rent them to Meskwaki farmers, and as early as 1948 some Meskwaki people considered organizing a crafts cooperative that could reduce overhead by purchasing supplies in bulk and working together. They launched this idea in 1955, when a group of Red Earth People partnered with the Fox Project anthropologists to launch a business called Tamacraft. Using grant funds for startup capital, more than a dozen Meskwaki artisans created paint-by-numbers kits, holiday greeting cards, and other crafts.[69]

For a few years, Tamacraft appeared a resounding success, with Meskwaki crafts selling nationwide. In 1961, it grossed over $10,000 in sales—around $102,000 today—for its Meskwaki members.[70] The next year, however, Tamacraft found itself in financial trouble, in part because the Fox Project anthropologists who lent administrative capacity had left the Settlement, and in part because some disagreements began to percolate over who could participate in the program. Meskwaki workers successfully managed the business on their own for several years, but the program lacked the capital it needed to grow and eventually went under.[71]

SHARING POWER

The State of Iowa continued to extend services to the Meskwaki Nation throughout the 1960s. For example, using BIA contract funds, the Iowa Department of Social Welfare supported foster care and other programs for Meskwaki children.[72] Yet a major obstacle remained. The 1948 law and order bill had only related to criminal jurisdiction. This left state and local agencies powerless to assist the tribe in civil cases. These could include anything from noncriminal child neglect to personal or property suits between tribal members, between Natives and non-Natives, or between the Meskwaki Nation and surrounding municipalities. The tribe, meanwhile, had little say in foster care and other social services, which frustrated tribal, state, and federal officials throughout the 1950s and 1960s.[73]

Under a termination-era federal law called Public Law 280 (PL-280), the State of Iowa could have unilaterally extended its civil jurisdiction over the Meskwaki Nation. Although the provision had been modeled in part on the 1948 Meskwaki criminal jurisdiction law, Iowa had never taken advantage of PL-280, primarily because Tama County did not want to pay for civil services and because many Meskwaki people, wary of yet another form of "state control," were initially tepid.[74]

The Meskwaki Nation's attitude had changed by the late 1960s. When the BIA encouraged the state legislature to invoke PL-280 for civil jurisdiction in 1967, the tribe assented.[75] The rapport between the tribe and the state had improved substantially since the 1940s. In addition to offering more services to tribal members, Iowa had so far declined to invoke PL-280 without consulting the tribe. This signaled a willingness to negotiate with tribal leaders and find a cooperative solution. As a result, it seems, Meskwaki leaders had greater faith in the state and its motives. The two entities worked together to make Iowa programs accessible to the tribe.[76]

The bill that authorized the transfer of the Meskwaki Nation into the state's civil jurisdiction was, effectively, a power sharing agreement between the two entities. The document, for example, preserved the tribe's right to settle disputes between its members. The tribe also convinced the state to appoint and pay for "legal council . . . for Indians in matters pertaining to dependency, neglect, delinquency, care or custody of minors."[77] In short, the Meskwaki Nation negotiated to protect its authority over some aspects of Settlement life while making its members eligible for state aid programs. With the agreement in place, the Meskwaki Nation used BIA funds to contract with state agencies for foster care and similar services.[78] That arrangement was a harbinger of a new era in Indigenous political history.

CREATING OPPORTUNITIES

The Meskwaki Nation's ability to contract with Iowa for its services in the late 1960s was emblematic of yet another reorientation of federal Indian policy—this time, toward "self-determination." The termination policy had proven a catastrophe for Indigenous Americans. According to anthropologist George Pierre Castile, however, its consequences went largely unnoticed by the general public. Without a strong push from their constituents, and echoing a pattern that had reverberated across the twentieth century, Congress hesitated to embrace new Indian policies. As a result, Native America looked to the executive branch for policy changes, and there were signs of transition in the 1960s. President John F. Kennedy, for example, appointed a former Arizona senator, Stewart Udall, as secretary of the interior. During Udall's tenure, the BIA tried to fold Indigenous peoples into the "New Frontier" and "Great Society" agendas of the John F. Kennedy and Lyndon B. Johnson presidencies, which attempted to extend the successes of American capitalism to the most poverty-stricken corners of the nation.[79]

In Indian Country, tracking the success of these policies has proven elusive. On one hand, as in the Indian New Deal of the 1930s, Great Society programs buoyed many struggling tribal economies but did not end reservation poverty. On the other, by funneling resources directly to Native communities, many federal programs in the 1960s afforded administrative control to tribes rather than the BIA. This continued to strengthen tribes' abilities to manage their own affairs and lent vital experience navigating the federal bureaucracy—thereby marking the rise of the era of "self-determination."[80]

By the time Richard Nixon became president in 1969, the language of self-determination had already taken root. In a special message to Congress in 1970, Nixon argued that it was "long past time that the Indian policies of the Federal government began to recognize and build upon the capacities and insights of the Indian people" and called for "a new era in which the Indian future is determined by Indian acts and Indian decisions."[81] With Congress's support, the Nixon administration supported some significant changes. These included laws like the Alaska Native Claims Settlement Act of 1971, which sought to resolve decades of outstanding issues for Indigenous peoples in Alaska, and the Menominee Restoration Act, which reversed the termination of the Menominee Tribe of Wisconsin.[82]

Yet the turn toward self-determination was a slow and complicated process for Native America. By the end of Nixon's presidency, tensions surrounding militant Indigenous activism—which highlighted Native peoples' ongoing dissatisfaction with many aspects of their situation—and the brewing Watergate scandal mired much of Nixon's agenda in gridlock. Facing steep political challenges, the Nixon administration chose to focus on executive policy changes rather than legislative reforms for Indian affairs.[83] Such reforms would not take place until 1975, when President Gerald Ford signed the Indian Self Determination and Education Assistance Act. This legislation expanded tribes' abilities to administer programs via federal contracts and is often viewed as a major turning point in formalizing the Indigenous self-determination policy.[84]

BUILDING CAPACITY

The Meskwaki Nation, like other tribes, had been creating opportunities for self-determination long before the federal government changed its approach. The tribe had staved off termination in 1953, maintaining its eligibility for federal support—however minimal. Three years later, a BIA memo reported that the Meskwaki tribal council had reasserted "full responsibility" for managing leases and assignments of Settlement land and managing treaty annuities, tribal finances, operations, and elections. Since about the 1930s, the tribe had been incrementally rebuilding its capacity for self-determination. This enabled the Red Earth People to fill the void left by the diminishment of federal support in the 1950s, and the tribe focused its energies on state-level issues into the 1960s.[85]

The Meskwaki Nation, of course, never stopped dealing with the BIA, and Meskwaki leaders seized the opportunity to reengage with federal affairs after LBJ signed a law creating the Office of Economic Opportunity (OEO) in 1964. This agency was tasked with proctoring the "War on Poverty," which became the centerpiece of the Great Society. The OEO housed well-known programs like the Job Corps, Head Start, and Volunteers in Service to America (VISTA), many of which operated (and still exist) in Indigenous communities.[86] Importantly, OEO programs emphasized what the agency called "maximum feasible participation" by community members, and, as Charles Wilkinson points out, for the first time ever—and in contrast to the New Deal—tribal governments could receive direct federal grants without having them funneled through the BIA.[87] Although most OEO programs had not been created with Native communities in mind,

Native peoples worked within them, experimenting with ways to secure federal funds to support tribal initiatives. In this way, the OEO became a laboratory for self-determination.[88]

Like other tribes, the Meskwaki Nation spent much of the 1960s utilizing Great Society programs to build capacity, provide services to the Red Earth People, and continue strengthening its control over tribal governance. There were missteps along the way. A BIA review in 1964, for example, found that the tribe's financial records had not been maintained in keeping with federal standards. This nearly disqualified the Meskwaki Nation from certain programs. In response, the tribal council hired an accounting firm to conduct an internal audit and devise a more effective bookkeeping system.[89] Two years later, a backlog of tribal business built up after a political spat denied several council meetings a quorum. The council eventually got back to business and set about applying for grant funds to support its operations as well as community welfare and improvement projects.[90]

The Meskwaki Nation exercised its sovereignty in other ways. It conducted diplomacy with other Native Nations, including the Passamaquoddy Tribe, a delegation from which Meskwaki leaders hosted on the Settlement in early 1969. The Passamaquoddy representatives were part of a federally unrecognized tribe in Maine who were preparing to launch a major land claim. Within eleven years, the Passamaquoddy Tribe would achieve federal recognition and receive sizable restitution for lost property. In the sixties, however, Passamaquoddy and Meskwaki leaders simply believed that their Nations shared "common problems and goals," as one BIA report read, and wanted to learn from similar experiences. The next summer, Passamaquoddy leaders reciprocated the offer, inviting Meskwaki leaders to their homeland for a follow-up meeting.[91]

The tribe also provided oversight for federal activities on Meskwaki land. In October 1969, the council authorized the BIA to negotiate with a white man who wanted to salvage fallen walnut trees on the Settlement. The tribe retained the final approval over this contract.[92] That same year, the council rejected a Public Health Service scientist's request to conduct a house-to-house survey of Meskwaki people's sanitary practices. The Red Earth People had participated in a similar study once before but found it too intrusive, so the council turned it down.[93]

In keeping with President Nixon's "special message," by the end of 1970, the Minneapolis Area Office that oversaw the Settlement described its mission as being focused on "Indian self-sufficiency through self-determination."[94] But the Meskwaki Nation was already involved in various expressions of sovereignty and self-determination. Unlike the termination era, in which tribal self-sufficiency was a rationale for reducing federal support, under the new policy framework, the BIA remained involved in assisting the tribe as it worked through numerous issues. In the 1960s and early 1970s, the Meskwaki Nation focused on reducing its unemployment rate and increasing the standard of living for the Red Earth People.[95]

INVESTING IN PEOPLE AND PROPERTY

In the early 1960s, it became clear that the Red Earth People's experiment with off-Settlement wage work had failed. The tribal economy was worse than it had been during the depths of the Great Depression. Around half of the tribe was unemployed. The BIA offered assistance where it could and, in 1961, used an industrial development initiative to get around fifty tribal members seasonal jobs at a broom company in nearby Waterloo and a door and window factory in Tama.[96] As the OEO expanded programs a few years later, it focused less on opening up short-term jobs and more on tackling structural problems like low educational attainment and addiction. It provided a VISTA worker to help community members apply for jobs, coordinate educational programming, and make referrals for counseling services.[97] Federal scholarships expanded access to higher education for a handful of Meskwaki students.[98] Challenges, however, remained entrenched.

Tribal members continued to cobble together a living from state and federal assistance programs, the powwow, gardening, and the sale of arts and crafts.[99] By 1967, the combined efforts of state and federal programs—and the Red Earth People's participation in them—had driven the unemployment rate down to around 20 percent, and most Meskwaki families had an automobile and a television set. These consumer comforts highlighted the improvement of the Meskwaki economy. The tribe's unemployment rate, meanwhile, was about half that of the average across Native Nations. It nonetheless remained frustratingly higher than the 4 percent average enjoyed by the rest of the United States. And most Meskwaki families depended heavily on state and federal assistance to make ends meet.[100]

Out of necessity, the tribe refined its ability to capture federal grants and invest them in the Settlement. Many of the roads and buildings on the Settlement had suffered from nearly forty years of minimal and sporadic management. Federal grants had improved some housing and sanitation, but only the school received regular maintenance. By the late 1960s, most Meskwaki houses were modest but had at least some electric service, and most were heated by woodstoves. Most had wells close by, although six families had to carry their water more than a mile.[101] Meskwaki leaders created a Tribal Housing Authority (THA) in 1967, which used BIA grants to build eight more houses, which received water and sewage services through the Public Health Service. The THA managed and rented these homes to Meskwaki families.[102] A few years later, the tribe assumed control over water and sewage management after a federal project helped revamp the Settlement's wastewater system.[103]

The tribal council also created a community development fund filled primarily from federal grants.[104] Tribal members could make project recommendations, and the tribe renovated the toilets on the powwow grounds, repaired roads and fences on the Settlement, restored the cemetery, and salvaged materials from dilapidated buildings. The fund even helped the tribe buy office supplies and recreational equipment for Meskwaki children.[105]

In the 1960s, the Meskwaki Nation also settled outstanding legal claims against the federal government. For decades, tribal members like the elder Young Bear had been arguing that the Meskwaki Nation had not received a fair share of the annuity payments from the series of nineteenth-century treaties that sold off vast tracts of Sauk and Meskwaki territory. Such claims were not unusual, and after Congress created the Indian Claims Commission (ICC) in the 1940s, the body began adjudicating Native land claims. The ICC settled hundreds of suits between then and its closure in 1978, although some cases continued after that time. Although it resolved some cases, the ICC faced heavy criticisms for being inefficient and only partially compensating tribes for dispossessed property, and for the commission's ability to deny claims outright.[106]

The Meskwaki Nation's claims dealt with the US government's early insistence that removal treaties with the Sauk and Meskwaki Nations be negotiated with the combined "Sac & Fox Tribe." For this reason, the Meskwaki Nation had to file its ICC claims in conjunction with the two other federally recognized Sauk and Meskwaki tribes: the Sac and Fox Nation of Oklahoma and the Sac and Fox Nation of the Missouri in Kansas and Nebraska.[107] In the 1950s, the tribes hired a Chicago-based law firm, which filed twelve ICC petitions on behalf of all three tribes. When these cases were finally settled years later, the three Nations split the restitution based on the size of each community and its stake in specific parcels of ceded land.[108]

The Meskwaki Nation's use of one such claim was indicative of the tribe's deep interest in providing for its people in an era of need and improving the Settlement in the context of self-determination. Congress paid out two of the ICC cases in 1967. The Meskwaki Nation received 36.91 percent of the reimbursement, while the Sac and Fox Tribes of Oklahoma, Kansas, and Nebraska received 51.7 and 11.39 percent, respectively.[109] The Meskwaki tribal council divvied up 40 percent of its share, making a modest per capita payment to every tribal member. The tribe then put the remaining $85,000—or just over $750,000 today—in the community development fund. Over the next few years, the tribe would devote over 70 percent of those funds to infrastructure projects like repairing fences, building and remodeling houses, and purchasing heavy equipment for road maintenance. The remainder went to a tribal death benefits program, educational grants, and other expenses.[110]

After escaping termination, the Meskwaki Nation spent two decades expanding its capacity for self-determination. It strengthened its rapport with the state government and took advantage of numerous state and federal programs while the US government slowly turned its focus toward supporting, rather than abandoning, the nation-to-nation relationship between tribes and the United States. Meskwaki sovereignty, to be sure, remained constrained by the interweaving of local, state, federal, and tribal relations. The Red Earth People lived amid an improving, but still weak, economy. But, building on lessons learned during and since the Indian New Deal, the tribe harnessed new opportunities to reclaim its authority over local decision-making. In the 1950s and 1960s, the Meskwaki Nation negotiated for access to vital assistance programs and invested in the Red Earth

People and their Settlement. Literally and figuratively, these steps laid the groundwork for coming efforts to reinvest in the on-Settlement economy.

None of these achievements came easily, and the strengthening of Meskwaki self-determination and the tribal economy faced many obstacles. Broader social and political acrimony in the late 1960s and 1970s tested the limits of local, state, and tribal cooperation. At the same moment that the Meskwaki Nation was undergoing a revitalization of its rights to sovereignty, new challenges exposed the lingering vulnerabilities of Meskwaki sovereignty at the dawn of the age of self-determination.

ONE FROZEN SQUIRREL

A single gunshot cracked through the Settlement forest on September 8, 1968. It killed a squirrel. After collecting his game, a Meskwaki hunter named Orrie Lasley encountered a state conservation officer. The state small game season did not begin until September 15, so the ranger arrested Lasley and charged him with "violating the laws of the state of Iowa by unlawfully having in his possession one squirrel in closed season."[111] Local newspapers covered "the squirrel case," as it came to be known, with an intensity reserved only for the most salacious of small-town scandals.

Lasley's two-hour trial took place in a courtroom "filled to overflowing, with many citizens," more than half of whom were Meskwaki, "lining the walls." Lasley did not deny slaying the squirrel. Quite the opposite, he froze the rodent and toted it to trial as evidence. There, Lasley's attorney argued that the hunt was not illegal, for several reasons. First, the lawyer cited the 1804 Sauk and Meskwaki removal treaty, Article 7 of which stated that "as long as the lands which are now ceded to the United States remain their property," members of the Sauk and Meskwaki Nations "shall enjoy the privilege of living and hunting upon them."[112] Later removal treaties had taken Iowa out of Meskwaki ownership, and the last of them—the 1842 treaty—did not mention hunting at all. But, Lasley's defense argued, when the tribe had purchased the Settlement, the land had become tribal property once again, thereby reinstating Meskwaki hunting rights. The defense also used local precedent to bolster its case. Tribal members, after all, had been freely hunting on the Settlement for generations, and, even though few relied on hunting for subsistence as their elders had, they retained rights, in law and practice, to hunt tribal land at will.[113]

In the end, it was the defense's third argument, focused on a technicality, that spared Orrie Lasley. Citing the Iowa legal code, Lasley's attorney argued that, at the time of the hunt, the state conservation commission had not yet announced the official dates of the small game season, so Lasley had not actually violated the law. The court agreed and found Lasley innocent.[114]

The county attorney quickly refiled the case. He admitted that "the squirrel does not seem to be worth a court fight" but argued that "a point of law must be decided."[115] At a second trial in late November, Lasley was again acquitted on technicalities. But that case also failed to answer the state's questions about the applicability of game laws on the Settlement. Although the county attorney decided to retire rather than launch a third prosecution, his questions about the applicability of state game laws to the Meskwaki Nation lived on.[116]

That the fate of a frozen rodent garnered so much attention was emblematic of the fever pitch that tensions between Native and non-Native Americans, particularly in border towns like Tama, had reached in the late 1960s and early 1970s. Across the country, Indigenous activists ardently decried more than a century of maltreatment at the hands of the federal government. The Indians of All Tribes famously occupied Alcatraz Island from late 1969 to the summer of 1971. The American Indian Movement (AIM) briefly took over the BIA headquarters in Washington, DC, in 1972, and the next year they faced down law enforcement during a long siege at Wounded Knee, South Dakota. Native activism drew widespread attention during this time and attracted celebrity support. Other Indigenous Americans, some affiliated with activist organizations and others acting on their own, held "fish-in" protests, in which they intentionally violated state game laws to raise awareness of treaty-based hunting and fishing rights. Natural resources had become both a symbolic and pragmatic issue around which Native communities from across the nation would continue to rally for decades.[117]

Tensions flared on and near the Meskwaki Settlement. Racially motivated late-night brawls often broke out in Tama bars. The county had made numerous attempts to ban Native people from drinking alcohol since the 1950s. At one point it had even tried banning Meskwaki people from local taverns. That provision "died a quick, quiet death" after both tribal members and local whites decried it as discriminatory, and Iowa repealed an old state ban on selling liquor to Native people in 1967.[118]

Racial violence flared in the summer of 1973, when a group of whites severely beat three Native men with baseball bats until they were left, bleeding and unconscious, outside a downtown Tama watering hole. Only one assailant was convicted. He spent two years in prison for assault. A month later, a Meskwaki man killed a white man in an altercation and was imprisoned for second-degree murder. Although AIM never had a strong presence on the Meskwaki Settlement, a few tribal members had ties to the organization, and, amid the chaos in 1973, a group of AIM activists came to town and pressured law enforcement to prosecute the other men involved in the earlier assault on the three Meskwaki men. In response, the city council closed local bars and suspended liquor sales until the activists left town.[119]

Confrontations in and over the schools also tested the limits of Tama County's fragile race relations. Despite the tribe's continued overtures to keep the Settlement day school open, the BIA had substantially reduced its budget by the late 1960s.[120] In 1968, the BIA decided to close the Settlement school for good. As they had in 1953, Meskwaki parents organized a resistance campaign, reaching out to white allies across Iowa for support. The tribal council filed a federal lawsuit to keep the school open, and two Meskwaki leaders testified before Congress. The tribe, meanwhile, began developing plans for a tribally run bilingual school.[121]

The controversy led to tense meetings between the tribal council and the BIA. In one oft-repeated episode, a frustrated BIA official allegedly told a group of Red Earth People that he could "terminate you guys right now! I can terminate this school!" A tribal member, the story goes, responded that "only the Manitou," or spirit being "that created us can terminate us." The agent died in a plane crash shortly after takeoff on his return flight to Minnesota. Many tribal members took the event as a sign of "divine intervention" in defense of their school.[122]

The courts eventually reopened the Meskwaki school. The BIA continued to contract teachers and administrators from Tama. The new teachers, however, were ill-equipped to teach Native culture or history and did not offer any cultural programming, which furthered the rift. In 1975, Meskwaki high school students, complaining of bullying by teachers and students, staged a walkout. The incident received extensive media attention, and the protest led to the creation of a Native American club, some cultural trainings for white teachers, and the hiring of several Meskwaki teachers' aides.[123]

In the context of the activism and tension of the time, Orrie Lasley's "squirrel case," along with other game cases, reflected the ongoing disputes about authority over the Meskwaki Settlement. In a context of local and national debate over treaty rights, state conservation officers continued to arrest tribal members for game-related infractions after the squirrel case. By 1974, members of the Meskwaki Nation had raised the issue with the Native American Rights Fund (NARF), a recently founded Colorado-based public interest law firm that specialized in Indigenous issues. NARF quickly filed a federal lawsuit. Hoping to clear up the issue, the next year the United States also requested that a federal judge in Cedar Rapids allow members of the Meskwaki community to hunt on the Settlement without state licenses.[124]

The district court at Cedar Rapids ultimately consolidated the two suits into a single case called *Sac and Fox Tribe of the Mississippi in Iowa v. Licklider*. The tribe and the federal government were co-plaintiffs against Les Licklider, chairman of the state conservation commission, and other officials. The Meskwaki Nation and the United States argued that the Settlement was a reservation, and therefore immune to state game laws, and that the 1842 treaty implicitly protected tribal game rights. Iowa, on the other hand, argued that the 1842 treaty did not specifically address hunting and fishing, that the tribe had violated the treaty by failing to leave Iowa in the 1840s and 1850s, and that the law and order bill enacted in 1948 had left all state crimes committed by members of the Meskwaki community under Iowa's purview. The court agreed with the state and, in November 1976, declared the tribe subject to state conservation laws. In 1978, the decision was affirmed on appeal.[125]

The Meskwaki Nation lost *Sac and Fox v. Licklider*. The case, however, illuminates the many transitions in the relationship between the Meskwaki Nation, the federal government, and the State of Iowa that had occurred over the course of more than a century. In the nineteenth century, the United States systematically dispossessed the Meskwaki Nation and its Sauk allies and refused to view the two tribes as separate from one another. It chased the Red Earth People across their homeland. It attempted to deport them to the Osage River reservation. When that failed, the United States refused to recognize Meskwaki sovereignty for a decade. In the generations that followed, federal agents used every tool in their considerable arsenal to undercut Meskwaki authority and control tribal land and lives.

For its part, the State of Iowa had once helped facilitate the Meskwaki Nation's desire to resettle on their old homeland within its boundaries. It supported the tribe when the Red Earth People pitted their land's unusual legal status against federal incursions in the nineteenth century. After Iowa stopped supporting the tribe in this way, the federal government slowly ground down Meskwaki political power in the early twentieth century and nearly extinguished the tribe in the termination era. In the late 1960s and 1970s—the same era in which both the state and federal government were offering unprecedented programmatic support to the Red Earth People— the United States was an ally in the Meskwaki Nation's fight to defend its game rights against Iowa's assertion of jurisdiction on tribal land.

This new configuration illustrated the amorphous and constant realignment of political alliances between the tribe and the state and federal governments that surrounded it. Yet *Sac and Fox v. Licklider* also represented a final step in the decades-long transformation in the ways in which the Red Earth People deployed the Settlement toward political ends. In the nineteenth century, the Settlement's anomalous history and legal status had protected the tribe from various allotment and assimilation programs. A few decades later, Meskwaki elders argued that the Settlement could not be subject to federal policies such as the Indian Reorganization Act. Faced with new federal programs that invested in Settlement land and provided necessary relief to their families, many Red Earth People began to argue that the federal trust responsibility applied to their property. All this while shrewdly navigating local, state, and federal politics; selectively embracing federal, state, and local programs; and negotiating terms that protected tribal sovereignty *and* increased access to beneficial state and federal services.

Then, faced with a battle over treaty-based hunting and fishing rights in the late 1970s, the Meskwaki Nation teamed up with its longtime political rival, the United States, in a lawsuit against the tribe's on-again, off-again ally, the State of Iowa. There, in a stark turnaround from the rhetoric of the early twentieth century, the Meskwaki Nation argued explicitly that the Settlement was both a privately owned tribal commune *and* an Indian reservation, subject to federal jurisdictional protections like any other.

Epilogue
Recovery

> This land base could well provide the basis not only for training and employing our people, but developing the basis for our own econom[y].
>
> —Meskwaki Tribal Council, 1978

On a blistering summer day, humidity pulsed from the lush and leafy trees lining Meskwaki Road. In the passenger seat sat Johnathan Buffalo, the Meskwaki Nation's tribal historic preservation officer. One arm rested casually on the window, and his ponytail drooped over a gray cardigan while keys dangled from his signature beaded lanyard. As we roamed the Settlement in the summer of 2014, Buffalo told me how the place had changed in his sixty years. Was the landscape different from when he was a child? "Yes and no," Buffalo replied. "The roads are better. They were smaller and more dirt-like" when he was young. This, the Settlement's main thoroughfare, had been paved for the first time only months before. "Basically, the land looks the same" as it did a half century ago, even if some houses were, as he said, "a little bit better."[1]

Buffalo had noticed, however, that his community's activity "[had] gradually been moving up hill." The Settlement's southern edge—the watery lowlands on the banks of the Iowa River near the powwow grounds—had hosted the Meskwaki central village a century ago. Many families have remained just above the floodplain, where their ancestors first settled after the 1901 smallpox outbreak. But eventually the bustle of daily business crept about a half mile north toward an area that, by the 1930s, contained a general store, the meeting place of the Meskwaki tribal council, and a small cluster of houses perched along the iron railroad tracks that bisect the Settlement. At midcentury, living in the Settlement's northern portion posed many challenges. Even though the increase in elevation from the river bottom to the Settlement's apex is less than 300 feet, it took time for running water and other amenities to make the climb. Yet as the Meskwaki population grew and infrastructure improved, more community members settled higher up on the Settlement, near Highway 30, which connects the cities of Ames, to the west, and Cedar Rapids, to the east.[2]

As my car neared the center of the Meskwaki community, Buffalo pointed to the brick and asphalt complex that I visited regularly during my explorations into the Meskwaki past. Built in the 1970s, it housed the Meskwaki tribal center, where the council met and tribal administrative offices were located, and the seniors' center, which was next door to Buffalo's office at the Meskwaki Historic Preservation Office, which included a small library and museum. The tribal courthouse sat about fifty yards away, right next to economic development and other divisions of the Meskwaki government. Together, these buildings formed a half-moon nestled against a woody hillside.

A green space flying the American and Meskwaki flags welcomed visitors to the sovereign Meskwaki Nation. "You gotta think of this as our capital," Buffalo said. "Wherever the capital is, [that's] where the [community's] main activity is ... political, cultural, not necessarily religious, but the political activity, the gravity of that changes" over the years. It had once been in the village by the river, and it had slowly migrated north. As we drove, the tribe was pondering whether to build a new tribal center even farther north, next to the Meskwaki Bingo Casino Hotel (MBCH), a dazzling recreational complex on Highway 30. If that happened, Buffalo predicted, most activity would move again, this time to the highway and near the school at the Settlement's summit.[3]

In the decade since we made that drive, the tribe has not yet made that change. No matter. That plan was just one of many dramatic changes the Meskwaki Nation had undergone over the last fifty years.

COMING HOME

The Meskwaki economy continued to struggle throughout the 1970s. Despite their efforts to reduce unemployment and invest in the Settlement, the Red Earth People earned only a little over two-thirds of the average income in Tama County. In 1978, more than half of Meskwaki houses lacked plumbing and barely 70 percent had access to a telephone. Nearly a third of the Red Earth People were unemployed, and only six of the roughly six hundred Meskwaki living on or near the Settlement made more than $10,000 per year. The tribal council had tried for years to build a self-sustainable economy on the Settlement. But these efforts were, in the council's own words, "constrained by lack of funding and the fractionalized nature of government programming."[4]

By the middle of the 1970s, the United States' postwar economic boom had peaked, and stagflation began to set in. An agricultural boom kept Iowa's economy in relatively good health.[5]

Iowa's prosperity, however, still did not extend to the Settlement. The Meskwaki Nation tried to rectify what it called the considerable irony of their predicament: that despite the relative prosperity and "bright future" projected for the rest of Iowa, "the [Meskwaki] people have not been a part of [the state's] growth and development."[6]

In September 1978, the council submitted a comprehensive plan to the Economic Development Administration (EDA) central office in Denver, Colorado. Aware that off-Settlement wage work had not brought prosperity to its people, the tribe drew upon lessons gleaned over the course of more than forty years. As the tribal council told the EDA, it wanted to "take advantage of our natural resources and human potential," but do so in a way "that [ensured] our culture [would] grow and flourish."[7]

To do so, the plan sought to contract with federal agencies to take over tribal services and repair Settlement infrastructure. The tribe hoped to use EDA and BIA funds to build forty new homes, a new school serving kindergarten through eighth grade, and a "core administrative unit" that would provide offices for a variety of tribal departments. The council also wanted to extend plumbing to every home on the Settlement and revamp the sewage disposal and treatment system that ran beneath tribal land.[8]

EPILOGUE   231

With these updates underway, the Meskwaki Nation would incentivize tribal members to reengage in an on-Settlement economy. The tribe wanted to maximize timber production in its forests and start a large-scale agribusiness enterprise on 1,400 acres of Meskwaki farmland. Non-arable land, the council believed, could be used to build "shops, services, or light industry," some of which could focus on tribal crafts like leatherwork, painting, and beadwork, from which the community could draw revenue. These changes, the council argued, would fundamentally restructure the Meskwaki economy. Their plan was to invest in the "human potential" of the Meskwaki Nation by administering its own programs and educating its people. The Red Earth People could finally trade long commutes to low-wage jobs for education, training, and economic development at home. This could deliver prosperity to the Settlement on Meskwaki terms.[9]

In a poignant passage, the tribal council declared that "we do not wish to see our resources exploited by those who do not understand what the land means to us; nor do we wish others to exploit our people to the point where our Tribe becomes part of a historical yesterday." The council expressed a collective belief that "this land base"—the Meskwaki Settlement—"could well provide the basis not only for training and employing our people, but developing the basis for our own econom[y]."[10]

The document reads with the spirit of pragmatic optimism with which the Meskwaki Nation, like many Native communities, faced the early years of self-determination. But with limited capital and a persistently high unemployment rate, the tribe had few resources with which to launch its plan.[11] After slow federally subsidized growth in the mid-1980s, one endeavor finally caught on: the Meskwaki Nation started a small-scale bingo hall in a converted gymnasium. As this endeavor grew, the tribe hired a management firm to run a 500-slot casino a few years later. Gaming revenue leaped from about $1.4 million to some $30 million by 1993. The tribe added a hotel, a spa, and several eateries and expanded its gaming floor in 1998.[12] By 2005, the MBCH was pulling in $135 million annually for the Meskwaki Nation.[13]

The development of the MBCH mirrored the national rise of tribal gaming at the end of the twentieth century. In 1979, the Seminole Tribe of Florida established a bingo hall on some of its property, it set a precedent that would reshape tribal economies throughout the United States. Over the next few years, many Native Nations, like the Meskwaki Nation, followed suit. Although only a small number of tribal casinos returned profits, Native gaming quickly garnered the attention of local and state governments. Various states sued Native Nations in the 1980s, claiming that tribes could not maintain casinos that were not permitted under state law. Tribes, on the other hand, reminded states that the very treaties that had taken Native homelands had preserved their sovereign rights to conduct business on tribal land outside state law.[14]

In February 1987, the US Supreme Court handed down a decision that protected the rights of two bands of California's Mission Indians to operate high-stakes casinos on their land. While this decision preserved Native gaming rights, the federal government still faced relentless pressure from states to regulate tribal casinos. In response, Congress crafted the Indian Gaming Regulatory Act (IGRA), which became law in 1988. Governed by IGRA, the National Indian Gaming Commission (NIGC) regulates tribal casinos.[15] The MBCH offers high-stakes slot machines, roulette, blackjack, and similar games of chance along with a bingo hall, restaurants, and hospitality services.

Under IGRA, the tribe must negotiate a gaming compact with the state, and unlike some agreements, the Meskwaki compact does not give Iowa a cut of Meskwaki gaming revenues. Completed in 1992 and updated in 2004, the document simply requires the Meskwaki Nation to repay the state for the cost of oversight and regulation of MBCH operations.[16] The same logic that the tribe deployed in *Sac and Fox v. Licklider*—that the privately purchased Meskwaki Settlement is an Indian reservation for the purposes of securing the federal trust responsibility—enabled the tribe to open its casino. IGRA created the mechanism through which the tribe could negotiate a lucrative compact on a sovereign-to-sovereign basis with the State of Iowa. Together, these developments created the business opportunities that allowed the Meskwaki Nation to enact a version of its 1978 economic development plan and invest heavily in a Settlement-based economy.

The rise of Indigenous gaming, both on the Meskwaki Settlement and nationally, proved a major break from long-established patterns throughout Indian Country. For a small number of Native Nations, gaming brought enormous wealth. For most, however, it created new opportunities for capacity building and established a handful of jobs in economically strapped communities struggling with deep socioeconomic disadvantages. In recent years, "sovereignty" has "take[n] material form and [been] built with material resources," and in many parts of Indian Country the assets and opportunities introduced in the casino era slowly became sources for the replenishment of tribal sovereignty.[17]

In the Meskwaki Nation, a direct line runs through the tribe's patient and strategic negotiation of its land ownership from the 1850s to the establishment of the tribal casino more than a century later. As this line squiggles and scrawls, it reflects both prescient choices and the wild contingencies of history. Had, for example, the Meskwaki Settlement not been transferred into federal trust in 1896 (a move many Red Earth People opposed at the time) or the tribe not embraced the federal trust responsibility in the termination era (which the federal government tried to erase), the Settlement may not have been eligible for the establishment of Meskwaki gaming enterprises in the 1980s and 1990s. Historians generally avoid such counterfactuals, but, in this case, Meskwaki history stands as a reminder of the long shadows cast as Indigenous peoples and other stakeholders make decisions about Native land.

MESKWAKI SOVEREIGNTY IN THE CASINO ERA

In the mid-2000s, an anthropologist named Douglas Foley, who had grown up near the Settlement and had written a book on race relations in Tama County during his youth, returned home. He described the impact of economic development on the Settlement. The tribe, for example, made per capita payments, or "per caps," to enrolled members based on its revenues. For the first time in centuries, tribal members have a steady income comparable to that of neighboring communities, especially when they combine it with full-time work, either on or off the Settlement.[18] The casino has also created jobs. By the early 2000s, the MBCH was, at 1,250 workers, Tama County's largest employer.[19]

After five years of planning, the tribe also formed Meskwaki Inc., in 2011. Modeled after other tribal holdings companies, Meskwaki Inc. is tasked with diversifying the tribe's business portfolio and, according to its website, the company's "mission is to use the Tribe's various economic and legal advantages to develop and operate successful tribally-owned business enterprises; to provide meaningful jobs and opportunities for Tribal Citizens; and, to provide the Tribe with an adequate income stream from its business operations so the Tribe may reach total economic self-sufficiency." Meskwaki Inc. operates six businesses in the transportation, manufacturing, energy, pest management, and government services sectors. The tribe also bought the Pinnacle Bank in nearby Marshalltown to better control its finances.[20]

Despite its many achievements, the Meskwaki Nation still faces many challenges. Along with bringing wealth, greater sovereign power, and an increased capacity for self-determination, gaming revenues have fomented discord both within the Meskwaki community and between the tribe and local residents. According to Foley, some tribal members worried that sudden wealth could disincentivize education and work, exacerbate substance abuse and other social ills, or erode engagement in customs and traditions.[21] Money has also inflamed questions over tribal enrollment and membership, and the community has wrestled with who can be enrolled, and how best and to whom to distribute the tribe's wealth.[22]

The Red Earth People's success also earned mixed reviews in Tama County. The tribe's businesses created many local jobs in a rural area hamstrung by deindustrialization and farm crises over the last few decades.[23] Yet the MBCH became a recreational hub for area residents, and the tribe has contributed to various charitable causes in and around Tama County.[24] Locals, however, also harbor some frustration. Foley, for example, noted that many non-Natives seemed offput at the idea that, by opening a casino, the tribe would be profiting off their vices.[25] Others complained that the tribe gets "special rights" in the form of tax breaks and unfair economic advantages.[26] This rhetoric has roots that extend back, at least, to the era of Native American activism that took off after World War II. In border town communities across Indian Country, non-Native—and often politically conservative—groups have framed Indigenous treaty rights, and all that flows from them, as unfair advantages for Native Americans.[27]

Backlash politics of this kind have also led to the perpetuation of common misconceptions, like the assumption that tribal members—on the Settlement and elsewhere—do not pay any taxes.[28] This fails to recognize that because the Meskwaki Nation owns its businesses as a sovereign government, not just a private corporation, 100 percent of its revenues are, in a sense, taxed by the tribe at the front end. The tribe distributes the remainder as per caps only *after* money has been taken out to fund health care, public works, and other governmental services.[29] Meanwhile, Meskwaki people are subject to federal income taxes, and only the income from per caps and on-Settlement jobs are exempt from state taxes.[30]

Another complaint—which has been used more frequently and across the nation in the era of Landback—some locals argue that when the tribe buys land and places it in trust, this deprives the county of tax revenue.[31] The Meskwaki Nation paid Iowa property taxes for 119 years. In 1976, a US Supreme Court case out of Minnesota found that states could not levy taxes on tribally owned federal trust land. Since then, the Settlement has been exempt from most property taxes.[32] In 2010, the Tama County Board of Supervisors tried to prevent a 257-acre Meskwaki purchase from being placed in federal trust. The tribe responded by pointing out that tax releases for trust land make up "a small percentage of all such exemptions in Tama County." Tribal land, it continued, was only one of fifteen categories for property tax exemption, and the money lost from the acreage in question amounted to only ".00000944%" of the county's overall tax revenue. Finally, the tribe noted that it had contributed some $80,000 to Tama County for a variety of services like waste removal and fire and ambulance services, which offset the cost. The county eventually backed down, and the BIA authorized the transfer.[33]

Despite these challenges, the Meskwaki Nation has used its business ventures to fund the recovery of the Red Earth People, strengthen Meskwaki sovereignty, and create numerous opportunities for self-determination. The tribe has more than doubled the size of the Settlement since the 1980s, increasing it to some 8,600 acres. It has invested heavily in housing, education, and health care. After purchasing a large tract of land on the north side of Highway 30, the tribe expanded its housing program. Members can apply for a tribally subsidized house and driveway. Even the largest two-floor homes maintain a modest aesthetic designed to discourage competition over the grandeur of Meskwaki houses.[34] Land assignments are not organized into cookie-cutter neighborhoods and continue to be spread out along major roads like Red Earth Drive. Families, as Buffalo told me, still informally demarcate their land: where a Meskwaki family stops mowing the lawn is roughly where their parcel ends.[35]

The 1978 plan would have maximized usage of every available natural resource, but the casino took pressure off the Settlement landscape. By 2015, around 70 percent of the Settlement was open space for people and wildlife to use as they wished. It was, as one tribal employee told me, "a very serene place geographically" that consisted of wetlands, grasslands, and forests."[36] The tribe no longer leased farmland to any non-Natives and had only one agricultural lease with a Meskwaki farmer. More than 300 acres of formerly leased land contained a pheasant sanctuary under a US Department of Agriculture conservation reserve program.[37]

The Settlement, meanwhile, is no longer the only piece of the Iowa homeland under Meskwaki ownership. An elderly non-Native couple donated a 775-acre parcel of land to the tribe in 1990. The couple wanted to donate the land—located about 160 miles northwest of the Settlement, near the town of West Bend—to Iowa as a hunting-free nature preserve. When the state refused their terms, the couple gifted it to the tribe, which has "lightly managed" the property in Palo Alto County ever since.[38]

The tribe also has several departments that make sure the community is as livable, navigable, and connected to the outside world as possible. Public Works maintains roads, buildings, and waterways while the Housing Authority keeps Meskwaki homes available and comfortable. In spring 2012, the tribe launched a million-dollar broadband-fiber project to bring high-speed internet to the nearly two hundred homes on the Settlement as well as tribal government facilities.[39]

The Meskwaki Natural Resources office also introduced a small herd of about twenty bison on the South Farm, the acreage that the tribe formerly leased to whites to fund its property taxes. Though the tribe maintains these animals primarily for cultural purposes, it periodically distributes meat to Settlement families.[92] Since 2011, AmeriCorps VISTAs have partnered with the Meskwaki Food Sovereignty Initiative (MFSI), a community gardening project that sought to "provide those conditions and resources, on a continual basis, that allow the Meskwaki to survive as a viable people and culture."[93] The MFSI began by planting several gardens to supply fresh produce to Meskwaki families. It sold surplus yields to the casino's restaurants. The project also promoted healthy eating and offered sustainable gardening classes.[40] In 2013, the MFSI created the Red Earth Gardens, which, according to the tribe's website, is "a 40-acre self-sustaining farm," and "in 2022 the tribe began growing and harvesting CBD grade hemp through its new production/manufacturing corporation."[41]

Meskwaki children can now receive their entire K–12 education in a school the tribe built on the Settlement in 2001 and expanded in 2009. Education disputes with the BIA and Tama County continued into the 1990s, leading the tribe to invest federal funding and significant portions of its revenues on education. Aside from educating Meskwaki students on tribal land, they have created a curriculum that reinforces community values, and the school offers a pre-K Meskwaki language immersion program and offers language training to children and adults.[42]

The State of Iowa also became the first state to pass a law protecting Native remains, in 1976, after a Dakota woman living in Iowa, Maria Pearson, pushed Iowa to address problems with the state's handling of Indigenous burial sites. Her efforts were precursors to the development of the Native American Graves Protection and Repatriation Act of 1990 (NAGPRA), which protects Native remains across the United States.[43] Since then, the Meskwaki Nation has cultivated a positive relationship with Iowa's Office of the State Archaeologist and the State Historical Society. State archaeologists consult with the Tribal Historic Preservation Department on myriad aspects of NAGPRA compliance. Cultural resources specialists work with the tribe to preserve many of the Meskwaki artifacts obtained by Edgar Harlan in the early twentieth century. One signal of the amicable relationship between the Meskwaki Nation and state cultural offices came in 2015, when the State Historical Society returned the bear claw necklace that had been sold by Sam Slick in 1931.[44]

Both the 1976 burials act and the exemption of the Meskwaki Nation from state property taxes arrived while the Meskwaki Nation and the United States were suing Iowa for the tribe's rights to regulate hunting and fishing on sovereign land. Following *Sac and Fox v. Licklider*, the state retained jurisdiction over these issues. In the late 1990s, empowered by the restoration of its economic might and the enhanced political influence it supports, the Meskwaki Nation negotiated an agreement with the Iowa Department of Natural Resources returning jurisdiction over hunting and fishing on the Settlement to the tribe. In 2002, the Meskwaki Nation assumed authority over hunting and fishing on tribal land as long as it agreed to craft regulations that complied with federal conservation laws.

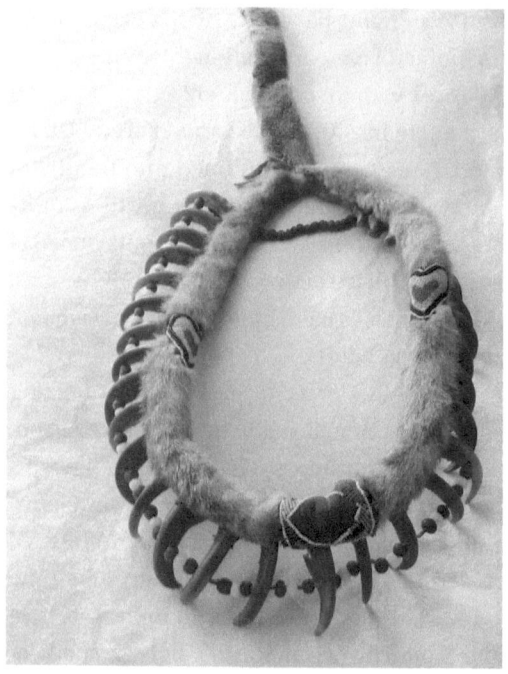

Sam Slick sold this bear claw necklace to the State Historical Society of Iowa during the Great Depression. The Meskwaki Historic Preservation Office has been slowly reclaiming other necklaces and cultural items from museums and repositories across the country. The tribe brought this one home in 2015. Photo courtesy of the Meskwaki Historic Preservation Office.

By agreeing to federal compliance, the tribe gained the authority to deputize state conservation officers if needed, as well as to determine "licenses and fees, bag and possession limits, seasons" and other regulations "in ways consistent with conservation purposes as well as tribal custom."[45]

The tribe has also created its own police force and court system. Meskwaki leaders began thinking about reestablishing the tribal court as early as 1963.[46] Explorations into the matter continued off and on for years, and in 1977 the council passed a resolution declaring the community's rights, capacity, and intention to manage its own justice system.[47] The issue arose again in the early 2000s after the tribe expressed concerns that Tama County was unfairly overcharging the tribe for law enforcement. After discussions with the county failed to address the issue, the Meskwaki Nation reignited its efforts to handle law and order on its own.[48]

In 2005, the tribal council began drafting a penal code and appointed a Meskwaki chief justice and two non-Native associate judges. The court heard only civil cases—divorces, juvenile matters, and child welfare and custody claims, among others—for the first couple of years. The tribe pursued funding to create a tribal police force and extend its authority to criminal matters.[49] The Meskwaki Police Department, consisting of a half dozen officers, most of them non-Native, began its patrols in October 2006.[50] The federal government still has jurisdiction over major crimes. On the whole, the State of Iowa has recognized the effectiveness of the Meskwaki police force. A woman was charged, for example, with assaulting a Meskwaki officer in 2011. As part of her defense, her attorneys argued that tribal police do not fall under state statutes protecting law enforcement officers. A state district court judge, however, held that tribal police have the same authority and protections as other police.[51] In June 2015, the Iowa legislature endorsed the repeal of the 1948 law and order bill, formally asking Congress to return Meskwaki jurisdiction to the tribe.[52] In 2018, Congress repealed the 1948 act, thereby restoring tribal jurisdiction over minor crimes committed between tribal members on the Settlement. This, however, did not end questions over criminal jurisdiction on Meskwaki land: in 2019, the Iowa Supreme Court found that the state, not the tribe, should prosecute crimes involving non-Natives on the Settlement.[53] If nothing else, these developments suggest that the long-running debate over the Meskwaki Settlement's "peculiar condition" is far from over.

THE RAID

On the morning of May 23, 2003, federal marshals stormed the Meskwaki casino. Sparked by an intense political dispute over tribal leadership, the raid led to the closure of the MBCH. More than 1,200 employees were laid off, and the Meskwaki Nation hemorrhaged some $3 million in weekly revenue for several months as the tribe and the NIGC sought a solution.[54]

The closure garnered national media attention, and observers sat shocked by the Red Earth People's willingness to lose incredible amounts of money while they resolved internal differences.[55] The dispute began in the autumn of 2002, when some three hundred Red Earth People signed a petition recalling the tribal council, alleging a lack of transparency, nepotism, and other abuses of power.[56] The tribal council refused to set new elections or fire some employees accused of corruption. One tribal elder, who held hereditary political power dating back to the chief's council, appointed a council. Although well respected as a spiritual leader and elder, this person was not deeply enmeshed in tribal politics. This person avoided using the crisis to undermine the Meskwaki Constitution; they used it only to try to get the tribe back on track. The elected council refused to budge, and the BIA initially declined to get involved, citing tribal sovereignty.[57]

But, when the turmoil began to threaten the casino's operations, and therefore the livelihoods of the many non-Native casino employees, the State of Iowa threatened to back out of its gaming compact with the tribe, which could have permanently shuttered the tribal casino. The Red Earth People attempted to elect a new council outside the constitutionally elected one already in place, but the BIA and the sitting council refused to recognize its results.[58] This led to federal lawsuits between the two councils. Months crept by as the tribe attempted to resolve the dispute and the NIGC kept the MBCH shut.[59] Finally, the Red Earth People elected a new council in the fall of 2003. Only once it had been seated did the BIA and the NIGC allow the casino to reopen. It resumed operations on New Year's Eve. This high-profile affair inflamed tensions within the community as well as external perceptions of the discordant nature of Meskwaki politics. The shutdown provided fodder for stereotypes of tribal corruption and chaos.[60]

Viewing this episode in the context of the longer arc of Meskwaki history, however, casts it in a different light. Over the last four centuries, Meskwaki people have lived the remarkable story of a small Indigenous community working against overwhelming threats to its land, culture, and political authority. With all the Red Earth People have endured and overcome, through patient political strategies and a deep commitment to their shared Settlement, the casino shutdown reminds us that Indigenous history in the United States is not a story of continual, steady improvement from the devastating mistakes of yesterday.[61] It is at once haunted by the deep legacies of history and constrained by the tortuous legal and political framework within which Native Nations must operate. But, through it all, Indigenous history has been and continues to be shaped by the decisions and strategies of Native people, in all their cunning and imperfection. And, in the long arc of Meskwaki history, the shutdown appears as merely one particularly acerbic chapter in a long-running and constantly evolving conversation about the nature and limitations of Meskwaki sovereignty and the many forms of Meskwaki self-determination.

* * *

The old story that followed Wisaka's arrow from the red earth of the Eastern Seaboard to a shimmering sea of tallgrass prairie explained how the Meskwaki Nation came to Iowa and, along the way, created a homeland amid deep uncertainty. There, the Red Earth People learned to live and grow, finding sustainability and a mooring for their community, which has endured for centuries under nearly constant assault, first by Europeans and Indigenous enemies, and later by the United States and its component parts.

In May 1992, the Meskwaki Nation held its first "Proclamation Day" celebration, an annual event that commemorates the tribe's formal return to Iowa in the 1850s and acts like a Meskwaki Nation Independence Day. (In recent years, it has often just been called "Meskwaki Nation Day.") In the resolution announcing that first holiday, the tribal council unanimously declared that their people were "forever grateful for the foresight and spirit that the tribal leaders who purchased the original lands had for the future of the" Meskwaki Nation.[62]

Exactly 150 years before the first Proclamation Day, the 1842 treaty took the remaining Iowa homelands from the Red Earth People. As that decision loomed, Wapello worried that "this land is all we have. When it is gone, we shall have nothing left." A few years later, a Meskwaki man rode a horse to an Iowa farm and offered to negotiate.

I wonder how well Wapello and that diplomat rest, knowing how much has returned since the Red Earth People reclaimed their land.

Acknowledgments

Writerly convention seems to hold that one should save their strongest, most poignant thanks for last. But my wonderful little family is at the front of this line. Together, my wife Samantha and I have been bouncing around the prairies and mountains for sixteen years. We relocated twice in support of this project, for which (among many other things) I will always be indebted to her. Along the way, we've expanded our little family unit to include our scruffy dog Nigel and our lovely daughter Stevie, in that order. They are my world. This book is for them.

I am grateful to many other people who shaped my thinking and otherwise supported this book over the course of many years. At the University of Iowa, I was fortunate to have a thoughtful group of faculty advisors. Thank you to my dissertation committee members: Jacki Thompson Rand, who was my primary advisor and has become a dear friend; Tyler Priest; Erica Prussing; Jim Giblin; and James F. Brooks. Others influenced this project in ways large and small. They include Phil Round, Steve Warren, Nick Brown, Tom Arne Mitrød, Colin Gordon, Landon Storrs, Omar Valerio-Jiménez, Cathy Komisaruk, Jen Sessions, Alyssa Park, Linda Kerber, and Lisa Heineman. Graduate student friends and colleagues, including Allison Wells, Paul Renfro, Chris McFadin, Kelsey Potdevin, Colleen Davis, Mary Wise, Kelly Nussbaum, David De La Torre, Christina Jensen, Noaquia Callahan, Josh Miner, Jason Sprague, Josh Cochran, Marlino Mubai, John Eicher, Heather Wacha, Youlia Tzenova, Mike Maciejewski, Josh and Sarah Pederson, Ben Morton, Gyorgy Toth, and many others, helped me learn and made graduate school a great experience.

In Iowa City, I found endless support and camaraderie at the State Historical Society's downtown office and the Obermann Center for Advanced Studies. At SHSI-IC, Mary Bennett championed my work from the very beginning, while Marvin Bergman and Charles Scott provided vital support. Teresa Mangum, Jennifer New, Neda Hatami, Chuck Connerly, Carolyn Colvin, Jennifer Teitle, and Erin Hackathorn and their colleagues at the Obermann Center helped me articulate an approach to publicly engaged scholarship that continues to inform my life and work to this day.

I completed this book as a visiting scholar in the History Department at the University of Montana. There, I had the good fortune of working with a wonderful group of faculty and students, including Kyle Volk, Scott Arcenas, Tobin Shearer, Jody Pavilack, Jeff Wiltse, John Eglin, Anya Jabour, Donna McCrea, Kym MacEwan, Michael Larmann, Harry Devoe, Chris Varney, Lance Foster, Nick Ambs, Alex LeVan, Cassidy VanderVoort, Hazel Videon, James Compton, Jacob Schmidt, Alexandra Ore, Dagny Walton, Mitchell Morris, Kellen Neighbors, Ian Thomas, Rory Johnson, Malinda Gaudry, Paige Moriarty, Dylan Haring, and more. Many of these individuals participated in a Lockridge Workshop session devoted to an early draft of my introduction, which sharpened it immeasurably. Dylan Yonce, Claire Rydell Arcenas, Leif Fredrickson, and Wade Davies graciously read a near-final draft of the full manuscript and offered some vital final advice. I am grateful to you all and count my time in Missoula among the best years of my life.

Administrative staff make the world go 'round. They are the unsung heroes of university departments, and I am grateful to Patricia Goodwin, Sheri Sojka, Heather Roth, Laura Jones, and Cady Card-Andrew for their help navigating the ins and outs of the University of Iowa and the University of Montana.

In addition to colleagues at those institutions, I benefited from an incredibly generous community of other scholars, many of whom read drafts, shared insights or encouragement over the phone, or created the intellectual foundation on Meskwaki history upon which I have attempted to build. Many thanks to Doug Foley, R. David Edmunds, Judy Daubenmier, Erik Gooding, Royce Kurtz, Jacob Manatowa-Bailey, Bob Burchfield, Josh Sales, C. Joseph Genetin-Pilawa, Robert Wellman Campbell, Jared Orsi, Doug Kiel, Greg Olson, Dave Beck, Shepard Forman, Jon Funabiki, Elizabeth Fenn, David Wilkins, Paul Kelton, Mark Fiege, and Janet Ore. Endless thanks to Margaret Lee, who finished reviewing my page proofs from the hospital, just before delivering her son Peter Brennan Lee. (Welcome, Peter!)

The University of Oklahoma Press has been a wonderful and patient supporter of this project. Leisl Carr-Childers, Michael Childers, and Adam Kane graciously invited me into the "Environment in Modern North America" series, and I hope my contribution meets their high standards. Over time, I was helped along by Alessandra Tamulevich, Joe Schiller, and Helen Robertson, the latter two of whom guided this project across the finish line, but not before making it a better book. The brilliant copyeditor Stephanie Marshall Ward cleaned and sharpened my writing and Amron Lehte produced a clear and helpful index. The press also identified stellar peer reviewers who offered vital feedback on this project as either a book proposal or full manuscript. These included Emily Moore, Larry Nesper, William Bauer, and one anonymous reader. Thanks to you all for your time and suggestions, which strengthened this work.

The staff at numerous archives helped bring the Meskwaki Nation's story to life. Thank you to Becki Plunkett, Sharon Avery, Kathy Gourley, Jeffrey Dawson, and Jerome Thompson at the State Historical Society of Iowa's main office in Des Moines; Glenn Longacre, Scott Forsythe, Martin Tuohy, MaryFrances Ronan, and Lori Cox-Paul at the National Archives branches in Chicago, Washington, DC, and Kansas City; Denise Anderson at the University of Iowa Special Collections; Bradley Kuennen at the Special Collections and University Archives at Iowa State University; Mark McFate and Chris Jones at Grinnell College Special Collections and Archives; Harrison Phillis in the Special Collections at the Thomas Tredway Library at Augustana College; Dave Osbourne, Michelle McCormick-Corbine, and Scott Sufficool at the Bureau of Indian Affairs; and Tim Osumi at the National Indian Gaming Commission.

Over the years, I have benefited from financial support from numerous organizations. The research, writing, and publication of *Red Earth Nation* was funded by grants from the State Historical Society of Iowa, the American Historical Association, the Phillips Fund for Native American Research at the American Philosophical Society, and the Windrose Fund of the Common Council Foundation. The following organizations at the University of Iowa also funded this project: the Executive Council of Graduate and Professional Students, the Graduate Student Senate, the American Indian and

Native Studies Program, the History Department, the Graduate College, and the Center for Global and Regional Environmental Research (which made both a research grant and a book subvention grant). Thank you all for your generous support.

Portions of this book have also been published as scholarly articles, first in "Settlement Sovereignty: The Meskwaki Fight for Self-Governance, 1856–1937," *Annals of Iowa* 73, no. 4 (Fall 2014): 311–47, published by the State Historical Society of Iowa and used by permission. Other sections first appeared in "Building the Red Earth Nation: The Civilian Conservation Corps – Indian Division on the Meskwaki Settlement," *Native American and Indigenous Studies* 2, no. 2 (Fall 2015): 106-33, published by the University of Minnesota Press in partnership with the Native American and Indigenous Studies Association and used by permission. Additionally, a summary of some of the book's main ideas appeared in "Can the Indigenous #Landback Movement Secure Self-Determination?" *Washington Post*, April 26, 2022. My thanks to these outlets for sharing my work and helping present small portions of the story told here.

An enormous group of friends and mentors inspired me to undertake this project, encouraged me not to give up, and taught me how to approach it in a spirit of responsibility and reciprocity. Thank you to Eric Abrahamson, Lois Facer, Sam Hurst, Craig Howe, Josh Houy, Randal Iverson, Ray Graham, Mitchell Stone, Mike Kaiser, Ashley and Dillon Julius, Rochelle and Andrew Zens, Heather Dawn Thompson, Tatewin Means, Beverly Stabber-Warne, Amy Sazue, Valeriah Big Eagle, Bobbie Koch, Violet Catches, Kibbe Brown, Casey Peterson, Robin PetersonLund, and many other friends in and around the Black Hills.

My extended family has also been a source of love, support, and much-needed distraction. Thank you to my parents, Steve and Sheri, and in-laws, Matt and Karen; my siblings and their partners Chris Zimmer, Emily Acker, Waylon Zimmer, Sarah Zimmer, Adam Heck, Samantha Blodgett, Kyle Heck, and all their families; and our sprawling network of aunts, uncles, cousins, and other relatives. I also owe deep gratitude to my other family, which includes Michael, Jacquie, and Skylar Phillips and Lily Mendoza, Cameron Ducheneaux, Madge Ducheneaux, and their families. And, of course, a note of remembrance and thanks to the always-smiling Shamus O'Daniel, who we lost too soon.

Finally, and with deep gratitude, I thank members of the Meskwaki community who helped this project along. Johnathan Lantz Buffalo and Dawn Suzanne (Buffalo) Wanatee read the manuscript and contributed immensely in many ways over the years, including writing the moving foreword to this book. Mary Young Bear is a friend and gentle guide, whose brilliant drawings appeared herein. I am also grateful to the late Donald Wanatee, Leah Slick-Driscoll, Matt Bear, Nathan Bear, Conrad Brown, Marion Wanatee, Ray Young Bear, Preston Duncan, Yolanda Pushetonequa, Alex Walker, Christina Black Cloud, Dalyn Wabaunasee, and Stephanie Bad Soldier-Snow for their inspiration and support, in ways subtle and overt. I would also like to thank the many Meskwaki folks, not named here, who attended talks and otherwise engaged in the process of creating this book over the years. This is your story. It has been an honor to help tell.

Sources and Abbreviations

BA	Buffalo Archive, Meskwaki Settlement, Iowa
CUL	Cornell University Library, Division of Rare and Manuscript Collections
SAE	Samuel A. Elliot Collection
ISUSC	Iowa State University Special Collections
CF Papers	Charles Friley Papers
EH Papers	Elizabeth Hoyt Papers
RHMF Papers	R. H. Moore Family Papers
JLCE	"Journals of the Lewis and Clark Expedition," Center for Digital Research in the Humanities, University of Nebraska–Lincoln, https://lewisandclarkjournals.unl.edu.
MHCD	Mary Bennett, Johnathan Lantz Buffalo, Dawn Suzanne Wanatee, "Meskwaki History" CD-ROM (Iowa City: State Historical Society of Iowa, 2004).
MHPO	Meskwaki Historic Preservation Office
IRA	Box, "Indian Reorganization Act"
MO	"Meskwaki Obituaries" Binder
NARA-CH	National Archives and Records Administration, Chicago
RG75, BIA	Record Group 75, Bureau of Indian Affairs
SFA	Sac & Fox Agency, Tama, Iowa
NARA-DC	National Archives and Records Administration, Washington, DC
RG 75	Record Group 75, Bureau of Indian Affairs
MAO	Minneapolis Area Office, Minneapolis, MN
SFAFO	Sac & Fox Area Field Office

SHSI-DM	State Historical Society of Iowa, Des Moines
	ERH Papers — Edgar R. Harlan Papers
	ZMS Files — Zella M. Schermerhorn Research Files
	RG 043 — Record Group 043
SHSI-IC	State Historical Society of Iowa, Iowa City
UCSCRC	University of Chicago Special Collections Research Center
	STP — Sol Tax Papers Microfilm
UISC	University of Iowa Special Collections
	LAH Papers — Leo A. Hoegh Papers

ORAL HISTORY INTERVIEWS

Donald Wanatee, July 20, 2014, and July 24, 2014, Meskwaki Settlement.
Johnathan Buffalo, July 16, 2014, Meskwaki Settlement.
Mary Young Bear, May 28, 2015, Meskwaki Settlement.
Nathan and Matthew Bear, September 9, 2014, Meskwaki Settlement.
Preston Duncan, July 16, 2014, and July 31, 2014, Meskwaki Settlement.
Ray Young Bear, March 22, 2015, Meskwaki Settlement.
Elizabeth Roberts, Donald Wanatee, Marion Davenport, and Darrell Wanatee, March 19, 2015, Meskwaki Settlement.

Notes

PREFACE

1. Vine Deloria Jr., *Custer Died for Your Sins: An Indian Manifesto* (Norman: University of Oklahoma Press, 1988), 78–100.

2. See "AHR Exchange: Living with the Past: Thoughts on Community Collaboration and Difficult History in Native American and Indigenous Studies," *American Historical Review* 125, no. 2 (April 2020): 517–51, which offers thoughtful essays by leading scholars, including David J. Silverman, Christine M. Delucia, Alyssa Mt. Pleasant, Philip J. Deloria, and Jean M. O'Brien. See also Alyssa Mt. Pleasant, Caroline Wigginton, and Kelly Wisecup, "Materials and Methods in Native American and Indigenous Studies: Completing the Turn," *William and Mary Quarterly*, 3d ser., 75, no. 2 (April 2018): 207–36.

3. Clint Carroll, *Roots of Our Renewal: Ethnobotany and Cherokee Environmental Governance* (Minneapolis: University of Minnesota Press, 2015), xi–xii.

4. I am also guided by public historians' concept of "shared inquiry." See for example Michael Frisch, *A Shared Authority: Essays on the Craft and Meaning of Oral and Public History* (Albany: SUNY Press, 1990); Katharine T. Corbett and Howard S. Miller, "A Shared Inquiry into Shared Inquiry," *The Public Historian* 28, no. 1 (February 2006): 15–38.

5. For a description of the various words people have used to describe the Meskwaki Nation over the last several hundred years, see Judith Daubenmier, *The Meskwaki and Anthropologists: Action Anthropology Reconsidered* (Lincoln: University of Nebraska Press, 2008), 317–18, n. 1; Erik D. Gooding, "The Return to *Nekotosiye*: Meskwaki Village Life, 1857–1902," 2018, unpublished manuscript, used and cited with Gooding's permission, copy in the author's possession, 1–2. I also use the terms "Sauk Nation" and "Yellow Earth People" to refer to the Asakiwaki people, whose name translates to "People of the Yellow Earth." Finally, throughout the text, I eliminate the hyphens that often appear in Meskwaki people's names in source material, and only for readability. Rather than Ma-sqa-see, for example, I use Masqasee.

6. See Christine Delucia, Doug Kiel, Katrina Phillips, and Kiara Vigil, "Histories of Indigenous Sovereignty in Action: What Is It and Why Does It Matter?" *American Historian*, March 2021, https://www.oah.org/tah/issues/2021/native-american-history-and-sovereignty/histories-of-indigenous-sovereignty-in-action-what-is-it-and-why-does-it-matter/; Jessica R. Cattelino, *High Stakes: Florida Seminole Gaming and Sovereignty* (Durham, NC: Duke University Press, 2008); Joanne Barker, ed., *Sovereignty Matters: Locations of Contestation and Possibility in Indigenous Struggles for Self-Determination* (Lincoln: University of Nebraska Press, 2005); Frank Pommersheim, *Broken Landscape: Indians, Indian Tribes, and the Constitution* (New York: Oxford University Press, 2009), 46; Daniel M. Cobb and Loretta Fowler, eds., *Beyond Red Power: American Indian Politics and Activism since 1900* (Albuquerque, NM: School for Advanced Research Press, 2007); Kevin Bruyneel, *The Third Space of Sovereignty: The Post-Colonial Politics of US/Indigenous Relations* (Minneapolis: University of Minnesota Press, 2007); Gregory Evans Dowd, *War under Heaven: Pontiac, the Indian Nations, and the British Empire* (Baltimore: Johns Hopkins University Press, 2002), 3.

INTRODUCTION

1. David Butler, "Old Indian Town," August 18, 1905, reprinted in "Meskwaki Proclamation Day Brochure: 'Old Indian Town,'" July 13, 1857, State Historical Society of Iowa, https://history.iowa.gov/history/education/educator-resources/primary-source-sets/right-to-vote-suffrage-women-african/meskwaki-proclamation-day; J. R. Caldwell, ed., *A History of Tama County Iowa*, Vol. 2 (Chicago: Lewis Publishing Company, 1910), 764.

2. Butler, "Old Indian Town."

3. The names of these Meskwaki men are spelled as they appear on a transcription of the Meskwaki land deed in Butler. "Old Indian Town."

4. Steven C. Cross, "History and the Constitution: The Drafting of Iowa's Constitution," State Library of Iowa: Iowa Publications Online, accessed June 8, 2018, http://publications.iowa.gov/135/1/history/7-6.html; Silvana R. Siddavi, "Principle, Interest, and Patriotism All Combined: The Fight over Iowa's Capital," *Annals of Iowa* 64, no. 2 (Spring 2005): 137.

5. See Landback, NDN Collective, accessed February 25, 2022, https://landback.org.

6. B. Toastie, "6 Questions about the Landback Movement, Answered," *High Country News*, September 2022, 38–39.

7. Dani Anguiano, "Native American Tribes Reclaim California Redwood Land for Preservation," *Guardian*, January 25, 2022, https://www.theguardian.com/us-news/2022/jan/25/native-american-tribes-california-redwood-preservation; "Our Work," Intertribal Sinkyone Wilderness Council, accessed March 10, 2022, https://sinkyone.org/achievements. See also Shirley Sneve, "Tribes Reclaiming

Lands 'Actually Happening,'" *Indian Country Today*, January 15, 2021, https://indiancountrytoday.com/news/tribes-reclaiming-lands-actually-happening.

8. Alice Hamilton, "Native American Tribe in Maine Buys Back Island Taken 160 Years Ago," *Guardian*, June 4, 2021, https://www.theguardian.com/us-news/2021/jun/04/native-american-tribe-maine-buys-back-pine-island.

9. Mario Koran, "Northern California Esselen Tribe Regains Ancestral Land after 250 Years," *Guardian*, July 28, 2020, https://www.theguardian.com/us-news/2020/jul/28/northern-california-esselen-tribe-regains-land-250-years. The Esselen Tribe is not federally recognized, although land reclamation is a component of its ongoing efforts to gain recognition. See Philip Blair Laverty, "Recognizing Indians: Place, Identity, History, and the Federal Acknowledgment of the Ohlone/Costanoan-Esselen Nation" (PhD diss., University of New Mexico, 2010).

10. "Final Piece of Pe' Sla Purchased by Tribes," *Indian Country Today*, December 3, 2014, http://indiancountrytodaymedianetwork.com/2014/12/03/final-piece-pe-sla-purchased-tribes-158106; Christina Rose, "Pe' Sla Guarantees Sacred Land Will Be Used for Ceremonies," *Indian Country Today*, December 21, 2012, http://indiancountrytodaymedianetwork.com/2012/12/21/pe-sla-purchase-guarantees-sacred-land-will-be-used-ceremonies-146500; "Bureau of Indian Affairs Places Sacred Site in Black Hills in Trust," *Z News*, March 17, 2016, http://www.indianz.com/News/2016/020719.asp.

11. See Remembering the Children: Wakȟáŋyeža Wičhákiksuyapi, accessed September 5, 2023, www.rememberingthechildren.org. I was a volunteer historian for the Rapid City Indian Boarding School Lands Project from 2015–2023. That project has also received grant funding from NDN Collective.

12. "Interior Transfers National Bison Range Lands in Trust for the Confederated Salish and Kootenai Tribes" (press release), US Department of the Interior, June 23, 2021, https://www.doi.gov/pressreleases/interior-transfers-national-bison-range-lands-trust-confederated-salish-and-kootenai; Anna V. Smith, "Reclaiming the National Bison Range," *High Country News*, January 26, 2021, https://www.hcn.org/issues/53.2/indigenous-affairs-tribes-reclaiming-the-national-bison-range.

13. See "Program History: Land Buy-Back Program for Tribal Nations," US Department of the Interior, accessed November 20, 2023, https://doi.gov/buybackprogram. See also US Senate, *Cobell v. Salazar Settlement Agreement: Hearing before the Committee on Indian Affairs*, 11th Congress, 1st Session, December 17, 2009 (Washington, DC: Government Printing Office, 2010).

14. "Interior Announces Revised Strategy, Policies to More Effectively Reduce Fractionation of Tribal Lands," US Department of the Interior, July 31, 2017, updated September 29, 2021, https://www.doi.gov/pressreleases/interior-announces-revised-strategy-policies-more-effectively-reduce-fractionation.

15. See "Issues," Indian Land Tenure Foundation, accessed March 24, 2022, https://iltf.org/land-issues/issues/; Harvard Project on American Indian Economic Development, *The State of the Native Nations: Conditions under US Policies of*

Self-Determination (New York: Oxford University Press, 2007), 101. The 114 million figure does not include lands owned by non-Indians within reservation boundaries.

16. See Landback, NDN Collective.

17. This summary is based on numerous private conversations with Indigenous thinkers, advocates, and leaders over several years.

18. See, for example, Shiri Pasternak, *Grounded Authority: The Algonquins of Barriere Lake against the State* (Minneapolis: University of Minnesota Press, 2017); Michael E. Harkin and David Rich Lewis, eds., *Native Americans and the Environment: Perspectives on the Ecological Indian* (Lincoln: University of Nebraska Press, 2007); Winona LaDuke, *All Our Relations: Native Struggles for Land and Life* (Cambridge, MA: South End Press, 1999); Christopher Vecsey and Robert W. Venables, eds., *American Indian Environments: Ecological Issues in Native American History* (Syracuse, NY: Syracuse University Press, 1980); John Bierhorst, *The Way of the Earth: Native America and the Environment* (New York: Harper Collins, 1994); Nancy C. Unger, *Beyond Nature's Housekeepers: American Women in Environmental History* (New York: Oxford University Press, 2012), 13–29; Shepard Krech III, *The Ecological Indian: Myth and History* (New York: W. W. Norton, 1999); J. Donald Hughes, *American Indian Ecology* (El Paso: Texas Western Press, 1983); Richard White, *The Roots of Dependency: Subsistence, Environment, and Social Change among the Choctaws, Pawnees, and Navajos* (Lincoln: University of Nebraska Press, 1983).

19. Stephanie Bad Soldier-Snow, email to the author, March 3, 2022. See also Enrique Salmon, "Kincentric Ecology: Indigenous Perceptions of Human-Nature Relationship," *Ecological Applications* 10, no. 5 (October 2000): 1327–32.

20. Clint Carroll, *Roots of Our Renewal: Ethnobotany and Cherokee Environmental Governance* (Minneapolis: University of Minnesota Press, 2015), 8.

21. Glen Sean Coulthard, *Red Skin, White Masks: Rejecting the Colonial Politics of Recognition* (Minneapolis: University of Minnesota Press, 2013), 13 (emphasis original). See also Robin Wall Kimmerer, *Braiding Sweetgrass: Indigenous Wisdom, Scientific Knowledge, and the Teachings of Plants* (Minneapolis: Milkweed Editions, 2020); Nicholas Anthony Brown, "Continental Land Back: Managing Mobilities and Enacting Relationalities in Indigenous Landscapes," *Mobilities* 17, no. 2 (2022), DOI:10.1080/17450101.2021.2012503; Jean Dennison, *Colonial Entanglement: Constituting a Twenty-First-Century Osage Nation* (Chapel Hill: University of North Carolina Press, 2012).

22. Mali Obomsawin, "Kihtahkomikumon (Our Land)—#IslandBack in Passamaquoddy Territory," uploaded to Vimeo by Sunrise Media Collective, April 15, 2021, https://vimeo.com/537535470.

23. Craig Howe, "Keep Your Thoughts above the Trees: Ideas on Developing and Presenting Tribal Histories," in *Clearing a Path: Theorizing the Past in Native American Studies*, ed. Nancy Shoemaker (New York: Routledge, 2002), 161; Rosalyn LaPier, "Land as Text: Reading the Land," *Environmental History* 28, no. 1 (January 2023): 40–46.

24. See Nick Estes, *Our History Is the Future: Standing Rock versus the Dakota Access Pipeline and the Long Tradition of Indigenous Resistance* (New York: Verso, 2019); Arthur Manuel and Grand Chief Ronald Derrickson, *The Reconciliation Manifesto: Recovering the Land, Rebuilding the Economy* (Toronto: James Lorimer, 2017), esp. 212–64.

25. Nina Totenberg, "Supreme Court Hands Defeat to Native American Tribes in Oklahoma," *All Things Considered*, NPR, June 29, 2022, https://www.npr.org/2022/06/29/1108717407/supreme-court-narrows-native-americans-oklahoma. See also Pasternak, *Grounded Authority*, 3–4.

26. See Doug Kiel, "Nation vs. Municipality: Indigenous Land Recovery, Settler Resentment, and Taxation on the Oneida Reservation," *Native American and Indigenous Studies* 6, no. 2 (Fall 2019): 51–73; Albert Bender, "Following McGirt Decision, Oneida Nation Case Continues String of Indigenous Court Victories," *Z News*, September 30, 2020, https://www.indianz.com/News/2020/09/03/following-mcgirt-decision-oneida-nation.asp.

27. Gregory Korte, "Obama Administration Renames Mount McKinley to Denali," *USA Today*, August 15, 2020, https://www.usatoday.com/story/news/politics/2015/08/30/obama-rename-nations-tallest-mountain/71426656/.

28. Miguel Otarola, "Minnesota DNR Can Rename Lake Calhoun as Bde Maka Ska, High Court Rules," *Star-Tribune* (Minneapolis), May 13, 2020, https://www.startribune.com/bde-maka-ska-name-stays-supreme-court-says/570435552/.

29. See, for example, Suzanne Keeptwo, *We All Go Back to the Land: The Who, Why, and How of Land Acknowledgements* (Edmonton, AB: Brush Education, 2021); Graeme Wood, "'Land Acknowledgements' Are Just Moral Exhibitionism," *Atlantic*, November 28, 2021, https://www.theatlantic.com/ideas/archive/2021/11/against-land-acknowledgements-native-american/620820/.

30. See Edgar Villanueva, *Decolonizing Wealth: Indigenous Wisdom to Heal Divides and Restore Balance* (Oakland, CA: Barrett-Koehler, 2018), 165; Christina L. Lyons, "Native American Rights," *CQ Researcher*, November 19, 2021, http://library.cqpress.com/cqresearcher/cqresrre2021111900; Kristen T. Ruppel, *Unearthing Indian Land: Living with the Legacies of Allotment* (Tucson: University of Arizona Press, 2008), 5–6.

31. Robert Lee, "Sources and Interpretations: 'A Better View of the Country': A Missouri Settlement Map by William Clark," *William and Mary Quarterly*, 3d ser., 79, no. 1 (January 2022): 91. See also Claudio Saunt, *Unworthy Republic: The Dispossession of Native Americans and the Road to Indian Territory* (New York: W. W. Norton, 2020); Allan Greer, *Property and Dispossession: Natives, Empires, and Land in Early Modern North America* (New York: Cambridge University Press, 2018); Christine M. DeLucia, *Memory Lands: King Philip's War and the Place of Violence in the Northeast* (New Haven, CT: Yale University Press, 2018); John P. Bowes, *Land Too Good for Indians: Northern Indian Removal* (Norman: University of Oklahoma Press, 2016); Ned Blackhawk, *The Rediscovery of America: Native Peoples and the Unmaking of US History* (New Haven, CT: Yale University Press, 2023).

32. Rory Taylor, "Trump Administration Revokes Reservation Status for Mashpee Wampanoag Tribe Amid Coronavirus Crisis," *Vox*, April 2, 2020, https://www.vox.com/identities/2020/4/2/21204113/mashpee-wampanoag-tribe-trump-reservation-native-land; Doug Fraser, "'This News Is So Welcome': Mashpee Wampanoag Tribe Can Retain Reservation Land," *Cape Cod Times*, December 2, 2021, https://www.capecodtimes.com/story/news/2021/12/22/mashpee-wampanoag-tribe-can-retain-reservation-land-taunton/9001309002.

33. "Biden Restores Protections for Bears Ears Monument, 4 Years After Trump Downsized It," NPR, October 8, 2021, https://www.npr.org/2021/10/07/1044039889/bears-ears-monument-protection-restored-biden; Maxine Joselow, "Native Americans to Co-manage National Monument for the First Time," *Washington Post*, June 20, 2022, https://www.washingtonpost.com/climate-environment/2022/06/20/bears-ears-national-monument-tribes/.

34. "Interior and Agriculture Departments Take Action to Strengthen Tribal Co-stewardship of Public Lands and Waters," US Department of the Interior, November 15, 2021, https://www.doi.gov/pressreleases/interior-and-agriculture-departments-take-action-strengthen-tribal-co-stewardship.

35. For an elaboration of the ongoing challenges to tribal sovereignty embedded in federal law, see Peter d'Errico, *Federal Anti-Indian Law: The Legal Entrapment of Indigenous Peoples* (New York: Bloomsbury, 2022).

36. Robert J. Miller, *Native America, Discovered and Conquered: Thomas Jefferson, Lewis & Clark, and Manifest Destiny* (Westport, CT: Praeger, 2006), xvii. See also Lindsay G. Robertson, *Conquest by Law: How the Discovery of America Dispossessed Indigenous Peoples of Their Lands* (New York: Oxford University Press, 2005).

37. See Stuart Banner, *How the Indians Lost Their Land: Law and Power on the Frontier* (Cambridge, MA: Harvard University Press, 2005), 135–37; Michael A. Blaakman, "'Haughty Republicans,' Native Land, and the Promise of Preemption," *William and Mary Quarterly* 78, no. 2 (April 2021): 244.

38. "Land Tenure Issues," Indian Land Tenure Foundation, accessed March 15, 2022, https://iltf.org/land-issues/issues/.

39. Harvard Project, *State of the Native Nations*, 101–103.

40. Naomi Schaefer Riley, "One Way to Help Native Americans: Property Rights," *Atlantic*, July 30, 2016, https://www.theatlantic.com/politics/archive/2016/07/native-americans-property-rights/492941/. See also Villanueva, *Decolonizing Wealth*, 165. Riley and Villanueva both credit Hernando de Soto with coining the term "dead capital." See also Duane Champagne, "The Crisis for Native Governments in the Twenty-First Century," in *The Future of Indigenous Peoples: Strategies for Survival and Development*, ed. Duane Champagne and Ismael Abu-Saad (Los Angeles: University of California, 2003), 205–18.

41. Indian Land Tenure Foundation, "From Removal to Recovery: Land Ownership in Indian Country," *Message Runner* 4 (Fall 2009): 12. For a detailed examination

of the history and implications of federal land policies related to fractionation and allotment, see Ruppel, *Unearthing Indian Land*, esp. 1–68.

42. Here I am inspired, in phrase as well as the spirit of creatively analyzing different models for managing and utilizing Indigenous lands, by Beth Rose Middleton, *Trust in the Land: New Directions in Tribal Conservation* (Tucson: University of Arizona Press, 2011).

43. Malcom Ebright, Rick Hendricks, and Richard W. Hughes, *Four Square Leagues: Pueblo Indian Land in New Mexico* (Albuquerque: University of New Mexico Press, 2014), esp. 49–88.

44. Brad D. E. Jarvis, *The Brothertown Nation of Indians: Land Ownership and Nationalism in Early America, 1740–1840* (Lincoln: University of Nebraska Press, 2010), 2. See also "About Our Heritage and Culture," Brothertown Indian Nation, Eayamquittoowauconnuck, accessed February 24, 2022, https://www.brothertownindians.org.

45. Khaled J. Bloom, "An American Tragedy in the Commons: Land and Labor in the Cherokee Nation, 1870–1900," *Agricultural History* 76, no. 3 (Summer 2002): 497–523; James W. Parins, "The Shifting Map of Cherokee Land Use Practices in Indian Territory," *ELOHI*, January 2012, 13–19, http://journals.openedition.org/elohi/197.

46. See "Ottawa Tribe of Oklahoma," Southern Plains Tribal Health Board, accessed March 8, 2022, https://www.spthb.org/about-us/who-we-serve/ottawa-tribe-of-oklahoma. See also David Grann, *Killers of the Flower Moon: The Osage Murders and the Birth of the FBI* (New York: Vintage, 2017), 54–56; Bryce Obermeyer, *Delaware Tribe in a Cherokee Nation* (Lincoln: University of Nebraska Press, 2009).

47. "The Strong People," Jamestown S'Klallam People, accessed February 24, 2022, https://jamestowntribe.org. See also Joseph H. Stauss, *The Jamestown S'Klallam Story: Rebuilding a Northwest Coast Indian Tribe* (Sequim, WA: Jamestown S'Klallam Tribe, 2002); Middleton, *Trust in the Land*, 163–174.

48. Tanis C. Thorne, "The Removal of the Indians of El Capitan to Viejas: Confrontation and Change in San Diego Indian Affairs in the 1930s," *Journal of San Diego History* 56, no. 1 (Winter/Spring 2010): 45–46.

49. Lawrence C. Kelly, "The Indian Reorganization Act: The Dream and the Reality," *Pacific Historical Review* 44, no. 3 (August 1975): 294–95. See also "Rosebud Sioux Tribe Tribal Land Enterprise: Serving the Oyate Since 1943," accessed November 20, 2023, https://www.rsttle.com.

50. Harvard Project, *State of the Native Nations*, 103.

51. See for example Martha C. Knack, "The Saga of Tim Hooper's Homestead: Non-Reservation Shoshone Indian Land Title in Nevada," *Western Historical Quarterly* 39, no. 2 (Summer 2008), esp. 126–28.

52. Daniel Heath Justice and Jean M. O'Brien, *Allotment Stories: Indigenous Land Relations under Settler Siege* (Minneapolis: University of Minnesota Press, 2022).

53. Doug Kiel, in conversation with the author, August 11, 2022.

54. See Duane Champagne, "UNDRIP (United Nations Declaration on the Rights of Indigenous Peoples): Human, Civil, and Indigenous Rights," *Wicazo Sa Review* 28, no. 1 (Spring 2013): 9–22; Francesca Merlan, "Indigeneity: Global and Local," *Current Anthropology* 50, no. 3 (June 2009) 303–31; Cher Weixa Chen, "Indigenous Rights in International Law," *Oxford Research Encyclopedia of International Studies*, November 20, 2017, https://oxfordre.com/internationalstudies/view/10.1093/acrefore/9780190846626.001.0001/acrefore-9780190846626-e-77.

55. I am guided here by Dan Flores's suggestion that "the perspective of the *longue durée* is essential to environmental history." See Dan Flores, "Bison Ecology and Bison Diplomacy: The Southern Plains from 1800 to 1850," *Journal of American History* 78, no. 2 (September 1991): 467.

56. I am informed here by Kevin Bruyneel, *The Third Space of Sovereignty: The Post-Colonial Politics of US/Indigenous Relations* (Minneapolis: University of Minnesota Press, 2007); Dennison, *Colonial Entanglement*; and Pasternak, *Grounded Authority*.

57. Douglas Firth Anderson, "Wapello (ca. 1787–March 15, 1842)," Biographical Dictionary of Iowa, Digital Press Editions, University of Iowa, accessed February 25, 2022, http://uipress.lib.uiowa.edu/bdi/DetailsPage.aspx?id=394.

CHAPTER 1

1. Oral tradition adapted from Johnathan Lantz Buffalo, "Oral History of the Meskwaki," *The Wisconsin Archeologist, from the Great Lakes to the Great Plains: Meskwaki Archaeology and Ethnohistory* 89, no. 1–2 (January–December 2008): 3–5.

2. Michael Witgen, "The Native New World and Western North America," *Western Historical Quarterly* 43, no. 3 (Autumn 2012): 297.

3. John W. Hall, *Uncommon Defense: Indian Allies in the Black Hawk War* (Cambridge, MA: Harvard University Press, 2009), 3.

4. Donald Wanatee, "Effects of Euroamerican Incursions on the Social, Linguistic, Economic, and Religious Aspects of the Meskwaki throughout the Great Lakes Region," *Wisconsin Archeologist* 89, no. 1–2 (January–December 2008): 202.

5. Buffalo, "Oral History," 5.

6. Wanatee, "Effects of Euroamerican Incursions," 200. See also Jeffrey A. Behm, "The Meskwaki in Eastern Wisconsin: Ethnohistory and Archaeology," *Wisconsin Archeologist* 89, no. 1–2 (January–December 2008): 10–11; Barbara Alice Mann, *President by Massacre: Indian-Killing for Political Gain* (Santa Barbara, CA: ABC-CLIO, 2019), 261.

7. Buffalo, "Oral History," 3–4; Donald Wanatee, "Effects of Euroamerican Incursions," 200.

8. Buffalo, "Oral History," 3–4.

9. R. David Edmunds and Joseph L. Peyser, *The Fox Wars: The Mesquakie Challenge to New France* (Norman: University of Oklahoma Press, 1993), 8–10.

NOTES TO CHAPTER 1

10. Edmunds and Peyser, *Fox Wars*, 8–10. See also Patrick J. Jung, *The Black Hawk War of 1832* (Norman: University of Oklahoma Press, 2007), 13–14. See also State Historical Society of Iowa, "History of the Meskwaki Timeline," 2004, https://history.iowa.gov/history/education/educator-resources/primary-source-sets/westward-expansion-and-native-americans/timeline-meskwaki.

11. Behm, "Meskwaki in Eastern Wisconsin," 7. See page 14 for a detailed list of Meskwaki villages in Wisconsin between the 1650s and 1730s.

12. Buffalo, "Oral History," 3.

13. Behm, "Meskwaki in Eastern Wisconsin," 18.

14. Ryan J. Howell, "The Meskwaki Settlement at Prairie du Chien, 1730–1780," *Wisconsin Archaeologist* 89, no. 1–2 (January–February 2008): 119–120.

15. Hall, *Uncommon Defense*, 3. On early Indigenous migrations, see for example Stephen Warren, *The World the Shawnees Made: Migration and Violence in Early America* (Chapel Hill: University of North Carolina Press, 2014).

16. Howell, "Meskwaki Settlement at Prairie du Chien, 1730–1780," 119.

17. Hall, *Uncommon Defense*, 3. See also Cornelia F. Mutel, *The Emerald Horizon: The History of Nature in Iowa* (Iowa City: University of Iowa Press, 2008).

18. Michael D. Green, "'We Dance in Opposite Directions': Mesquakie (Fox) Separatism from the Sac and Fox Tribe," *Ethnohistory* 30, no. 3 (Summer 1983): 130.

19. Buffalo, "Oral History," 3–4.

20. Cynthia L. Peterson, John G. Hedden, and Cindy L. Nagel, "Archaeology of the Meskwaki Fur Trade in Iowa, 1835–1845," *Wisconsin Archeologist* 89, no. 1–2 (January–February 2008): 163; Behm, "Meskwaki in Eastern Wisconsin," 7. See also Richard White, *The Middle Ground: Indians, Empires, and Republics in the Great Lakes Region, 1650–1815* (New York: Cambridge University Press, 1991).

21. For a detailed account of the siege, see Edmunds and Peyser, *Fox Wars*, 55–74.

22. Jung, *Black Hawk War*, 13–14.

23. Peterson, Hedden, and Nagel, "Archaeology of the Meskwaki Fur Trade," 163.

24. Jung, *Black Hawk War*, 13; Behm, "The Meskwaki in Eastern Wisconsin, 7.

25. Jung, *Black Hawk War*, 13–14; Green, "We Dance," 130.

26. Jung, *Black Hawk War*, 13. On translation of the Sauk Nation's name, see Johnathan Buffalo, interviewed by Nicholas A. Brown, in Nicholas A. Brown and Sarah E. Kanouse, *Re-Collecting Black Hawk: Landscape, Memory, and Power in the American Midwest* (Pittsburgh: University of Pittsburgh Press, 2015), 68.

27. Green, "We Dance," 130; Lucy Eldersveld Murphy, *Great Lakes Creoles: A French-Indian Community on the Northern Borderlands, Prairie du Chien, 1750–1860* (New York: Cambridge University Press, 2014), 26. See also Buffalo, interviewed by Brown, in *Re-Collecting Black Hawk*, 68.

28. Behm "Meskwaki in Eastern Wisconsin," 8.

29. Jung, *Black Hawk War*, 14. Wanatee, "Effects of Euroamerican Incursions," 202.

30. Jung, *Black Hawk War*, 13.

31. Jung, *Black Hawk War*, 19.

32. Edmunds and Peyser, *Fox Wars*, 48–49; Erik D. Gooding, "The Return to *Nekotosiye*: Meskwaki Village Life, 1857–1902," 2018, unpublished manuscript, used and cited with Gooding's permission, copy in the author's possession, 19.

33. Johnathan L. Buffalo, "Historical Overview of the Adoption of the Indian Reorganization Act of 1934 by the Sac and Fox of the Mississippi in Iowa," 1, IRA, MHPO.

34. Buffalo, "Historical Overview," 1–2; W. R. Lesser, "Report of Agent in Iowa," in *Fifty-Ninth Annual Report of the Commissioner of Indian Affairs to the Secretary of the Interior* (Washington, DC: Government Printing Office, 1890), 103–106.

35. Jung, *Black Hawk War*, 19.

36. Green, "We Dance," 130.

37. Behm, "Meskwaki in Eastern Wisconsin," 14; Green, "We Dance," 130; "Mesquakie," *Goldfinch* 3, no. 13 (February 1992): 18; Royce Kurtz, "Timber and Treaties," *Forest & Conservation History* 35, no. 2 (April 1991): 58. See also Royce Delbert Kurtz, "Economic and Political History of the Sauk and Mesquakie: 1780's–1845" (PhD diss., University of Iowa, 1986).

38. Green, "We Dance," 130.

39. Murphy, *Great Lakes Creoles*, 27; Jung, *Black Hawk War*, 14.

40. S. S. Hebberd, *History of Wisconsin under the Dominion of France* (Madison, WI: Midland Publishing, 1890), 84. Different iterations of this quote appear across the literature on Meskwaki history. See for example Edmunds and Peyser, *Fox Wars*, 70; Irving Bernadine Richman, *Ioway to Iowa: The Genesis of a Corn and Bible Commonwealth* (Iowa City: State Historical Society of Iowa, 1931), 55.

41. For overviews of the causes, action, and immediate outcomes of the Seven Years' War, see Daniel Baugh, *The Global Seven Years' War, 1754–1763* (New York: Pearson Press, 2011); Fred Anderson, *Crucible of War: The Seven Years' War and the Fate of Empire in British North America, 1754–1766* (New York: Knopf, 2000).

42. Walter R. Echo-Hawk, *In the Courts of the Conqueror: The 10 Worst Indian Law Cases Ever Decided* (Golden, CO: Fulcrum, 2010), 17–18.

43. See Anderson, *Crucible of War*; Warren R. Hofstra, ed., *Cultures in Conflict: The Seven Years' War in North America* (Lanham, MD: Rowman & Littlefield, 2007).

44. Buffalo, "Oral History," 4. Patrick Jung argues that the Meskwaki and Sauk Nations had close, early bonds with the Spanish by the 1760s and slowly allied themselves with the British in the decades that followed. See Jung, *Black Hawk War*, 14–15, 18.

45. Hall, *Uncommon Defense*, 4.

46. Hall, *Uncommon Defense*, 4; Jung, *Black Hawk War*, 14.

47. Murphy, *Great Lakes Creoles*, 27. See also Susan Sleeper-Smith, *Indian Women and French Men: Rethinking Cultural Encounter in the Western Great Lakes* (Amherst: University of Massachusetts Press, 2001); Lucy Eldersveld Murphy, *A Gathering of Rivers: Indians, Metis, and Mining in the Western Great Lakes, 1737–1832* (Lincoln: University of Nebraska Press, 2000).

48. Jung, *Black Hawk War*, 15.
49. William Clark, June 13, 1804, and annotations, JLCE.
50. Clark, Winter 1804–1805, JLCE.
51. Otoe-Missouria Tribe, "Who We Are: Otoe & Missouria, Five Hundred Years of History," accessed July 6, 2022, https://www.omtribe.org/who-we-are/history/.
52. Greg Olson, *Ioway Life: Reservation and Reform, 1836–1870* (Norman: University of Oklahoma Press, 2016), 7. For deep explorations of the role and meanings of Indigenous violence in the West, see for example Ned Blackhawk, *Violence over the Land: Indians and Empires in the Early American West* (Cambridge, MA: Harvard University Press, 2008); James F. Brooks, *Mesa of Sorrows: A History of the Awat'ovi Massacre* (New York: W. W. Norton, 2017); Karl Jacoby, *Shadows at Dawn: An Apache Massacre and the Violence of History* (New York: Penguin, 2009).
53. See Stuart Banner, *How the Indians Lost Their Land: Law and Power on the Frontier* (Cambridge, MA: Harvard University Press, 2005), 85–111; "The Royal Proclamation—October 7, 1763, By the King. A Proclamation George R.," The Avalon Project of Yale Law School's Lillian Goldman Law Library, accessed June 14, 2022, https://avalon.law.yale.edu.
54. Hall, *Uncommon Defense*, 4.
55. Hall, *Uncommon Defense*, 32.
56. Buffalo, "Oral History," 5–6.
57. Hall, *Uncommon Defense*, 4.
58. Jung, *Black Hawk War*, 14–15.
59. Buffalo, "Oral History," 6.
60. Jung, *Black Hawk War*, 13.
61. Colin G. Calloway, "The Continuing Revolution in Indian Country," in *Native Americans and the Early Republic*, eds. Frederick E. Hoxie, Ronald Hoffman, and Peter J. Albert (Charlottesville, VA: United States Capitol Historical Society and the University Press of Virginia, 1999), 13.
62. See for example Elizabeth A. Fenn, *Encounters at the Heart of the World: A History of the Mandan People* (New York: Hill and Wang, 2014); Pekka Hämäläinen, *The Comanche Empire* (New Haven, CT: Yale University Press, 2009); Pekka Hämäläinen, *Lakota America: A New History of Indigenous Power* (New Haven, CT: Yale University Press, 2019); Andrew Lipman, *The Saltwater Frontier: Indians and the Contest for the American Coast* (New Haven, CT: Yale University Press, 2015).
63. Hall, *Uncommon Defense*, 32.
64. See Banner, *How the Indians Lost Their Land*, 112–45; John P. Bowes, *Land Too Good for Indians: Northern Indian Removal* (Norman: University of Oklahoma Press, 2016), 21–22.
65. Banner, *How the Indians Lost Their Land*, 112–13, 126–32.
66. Woody Holton, *Unruly Americans and the Origins of the Constitution* (New York: Hill & Wang, 2007), 143–44.
67. Jung, *Black Hawk War*, 16.

68. "Northwest Ordinance, July 13, 1787: An Ordinance for the Government of the Territory of the United States Northwest of the River Ohio," Avalon Project, Yale Law School, accessed February 28, 2023, https://avalon.law.yale.edu/18th_century/nworder.asp.

69. Bowes, *Land Too Good for Indians*, 50.

70. U.S. Const., art. I, § 8.

71. Jung, *Black Hawk War*, 15–16.

72. Holton, *Unruly Americans*, 268.

73. Stephen L. Pevar, *The Rights of Indians and Tribes: The Authoritative ACLU Guide to Indian and Tribal Rights* (New York: New York University Press, 2004), 6; Holton, *Unruly Americans*, 269.

74. Jung, *Black Hawk War*, 16.

75. Jung, *Black Hawk War*, 13.

76. Jung, *Black Hawk War*, 16.

77. Pevar, *Rights of Indians and Tribes*, 6; Holton, *Unruly Americans*, 143–44.

78. Clark, Winter 1804–1805, JLCE.

79. Kurtz, "Economic and Political History," 21–28.

80. See Geo F. Robeson, "Fur Trade in Early Iowa," *Palimpsest* 6, no. 1 (Iowa City: State Historical Society of Iowa, 1925): 14–18; Laura Rigal, "Watershed Days on the Treaty Line, 1836–1839," *Iowa Review* 39, no. 2 (Fall 2009): 205–6.

81. Clark, October 1, 1804, JLCE.

82. See James M. Collins, "Meskwaki Mining in the Upper Mississippi River Lead District During the Era of Julien Dubuque," *Wisconsin Archaeologist* 89, no. 1–2 (January–February 2008): 150.

83. Collins, "Meskwaki Mining," 150; Claudio Saunt, *Unworthy Republic: The Dispossession of Native Americans and the Road to Indian Territory* (New York: W. W. Norton, 2020), 144.

84. John Broihahn, "Meskwaki Mining Metamorphosis: Mining Archival and Archaeological Resources for Insights on Meskwaki Mining and Smelting in Upper Mississippi Valley Lead Fields," *Wisconsin Archaeologist* 89, no. 1–2 (January–February 2008): 102.

85. Broihahn, "Meskwaki Mining Metamorphosis," 101.

86. Broihahn, "Meskwaki Mining Metamorphosis," 103–4; Shirley J. Schermer, "The Archaeology of the Mines of Spain: The Meskwaki and Julien Dubuque," *Wisconsin Archeologist* 89, no. 1–2 (January–February 2008): 132.

87. Broihahn, "Meskwaki Mining Metamorphosis," 105–11. See also Lucy Eldersveld Murphy, "'Their Women Quite Industrious Miners': Native American Lead Mining in the Upper Mississippi Valley, 1788–1832," in *Enduring Nations: Native Americans in the Midwest*, ed. R. David Edmunds (Urbana: University of Illinois Press, 2008): 36–53; Murphy, *Gathering of Rivers*, 82.

88. Saunt, *Unworthy Republic*, 144.

89. Broihahn, "Meskwaki Mining Metamorphosis," 104.

90. Schermer, "Archaeology of the Mines of Spain," 136.

91. Arthur G. Leonard, "History of Lead and Zinc Mining in Iowa," *Annals of Iowa* 3 (1897): 63–66. Murphy, "Their Women," 39; Collins, "Meskwaki Mining," 153.

92. Saunt, *Unworthy Republic*, 144.

93. David M. Stothers and Patrick M. Tucker, *The Fry Site: Archaeological and Ethnohistorical Perspectives on the Maumee River Ottawa of Northwest Ohio* (University of Toledo Laboratory of Archaeology Occasional Monographs) no. 2 (2006): 214.

94. There were also 4,800 Sauk people that year. See Mann, *President by Massacre*, 261.

95. Broihahn, "Meskwaki Mining Metamorphosis," 103, 113.

96. Colin G. Calloway, *Pen & Ink Witchcraft: Treaties and Treaty Making in American Indian History* (New York: Oxford University Press, 2013), 5.

97. See Anthony F. C. Wallace, *Jefferson and the Indians: The Tragic Fate of the First Americans* (Cambridge, MA: Belknap Press, 1999), esp. 206–75.

98. National Archives and Records Administration, "The Louisiana Purchase, Transcriptions: Treaty between the United States of America and the French Republic," American Originals, 1996, https://www.archives.gov/exhibits/american _originals/louistxt.html.

99. Hall, *Uncommon Defense*, 32. See also Bowes, *Land Too Good for Indians*, 23, 29.

100. Clark, March 25, 1804, JLCE.

101. David Lavender, *The Way to the Western Sea: Lewis and Clark across the Continent* (Lincoln: University of Nebraska Press, 2001), 95.

102. See Richard White, "The Fictions of Patriarchy: Indians and Whites in the Early Republic," in *Native Americans and the Early Republic*, eds. Frederick E. Hoxie, Ronald Hoffman, and Peter J. Albert (Charlottesville, VA: United States Capitol Historical Society and the University Press of Virginia, 1999), 62–84; Francis Paul Prucha, *The Great Father: The United States Government and the American Indians*, (Lincoln: University of Nebraska Press, 1984), xxviii.

103. Hall, *Uncommon Defense*, 4.

104. Lavender, *Way to the Western Sea*, 95–96.

105. Buffalo, "Oral History," 5.

106. Bowes, *Land Too Good for Indians*, 53.

107. See Stephen J. Rockwell, *Indian Affairs and the Administrative State in the Nineteenth Century* (New York: Cambridge University Press, 2010), 38–88; Bowes, *Land Too Good for Indians*, 55.

108. Green, "We Dance," 130

109. Kathleen Duval, *The Native Ground: Indians and Colonists in the Heart of the Continent* (Philadelphia: University of Pennsylvania Press, 2006), 184.

110. Wallace, *Jefferson and the Indians*, 249.

111. Jung, *Black Hawk War*, 18–20.

112. Jung, *Black Hawk War*, 20. See also B. L. Wick, "The Struggle for the Half-Breed Tract," *Annals of Iowa* 7, no 1 (1905): 16. Historians disagree about tribal

representation in the signing of the Treaty of 1804. Michael Green, for example, argues that it was signed "by four Sauks and no Mesquakies," while B. L. Wick, writing in the early twentieth century, writes that "five Indian chiefs of the Fox and Sac nation" signed the document. Johnathan Buffalo argues that it was "signed by a Sauk band and one Meskwaki." The treaty itself shows that five Native men and William Henry Harrison signed the document. See Green, "We Dance," 130; Wick, "Struggle for the Half-Breed Tract," 16; Buffalo, interviewed by Brown, 65; "Treaty between the United States Government and the Sauk and Fox Indians Signed at Saint Louis in the District of Louisiana on November 11, 1804 (Ratified Indian Treaty #43, 7 STAT 84), Ratified Indian Treaty 43, Sauk and Fox-St. Louis in the District of Louisiana, November 3, 1804, Indian Treaties, 1722-186, General Records of the United States Government, Record Group 11, NARA-DC, accessed May 11, 2022, https://www.docsteach.org/documents/document/sauk-and-fox-treaty. See also Scott Richard Lyons, *X-Marks: Native Signatures of Assent* (Minneapolis: University of Minnesota Press, 2010).

113. Jung, *Black Hawk War*, 20.

114. Jung, *Black Hawk War*, 18–20.

115. In his autobiography, Makataimeshekiakiak (Black Hawk) twice notes that Quashquame told him personally that he "never had consented to the sale of our village." Quashquame, quoted by Makataimeshekiakiak, in Roger L. Nichols, ed., *Black Hawk's Autobiography* (Ames: Iowa State University Press, 1999), 50. See also 53.

116. Jung, *Black Hawk War*, 20–22.

117. See "Treaty between the United States Government and the Sauk and Fox Indians Signed at Saint Louis in the District of Louisiana on November 11, 1804" (Ratified Indian Treaty #43, 7 STAT 84), November 3, 1804, Ratified Indian Treaty 43: Sauk and Fox - St. Louis in the District of Louisiana, November 3, 1804, Indian Treaties, 1722–1869, General Records of the United States Government, Record Group 11, National Archives Building, Washington, DC, accessed June 20, 2022, https://www.docsteach.org/documents/document/sauk-and-fox-treaty. See also Angela Keysor, "Emergence of a Distinct Legal Identity from the Forces of Assimilation: The Mesquakie Indians and the Fight for Citizenship, 1842–1912," unpublished manuscript available on MHCD, no page numbers.

118. Buffalo, interviewed by Brown, 68.

119. Wallace, *Jefferson and the Indians*, 251.

120. See Bethel Saler, *The Settler's Empire: Colonialism and State Formation in America's Old Northwest* (Philadelphia: University of Pennsylvania Press, 2015), 1–12.

121. See "Treaty between the United States Government and the Sauk and Fox Indians signed at Saint Louis in the District of Louisiana on November 11, 1804." The US government still formally recognizes three groups of Sauk and Meskwaki descendants in the language of this two-century-old misnomer: The Sac and Fox Tribe of the Mississippi in Iowa (Meskwaki Nation), the Sac and Fox Nation of Missouri in Kansas and Nebraska, and the Sac and Fox Nation of Oklahoma.

122. Here I follow Robert Lee, who uses an 1816 American land grab in Missouri to demonstrate how treaties did not simply "legally tidy up settler floods." Instead, treaties themselves became the mechanisms that usurped specific tracts of Indigenous land while setting the stage for further land seizures. See Robert Lee, "Sources and Interpretations: 'A Better View of the Country': A Missouri Settlement Map by William Clark, *William and Mary Quarterly*, 3d ser., 79, no. 1 (January 2022): 114.

123. Several historians have traced the roots of later disagreements between Sauk and Meskwaki leaders to the 1804 treaty. See for example Edmunds and Peyser, *Fox Wars*, 206; Green, "We Dance," 130–32; Jung, *Black Hawk War*, 19.

124. For a complete list, as well as the full text, of all treaties between the United States and the Sauks and the Red Earth People, see "Meskwaki History: Relations with United States Government," MHCD.

125. Green, "We Dance," 130. For other examples of separate Native Nations forced to share reservations, see for example Robert J. Bigart, *Providing for the People: Economic Change among the Salish and Kootenai Indians, 1875–1910* (Norman: University of Oklahoma Press, 2020); Jeffrey Ostler, *The Lakotas and the Black Hills: The Struggle for Sacred Ground* (New York: Viking, 2010); Paul Vandevelder, *Coyote Warrior: One Man, Three Tribes, and the Trial that Forged a Nation* (New York: Little, Brown, and Company, 2004).

126. See J. B. Patterson, ed., *Autobiography of Ma-Ka-Tai-Me-She-Kia-Kiak, or Black Hawk, by Black Hawk, Embracing the Traditions of His Nations, Various Wars in Which He Had Been Engaged, and His Account of the Cause and General History of Black Hawk War, His Surrender, and Travels through the United States* (Rock Island, IL: J. B. Patterson, 1882), https://www.gutenberg.org/files/7097/7097-h/7097-h.htm. This quote is also stated as "it has been the origin of all our difficulties." See Black Hawk, quoted in Jung, *Black Hawk War*, 12; Nichols, *Black Hawk's Autobiography*, 18.

CHAPTER 2

1. John P. Bowes, *Land Too Good for Indians: Northern Indian Removal* (Norman: University of Oklahoma Press, 2016), 31–34.

2. Bowes, *Land Too Good for Indians*, 31–34; Patrick J. Jung, *The Black Hawk War of 1832* (Norman: University of Oklahoma Press, 2007), 27; John W. Hall, *Uncommon Defense: Indian Allies in the Black Hawk War* (Cambridge, MA: Harvard University Press, 2009), 32.

3. Hall, *Uncommon Defense*, 68.

4. Jung, *Black Hawk War*, 17, 26–27.

5. William T. Hagan, *The Sac and Fox Indians* (Norman: University of Oklahoma Press, 1958), 84; Jung, *Black Hawk War*, 24.

6. Jung, *Black Hawk War*, 27.

7. Bowes, *Land Too Good for Indians*, 31–34.

8. Jung, *Black Hawk War*, 29–30.

9. Cynthia L. Peterson, John G. Hedden, and Cindy L. Nagel, "Archaeology of the Meskwaki Fur Trade in Iowa, 1835–1845," *Wisconsin Archeologist* 89, no. 1–2 (January–February 2008): 163.

10. Jung, *Black Hawk War*, 29–31; Peterson, Hedden, and Nagel, "Archaeology of the Meskwaki Fur Trade," 163; Hall, *Uncommon Defense*, 32; Robert Lee, "Sources and Interpretations: 'A Better View of the Country': A Missouri Settlement Map by William Clark, *William and Mary Quarterly*, 3d ser., 79, no. 1 (January 2022): 108.

11. Hall, *Uncommon Defense*, 32, 35, 68. Bowes, *Land Too Good for Indians*, 54.

12. Jung, *Black Hawk War*, 22, 32.

13. Thomas Forsyth, quoted in both Hagan, *Sac and Fox Indians*, 84, and Jung, *Black Hawk War*, 22.

14. See Royce Kurtz, "Timber and Treaties," *Forest & Conservation History* 35, no. 2 (April 1991): 59.

15. Jung, *Black Hawk War*, 22, 31.

16. See Angela Keysor, "Emergence of a Distinct Legal Identity from the Forces of Assimilation: The Mesquakie Indians and the Fight for Citizenship, 1842–1912," unpublished manuscript available on MHCD, no page numbers.

17. Lee, "Better View of the Country," 89.

18. Lee, "Better View of the Country," 89–120; see 105 for the quote.

19. Erik D. Gooding, "The Return to *Nekotosiye*: Meskwaki Village Life, 1857–1902," 2018, unpublished manuscript, used and cited with Gooding's permission, copy in the author's possession, 1–2; State Historical Society of Iowa/Meskwaki Nation Historic Preservation Office, "Timeline of How the Meskwaki and Sauki Became Three Separate 'Sac & Fox' Tribes," 2004, https://history.iowa.gov/history/education/educator-resources/primary-source-sets/westward-expansion-and-native-americans/meskwaki-fox-sac.

20. Kathleen Duval, *The Native Ground: Indians and Colonists in the Heart of the Continent* (Philadelphia: University of Pennsylvania Press, 2006), 217.

21. Bowes, *Land Too Good for Indians*, 44.

22. Hall, *Uncommon Defense*, 63

23. Barbara Alice Mann, *President by Massacre: Indian-Killing for Political Gain* (Santa Barbara, CA: ABC-CLIO, 2019), 261.

24. "Population of Missouri by Counties and Minor Civil Divisions," *Census Bulletin* 32 (Washington, DC: Twelfth Census of the United States, 1901), 1. See https://www2.census.gov/library/publications/decennial/1900/bulletins/demographic/32-population-mo.pdf.

25. Mann, *President by Massacre*, 261.

26. Hall, *Uncommon Defense*, 63.

27. Hall, *Uncommon Defense*, 70–72.

28. Hall, *Uncommon Defense*, 74–77; John Broihahn, "Meskwaki Mining Metamorphosis: Mining Archival and Archaeological Resources for Insights on Meskwaki

Mining and Smelting in Upper Mississippi Valley Lead Fields," *Wisconsin Archaeologist* 89, no. 1–2 (January–February 2008): 103, 113.

29. Hall, *Uncommon Defense*, 76–77.

30. Peterson, Hedden, and Nagel, "Archaeology of the Meskwaki Fur Trade in Iowa, 1835–1845," 162.

31. Settlers called this parcel of land the Half-Breed Tract. This crude moniker has persisted in much of the historical literature and in popular memory. I avoid this term and instead refer to it here as the "Mixed-Race Reserve," while also recognizing, as Matthew Hill has noted, that the term "half-breed" was used in the 1820s and 1830s to describe people of ambiguous racial backgrounds and statuses, not necessarily just those who were of white and Indigenous heritage. See Matthew Hill, "'Half-Breeds,' Squatters, Land Speculations, and Settler Colonialism in the Des Moines–Mississippi Confluence" (MA Thesis, University of Northern Iowa, 2019); B. L. Wick, "The Struggle for the Half-Breed Tract," *Annals of Iowa* 7, no 1 (1905): 16–29; Lawrence Barkwell, "Iowa Half Breed Tract," Metis Museum of Canada, accessed July 13, 2022, https://www.metismuseum.ca/; J. A. Swisher, "The Half-Breed Tract," *Palimpsest* 14, no. 2 (February 1933): 69–76.

32. Hall, *Uncommon Defense*, 71–77; Kurtz, "Timber and Treaties," 58–59.

33. See Hall, *Uncommon Defense*, 76–77; Jung, *Black Hawk War*, 47–49.

34. Swisher, "Half-Breed Tract," 73–74.

35. Hall, *Uncommon Defense*, 89–90. For a summary of the Black Hawk War, see also Jeffrey Ostler, *Surviving Genocide: Native Nations and the United States from the American Revolution to Bleeding Kansas* (New Haven: Yale University Press, 2019), 297–308.

36. Jung, *Black Hawk War*, 61.

37. Jung, *Black Hawk War*, 56, 75–76.

38. See Claudio Saunt, *Unworthy Republic: The Dispossession of Native Americans and the Road to Indian Territory* (New York: W. W. Norton, 2020), 144–47; Michael D. Green, "'We Dance in Opposite Directions': Mesquakie (Fox) Separatism from the Sac and Fox Tribe," *Ethnohistory* 30, no. 3 (Summer 1983): 132. For a detailed account of the action of the war, see Jung, *Black Hawk War*, esp. 69–160; Kerry A. Trask, *Black Hawk* (New York: Henry Holt, 2006), esp. 163–239.

39. Jung, *Black Hawk War*, 32; Hall, *Uncommon Defense*, 89–100.

40. Hall, *Uncommon Defense*, 95. Here I borrow from Hall, who titled Chapter 9 of *Uncommon Defense* "An Indian War."

41. Hall, *Uncommon Defense*, 253.

42. Bowes, *Land Too Good for Indians*, 42–44, quote on 44.

43. Ostler, *Surviving Genocide*, 307.

44. See Stephen L. Pevar, *The Rights of Indians and Tribes: The Authoritative ACLU Guide to Indian and Tribal Rights* (New York: New York University Press, 2004), 7; Walter R. Echo-Hawk, *In the Courts of the Conqueror: The 10 Worst Indian Law Cases Ever Decided* (Golden, CO: Fulcrum, 2010), 55–127; Frank Pommersheim, *Broken*

Landscape: Indians, Indian Tribes, and the Constitution (New York: Oxford University Press, 2009), 87–124; David E. Wilkins, *American Indian Sovereignty and the US Supreme Court: The Masking of Justice* (Austin: University of Texas Press, 1997); Ronald N. Satz, *American Indian Policy in the Jacksonian Era* (Lincoln: University of Nebraska Press, 1974).

45. Hall, *Uncommon Defense*, 93. Here, I utilize Saunt's term from *Unworthy Republic*, "deportation," as a descriptor for Indian removal. On major trends in federal Indian policy in the nineteenth century, see Frederick E. Hoxie, *A Final Promise: The Campaign to Assimilate the Indians, 1880–1920* (New York: Cambridge University Press, 1989); Janet A. McDonnell, *The Dispossession of the American Indian, 1887–1934* (Bloomington: Indiana University Press, 1989); C. Joseph Genetin-Pilawa, *Crooked Paths to Allotment: The Fight over Federal Indian Policy after the Civil War* (Chapel Hill: University of North Carolina Press, 2012).

46. See Theda Perdue and Michael D. Green, *The Cherokee Nation and the Trail of Tears* (New York: Viking, 2007); and Perdue, "The Legacy of Indian Removal," *Journal of Southern History* 78, no. 1 (Feb. 2012): 3–36; Gregory D. Smithers, *The Cherokee Diaspora: An Indigenous History of Migration, Resettlement, and Identity* (New Haven, CT: Yale University Press, 2015).

47. Susan E. Gray, "Stories Written in the Blood: Race and Midwestern History," in *The American Midwest: Essays on Regional History*, ed. Andrew R. L. Cayton and Susan E. Gray (Bloomington: Indiana University Press, 2001), 124–26.

48. Bowes, *Land Too Good for Indians*, 5.

49. Cornelia F. Mutel, *The Emerald Horizon: The History of Nature in Iowa* (Iowa City: University of Iowa Press, 2008), 41.

50. Mutel, *Emerald Horizon*, 36–42.

51. Green, "We Dance," 132.

52. Green, "We Dance," 132.

53. *Denison Review* (Denison, IA), September 4, 1914.

54. Green, "We Dance," 134. See also Lucy Eldersveld Murphy, *Great Lakes Creoles: A French-Indian Community on the Northern Borderlands, Prairie du Chien, 1750–1860* (New York: Cambridge University Press, 2014), 251–61; Wick, "The Struggle for the Half-Breed Tract," 16–29.

55. Kurtz, "Timber and Treaties," 61–63; Laura Rigal, "Watershed Days on the Treaty Line, 1836–1839," *Iowa Review* 39, no. 2 (Fall 2009): 206.

56. Kurtz, "Timber and Treaties," 61–63. See also Rigal, "Watershed Days," 206.

57. Kurtz, "Timber and Treaties," 59–61.

58. Peterson, Hedden, and Nagel, "Archaeology of the Meskwaki Fur Trade in Iowa," 167.

59. Peterson, Hedden, and Nagel, "Archaeology of the Meskwaki Fur Trade in Iowa," 167; Royce Delbert Kurtz, "Economic and Political History of the Sauk and Mesquakie: 1780s–1845" (PhD diss., University of Iowa, 1986), 120–23.

60. Peterson, Hedden, and Nagel, "Archaeology of the Meskwaki Fur Trade in Iowa," 162, 167.

NOTES TO CHAPTER 2

61. Bill Sherman, "Tracing the Treaties: How They Affected American Indians and Iowa," *Iowa History Journal*, accessed July 18, 2022, http://iowahistoryjournal.com/tracing-treaties-affected-american-indians-iowa/.

62. See Jung, *Black Hawk War*, 12, 31, 187–89; Peterson, Hedden, and Nagel, "Archaeology of the Meskwaki Fur Trade in Iowa," 163, 167; Green, "We Dance," 133–38; R. David Edmunds and Joseph L. Peyser, *The Fox Wars: The Mesquakie Challenge to New France* (Norman: University of Oklahoma Press, 1993), 206; Hagan, *Sac and Fox Indians*, 205–224; Kurtz, "Economic and Political History," 276–91.

63. See also Rigal, "Watershed Days," 206.

64. Mann, *President by Massacre*, 261; Kurtz, "Timber and Treaties," 60–61. These estimates are challenged by Peterson, Hedden, and Nagel, who cite an 1840 letter by a government official that placed the Meskwaki population at 2,446 people, spread over three main Meskwaki villages, in 1838. I follow the lower consensus by other sources, aware of the possibility that the official mistakenly counted the total number of people—which could have included Sauk people and other visitors, not just Meskwaki people—living in the Meskwaki villages at that time. See also Kurtz, "Economic and Political History," 30–36.

65. Peterson, Hedden, and Nagel, "Archaeology of the Meskwaki Fur Trade in Iowa," 176.

66. Ostler, *Surviving Genocide*, 7–8, 352–53.

67. "Artifact: Bear Claw Necklace," MHCD; "Meskwaki Tribe Places Historic Bear Claw Necklace on Display," *Z News*, March 19, 2014, http://www.indianz.com/News/2014/012936.asp.

68. Here I draw upon Kurtz, "Timber and Treaties," 63, who has called the Sauk and Meskwaki treaty decision a "stopgap" solution.

69. *Oxford Weekly Leader* (Oxford, IA), August 7, 1869; Mary Alecia Owen, *Folk-Lore of the Musquakie Indians of North America and Catalogue of Musquakie Beadwork and Other Objects in the Collections of the Folk-Lore Society* (London: David Nutt, 1904), 26.

70. Owen, *Folk-Lore*, 33.

71. *Oxford Weekly Leader* (Oxford, IA), August 7, 1869; Owen, *Folk-Lore*, 26.

72. See James W. Grimes, "The Sac and Fox Indian Council of 1841," *Annals of Iowa* 12, no. 5 (July 1920): 321–31, available from the Northern Illinois University Digital Library, https://digital.lib.niu.edu/islandora/object/niu-prairie%3A2062.

73. Hartley Crawford, quoted in James Grimes, "Sac and Fox Indian Council of 1841," 323–24.

74. See Grimes, "Sac and Fox Indian Council of 1841," 323–25. See also Green, "We Dance," 134.

75. Wishecomacquet, quoted in Grimes, "Sac and Fox Indian Council of 1841," 327.

76. See Kishkekosh and Wishewahka, quoted in Grimes, "Sac and Fox Indian Council of 1841," 327–28. See also Kurtz, "Timber and Treaties," 56.

77. Poweshiek, quoted in Grimes, "Sac and Fox Indian Council of 1841," 327.

78. Jung, *Black Hawk War*, 22, 32. See also Paul W. Gates, "The Homestead Act: Free Land Policy in Operation, 1862–1935," in *Land Use Policy in the United States*, ed. Howard W. Ottoson (Washington, DC: BeardBooks, 1963), 28–46.

79. Wapello quoted in Grimes, "Sac and Fox Indian Council of 1841," 329.

80. Grimes, "Sac and Fox Indian Council of 1841," 330–31.

81. Benjamin F. Shambaugh, ed., "The Sac and Fox Indians and the Treaty of 1842," *Iowa Journal of History and Politics* 10, no. 2 (April 1912), 261.

82. See John Beach, "The Sac and Fox Indian Council of 1841," *Annals of Iowa* 12, no. 5 (July 1920): 332–45, available from the Northern Illinois University Digital Library, https://digital.lib.niu.edu/islandora/object/niu-prairie%3A2062.

83. John Chambers to J. G. Spencer, October 13, 1842, in "Ratified Treaty No. 243, Documents Relating to the Negotiation of the Treaty of October 11, 1842, with the Sauk and Fox Indians," pages 4–5, University of Wisconsin Digital Collections, accessed July 20, 2022, https://search.library.wisc.edu/digital/AHistory. Emphasis in original. Historians have tended to emphasize leadership disputes between tribal leaders. See Green, "We Dance," 130–32, 138; Jung, *Black Hawk War*, 19.

84. Chambers, quoted in Beach, "Sac and Fox Indian Council of 1842," 332.

85. Chambers, quoted in Beach, "Sac and Fox Indian Council of 1842," 332.

86. Poweshiek, quoted in Beach, "Sac and Fox Indian Council of 1842," 335.

87. Wishecomaque, quoted in Beach, "Sac and Fox Indian Council of 1842," 335–36. In his minutes of the negotiations, Beach spells "Wishecomacquet" as "Wishecomaque."

88. Chambers to Spencer, October 13, 1842; Chambers, quoted in Beach, "Sac and Fox Indian Council of 1842," 336–37.

89. Green, "We Dance," 135. See 134 on the bribes.

90. "Sac and Fox Treaty, 1842: Treaty with the Sauk and Foxes, 1842, October 11, 1842," State Historical Society of Iowa, https://iowaculture.gov/sites/default/files/history-education-pss-voting-1842-transcription.pdf.

91. Clark, Winter 1804–1805, JLCE.

92. Keokuk, quoted in Beach, "Sac and Fox Indian Council of 1842," 338–39; Chambers, quoted in Beach, "Sac and Fox Indian Council of 1842," 332; Chambers, quoted in Beach, "Sac and Fox Indian Council of 1842," 332; "Legal Status of the Musquakies: From the Attorney General's Report to Governor Cummins," 1905, folder 19, box BL21, SHSI-IC; Sherman, "Tracing the Treaties"; Chambers to Spencer, October 13, 1842, 4, 8; Beach, "Sac and Fox Indian Council of 1842," 344.

93. Chambers to Spencer, October 13, 1842; Chambers, quoted in Beach, "Sac and Fox Indian Council of 1842," 336–37.

94. "Sac and Fox Treaty, 1842"; Chambers, quoted in Beach, "Sac and Fox Indian Council of 1842," 332, emphasis added.

95. Green, "We Dance," 134–35 estimates the 1842 treaty cession at 11 million acres. Divided by the purchase price of $1.05 million, this is about $10.39 per acre.

96. Shambaugh, "The Sac and Fox Indians and the Treaty of 1842," 264.

97. J. Leland Mitchell, "Crying in the Bottoms," *Palimpsest* 26, no. 8 (August 1945), 241.

98. Ambrose Cowperthwaite Fulton, *A Life's Voyage: A Diary of a Sailor on Sea and Land, Jotted Down During a Seventy-Years' Voyage* (New York, 1898), 542.

99. *Daily Gate City and Constitution-Democrat* (Keokuk, IA), April 17, 1920.

CHAPTER 3

1. John Beach to Thomas Harvey, September 1, 1846, from the *Annual Report of the Commissioner of Indian Affairs, 1846*, quoted in Johnathan Buffalo, "A Narrative of Chronology and Perspectives on the Removal and Return of the Meskwaki to Iowa: 1839–1857," accessed July 25, 2022, https://www.meskwaki.org/wp-content/uploads/2021/03/Meskwaki-A-Narrative-of-Chronology-and-Perspectives.pdf.

2. Cynthia L. Peterson, John G. Hedden, and Cindy L. Nagel, "Archaeology of the Meskwaki Fur Trade in Iowa, 1835–1845," *Wisconsin Archeologist* 89, no. 1–2 (January–February 2008): 176.

3. Michael D. Green, "'We Dance in Opposite Directions': Mesquakie (Fox) Separatism from the Sac and Fox Tribe," *Ethnohistory* 30, no. 3 (Summer 1983): 134–35. On Indian removal, see Stephen J. Rockwell, *Indian Affairs and the Administrative State in the Nineteenth Century* (New York: Cambridge University Press, 2010), 38–102, 159–216. See Stuart Banner, *How the Indians Lost Their Land: Law and Power on the Frontier* (Cambridge, MA: Harvard University Press, 2005), 191–227; Theda Perdue and Michael D. Green, *The Cherokee Nation and the Trail of Tears* (New York: Viking, 2007); Theda Perdue, "The Legacy of Indian Removal," *Journal of Southern History* 78, no. 1 (February 2012): 3–36; Robert Marshall Utley, *The Indian Frontier, 1846–1890* (Albuquerque: University of New Mexico Press, 2003), 33–58; Mark David Spence, *Dispossessing the Wilderness: Indian Removal and the Making of the National Parks* (New York: Oxford University Press, 1999).

4. Harold P. Dickey and Harold Penner, "Soil Survey of Osage County, Kansas," United States Department of Agriculture Soil Conservation Service (Washington, DC: Government Printing Office, March 1985): 1, 27. See also Green, "We Dance," 136; Peterson, Hedden, and Nagel, "The Meskwaki Fur Trade in Iowa," 176.

5. In addition to the works cited earlier in this volume, see for example Kim Tallbear, "Caretaking Relations, Not American Dreaming," *Kalfou* 6, no. 1 (Spring 2019): 24–41; Kyle Pows Whyte, "Time as Kinship," in *The Cambridge Companion to Environmental Humanities*, ed. Jeffery Cohen and Stephanie Foote (New York: Cambridge University Press, 2021), 39–55.

6. William Jones, "Notes on the Fox Indians," *Journal of American Folklore* 24, no. 91 (January–March 1911), 219. Jones's account is based on a conversation with a Meskwaki person who was describing why their people preferred Iowa to the surrounding territories. See also Erik D. Gooding, "The Return to *Nekotosiye*: Meskwaki

Village Life, 1857–1902," 2018, unpublished manuscript, used and cited with Gooding's permission, copy in the author's possession, 13.

7. Johnathan Lantz Buffalo, "Oral History of the Meskwaki," *The Wisconsin Archeologist, from the Great Lakes to the Great Plains: Meskwaki Archaeology and Ethnohistory* 89, no. 1–2 (January–December 2008): 5.

8. *Daily Gate City* (Keokuk, IA), February 18, 1916; Johnathan Buffalo and Dawn Suzanne Wanatee, "1846–1856: The Iowa Journey," MHCD.

9. John R. Chenault, "No. 33 Sac and Fox Agency," in *Annual Report of the Commissioner of Indian Affairs Transmitted with the Message of the President at the Opening of the Second Session of the Thirty-Second Congress, 1852* (Washington, DC: Robert Armstrong, 1852), 91–94; See also Peterson, Hedden, and Nagel, "Archaeology of the Meskwaki Fur Trade in Iowa," 173; Gooding, "Return to *Nekotosiye*," 5; Jeffrey Ostler, *Surviving Genocide: Native Nations and the United States from the American Revolution to Bleeding Kansas* (New Haven: Yale University Press, 2019), 353.

10. See Ostler, *Surviving Genocide*, 288–358.

11. Green, "We Dance," 135–36.

12. Gooding, "Return to *Nekotosiye*," 4.

13. John H. Hauberg, interview with James Poweshiek, translated by William Poweshiek, Black Hawk State Park, Rock Island, Illinois, September 5, 1942, in folder "Native American Interview with James Poweshiek," box 7, MHPO.

14. Green, "We Dance," 136.

15. A. R. Howbert, quoted in Johnathan L. Buffalo, "1867–1886: The New Neighbors," MHCD.

16. Green, "We Dance," 137.

17. Green, "We Dance," 133; Peterson, Hedden, and Nagel, "The Meskwaki Fur Trade in Iowa," 173–175.

18. Peterson, Hedden, and Nagel, "The Meskwaki Fur Trade in Iowa," 176.

19. Peterson, Hedden, and Nagel, "The Meskwaki Fur Trade in Iowa," 136–37.

20. Jones, "Notes on the Fox Indians," 219.

21. Walter R. Echo-Hawk, *In the Courts of the Conqueror: The 10 Worst Indian Law Cases Ever Decided* (Golden, CO: Fulcrum, 2010), 137.

22. See Howard Lamar, *Dakota Territory, 1861–1889: A Study of Frontier Politics* (New Haven, CT: Yale University Press, 1956).

23. Horace M. Rebok, "The Last of the Mus-qua-kies," *Iowa Historical Record* 17, no. 3 (July 1901): 332; Green, "We Dance," 137.

24. Green, "We Dance," 137.

25. "Indian Disturbances," *Racine Advocate*, July 26, 1848, quoted in Buffalo, "Narrative of Chronology and Perspectives," 5.

26. Thomas Peter Christensen, *The Iowa Indians: A Brief History* (Iowa City: Athens Press, 1954), 69.

27. Green, "We Dance," 137; Peterson, Hedden, and Nagel, "The Meskwaki Fur Trade in Iowa," 176.

28. Peter Hoehnle, "Die Colonisten und die Indianer: The Unusual Relationship between the Meskwaki Nation and the Amana Society," *Iowa Heritage Illustrated* 92, no. 3–4 (Fall & Winter 2011): 90–100.

29. Green, "We Dance," 137; Peterson, Hedden, and Nagel, "The Meskwaki Fur Trade in Iowa," 176.

30. James W. Grimes to A. C. Dodge, G. W. Jones, J. B. Cook, and B. Henn, January 3, 1855, reprinted as "Apprehended Indian Troubles: Unpublished Letter by Gov. James W. Grimes," in *Annals of Iowa* 2, no. 8 (January 1897): 627–30.

31. James W. Grimes to Franklin Pierce, December 3, 1855, reprinted as "Apprehended Indian Troubles: Unpublished Letter by Gov. James W. Grimes," in *Annals of Iowa* 3, no. 2 (July 1897): 135.

32. Grimes to Pierce, December 3, 1855.

33. Paul N. Beck, *Inkpaduta: Dakota Leader* (Norman: University of Oklahoma Press, 2008), 51–74.

34. On the US-Dakota War of 1862, see Gary Clayton Anderson and Alan R. Woolworth, eds., *Through Dakota Eyes: Narrative Accounts of the Minnesota Indian War of 1862* (St. Paul: Minnesota State Historical Society Press, 1988); Mark Diedrich, *Little Crow and the Dakota War* (Rochester, MN: Coyote Books, 2006). See also J. H. Denison to Samuel Kirkwood, September 20, 1861; D. J. Langdon to M. Stone, November 6, 1864; both in folder "Governor, Correspondence, Indian Affairs 1860–1887," box 3, all RG 043, SHSI-DM.

35. Green, "We Dance," 137.

36. Duren H. Ward, "Meskwakia," *Iowa Journal of History and Politics* 4, no. 2 (April 1906): 180; Royce Delbert Kurtz, "Economic and Political History of the Sauk and Mesquakie: 1780s–1845" (PhD diss., University of Iowa, 1986), 264; Gooding, "Return to *Nekotosiye*," 5. In some sources, Mamiwanige's and Patagoto's names are spelled "Mamiwanike" and "Patakoto" or "Betikotowa."

37. Marion Petition to the US Congress, 1852, quoted in Buffalo, "Narrative of Chronology and Perspectives," 12.

38. Peterson, Hedden, and Nagel, "Meskwaki Fur Trade in Iowa," 176.

39. Grimes to Pierce, December 3, 1855; "Aged Papers Tell Story of Mesquakies," *Tama News-Herald*, July 11, 1957. See also Green, "We Dance," 137; Peterson, Hedden, and Nagel, "Meskwaki Fur Trade in Iowa," 176.

40. James M. Berry, June 23, 1852, quoted in Buffalo, "Narrative of Chronology and Perspective," 13.

41. Green, "We Dance," 137.

42. Green, "We Dance," 71–72.

43. Dorothy Schwieder, *Iowa: The Middle Land* (Iowa City: University of Iowa Press, 1996), 16, 71–72.

44. Schwieder, *Iowa*, 72.

45. Green, "We Dance," 137.

46. Green, "We Dance," 137.

47. "Indians Reside in the State: An Act Permitting Certain Indians to Reside within the State," in *Acts, Resolutions, and Memorials Passed at the Fifth General Assembly of the State of Iowa Which Convened at Iowa City on the Second Day of July, Anno Domini, 1856* (Iowa City: P. Moriarty, 1856), 274; Green, "We Dance," 137.

48. Donald Wanatee in discussion with the author, June 20, 2014. For a slightly different version, see Ray A. Young Bear, *Black Eagle Child: The Facepaint Narratives* (New York: Fire Keepers, 1992), 47–48.

49. J. R. Caldwell, ed., *A History of Tama County Iowa*, Vol. 2 (Chicago: Lewis Publishing Company, 1910), 764; Cynthia L. Peterson, "History of the 1846 Meskwaki Village in Tama County," report to Johnathan Buffalo, Meskwaki Historic Preservation Office, March 16, 2012, document in the author's possession.

50. "Beginnings of County History Told from Old Books at News-Herald," *Tama News-Herald*, May 19, 1949.

51. Field notes of Samuel W. Durham, quoted in Peterson, "History of the 1846 Meskwaki Village."

52. Facsimile and transcript of the 1857 deed for the purchase of the original eighty acres of the Meskwaki Settlement, in "Meskwaki Documents," MHCD.

53. Iowa secretary of state field notes, "Township 83N, Range 15W," microfilm reel 108C; "Range 14–22W," microfilm reel 108D; "Iowa Secretary of State Plats, Range 1E, Township 77N-Range 20W, Township 100 North," all SHSI-IC. See also R. David Edmunds and Joseph L. Peyser, *The Fox Wars: The Mesquakie Challenge to New France* (Norman: University of Oklahoma Press, 1993), 34.

54. Ward, "Meskwakia," 180.

55. "Indians About," *Daily Hawk-Eye and Telegraph*, February 5, 1857.

56. "The Plaint of the Savage," *New York Times*, February 18, 1857.

57. See Buffalo, "Narrative of Chronology and Perspectives," 15.

58. Young Bear, "Notes on Me-Skw-ki History," quoted in Buffalo, "Narrative of Chronology and Perspectives," 14.

59. David Butler, "Old Indian Town," August 18, 1905, reprinted in "Meskwaki Proclamation Day Brochure: 'Old Indian Town,' July 13, 1857," State Historical Society of Iowa, https://history.iowa.gov/history/education/educator-resources/primary-source-sets/right-to-vote-suffrage-women-african/meskwaki-proclamation-day. See also Stephen Warren, "'To Show the Public We Were Good Indians': Origins and Meanings of the Meskwaki Powwow," *American Indian Culture and Research Journal* 33, no. 4 (January 2009): 4–5.

60. Huron H. Smith, "Ethnobotany of the Meskwaki Indians," *Bulletin of the Public Museum of the City of Milwaukee* 4, no. 2 (April 1928): 185.

61. "Meskwaki Proclamation Day: A Historical Perspective," MHCD. All of these Meskwaki men's names are spelled in various ways in the source documents. For example, "Matauaquah" also appears in the sources as "Matauequa." For consistency, I use "Matauaquah" in the main text.

62. Smith, "Ethnobotany," 186.

63. Butler, "Old Indian Town," 1905. See also Warren, "To Show the Public," 4–5.

64. Natalie F. Joffe, "The Fox of Iowa," in *Acculturation in Seven American Indian Tribes*, ed. Ralph Linton (London: D. Appleton-Century Company, 1940), 289.

65. Butler, "Old Indian Town."

66. Butler, "Old Indian Town."

67. Hauberg, interview with James Poweshiek, September 5, 1942.

68. Edmunds and Peyser, *Fox Wars*, 33–35; Allie B. Busby, *Two Summers Among the Musquakies, Relating to the Early History of the Sac and Fox Tribe, Incidents of their Noted Chiefs, Location of the Foxes, or Musquakies, in Iowa, with a Full Account of their Traditions and Ceremonies, and the Personal Experience of the Writer for Two and a Half Years among Them* (Vinton, IA: Herald Book and Job Rooms, 1886), 73, 95–96.

69. Gooding, "Return to *Nekotosiye*," 8. Gooding offers a detailed and thoughtful description of Meskwaki village life during this period, based on his deep research and more than two decades of interviews with tribal members. For descriptions of the seasonal round and daily routine at the Meskwaki central village, see pages 8–11 and 15–17.

70. Busby, *Two Summers*, 73. See also 95–96.

71. Busby, *Two Summers*, 71. See also Gooding, "Return to *Nekotosiye*."

72. Richard Frank Brown, "A Social History of the Mesquakie Indians, 1800–1963" (MA thesis, Iowa State University, 1964), 56–58; Buffalo and Wanatee, "The History of Meskwaki Land Purchases," MHCD.

73. See Buffalo, "Narrative of Chronology and Perspectives," 14, 1; Joffe, "Fox of Iowa," 289; Busby, *Two Summers*, 95–96.

74. Cornelia F. Mutel, *The Emerald Horizon: The History of Nature in Iowa* (Iowa City: University of Iowa Press, 2008), 22, describes the transition from rural to urban settlement in Iowa between 1850 and 2000. The year 1950 was a key turning point when "Iowa's urban population outstripped rural residents for the first time."

75. See Busby, *Two Summers*, 77. For information on the annual winter camps, see Brown, "Social History," 59–69; Judith Daubenmier, *The Meskwaki and Anthropologists: Action Anthropology Reconsidered* (Lincoln: University of Nebraska Press, 2008), 34; Gooding, "Return to *Nekotosiye*," 9.

76. Smith, "Ethnobotany," 187, 203–204, 269.

77. Joffe, "Fox of Iowa," 264.

78. Truman Michelson, ed., "The Autobiography of a Fox Indian Woman," Fortieth Annual Report of the Bureau of American Ethnology (Washington, DC: Government Printing Office, 1925), 297–335; Joffe, "Fox of Iowa," 263–65. See also Ives Goddard, "The Autobiography of a Meskwaki Woman: A New Edition and Translation," Memoir 18, Algonquin and Iroquoian Linguistics (2006), available at the MHPO.

79. Michelson, "Autobiography of a Fox Indian Woman," 297–335; Joffe, "Fox of Iowa," 263–65. See also Andrew C. Isenberg, *The Destruction of the Bison: An Environmental History, 1750–1920* (New York: Cambridge University Press, 2000), 47–53;

Nancy C. Unger, *Beyond Nature's Housekeepers: American Women in Environmental History* (New York: Oxford University Press, 2012), 13–29; Larry Nesper and James H. Schlender, "The Politics of Cultural Revitalization and Intertribal Resource Management: The Great Lakes Indian Fish and Wildlife Commission and the States of Wisconsin, Michigan, and Minnesota," in Michael E. Harkin and David Rich Lewis, eds., *Native Americans and the Environment: Perspectives on the Ecological Indian* (Lincoln: University of Nebraska Press, 2007), 277–303.

80. Joffe, "Fox of Iowa," 264, 303; Busby, *Two Summers*, 71; Leander Clark, "Sac and Foxes in Iowa," in *Report on Indian Affairs, by the Acting Commissioner, for the Year 1867* (Washington, DC: Government Printing Office, 1868), 347. Joffe, "Fox of Iowa," 263–64; Mary Alecia Owen, *Folk-Lore of the Musquakie Indians of North America and Catalogue of Musquakie Beadwork and Other Objects in the Collections of the Folk-Lore Society* (London: David Nutt, 1904), 26; Busby, *Two Summers*, 77; Brown, "Social History," 59–69; Daubenmier, *Meskwaki and Anthropologists*, 29–63; Gooding, "Return to *Nekotosiye*," 10.

81. Joffe, "Fox of Iowa," 263–64; Brown, "Social History," 60–61.

82. A.R.F., "The Indians of Iowa," *Daily Iowa State Register* (Des Moines), Nov. 18, 1869.

83. George L. Davenport to Kirkwood, September 26, 1862, folder "Governor, Correspondence, Misc. 1850-1887 Indian Affairs," box 3, RG 043, SHSI-DM.

84. Ward, "Meskwakia," 184.

85. See Echo-Hawk, *Courts of the Conqueror*, 123–60.

86. Richard Henry Pratt, quoted in Frederick E. Hoxie, *A Final Promise: The Campaign to Assimilate the Indians, 1880–1920* (New York: Cambridge University Press, 1989), xii. See also C. Joseph Genetin-Pilawa, *Crooked Paths to Allotment: The Fight over Federal Indian Policy after the Civil War* (Chapel Hill: University of North Carolina Press, 2012), 75; Jacki Thompson Rand, *Kiowa Humanity and the Invasion of the State* (Lincoln: University of Nebraska Press, 2008); Bethany R. Berger, "Red: Racism and the American Indian," *UCLA Law Review* 56 (2009): 591–656.

87. See Deborah A. Rosen, *American Indians and State Law: Sovereignty, Race, and Citizenship, 1790–1880* (Lincoln: University of Nebraska Press, 2007), xi; Vine Deloria Jr. and Clifford M. Lytle, *The Nations Within: The Past and Future of American Indian Sovereignty* (Austin: University of Texas Press, 1984), 3.

88. See Rosen, *American Indians and State Law*, 19–79; Bethany Ruth Berger, "After Pocahontas: Indian Women and the Law, 1830 to 1934," *American Indian Law Review* 21, no. 1 (1997): 1–62. See also Donald Fixico, "Federal and State Policies and American Indians," in *A Companion to American Indian History*, ed. Philip J. Deloria and Neal Salisbury (Malden, MA: Blackwell, 2004), 379–96.

89. "An Act Permitting Certain Indians to Reside within the State," in *Acts and Resolutions Passed at the Regular Session of the Seventh General Assembly of the State of Iowa, Which Convened at the Capitol, Des Moines, on the First Monday in January, A.D. 1858* (Des Moines: J. Tessdale, 1856), 51. See also Robert A. Birmingham, *Skunk Hill:*

A *Native Ceremonial Community in Wisconsin* (Madison: Wisconsin Historical Society Press, 2015).

90. Leander Clark, "Sacs and Foxes in Iowa," in *Message of the President of the United States and Accompanying Documents to the Two Houses of Congress at the Commencement of the Second Session of the Fortieth Congress, 1867* (Washington, DC: Government Printing Office, 1867), 25–26.

91. L. Edward Purcell, "The Mesquakie Indian Settlement in 1905," *Palimpsest* 55, no. 2 (March–April 1974): 36. See also correspondence between Leander Clark and Buren R. Sherman from July 1882, in folder "Correspondence, Miscellaneous Indian Affairs 1860–1887," box 3, RG 043, SHSI-DM. This is the second of two folders bearing this name in this box.

92. Lewis V. Bogy to Clark, November 17, 1866, quoted in Buffalo, "1867–1886: The New Neighbors." See also Warren, "To Show the Public," 5; Brown, "Social History," 42–46.

93. See Brian Klopotek, *Recognition Odysseys: Indigeneity, Race, and Federal Tribal Recognition Policy in Three Louisiana Indian Communities* (Durham, NC: Duke University Press, 2011), 2–3.

94. See Rand, *Kiowa Humanity*, 91.

95. Bogy to Clark, November 17, 1866; Warren, "To Show the Public," 5.

96. Gooding, "Return to *Nekotosiye*," 5.

97. Green, "We Dance," 138; Davenport to Kirkwood, September 26, 1862.

98. Purcell, "Mesquakie Settlement in 1905," 35.

99. Echo-Hawk, *Courts of the Conqueror*, 137; Colin G. Calloway, *Pen & Ink Witchcraft: Treaties and Treaty Making in American Indian History* (New York: Oxford University Press, 2013), 182–225.

100. See "From Washington," *Burlington Daily Hawk Eye*, November 8, 1865; quoted in Buffalo, "Narrative of Chronology and Perspectives," 19–21.

101. Joffe, "Fox of Iowa," 289; Green, "We Dance," 138.

102. See Hoxie, *Final Promise*, 2–3; Brown, "Social History," 60.

103. Owen, *Folk-Lore*, 26. One early newspaper account suggested that the Meskwaki Nation "own[ed] 240 acres of land in Tama county," but the details of tribal land ownership at that time are not clear. See Buffalo, "Narrative of Chronology and Perspectives," 19.

104. Ward, "Meskwakia," 187; Leander Clark to E. S. Parker, "Second Quarter Report, 1867," May 17, 1867, folder "Leander Clark–Correspondence 1866–1869, 1872 Copies of Letters," box BL 57, SHSI-IC. See also Joffe, "Fox of Iowa," 289.

105. Ward, "Meskwakia," 187; Clark to Parker, May 17, 1867. See also Joffe, "Fox of Iowa," 289.

106. Clark to E. B. Fenn, February 24, 1868, folder "Leander Clark–Correspondence 1866–1869, 1872 Copies of Letters," box BL 57, SHSI-IC. See also Frederick E. Hoxie, *This Indian Country: American Indian Activists and the Place They Made* (New York: Penguin, 2012), 181–223.

107. "Sac and Fox Treaty, 1842: Treaty with the Sauk and Foxes, 1842, October 11, 1842," State Historical Society of Iowa, https://iowaculture.gov/sites/default/files/history-education-pss-voting-1842-transcription.pdf, emphasis added; Chambers, quoted in John Beach, "The Sac and Fox Indian Council of 1841," *Annals of Iowa* 12, no. 5 (July 1920): 332. Available from the Northern Illinois University Digital Library, https://digital.lib.niu.edu/islandora/object/niu-prairie%3A2062.

108. Ward, "Meskwakia," 186–87.

109. Leander Clark, "Second Quarterly Report, 1867," quoted in John M. Zielinski, *Mesquakie and Proud of It* (Kalona, IA: Photo-Art Gallery Publications, 1976), 42.

110. Gooding, "Return to *Nekotosiye*," 16–17.

111. "Treaty with the Kiowa, Comanche, and Apache, October 21, 1867," Avalon Project, Yale Law School, https://avalon.law.yale.edu/19th_century/kicoap67.asp; "Fort Laramie Treaty, 1868," Avalon Project, Yale Law School, https://avalon.law.yale.edu/19th_century/nt001.asp.

112. Brown, "Social History," 59. Ward, "Meskwakia," 186–87.

113. See Martha C. Knack, "The Saga of Tim Hooper's Homestead: Non-Reservation Shoshone Indian Land Title in Nevada," *Western Historical Quarterly* 39, no. 2 (Summer 2008): 125–51; Peter Iverson, *The Navajo* (New York: Chelsea House Publishers, 2006), 43–49; William Wood, "The Trajectory of Indian Country in California: Rancherias, Villages, Pueblos, Missions, Ranchos, Reservations, Colonies, and Rancherias," *Tulsa Law Review* 44, no. 2 (Winter 2008): 356–59; Damon B. Akins and William J. Bauer Jr., *We Are the Land: A History of Native California* (Oakland: University of California Press, 2022).

CHAPTER 4

1. *History of Tama County, Iowa* (Springfield, IL: Union Publishing Company, 1883), 245.

2. *History of Tama County* (1883), 245.

3. Donald Wanatee, "The Lion, Fleur-de-lis, the Eagle, or the Fox: A Study of Government," in *The Worlds between Two Rivers: Perspectives on American Indians in Iowa*, ed. Gretchen M. Bataille, David M. Gradwohl, and Charles L. P. Silet (Ames: Iowa State University Press, 1978), 79. See also Natalie F. Joffe, "The Fox of Iowa," in *Acculturation in Seven American Indian Tribes*, ed. Ralph Linton (London: D. Appleton-Century Company, 1940), 311–12; Judith Daubenmier, *The Meskwaki and Anthropologists: Action Anthropology Reconsidered* (Lincoln: University of Nebraska Press, 2008), 48–57; *History of Tama County* (1883), 242.

4. Shiri Pasternak, *Grounded Authority: The Algonquins of Barriere Lake against the State* (Minneapolis: University of Minnesota Press, 2017), 3.

5. See Blue Clark, *Lone Wolf v. Hitchcock: Treaty Rights and Indian Law at the End of the Nineteenth Century* (Lincoln: University of Nebraska Press, 1994), 14; Sidney L. Harring, *Crow Dog's Case: American Indian Sovereignty, Tribal Law, and United*

States Law in the Nineteenth Century (New York: Cambridge University Press, 1994), 134–40.

6. See Boyd Cothran and C. Joseph Genetin-Pilawa, "Forum: Indigenous Histories of the Gilded Age and Progressive Era, An Introduction," *Journal of the Gilded Age of Progressive Era* 14 (2015): 503–11. See also Frederick Jackson Turner, *The Frontier in American History* (New York: Henry Holt, 1920); Walter Prescott Webb, *The Great Frontier* (Boston: Houghton Mifflin, 1952); Doug Kiel, "Untaming the Mild Frontier: In Search of New Midwestern Histories," *Middle West Review* 1, no. 1 (Fall 2014): 9–38.

7. Frederick E. Hoxie, *A Final Promise: The Campaign to Assimilate the Indians, 1880–1920* (New York: Cambridge University Press, 1989); x; C. Joseph Genetin-Pilawa, *Crooked Paths to Allotment: The Fight over Federal Indian Policy after the Civil War* (Chapel Hill: University of North Carolina Press, 2012), 2, 13–28; Philip J. Deloria, *Indians in Unexpected Places* (Lawrence: University Press of Kansas, 2006), 20–21.

8. See Jeffrey Ostler, *The Plains Sioux and US Colonialism from Lewis and Clark to Wounded Knee* (New York: Cambridge University Press, 2004), 66–67, 204–210, 227. See also Margaret D. Jacobs, "Indian Boarding Schools in Comparative Perspective: The Removal of Indigenous Children in the United States and Australia, 1880–1940," in *Boarding School Blues: Revisiting American Indian Educational Experience*, ed. Clifford E. Trafzer, Jean A. Keller, and Lorene Sisquouc (Lincoln: University of Nebraska Press, 2006), 215; Jacki Thompson Rand, *Kiowa Humanity and the Invasion of the State* (Lincoln: University of Nebraska Press, 2008), 58–92.

9. "Indians Reside in the State: An Act Permitting Certain Indians to Reside within the State," in *Acts, Resolutions, and Memorials Passed at the Fifth General Assembly of the State of Iowa Which Convened at Iowa City on the Second Day of July, Anno Domini, 1856* (Iowa City: P. Moriarty, 1856), 77.

10. Richard Frank Brown, "A Social History of the Mesquakie Indians, 1800–1963" (MA thesis, Iowa State University, 1964), 61–62.

11. Davenport to Sherman, June 14, 1882, in folder "Correspondence, Miscellaneous Indian Affairs 1860–1887," box 3, RG 043, SHSI-DM. This is the second of two folders bearing this name in this box, hereafter referred to as "Indian Affairs 1860–87, #2."

12. Davenport to Sherman, June 14, 1882, Indian Affairs 1860–87, #2.

13. Davenport to Sherman, June 14, 1882, Indian Affairs 1860–87, #2.

14. E. S. Stevens to Davenport, May 24, 1882, Indian Affairs 1860–87, #2.

15. George Davenport, quoted in *History of Tama County* (1883), 240. See also "Colonel George L'Oste Davenport," in *History of Tama County, Iowa, 1987* (Dallas, TX: Curtis Media Corporation, 1987), 235.

16. See Rand, *Kiowa Humanity*, 58–92; Jacobs, "Indian Boarding Schools," 215.

17. George L. Davenport, "Report of Agent in Iowa," in *Annual Report of the Commissioner of Indian Affairs to the Secretary of the Interior for the Year 1882* (Washington, DC: Government Printing Office, 1882), 91.

18. Brown, "Social History," 62.

19. Andrew Jackson to Kirkwood, July 22, 1872, folder "Governor, Correspondence-Miscellaneous, 1860–1887 Indian Affairs," box 3, RG 043, SHSI-DM. This is the first of two folders bearing this name in this box.

20. "To the Hon. Geo. W. M. Crary, Secretary of War," May 14, 1878; "To the Hon. Commission of Indian Affairs, Washington, DC," both quoted in Buffalo, "1867–1886: The New Neighbors," MHCD.

21. "To the Hon. Commission of Indian Affairs, Washington, DC," quoted in Buffalo "1867–1886: The New Neighbors," MHCD.

22. A. R. Howbert, 1873; T. A. Graham to John R. Rankin, April 30, 1878, both quoted in Buffalo, "1867–1886: The New Neighbors," MHCD.

23. Davenport to Sherman, July 12 and 22, 1882, Indian Affairs 1860–87, #2.

24. Clark to Sherman, July 6, 1882; O. H. Mills to Sherman, telegram, July 12, 1882, both in Indian Affairs 1860–87, #2.

25. Price to Sherman, April 8, 1882, Indian Affairs 1860–87, #2. See also Brown, "Social History," 62.

26. Price to Sherman, April 8, 1882, Indian Affairs 1860–87, #2.

27. Davenport to Sherman, June 14, 1882, Indian Affairs 1860-87, #2.

28. Enos Gheen to John D. C. Atkins, July 20, 1888, microcopy 595, roll 450, Indian Census Rolls, 1885–1940, Sac and Fox, IA, 1888–1910, National Archives Microfilm Publications (Washington, DC: 1965).

29. George L. Davenport, "Report of Agent in Iowa," August 26, 1881, in *Annual Report of the Commissioner of Indian Affairs to the Secretary of the Interior for the Year 1881* (Washington, DC: Government Printing Office, 1881), 105. Horace M. Rebok, "Report of Agency in Iowa," in *Annual Reports of the Department of the Interior for the Fiscal Year Ended June 30, 1898, Indian Affairs* (Washington, DC: Government Printing Office, 1898), 165. John H. Hauberg, interview with James Poweshiek, translated by William Poweshiek, Black Hawk State Park, Rock Island, Illinois, September 5, 1942, in folder "Native American Interview with James Poweshiek," box 7, MHPO; Ray A. Young Bear, interview with the author, March 22, 2015. Johnathan L. Buffalo, "Historical Overview of the Adoption of the Indian Reorganization Act of 1934 by the Sac and Fox of the Mississippi in Iowa," 1, IRA, MHPO, 3–5; Brown, "Social History," 62–63. See also Ray A. Young Bear, "Notes on Me-Skwa-Ki History," August 1905, quoted in John M. Zielinski, *Mesquakie and Proud of It* (Kalona, IA: Photo-Art Gallery Publications, 1976), 46; Ruth A. Gallaher, "The Tama Indians," *Palimpsest* 48, no. 7 (July 1967): 295–96 Erik D. Gooding, "The Return to *Nekotosiye*: Meskwaki Village Life, 1857–1902," 2018, unpublished manuscript, used and cited with Gooding's permission, copy in the author's possession, 22–23.

30. Wanatee, "Study of Government," 79; Buffalo, "Historical Overview," 3–5; Brown, "Social History," 62–63. See also Young Bear, "Notes on Me-Skwa-Ki History," 46; Gallaher, "Tama Indians," 295–96.

31. See "Muc-E-Push-E-To, Son of a Former Chief of the Sac and Fox Indians," n. p., November 1900, news clipping, MO, MHPO.

NOTES TO CHAPTER 4   281

32. Hauberg, interview with James Poweshiek, September 5, 1942. Oral histories that maintain the Old Bear claim to hereditary Meskwaki leadership still circulate the settlement. Descendants of this line, furthermore, have continued to serve in informal leadership capacities, both in ceremonies and in community affairs, even when their power has not been recognized by the Indian Office or, in more recent years, supported by a tribal election. Ray A. Young Bear, interview with the author, March 22, 2015. See also Daubenmier, *Meskwaki and Anthropologists*, 275–77; Rebok, "Report of Agency in Iowa," 1898, 165. Douglas E. Foley, *The Heartland Chronicles* (Philadelphia: University of Pennsylvania Press, 1995), 153–55.

33. See Audra Simpson, "On Ethnographic Refusal: Indigeneity, 'Voice,' and Colonial Citizenship," *Junctures* 9 (2007): 67–80.

34. See Loretta Fowler, *Arapahoe Politics, 1851–1978: Symbols in Crises of Authority* (Lincoln: University of Nebraska Press, 1982), 98; Buffalo, "Historical Overview," 4; Lloyd Fallers, "The Role of Factionalism in Fox Acculturation" in *Documentary History of the Fox Project, 1928–1959: A Program in Action Anthropology Directed by Sol Tax*, ed. Fred Gearing, Robert McC. Netting, and Lisa R. Peattie (Chicago: University of Chicago Press, 1960), 74.

35. George Bird Grinnell, *The Indians of To-day* (New York: Duffield, 1911), 283.

36. See Buffalo, "Historical Overview"; L. Edward Purcell, "The Mesquakie Indian Settlement in 1905," *Palimpsest* 55, no. 2 (March–April 1974): 39.

37. The Dawes Severalty Act of 1887 is also known as the "General Allotment Act" or simply the "Dawes Act." See Janet A. McDonnell, *The Dispossession of the American Indian, 1887–1934* (Bloomington: Indiana University Press, 1991); D. S. Otis, *The Dawes Act and the Allotment of Indian Lands* (Norman: University of Oklahoma Press, 1973); Emily Greenwald, *Reconfiguring the Reservation: The Nez Perces, Jicarilla Apaches, and the Dawes Act* (Albuquerque: University of New Mexico Press, 2002).

38. Stuart Banner, *How the Indians Lost Their Land: Law and Power on the Frontier* (Cambridge, MA: Harvard University Press, 2005), 256–92; Douglas E. Foley, "The Fox Project: A Reappraisal," *Current Anthropology* 40, no. 2 (April 1999): 187.

39. Thomas S. Free, "Agency of the Sac and Fox Indians in Iowa," in *Annual Report of the Commissioner of Indian Affairs to the Secretary of the Interior for the Year 1877* (Washington, DC: Government Printing Office, 1877), 114.

40. Free, "Agency of the Sac and Fox Indians in Iowa," 114.

41. Hiram Price to George L. Davenport, June 12, 1882, Indian Affairs 1860–87, #2. See also Angela Keysor, "Emergence of a Distinct Legal Identity from the Forces of Assimilation: The Mesquakie Indians and the Fight for Citizenship, 1842–1912," unpublished manuscript available on MHCD, no page numbers.

42. E. C. Ebersole, John R. Caldwell, and Horace M. Rebok, *History of the Indian Rights Association of Iowa and the Founding of the Indian Training School, Toledo, Iowa* (n.p., 1899), 5. Francis M. Drake, quoted in "Indians Claim Damages," *Annals of Iowa* 3, no. 2 (1897): 133.

43. Peter A. Dey, quoted in Irving Berdine Richman, *Ioway to Iowa: The Genesis of a Corn and Bible Commonwealth* (Iowa City: State Historical Society of Iowa, 1931), 219.

44. Donald Parman, *Indians and the American West in the Twentieth Century* (Bloomington: Indiana University Press, 1994), 4–5.

45. Johnathan Buffalo, "South Farm," *Meskwaki Nation Newsletter,* September 20, 2002, in binder "FY 2002 Newsletters," MHPO. See the appendix to this volume for the location of the South Farm in relation to the rest of the Settlement. On the 1888 issue, see Fallers, "Role of Factionalism," 72.

46. Wallace R. Lesser to Frank D. Jackson, December 6, 1895, folder 19, box 15, ZMS Files, SHSI-DM; Ebersole, Caldwell, and Rebok, *History of the Indian Rights Association,* 7.

47. Milton Remley to Frank D. Jackson, Nov. 15, 1895, folder 19, box 15, ZMS Files, SHSI-DM.

48. Lesser to F. D. Jackson, December 6, 1895, folder 19, box 15, ZMS Files, SHSI-DM.

49. Lesser to Jackson, December 6, 1895.

50. Horace M. Rebok to F. D. Jackson, September 6, 1895, folder 19, box 15, ZMS Files, SHSI-DM.

51. Rebok to Jackson, September 6, 1895; Remley to Jackson, Nov. 15, 1895.

52. Horace M. Rebok, "Report of Agency in Iowa, 1898," 167.

53. Horace M. Rebok, "Report of Agency in Iowa, 1898," 167. Even though the tribe accepted this lower settlement, Rebok's report states that Chicago & Northwestern continued to delay paying the tribe. Later annual reports do not indicate that the company paid in full.

54. "Son of Mekmewanke [Mamiwanige]" to Drake, February 13, 1896, translated by a Potawatomie person named Kitchkuwme, folder 19, box 15, ZMS Files, SHSI-DM.

55. "Indians Claim Damages," 130; Purcell, "Mesquakie Settlement in 1905," 36.

56. Matauequa and Pushetonequa, quoted in "Indians Claim Damages," 130–31.

57. Matauequa and Pushetonequa, quoted in "Indians Claim Damages," 130–31.

58. Charles H. Mills to E. G. Penrose, February 16, 1897, folder 19, box 15, ZMS Files, SHSI-DM.

59. Drake, quoted in "Indians Claim Damages," 133.

60. Charles H. Mills, "Transcript of Proceedings for the Establishment of 'Indian Road,'" February 16, 1897, folder 19, box 15, ZMS Files, SHSI-DM; Mills to Penrose, February 16, 1897.

61. Mucwesiessato [likely Moquibushito], Nahashee, and Byeakenawga to Drake, February 3, 1897, folder 19, box 15, ZMS Files, SHSI-DM.

62. Rebok to Drake, June 16, 1898, folder 19, box 15, ZMS Files, SHSI-DM.

63. Stephen Warren, "'To Show the Public We Were Good Indians': Origins and Meanings of the Meskwaki Powwow," *American Indian Culture and Research Journal* 33, no. 4 (January 2009): 4–6.

64. Horace M. Rebok, "Report of Agent in Iowa," in *Annual Report of the Secretary of the Interior for the Fiscal Year Ended June 30, 1895,* Vol. 2 (Washington, DC: Government Printing Office, 1896), 165–69.

65. Genetin-Pilawa, *Crooked Paths to Allotment*, 113; Benay Blend, "The Indian Rights Association, the Allotment Policy, and the Five Civilized Tribes, 1923–1936," *American Indian Quarterly* 7, no. 2 (Spring 1983): 67.

66. Ebersole, Caldwell, and Rebok, *History of the Indian Rights Association*, 22–23, 29–30; see also Warren, "To Show the Public," 6.

67. Ebersole, Caldwell, and Rebok, *History of the Indian Rights Association*, 6, 14.

68. Ebersole, Caldwell, and Rebok, *History of the Indian Rights Association*, 7.

69. Ebersole, Caldwell, and Rebok, *History of the Indian Rights Association*, 6; Ruth M. Gallaher, "Indian Agents in Iowa, Part II," *Iowa Journal of History and Politics* 14, no. 4 (October 1916): 590.

70. Ebersole, Caldwell, and Rebok, *History of the Indian Rights Association*, 7.

71. S. N. Fellows to Drake, December 23, 1895, folder "Governor, Correspondence-Miscellaneous, 1895–1897," box 3, RG 043, SHSI-DM.

72. Fallers, "Role of Factionalism," 72.

73. Ebersole, Caldwell, and Rebok, *History of the Indian Rights Association*, 6.

74. "Indians Claim Damages," 134.

75. "An Act Tendering to the United States Jurisdiction over Certain Indians Residing in Iowa and over Their Lands, and the Privilege of Purchasing Land in Tama County for Indian School Purposes," in *Acts and Resolutions Passed at the Regular Session of the Twenty-Sixth General Assembly of the State of Iowa* (Des Moines: F. B. Conaway): 114–15. On the size of Meskwaki land at that time, see Horace M. Rebok, "Report of Agent in Iowa," in *Annual Report of the Secretary of the Interior for the Fiscal Year Ended June 30, 1896*, Vol. 2 (Washington, DC: Government Printing Office, 1897), 159–60; Duren H. Ward, "Meskwakia," *Iowa Journal of History and Politics* 4, no. 2 (April 1906): 186–89.

CHAPTER 5

1. See Angela Keysor, "Emergence of a Distinct Legal Identity from the Forces of Assimilation: The Mesquakie Indians"; Lisa Dianne Lykins, "'Curing the Indian': Therapeutic Care and Acculturation at the Sac and Fox Tuberculosis Sanatorium, 1912–1942" (PhD diss., University of Kentucky, 2002). On the night Masqasee ran away, she was accompanied by another Meskwaki girl, who was also captured and returned to the school.

2. William G. Malin, "Report Concerning Indians in Iowa," *Annual Report of the Department of the Interior, for the Fiscal Year Ended June 30, 1899, Indian Affairs, Part I* (Washington, DC: Government Printing Office, 1899), 199; Keysor, "Emergence."

3. Lewis Lord, "How Many People Were Here Before Columbus?" *U.S. News and World Report*, August 18–25, 1997, 68–70. Benjamin Madley, "Reexamining the American Genocide Debate: Meaning, Historiography, and New Methods," *American Historical Review* 120, no. 1 (February 2015), 98, n. 1. The policies and methods of the US Census Bureau as they regarded American Indians shifted dramatically in the latter half of the nineteenth century. For further reading, see James P. Collins, "Native

Americans in the Census, 1860–1890," *Prologue* 38, no. 2 (Summer 2006), http://www.archives.gov/publications/prologue/2006/summer/indian-census.html.

4. Peter Hoehnle, "Die Colonisten und die Indianer: The Unusual Relationship Between the Meskwaki Nation and the Amana Society," *Iowa Heritage Illustrated* 92, no. 3–4 (Fall & Winter 2011): 91; W. R. Lesser, "Report of Agent in Iowa," in *Fifty-Ninth Annual Report of the Commissioner of Indian Affairs to the Secretary of the Interior* (Washington, DC: Government Printing Office, 1890) 106. I averaged the population reports from Indian agents from 1890 to 1901. See also Horace M. Rebok, "Report of Agency in Iowa," in *Annual Reports of the Department of the Interior for the Fiscal Year Ended June 30, 1898, Indian Affairs* (Washington, DC: Government Printing Office, 1898), 170.

5. *History of Tama County, Iowa* (Springfield, IL: Union Publishing Company, 1883), 239. Rebok, "Report of Agent in Iowa," in *Annual Report of the Secretary of the Interior for the Fiscal Year Ended June 30, 1895*, Vol. 2 (Washington, DC: Government Printing Office, 1896), 167; William G. Malin to William A. Jones, December 13, 1901, in unnamed bound volume, box 2 "Press Copies, Letters Sent 1899–1902," SFA, RG 75, NARA-CH.

6. Frederick E. Hoxie, *A Final Promise: The Campaign to Assimilate the Indians, 1880–1920* (New York: Cambridge University Press, 1989), xii–xiii.

7. Kevin Bruyneel, *The Third Space of Sovereignty: The Post-Colonial Politics of US/Indigenous Relations* (Minneapolis: University of Minnesota Press, 2007), 16.

8. See Walter R. Echo-Hawk, *In the Courts of the Conqueror: The 10 Worst Indian Law Cases Ever Decided* (Golden, CO: Fulcrum, 2010), 324; David Wallace Adams, *Education for Extinction: American Indians and the Boarding School Experience, 1875–1928* (Lawrence: University Press of Kansas, 1995); Blue Clark, *Lone Wolf v. Hitchcock: Treaty Rights and Indian Law at the End of the Nineteenth Century* (Lincoln: University of Nebraska Press, 1994); Charles F. Wilkinson, "Indian Claims Commission," in *Indian Self-Rule: First-Hand Accounts of Indian-White Relations from Roosevelt to Reagan*, ed. Kenneth R. Philp (Salt Lake City: Howe Brothers, 1986), 151–59.

9. Keysor, "Emergence." See also Andrew Kennard, "A Closer Look at the Experiences of the Meskwaki People at the Indian Training School at Toledo, Iowa," *Times-Delphic* (Drake University), October 21, 2021, https://nativenewsonline.net/sovereignty/a-closer-look-at-the-experiences-of-the-meskwaki-people-at-the-indian-training-school-at-toledo-iowa.

10. Keysor, "Emergence."

11. Allie B. Busby, *Two Summers among the Musquakies, Relating to the Early History of the Sac and Fox Tribe, Incidents of their Noted Chiefs, Location of the Foxes, or Musquakies, in Iowa, with a Full Account of Their Traditions and Ceremonies, and the Personal Experience of the Writer for Two and a Half Years among Them* (Vinton, IA: Herald Book and Job Rooms, 1886), 73; Erik D. Gooding, "The Return to *Nekotosiye*: Meskwaki Village Life, 1857–1902," 2018, unpublished manuscript, used and cited with Gooding's permission, copy in the author's possession, 26.

12. Judith Daubenmier, *The Meskwaki and Anthropologists: Action Anthropology Reconsidered* (Lincoln: University of Nebraska Press, 2008), 31; Keysor, "Emergence."

13. Charles Alexander Eastman (Ohiyesa), *From the Deep Woods to Civilization* (Mineola, NY: Dover Publications, 2003), 83; Stephen Warren, "'To Show the Public We Were Good Indians': Origins and Meanings of the Meskwaki Powwow," *American Indian Culture and Research Journal* 33, no. 4 (January 2009): 6. See also Keysor, "Emergence."

14. Eastman, *From the Deep Woods*, 84; Warren, "To Show the Public," 6.

15. For another example of the Indian Service pressuring tribes to select federally recognized leaders, see Loretta Fowler, *Arapahoe Politics, 1851–1978: Symbols in Crises of Authority* (Lincoln: University of Nebraska Press, 1982), 32–34.

16. MacBurnie Allinson, "Education and the Meskwaki" (PhD diss., Iowa State University, 1974), 71.

17. Richard Frank Brown, "A Social History of the Mesquakie Indians, 1800–1963" (MA thesis, Iowa State University, 1964), 70.

18. Johnathan L. Buffalo, "Historical Overview of the Adoption of the Indian Reorganization Act of 1934 by the Sac and Fox of the Mississippi in Iowa," 1, IRA, MHPO, 5; Brown, "Social History," 70.

19. *Yearbook and List of Active Members of the National Educational Association* (Winona, MN: National Education Association, 1903), 163.

20. George W. Nellis, "Report of Superintendent of Sac and Fox School," in *Annual Report of Department of the Interior, 1899* (Washington, DC: Government Printing Office, 1899), 202. See also Keysor, "Emergence."

21. Keysor, "Emergence."

22. See Peter M. Whiteley, *Deliberate Acts: Changing Hopi Culture Through the Oraibi Split* (Tucson: University of Arizona Press, 1988), 74–76; Jerrold E. Levy and Barbara Pepper, *Orayvi Revisited: Social Stratification in an "Egalitarian" Society* (Santa Fe: School of American Research Press, 1992), 92; John Kantner, *Ancient Puebloan Southwest* (New York: Cambridge University Press, 2004), 41.

23. Buffalo, "Historical Overview," 5; Brown, "Social History," 68–70; Keysor, "Emergence."

24. Keysor, "Emergence"; E. I. Wilcox to L. M. Shaw, January 20, 1899, folder 28, box 15, ZMS Files, SHSI-DM.

25. Keysor, "Emergence"; Rebok, "Report of Agency in Iowa, 1898," 164, 167.

26. Rebok, "Report of Agency in Iowa, 1898," 167. Rebok struggled to find a fourth tribal member willing to serve as a police officer for the OIA. See also Scott Riney, *The Rapid City Indian School, 1898–1933* (Norman: University of Oklahoma Press, 1999), 6–7.

27. B. L. Wick to Harlan, December 27, 1919, folder 49, ERH Papers, SHSI-DM; J. R. Caldwell, ed., *A History of Tama County Iowa*, Vol. 1 (Chicago: Lewis Publishing Company, 1910), 70; Thomas H. Ryan, ed., *History of Outagamie County, Wisconsin* (Chicago: Goodspeed Historical Association Publishers, 1911), 892.

28. The two cases described here are Ma-Ka-Ta-Wah-Qua-Twa v. Rebok, 111 F. 212 (N.D. Iowa, Cedar Rapids Division, October 24, 1900) and Y-Ta-Tah-Wah v. Rebok, 105 F. 257 (N.D. Iowa, Cedar Rapids Division, December 1, 1900). See Keysor, "Emergence"; "Horace M. Rebok," *Annals of Iowa* 20, no. 5 (July 1936): 394; Warren, "To Show the Public," 8–9.

29. William G. Malin to H. G. McMillan, bound volume, no title, box 2, "Press Copies of Letters Sent, Dec. 1899–Sept. 1902," SFA, RG 75, NARA-CH, hereafter "bound volume 2, Press Copies, 1899–1902"; Malin to A. B. Cummins, June 27, 1904, folder 28, box 15, ZMS Files, SHSI-DM.

30. Malin, "Report Concerning Indians in Iowa," 200. Caldwell, *A History of Tama County, Iowa*, Vol. 1, 512.

31. Malin to Cummins, August 12, 1905, folder 28, box 15, ZMS Files, SHSI-DM.

32. Keysor, "Emergence." See also "Peters v. Malin," *The Federal Reporter: Cases Argued and Determined in the Circuit Courts of Appeals and Circuit and District Courts of the United States*, November 1901–January 1902 (St. Paul: West Publishing Co.: 1902), 244–56.

33. Rebok, "Report of Agency in Iowa, 1898," 167.

34. See "Peters v. Malin," *Federal Reporter*, 244–56. Keysor, "Emergence."

35. See "Peters v. Malin," *Federal Reporter*, 244–56. Keysor, "Emergence."

36. Malin, "Report Concerning Indians in Iowa, 1899," 199–200. See Peters v. Malin 111 F. 244 (N.D. Iowa, Cedar Rapids Division, December 1, 1900). See also "Peters v. Malin," *Federal Reporter*, 244–56.

37. Ruth M. Gallaher, "Indian Agents in Iowa, Part II," *Iowa Journal of History and Politics* 14, no. 4 (October 1916): 592; Wick to Harlan, January 14, 1920, folder 49, ERH Papers, SHSI-DM; Daubenmier, *Meskwaki and Anthropologists*, 49–51.

38. Keysor, "Emergence"; Lykins, "Curing the Indian," 95; Gallaher, "Indian Agents Part II," 592; Wick to Harlan, January 14, 1920, folder 49, ERH Papers, SHSI-DM.

39. Gallaher, "Indian Agents Part II," 592; Wick to Harlan, January 14, 1920, folder 49, ERH Papers, SHSI-DM.

40. Keysor, "Emergence."

41. "Peters v. Malin," *Federal Reporter*, 250.

42. See David E. Wilkins, "The US Supreme Court's Explication of 'Federal Plenary Power': An Analysis of Case Law Affecting Tribal Sovereignty, 1886–1914," *American Indian Quarterly* 18, no. 3 (Summer 1994): 352–53; Echo-Hawk, *Courts of the Conqueror*, 198–99, 230–31.

43. "Peters v. Malin," *Federal Reporter*, 250.

44. William G. Malin to William Jones, December 13, 1901, bound volume 2, Press Copies, 1899–1902; Johnathan Buffalo, interview with Adeline Wanatee, March 1977, quoted in Mary Bennett, *An Iowa Album: A Photographic History, 1860–1920* (Iowa City: University of Iowa Press, 1990), 17.

45. Jonathan B. Tucker, *Scourge: The Once and Future Threat of Smallpox* (New York: Grove Press, 2001), 2. See also S. L. Kotar and J. E. Gessler, *Smallpox: A History*

(Jefferson, NC: McFarland & Company, 2013); Elizabeth A. Fenn, *Pox Americana: The Great Smallpox Epidemic of 1775–82* (New York: Hill and Wang, 2001), 3–11.

46. Tucker, *Scourge*, 2–3. See also Kurt Link, *The Vaccine Controversy: The History, Use, and Safety of Vaccinations* (Westport, CT: Greenwood Publishing Group, 2005), 43–47.

47. The impact, if any, of the smallpox epidemics of the 1780s and 1830s on the Sauk and Meskwaki Nations is a subject for further research. It appears that in the 1830s, some Sauk and Meskwaki people were vaccinated, thereby staving off the worst of the epidemic. I am indebted here to historian Paul Kelton, who shared some research notes on vaccination efforts among Indigenous tribes around the Great Lakes in the 1830s. None of these notes mentions the Sauk and Meskwaki Nations directly, but they show substantial rates of vaccination in the region. These vaccination rates, notably, declined in the 1840s and 1850s, possibly leaving a new generation of Meskwaki people vulnerable to the disease. The federal government's 1838 report for the tribes makes no mention of smallpox. Paul Kelton, email to the author, February 27, 2023; "No. 18: Extract from the Report of Joseph M. Street," *Annual Report of the Commissioner of Indian Affairs, 1838* (Washington, DC: War Department, Office of Indian Affairs, 1838), 490–94. See also J. Diane Pearson, "Lewis Cass and the Politics of Disease: The Indian Vaccination Act of 1832," *Wicazo Sa Review* 18, no. 2 (Autumn 2003): 13, 31 n. 14; Andrew C. Isenberg, "An Empire of Remedy: Vaccination, Natives, and Narratives in the North American West," *Pacific Historical Review* 86, no. 1 (February 2017): 84–113. On the epidemics of the 1780s and 1830s more generally, see Fenn, *Pox Americana* and Elizabeth A. Fenn, *Encounters at the Heart of the World: A History of the Mandan People* (New York: Hill and Wang, 2014).

48. H. J. Hamilton, "Statistical Reports of States and Cities of the United States—Yearly and Monthly," in *Public Health Report Issued by the Surgeon General, Public Health and Marine-Hospital*, Vol. 17, Part 1 (Washington, DC: Government Printing Office, 1902), 47.

49. Centers for Disease Control and Prevention, "Achievements in Public Health, 1900–1999: Impact of Vaccines Universally Recommended for Children, United States, 1990–1998," *Morbidity and Mortality Weekly Report* 48, no. 12 (April 1999): 243–48. J. H. Sams, "Smallpox—Diagnosis and Prevention," in *Twelfth Biennial Report of the Board of Health of the State of Iowa for the Period Ending June 30, 1903* (Des Moines: B. Murphy, 1904), 210–11.

50. Malin to Jones, December 13, 1901, bound volume 2, Press Copies, 1899–1902. Josiah Forrest Kennedy, ed., *Iowa Health Bulletin* 16, no. 9 (February 1903), 1. See also Philip L. Frana, "Smallpox: Local Epidemics and the Iowa State Board of Health, 1880–1900," *Annals of Iowa* 54, no. 2 (Spring 1995): 87–118.

51. Malin to Jones, October 29, 1901, bound volume 2, Press Copies, 1899–1902.

52. Malin to Jones, October 25, 1901. This is the first of two letters from Malin to Jones on this date. See also Malin to Jones, October 29, 1902, bound volume 2, Press Copies, 1899–1902.

53. Malin to Jones, December 4, 1901, bound volume 2, Press Copies, 1899–1902.

54. Malin to Jones, November 5, 1901; Malin to Jones, November 9, 1901, both in bound volume 2, Press Copies, 1899–1902.

55. Sams, "Smallpox," 213.

56. Malin to W. M. Beardshear, November 22, 1901, bound volume 2, Press Copies, 1899–1902.

57. *Tama News-Herald*, November 29, 1901; *Iowa State Bystander*, November 22, 1901.

58. Malin to Jones, February 26, 1902, bound volume "1-29-02, 9-12-02, Agency," box 2, Press Copies of Letters Sent, Dec. 1899–Sept. 1902, SFA, RG 75, NARA-CH, hereafter "1902 Agency, Press Copies 1899–1902."

59. Malin to W. B. Allison, November 13, 1901, bound volume 2, Press Copies, 1899–1902.

60. Malin to Jones, November 30, 1901; Malin to A. M. Linn, November 27, 1901, both in bound volume 2, Press Copies, 1899–1902.

61. Malin to Jones, December 16, 1901, bound volume 2, Press Copies, 1899–1902.

62. Malin to Jones, January 6, 1902, bound volume 2, Press Copies, 1899–1902; Malin to Jones, December 13, 1901, bound volume 2, Press Copies, 1899–1902; Malin to Axel Jacobson, February 1, 1902, 1902 Agency, Press Copies 1899–1902.

63. W. G. Malin, "Sac & Fox of Iowa Census, July 1, 1901," photocopy in binder "Sac and Fox of Iowa Census: 1901, 1902, 1911, 1913, 1914, 1915, 1919, 1920," MHPO; Thomas S. Free, "Agency of the Sac and Fox Indians in Iowa," in *Annual Report of the Commissioner of Indian Affairs to the Secretary of the Interior for the Year 1875* (Washington, DC: Government Printing Office, 1875), 290.

64. See Jeffery K. Taubenberger and David M. Morens, "1918 Influenza: The Mother of All Pandemics," *Emerging Infectious Diseases* 12, no. 1 (January 2006): 15; Alfred W. Crosby, *America's Forgotten Pandemic: The Influenza of 1918* (New York: Cambridge University Press, 2003), 206.

65. John Elflein, "Number of Novel Coronavirus (COVID-19) Deaths Worldwide as of October 5, 2022, by Country and Territory," Statista.com, https://www.statista.com/statistics/1093256/novel-coronavirus-2019ncov-deaths-worldwide-by-country/.

66. Johnathan Buffalo in conversation with the author, February 6, 2015; Warren, "To Show the Public," 3.

67. Malin to Jones, March 10, 1902, 1902 Agency, Press Copies 1899–1902.

68. Malin to R. G. Cousins, November 12, 1901, bound volume 2, Press Copies, 1899–1902. See also *Small-Pox: Its Prevention, Restriction, and Suppression* (Springfield: Illinois State Board of Heath, 1907), 24, 53–55.

69. Malin to Jones, March 10, 1902.

70. Malin to Jones, December 30, 1901, bound volume 2, Press Copies, 1899–1902.

71. Malin to Linn, February 27, 1902; Malin to Jones, March 4, 1902, both 1902 Agency, Press Copies 1899–1902.

72. Malin to Jones, March 10, 1902, 1902 Agency, Press Copies 1899–1902.

NOTES TO CHAPTER 5

73. Malin to Jones, December 16, 1901, 1902 Agency, Press Copies 1899–1902. Jim Peters is frequently referred to as being Meskwaki, though he was born into the Sauk community. He married a Meskwaki woman and lived on the Iowa Settlement for most of his life. See Duren J. H. Ward, "The Meskwaki People of To-day," *Iowa Journal of History and Politics* 4, no. 2 (Spring 1906): 201; Neil Schmitz, *White Robe's Dilemma: Tribal History in American Literature* (Amherst: University of Massachusetts Press, 2001), 50.

74. Malin to Linn, March 11, 1902, 1902 Agency, Press Copies 1899–1902.

75. Malin to Jones, April 2, 1902, 1902 Agency, Press Copies 1899–1902.

76. Malin to Linn, February 27, 1902; Malin to Malcolm V. Idell, February 28, 1901, 1902 Agency, Press Copies 1899–1902; Albert B. Cummins, "State of Iowa, Executive Department," proclamation dated June 7, 1902; A. F. Dawson to Cummins, February 21, 1903; Dawson to Cummins, April 9, 1903, all in folder 28, box 15, ZMS Files, SHSI-DM. Malin to Jones, December 10, 1901, bound volume 2, Press Copies, 1899–1902; Malin to Jones, December 5, 1901, bound volume 2, Press Copies, 1899–1902.

77. Malin to Cousins, December 11, 1901, bound volume 2, Press Copies, 1899–1902.

78. Malin to Linn, April 1, 1902, 1902 Agency, Press Copies 1899–1902.

79. For the first quote, see Thomas G. Dyer, *Theodore Roosevelt and the Idea of Race* (Baton Rouge: Louisiana State University Press, 1992), 81. For the second, see Charles Wilkinson, *Blood Struggle: The Rise of Modern Indian Nations* (New York: W. W. Norton, 2005), 43.

80. Warren, "To Show the Public," 3. William G. Malin, "Report Concerning Indians in Iowa," in *Annual Reports of the Department of the Interior for the Fiscal Year Ended June 30, 1902, Indian Affairs*, Part 1, *Report of the Commissioner and Appendixes* (Washington, DC: Government Printing Office, 1903), 215.

81. Warren, "To Show the Public," 10; Jay H. Bernstein, "First Recipients of Anthropological Doctorates in the United States, 1891–1930," *American Anthropologist* 104, no. 2 (June 2002): 558–60.

82. William Jones, "Fox Texts," *Publications of the American Ethnological Society*, Vol. 1 (Leiden, The Netherlands: E. J. Brill, 1907), 2. See also Johnathan L. Buffalo, "1901–1902: Tenaciously Clinging," MHCD; Gooding, "Return to *Nekotosiye*," 7.

83. Warren, "To Show the Public," 3.

84. Jonas M. Poweshiek, "Jonas M. Poweshiek: An Autobiography," *Annals of Iowa* 20, no. 6 (Fall 1936): 437.

85. Cornelia F. Mutel, *The Emerald Horizon: The History of Nature in Iowa* (Iowa City: University of Iowa Press, 2008), 20–21; Sharon E. Wood, *The Freedom of the Streets: Work, Citizenship, and Sexuality in a Gilded Age City* (Chapel Hill: University of North Carolina Press, 2005), 10.

86. Richard L. Forstall, ed., *Population of States and Counties of the United States, 1790–1990* (Washington, DC: Government Printing Office, 1996), 56–57.

87. Warren, "To Show the Public," 5.

88. L. Edward Purcell, "The Mesquakie Indian Settlement in 1905," *Palimpsest* 55, no. 2 (March–April 1974): 47.

89. John J. Sullivan, "Sac and Fox Agency and Sanatorium, Iowa," 9, Report to the Commissioner of Indian Affairs, SAE, # 9165 Series I, Board of Indian Commissioners Reports, Box 5C, CUL; C. M. Richards, "Tama Indians Abandon Wickiups for Modern Homes; Progress in Last Few Years was Greatest in History," *Toledo Chronicle*, December 15, 1927; Daubenmier, *Meskwaki and Anthropologists*, 29–30.

90. Daubenmier, *Meskwaki and Anthropologists*, 34. See also David A. Chang, *The Color of the Land: Race, Nation, and the Politics of Landownership in Oklahoma, 1832–1929* (Chapel Hill: University of North Carolina Press, 2010), 20–21.

91. Malin to Cummins, August 12, 1905, folder 28, box 15, ZMS Files, SHSI-DM. See also Rebok, "Report of Agency in Iowa, 1898," 168.

92. Gallaher, "Indian Agents Part II," 590.

93. Douglas E. Foley, *The Heartland Chronicles* (Philadelphia: University of Pennsylvania Press, 1995), 153; "John Tetapache, 1869–1948," news clipping, MO, MHPO.

94. Anonymous Meskwaki elder, quoted in Purcell, "Mesquakie Settlement in 1905," 45.

95. Malin to Cummins, June 27, 1904, folder 28, box 15, ZMS Files, SHSI-DM.

96. Malin to Cummins, August 12, 1905, folder 28, box 15, ZMS Files, SHSI-DM.

97. Malin to Cummins, August 12, 1905, folder 28, box 15, ZMS Files, SHSI-DM.

98. Jesse E. Wilson to Cummins, July 26, 1907, folder 28, box 15, ZMS Files, SHSI-DM.

99. Malin to Shaw, May 15, 1901, folder 28, box 15, ZMS Files, SHSI-DM; Wilson to Cummins, July 26, 1907.

100. Green to Cummins, July 21, 1908, folder 28, box 15, ZMS Files, SHSI-DM.

101. "Do We Need More Land?" *Meskwaki Booster* 4, no. 5 (February 1917), folder "Copies of the Mesquakie Booster, 1915–1916," box 327, RG 75, NARA-CH.

102. Daubenmier, *Meskwaki and Anthropologists*, 34; Peru Farver, "Reservation Post-War Program," March 1944, 3, folder "Postwar Reservation Program—Memoranda, Correspondence, Reports, Instructions, 1943–1944," box 303, "Decimal Files: Miscellaneous Correspondence, 944–995," SFA, RG 75, NARA-CH.

103. Robert L. Russell to Sells, March 10, 1917, folder "Correspondence, Sac & Fox Sanatorium, 1916–1917," box 26, SFA, RG 75, NARA-CH; "Reclamation of Whiskey Bottom," *Meskwaki Booster* 4, no. 2 (November 1916), folder "Copies of the Mesquakie Booster, 1915–1916," box 327, RG 75, NARA-CH.

104. Daubenmier, *Meskwaki and Anthropologists*, 30. "Boosters," in *Meskwaki Booster* 4, no. 8 (May 1917), folder "Copies of the Mesquakie Booster, 1915–1916," box 327, RG 75, NARA-CH.

105. R. G. Valentine to Tataposha, May 17, 1910, folder "Correspondence 1909–1922, Trust Funds and Land Allotment," box 26, "Correspondence with the Commissioner of Indian Affairs, 1899–1920," RG 75, NARA-CH.

106. Gallaher, "Indian Agents Part II," 593.
107. Orville J. Green to Cummins, October 4, 1907, folder 28, box 15, ZMS Files, SHSI-DM.
108. Caldwell, *History of Tama County*, Vol. 1 (1910): 70–72.
109. Robert G. Valentine, "Report of the Commissioner of Indian Affairs," in *Reports of the Department of the Interior for the Fiscal Year Ended June 30, 1910*, Vol. 2, *Indian Affairs, Territories* (Washington, DC: Government Printing Office, 1911), 52.
110. Valentine, "Report of the Commissioner," 52.
111. R. G. Valentine, "The Sac and Fox Indians in Iowa," in *Reports of the Department of the Interior for the Fiscal Year Ended June 30, 1910*, Vol. 2, *Indian Affairs, Territories* (Washington, DC: Government Printing Office, 1911), 52.
112. Valentine, "Report of the Commissioner," 52.
113. Daubenmier, *Meskwaki and Anthropologists*, 34.
114. Chakotakosee, quoted in Green to Valentine, November 19, 1909, folder "Correspondence 1909–1922, Trust Funds and Land Allotment," box 26, "Correspondence with the Commissioner of Indian Affairs, 1899–1920," RG 75, NARA-CH.

CHAPTER 6

1. William G. Malin, "Report Concerning Indians in Iowa," in *Annual Reports of the Department of the Interior for the Fiscal Year Ended June 30, 1901, Indian Affairs*, Part 1, *Report of the Commissioner and Appendixes* (Washington, DC: Government Printing Office, 1902), 240. My use of the term "subsistence" should not suggest that members of the Meskwaki community were not also engaged in other economic activities. Rather, as Chantal Norgaard puts it, "integration into the capitalist economy meant that [Native] subsistence was defined not just in terms of sustenance but also in terms of the goods or cash generated from the products of an individual's labor." See Chantal Norgaard, *Seasons of Change: Labor, Treaty Rights, and Ojibwe Nationhood* (Chapel Hill: University of North Carolina Press, 2014), 26.
2. Malin, "Report Concerning Indians in Iowa, 1903," 179.
3. Judith Daubenmier, *The Meskwaki and Anthropologists: Action Anthropology Reconsidered* (Lincoln: University of Nebraska Press, 2008).
4. I. D. C. Atkins to William Larrabee, February 24, 1888, folder 19, box 15, ZMS Files, SHSI-DM; Horace M. Rebok, "Report of Agent in Iowa," in *Annual Reports of the Department of the Interior for the Fiscal Year Ended June 30, 1897, Report of the Commissioner of the Indian Affairs* (Washington, DC: Government Printing Office, 1897), 147.
5. "Game Laws," Mesquakie Booster 4, no. 2 (November 1915), folder "Copies of the Mesquakie Booster, 1915–1916," box 327, RG 75, NARA-CH.
6. Ira D. Nelson to John Collier, March 9, 1942, folder "920 Hunting and Fishing, Misc. Correspondence," box 302, decimal correspondence files, SFA, RG 75, NARA-CH.

7. C.M. Ellis to Robert Lyon, December 17, 1916, folder "Reports and Statistics, Farmer's Report 1916–1918," box 324, "Annual and Program Reports, Including Census, 1910–1920," Tama Agency files, RG 75, NARA-CH; "Indians Not Giving Farmers Fair Deal," *Mesquakie Booster* 4, no. 2 (November 1915), folder "Copies of the Mesquakie Booster, 1915–1916," box 327, RG 75, NARA-CH.

8. Ira D. Nelson, "1936 Annual Statistical Report," 1–8, folder "Annual Reports 051, 1935–1943," box 114, decimal correspondence files, Sac & Fox Agency, RG 75, NARA-CH.

9. "Fox Day School Report of Attendance, Quarter Ending March 31, 1918," folder "Meskwaki Day School Quarterly Reports, 1916–1926," box 329, decimal correspondence files; "Mesquakie Day School Report of Attendance, Year Ending June 30, 1926," folder "Meskwaki Day School Quarterly Reports, 1916–1926," box 329; both SFA, RG 75, NARA-CH.

10. Richard Frank Brown, "A Social History of the Mesquakie Indians, 1800–1963" (MA thesis, Iowa State University, 1964), 71; Cole to Jacob Breid, February 12, 1931, folder "Charities and Benevolences-Rations (Food and Clothing), Misc. Correspondence, 1931–1933," box 293, decimal correspondence files, SFA, RG 75, NARA-CH; George Young Bear, "Mesquakie News Tells of History: George Young Bear Gives Facts About Indian Education," *Toledo Chronicle*, November 22, 1928. For a Meskwaki account of the assimilation project and the boarding school system, see Adeline Wanatee, "Education, the Family, and the Schools," in *The Worlds between Two Rivers: Perspectives on American Indians in Iowa*, ed. Gretchen M. Bataille, David M. Gradwohl, and Charles L. P. Silet (Ames: Iowa State University Press, 1978), 100–103.

11. Ira D. Nelson, "Annual Report, January 1, 1935," folder "Annual Reports 051, 1931–1935," box 113, decimal correspondence files, SFA; RG 75, NARA-CH; Sol Tax, "The Social Organization of the Fox Indians" (PhD diss., University of Chicago, 1935), reprinted in part in *Documentary History of the Fox Project, 1928–1959: A Program in Action Anthropology Directed by Sol Tax*, ed. Fred Gearing, Robert McC. Netting, and Lisa R. Peattie (Chicago: University of Chicago Press, 1960), 5.

12. See Louis S. Warren, *Buffalo Bill's America: William Cody and the Wild West Show* (New York: Random House, 2005); L. G. Moses, *Wild West Shows and the Images of American Indians 1883–1933* (Albuquerque: University of New Mexico Press, 1999).

13. Stephen Warren, "'To Show the Public We Were Good Indians': Origins and Meanings of the Meskwaki Powwow," *American Indian Culture and Research Journal* 33, no. 4 (January 2009), 5.

14. Benjamin F. Gue and Benjamin Franklin Shambaugh, *Biographies and Portraits of the Progressive Men of Iowa*, Vol. 11, *Leaders in Business, Politics, and the Professions* (Des Moines: Conway and Shaw, 1899), 353–54; Chris Rasmussen, *Carnival in the Countryside: The History of the Iowa State Fair* (Iowa City: University of Iowa Press, 2015), 68.

15. On powwows and Native American tourism, see the special issue "Native Peoples and Tourism," *Ethnohistory* 50, no. 3 (Summer 2003): 413–585; Philip J.

Deloria, *Indians in Unexpected Places* (Lawrence: University Press of Kansas, 2006); Clyde Ellis, Luke E. Lassiter, and Gary H. Dunham, eds. *Powwow* (Lincoln: University of Nebraska Press, 2005).

16. Daubenmier, *Meskwaki and Anthropologists*, 34–35. On Meskwaki people playing to Native stereotypes, see Lisa Peattie, "Being a Mesquakie Indian," in *Documentary History of the Fox Project, 1928–1959: A Program in Action Anthropology Directed by Sol Tax*, ed. Fred Gearing, Robert McC. Netting, and Lisa R. Peattie (Chicago: University of Chicago Press, 1960), 55.

17. Brown, "Social History," 63–64, 72–74. See also Daubenmier, *Meskwaki and Anthropologists*, 31, 34–35; Peattie, "Being a Mesquakie," 53–56; Tax, "Social Organization," 5.

18. See Warren, "To Show the Public," 20.

19. I determined this figure by dividing $13,300 by 360, the Settlement population as noted in "Statistical Annual Report, 1917, Sac & Fox Sanatorium, & Sac & Fox, Iowa," 4, folder "Statistical Records and Reports 1915–1917," box 324, SFA, RG 75, NARA-CH.

20. E. B. Merritt to James W. Good, [exact date obscured] 1918, folder "Correspondence 1909–1922, Trust Funds and Land Allotment," box 26, "Correspondence with the Commissioner of Indian Affairs, 1899–1920," RG 75, NARA-CH. Brown, "Social History," 73.

21. Ruth M. Gallaher, "Indian Agents in Iowa, Part II," *Iowa Journal of History and Politics* 14, no. 4 (October 1916): 585; Atkins to Larrabee, February 24, 1888.

22. Isaac C. Millard to Francis M. Drake, October 20, 1896, folder 19, box 15, ZMS Files, SHSI-DM; Gallaher, "Indian Agents Part II," 585.

23. O. J. Green to Albert B. Cummings, June 9, 1908, folder 28, box 15, ZMS Files, SHSI-DM.

24. Gallaher, "Indian Agents in Iowa II," 585; Green to Cummings, June 9, 1908. R. G. Valentine, "The Sac and Fox Indians in Iowa," in *Reports of the Department of the Interior for the Fiscal Year Ended June 30, 1910*, Vol. 2, *Indian Affairs, Territories* (Washington, DC: Government Printing Office, 1911), 52.

25. "Jim Poweshiek Dies After Life of Leadership and Service in Tribe," *Tama News-Herald*, October 9, 1950.

26. O. J. Green, "Census of the Sac and Fox of the Mississippi Indians in Iowa," June 30, 1910, folder "Tribal Census 1910–1913," box 324, SFA, RG 75, NARA-CH; "Willie Poweshiek, Prominent Indian, Dies of Pneumonia," March 1945, news clipping, MO, MHPO.

27. "James Poweshiek," folder "Surveys of Indian Industry, 1921–1926, (3 of 4)," box 1, "Surveys of Indian Industry," SFA, RG 75, NARA-CH, hereafter "Surveys of Indian Industry #3." On death of Mary Poweshiek, see "Willie Poweshiek, Prominent Indian."

28. "James Poweshiek"; "Willie Poweshiek, Prominent Indian." "Poweshiek Rites Held," October 9, 1950, news clipping in binder, "Meskwaki Obituaries," MHPO.

29. "James Poweshiek."

30. "James Poweshiek"; Clifford C. Taylor and Edgar B. Hurd, "Farm Organization and Farm Profits in Tama County, Iowa," *Iowa State College Research Bulletin* 88 (November 1925): 274.

31. Taylor and Hurd, "Farm Organization," 258–59, 267, 275.

32. Taylor and Hurd, "Farm Organization," 438.

33. Jonas M. Poweshiek, "Jonas M. Poweshiek: An Autobiography," *Annals of Iowa* 20, no. 6 (Fall 1936): 438–42. On Native Americans in World War I, see Donald Parman, *Indians and the American West in the Twentieth Century* (Bloomington: Indiana University Press, 1994), 59–60. At the time, the State Historical Society was called the Historical, Memorial, and Art Department of Iowa.

34. "Horace Poweshiek, 90, Buried; Prominent in Tribe's History," September 9, 1982, news clipping, MO, MHPO.

35. "Horace Poweshiek, 90, Buried; Prominent in Tribe's History," September 9, 1982, news clipping, MO, MHPO.

36. "Willie Poweshiek," Surveys of Indian Industry #3.

37. "Willie Poweshiek, Prominent Indian." "Willie Poweshiek, Prominent Indian, Dies of Pneumonia," March 1945, news clipping in binder, "Meskwaki Obituaries," MHPD.

38. "Willie Poweshiek," Surveys of Indian Industry #3.

39. Brenda J. Child, *Boarding School Seasons: American Indian Families, 1900–1940* (Lincoln: University of Nebraska Press, 1998), 7; "Willie Poweshiek," Surveys of Indian Industry #3. See also Lydia Whirlwind Soldier, "Memories," in *Shaping Survival: Essays by Four American Indian Tribal Women*, ed. Jack W. Marken and Charles L. Woodward (Lanham, MD: Scarecrow Press, 2002), 199–201.

40. "Mrs. Poweshiek Buried Friday," *Tama News-Herald*, March 27, 1969; "Willie Poweshiek."

41. D'Arcy McNickle, "The Indian New Deal as Mirror of the Future," in *Political Organization of Native North Americans*, ed. Ernest Schusky (Washington, DC: University Press of America, 1980), 109.

42. Lisa Dianne Lykins, "'Curing the Indian': Therapeutic Care and Acculturation at the Sac and Fox Tuberculosis Sanatorium, 1912–1942" (PhD diss., University of Kentucky, 2002), 105.

43. Johnathan L. Buffalo, "Historical Overview of the Adoption of the Indian Reorganization Act of 1934 by the Sac and Fox of the Mississippi in Iowa," 1, IRA, MHPO, 7–8.

44. Charles Davenport, quoted in Daubenmier, *Meskwaki and Anthropologists*, 39.

45. Buffalo, "Historical Overview," 7–8.

46. Daubenmier, *Meskwaki and Anthropologists*, 38–39.

47. E. B. Merritt to Harlan, May 6, 1920, folder 49ff, ERH Papers, SHSI-DM.

48. Merritt to Harlan, May 6, 1920; Daubenmier, *Meskwaki and Anthropologists*, 38–39; Buffalo, "Historical Overview," 9.

NOTES TO CHAPTER 6

49. Harlan to W. E. Albert, March 11, 1922, folder 49u, ERH Papers, SHSI-DM.
50. Harlan to Wick, January 1, 1920, folder 49, ERH Papers, SHSI-DM.
51. Buffalo, "Historical Overview," 10.
52. Cyrenus Cole to Charles H. Burke, March 28, 1927, folder 49ff, ERH Papers, SHSI-DM.
53. Jerome L. Thompson, "The Museum Curator and the Meskwaki: Edgar R. Harlan and the Indian Life School," 1–13, unpublished manuscript, folder "'Museum Curator and the Meskwaki: Edgar Harland and Indian School Life' by Jerome Thompson," box 101, MHPO; Rebecca Conard, *Benjamin Shambaugh and the Intellectual Foundations of Public History* (Iowa City: University of Iowa Press, 2002), 70.
54. Douglas E. Foley, *The Heartland Chronicles* (Philadelphia: University of Pennsylvania Press, 1995), 95. Edgar Harlan, "Comment upon a Visit to the Musquakie Indians, Tama, Iowa, March 14–15, 1922," folder 49a; Harlan to A. C. Willford, September 7, 1933, folder 49t, both ERH Papers, SHSI-DM; Dick Spencer III, "Powwow Time," *Palimpsest* 48, no. 7 (July 1967): 306.
55. "Young Bear Was Son of Last Indian Tribal Chief," n.d., news clipping, MO, MHPO.
56. Thompson, "Museum Curator," 2.
57. "Young Bear Was Son of Last Indian Tribal Chief."
58. "Young Bear," folder "Surveys of Indian Industry, 1921–1926, (4 of 4)," box 1, "Surveys of Indian
Industry," Sac & Fox Agency; RG 75; NARA-CH.
59. "Conference with Mr. Schenk, January 14, 1926, by Young Bear; Jonas Poweshiek, Interpreter; George Buff, Stenographer; Present Mr. Edgar Harlan"; "Conference October 4, 1929," both in folder 49t, ERH Papers, SHSI-DM.
60. "Minutes of Conference at House of Bill Wanatee, March 23, 1919," folder 49t, ERH Papers, SHSI-DM. See Foley, *Heartland Chronicles*, 130–32. Scholars have been skeptical of the motivations of people like Harlan and Svacina. Evidence suggests that the comradery between Harlan and at least some Meskwaki leaders was genuine. As Sam Lincoln said during an early meeting in 1919, "It is a good thing to help your friends and the Council think you are doing a good thing for them." Bill Wanatee told Harlan and Svacina that they were the first white people who really seemed willing to aid the tribe.
61. Thompson, "Museum Curator," 5.
62. Spencer, "Powwow Time," 306; Young Bear to Harlan, June 9, 1928, folder 49v, ERH Papers, SHSI-DM.
63. Harlan to Frank Wanatee, June 23, 1927, folder 49bb, ERH Papers, SHSI-DM; Thompson, "Museum Curator," 5–8; Harlan to Ida Priest, March 1, 1920, folder 49bb, ERH Papers, SHSI-DM.
64. Thompson, "Museum Curator," 8–9.
65. *Grand Lodge Bulletin, Iowa Masonic Library* 25 no. 3 (July 1924): 35. Grace Boston to Harlan, November 6, 1924, folder 49a, ERH Papers, SHSI-DM.

66. Harlan to Boston, November 10, 1924, folder 49a, ERH Papers, SHSI-DM.
67. Young Bear to Harlan, March 28, 1933, folder 49v, ERH Papers, SHSI-DM.
68. Thompson, "Museum Curator," 4.
69. Lykins, "Curing the Indian," 9, 133–34.
70. Harlan to Charles H. Burke, November 25, 1924, folder 49ff, ERH Papers, SHSI-DM.
71. Burke to Harlan, December 10, 1924, folder 49ff, ERH Papers, SHSI-DM.
72. "Conference with Mr. Schenk, January 14, 1926."
73. "Jack Old Bear #2"; "Jack Old Bear #1," both in folder "Surveys of Indian Industry, 1921–1926 (3 of 4)," box 1, "Surveys of Indian Industry," SFA, RG 75, NARA-CH. There are two successive reports on Jack Old Bear in this folder, referred to hereafter as "Jack Old Bear #1" and "Jack Old Bear #2."
74. Jack Old Bear to Cato Sells, October 11, 1920, Misc. 1915–1920, box 26, SFA, RG 75, NARA-CH.
75. Jacob Breid to Sells, October 27, 1920, Misc. 1915–1920, box 26, SFA, RG 75, NARA-CH.
76. Cathleen D. Cahill, *Federal Fathers and Mothers: A Social History of the United States Indian Service, 1868–1933* (Chapel Hill: University of North Carolina Press, 2011), 39.
77. Many scholars refer to these kinds of extended family networks as "lateral kinship" or explore them in the contexts of other tribes. See Brenda J. Child, *My Grandfather's Knocking Sticks: Ojibwe Family Life and Labor on the Reservation* (St. Paul: Minnesota Historical Society Press, 2014), 6; Beth H. Piatote, *Domestic Subjects: Gender, Citizenship, and Law in Native American Literature* (New Haven, CT: Yale University Press, 2013), 1–15.
78. Natalie F. Joffe, "The Fox of Iowa," in *Acculturation in Seven American Indian Tribes*, ed. Ralph Linton (London: D. Appleton-Century Company, 1940), 305.
79. Robert L. Russell, "Annual Report, 1916," in folder "Statistical Records and Reports, 1919–1920," box 324, "Annual and Program Reports, Including Census, 1910–1920," SFA, RG 75, NARA-CH.
80. Wick to Harlan, January 22, 1920, folder 49, ERH Papers, SHSI-DM.
81. See James H. Trewin, J. C. Mabry, and U. G. Whitney, eds., *Code of Iowa Containing All the Laws of a General Nature of the State of Iowa* (Des Moines: Homestead Company, 1919), 1966–67, esp. sections 6593 and 6596.
82. Wick to Harlan, January 22, 1920.
83. Ira D. Nelson, "1936 Annual Statistical Report," section 1, folder "Annual Reports 051, 1935–1943," box 114, decimal correspondence files, SFA, RG 75, NARA-CH.
84. "Jack Old Bear #2."
85. Spencer, "Powwow Time," 304–307.
86. *Denison Review* (Denison, IA), September 29, 1920; J. G. Stoddard to the Marshal of the Northern District of Iowa, September 17, 1920, folder "Mesquakie, Powwow Constitution, Court Case, etc., BL 65," box BL 341, "Svacina, Joseph,

Meskwaki Powwow, Svacina Family History," SHSI-IC; Johnathan L. Buffalo, "Green Corn Dance to Annual Powwow: A History of the Annual Meskwaki Powwow," MHCD; Foley, *Heartland Chronicles*, 131.

87. Harlan to Young Bear, July 12, 1925, folder 49v, ERH Papers, SHSI-DM.

88. "Meskwaki Powwow Association Statement of Purpose," printed in Spencer, "Powwow Time," 309.

89. "Constitution of the Meskwaki Indian Powwow Association," printed in Spencer, "Powwow Time," 307–8.

90. See Clyde Ellis, *A Dancing People: Powwow Culture on the Southern Plains* (Lawrence: University Press of Kansas, 2003), 108–11; Tisa Wenger, *We Have a Religion: The 1920s Pueblo Indian Dance Controversy and American Religious Freedom* (Chapel Hill: University of North Carolina Press, 2009).

91. Thomas A. Britten, *American Indians in World War I: At War and at Home* (Albuquerque: University of New Mexico Press, 1997), 59. See also Kenneth R. Philp, *John Collier's Crusade for Indian Reform, 1920–1954* (Tucson: University of Arizona Press, 1977), xiv.

92. See for example Renya K. Ramirez, *Standing Up to Colonial Power: The Lives of Henry Roe Cloud and Elizabeth Bender Cloud* (Lincoln: University of Nebraska Press, 2018); Stephen Kantrowitz, *Citizens of a Stolen Land: A Ho-Chunk History of the Nineteenth-Century United States* (Chapel Hill: University of North Carolina Press, 2023), 155–56.

93. *Indian Citizenship Act of 1924*, 68th Cong., 1st sess. (June 2, 1924); Kantrowitz, *Citizens of a Stolen Land*, 156; Kevin Bruyneel, *The Third Space of Sovereignty: The Post-Colonial Politics of US/Indigenous Relations* (Minneapolis: University of Minnesota Press, 2007), 97–122; Laughlin McDonald, *American Indians and the Fight for Equal Voting Rights* (Norman: University of Oklahoma Press, 2010).

94. Edgar Harlan to Mildred Hutchins, April 1, 1936, folder 49d, ERH Papers, SHSI-DM; Associated Press, "Story of the Tama Indians," *Boone News-Republican* (Boone, IA), April 5, 1928. See also Bruyneel, *Third Space*, 97–122; McDonald, *American Indians and the Fight for Equal Voting Rights*, 156.

95. Ramirez, *Standing Up to Colonial Power*, 3, 121–49.

96. "Meriam Report," quoted in Charles Wilkinson, *Blood Struggle: The Rise of Modern Indian Nations* (New York: W. W. Norton, 2005), 58.

97. Graham D. Taylor, *The New Deal and American Indian Tribalism: The Administration of the Indian Reorganization Act, 1934–1945* (Lincoln: University of Nebraska Press, 1980), 14.

98. Taylor, *New Deal and American Indian Tribalism*, 14.

99. Taylor, *New Deal and American Indian Tribalism*, 14.

100. *Toledo Chronicle*, May 9, 1929.

101. Nelson to John Collier, February 23, 1935, folder "Correspondence, Letters Sent-CCC-ID 1935," box 306, "CCC-ID Records, Letters Sent, 1933–1942," SFA, RG 75, NARA-CH; Buffalo, "Historical Overview," 11.

102. Buffalo, "Historical Overview," 12.

103. Charlotte T. Westwood, "Memorandum for Mr. Collier, Commissioner of Indian Affairs," January 29, 1937, IRA, MHPO.

104. "Congressman Dines in Indian Home, Hears Plaints to Great White Father," *Waterloo Daily Courier*, September 2, 1932.

105. "Congressman Dines in Indian Home."

106. McNickle, "The Indian New Deal as Mirror of the Future," 109.

107. "Sam Slick, 73, Dies on Indian Reservation," June 1947, news clipping, MO, MHPO.

108. Slick to Harlan, April 8, 1931; Slick to Harlan, April 13, 1931, both folder 49bb, ERH Papers, SHSI-DM.

CHAPTER 7

1. Preston Duncan in discussion with the author, July 16, 2014; "Child Birth, George Young Bear-Informant," 27; "Child Birth, Frank Showeta, Tom Scott—Interp.," 29, both on Reel 1, STP, UCSCRC.

2. Preston Duncan in discussion with the author, July 16, 2014.

3. Elizabeth Hoyt, "Tama: An American Conflict," ch. 2, p. 7, folder "Final Manuscript—Tama: An American Conflict, 1970," box 18a, EH Papers, ISUSC. This is a manuscript for Hoyt's book *Tama: An American Conflict* (Ames: Iowa State University, 1964), which had a limited print run. See also Judith M. Daubenmier, "Meskwaki Remember Action Anthropology," *Annals of Iowa* 62, no. 4 (Fall 2003): 451, n. 49.

4. See Brianna Theobald, *Reproduction on the Reservation: Pregnancy, Childbirth, and Colonialism in the Long Twentieth Century* (Chapel Hill: University of North Carolina Press, 2019), 7–13, 71–122.

5. Conrad Black, *Franklin Delano Roosevelt: Champion of Freedom* (New York: Public Affairs, 2003), 250.

6. Jason Scott Smith, *Building New Deal Liberalism: The Political Economy of Public Works, 1933–1956* (New York: Cambridge University Press, 2006), 1.

7. David M. Kennedy, "What the New Deal Did," *Political Science Quarterly* 124, no. 2 (2009): 251–68.

8. See Harry A. Kersey Jr., *The Florida Seminoles and the New Deal, 1933–1942* (Boca Raton: Florida Atlantic University Press, 1989), 14–15.

9. Kersey, *Florida Seminoles*, 200.

10. D. C. Johnson to Edgar Harlan, June 3, 1935, folder 49u, ERH Papers, SHSI-DM; "Indians to Get Old Age Help," *Tama News-Herald*, April 11, 1935; Nelson to Collier, January 8, 1936, folder "CCC-ID Correspondence, 1934–1936," box 307, SFA, RG 75, NARA-CH.

11. Virginia Davis, "A Discovery of Sorts: Reexamining the Origins of the Federal Indian Housing Obligation," *Harvard Blackletter Law Journal* 18 (2002): 228;

D. E. Livesay to Collier, February 25, 1937; Livesay to Collier, March 17, 1937, both in folder "Indian Relief and Rehabilitation Emergency Relief Records: 1935–1937," box 320, SFA, RG 75, NARA-CH.

12. "Mesquakies Given Rights of Individuals under A.A.A. Plan," *Tama News-Herald*, April 27, 1939. On the AAA, see Briggs Depew, Price V. Fishback, and Paul W. Rhode, "New Deal or No Deal in the Cotton South: The Effect of the AAA on the Agricultural Labor Structure," *Explorations in Economic History* 50, no. 4 (October 2013): 466–69.

13. Vine Deloria, Jr., "This Country Was a Lot Better Off When the Indians Were Running It," *New York Times*, March 8, 1970.

14. Jennifer McLerran, *A New Deal for Native Art: Indian Arts and Federal Policy, 1933–1943* (Tucson: University of Arizona Press, 2009), 3, 202; James S. Olson and Raymond Wilson, *Native Americans in the Twentieth Century* (Champaign: University of Illinois Press, 1984), 113–15; Vine Deloria Jr. and Clifford M. Lytle, *The Nations Within: The Past and Future of American Indian Sovereignty* (Austin: University of Texas Press, 1984), 220–22; Kenneth R. Philp, *John Collier's Crusade for Indian Reform, 1920–1954* (Tucson: University of Arizona Press, 1977), 113-34; Emily L. Moore, *Proud Raven, Panting Wolf: Carving Alaska's New Deal Totem Parks* (Seattle: University of Washington Press, 2018).

15. See Akim D. Reinhardt, "A Crude Replacement: The Indian New Deal, Indirect Colonialism, and Pine Ridge Reservation," *Journal of Colonialism and Colonial History*, 6 (2005), 1–56.

16. Alice Sherwood, "Report of Field Matron," September 30, 1916, folder "Reports and Statistics, Farmer's Report 1916–1918," box 324 "Annual and Program Reports, Including Census, 1910–1920," SFA, RG 75, NARA-CH. See also Richard Frank Brown, "A Social History of the Mesquakie Indians, 1800–1963" (MA thesis, Iowa State University, 1964), 74.

17. Jacob Breid, "1934 Annual Statistical Report," 3, folder "Annual Reports 051, 1931–1935," box 113, decimal correspondence files, SFA; RG 75; NARA-CH. See also Stephen Warren, "'To Show the Public We Were Good Indians': Origins and Meanings of the Meskwaki Powwow," *American Indian Culture and Research Journal* 33, no. 4 (January 2009): 21–23.

18. See for example David A. Chang, *The Color of the Land: Race, Nation, and the Politics of Landownership in Oklahoma, 1832–1929* (Chapel Hill: University of North Carolina Press, 2010),192–201.

19. Joseph Frazier Wall, *Iowa: A History* (New York: W. W. Norton, 1978), 176.

20. Cyrenus Cole to Charles A. Burke, March 28, 1927, folder 49ff, ERH Papers, SHSI-DM.

21. Breid, "1934 Annual Statistical Report," 3.

22. Orris C. Culver to A. C. Cooley, February 23, 1934, folder "Agricultural Extension 1930–1934," box 302, SFA, RG 75, NARA-CH.

23. Judith Daubenmier, *The Meskwaki and Anthropologists: Action Anthropology Reconsidered* (Lincoln: University of Nebraska Press, 2008), 30.

24. Douglas Metoxen Kiel, *Unsettling Territory: Oneida Nation Resurgence and Anti-Sovereignty Backlash*, forthcoming from Yale University Press, 2024, manuscript shared with the author.

25. Lisa Dianne Lykins, "'Curing the Indian': Therapeutic Care and Acculturation at the Sac and Fox Tuberculosis Sanatorium, 1912–1942" (PhD diss., University of Kentucky, 2002), 143–47.

26. Daubenmier, *Meskwaki and Anthropologists*, 31.

27. Edgar R. Harlan to H. D. Bernbrock, April 30, 1932; Halla M. Rhode, memorandum dated December 15, 1930, both in folder 49c, ERH Papers, SHSI-DM.

28. Daubenmier, *Meskwaki and Anthropologists*, 30.

29. Peru Farver, "Reservation Post-War Program," March 1944, 3, folder "Postwar Reservation Program—Memoranda, Correspondence, Reports, Instructions, 1943–1944," box 303, "Decimal Files: Miscellaneous Correspondence, 944–995," SFA, RG 75, NARA-CH. See Daubenmier, *Meskwaki and Anthropologists*, 30–31.

30. R. E. Buchanan to Charles E. Friley, February 22, 1943, folder "Tama Reservation," box 15, CF Papers, Friley Papers, ISUSC.

31. Daubenmier, *Meskwaki and Anthropologists*, 31.

32. "12,000 Qts. Vegetables Canned by Indian Women," *Tama News-Herald*, October 30, 1941; Daubenmier, *Meskwaki and Anthropologists*, 29–31; Ira D. Nelson, "Annual Forestry and Grazing Report, Fiscal Year Ending June 30, 1939," 3, folder "Annual Forest and Grazing Reports FY 1935 to 1939"; "CCC-ID Program Records, Forestry Reports, Monthly Reviews, 1935–1942"; Orpha Hoganson, "Report of the USIS Dairy Herd Improvement Association for the Short Year Period September 1 to December 31, 1939," folder "1932 Dairying, Misc. Correspondence," box 302; William Zimmerman to Nelson, January 30, folder "Hunting and Fishing Misc. Correspondence," box 302, "Decimal Files 904–941, 1930–1947," all in SFA, RG 75, NARA-CH.

33. Culver to Cooley, February 23, 1934.

34. "Annual Forestry Report, Fiscal Year 1935," 3; Hoganson, "Report of the USIS Dairy Herd Improvement Association, September 1 to December 31, 1939."

35. George Young Bear, "274 Mesquakies Get Annuities," *Tama News-Herald*, December 2, 1937; "Mesquakies Get Annuities," *Tama News-Herald*, December 2, 1937.

36. "Indians Make Sugar from Soft Maple," *Rock Valley Bee*, March 23, 1930; "Mesquakies Make Maple Sugar for Use in Trading," *Burlington Hawkeye*, March 27, 1932.

37. "Sugar Making by Iowa Indians," *Des Moines Register*, April 11, 1937.

38. "Little Tama Indians Will Learn How to Raise Chicks," n.p., n.d., news clipping in folder "4-H Club Material for Girls, Miss Louise Harpe-Toledo, IA," hereafter "4-H Club for Girls," box 303, SFA, RG 75, NARA-CH.

39. "Ne-No-Tal" simply translates to "Indian." See "4-H Club Narrative"; various undated newspaper clippings titled "4-H Club Started on Reservation"; "4-H Club Rally Held in Toledo on Wednesday"; "Ne-No-Tal 4-H Indian Girls in Sewing

Project"; "Mesquakie 4-H Ne-No-Tal Girls Enjoy Meeting"; "Mary Davenport Sits in 4-H Club Booth and Does Bead Work"; Nancy Davenport, "4-H Club Secretary's Book," all in "4-H Club for Girls," box 303, SFA, RG 75, NARA-CH.

40. Marlene Smith, "Adeline Wanatee Is Servant of Her People," *Waterloo Courier*, May 29, 1960.

41. Preston Duncan in discussion with the author, July 16, 2014. Elizabeth Hoyt claims there were only about 105 horses on the Settlement in 1935. See Hoyt, "Tama: An American Conflict," ch. 4, p. 4.

42. Donald Wanatee, in discussion with the author, June 27, 2014.

43. "Miller, July 16, Billy Waseskuk," 482, Reel 2, STP.

44. "Miller, July 16, Billy Waseskuk," 482, Reel 2, STP.

45. "Annual Statistical Report, Calendar Year 1939," 4, folder "Agriculture, Agency Farmer Misc. Correspondence, Reports, etc., 1936–1942," box 302, SFA, RG 75, NARA-CH.

46. "William J. Peterson to Give Main Address at Pow-Wow Sun. Afternoon," *Tama News-Herald*, August 18, 1938; "Thousands See Pow Wow; Peak Reached Sunday," *Tama News-Herald*, August 25, 1938.

47. "Thousands See Pow Wow."

48. "Indian Pow Wow Begins Today, Gov. Wilson to Speak Sunday," *Tama News-Herald*, August 14, 1941; "Pow Wow Makes Profit in Spite of Sunday Rain," *Tama News-Herald*, August 21, 1941.

49. See Philp, *Crusade*, 113–34; Kersey, *Florida Seminoles*; Deloria and Lytle, *Nations Within*; Reinhardt, "A Crude Replacement"; Graham D. Taylor, *The New Deal and American Indian Tribalism: The Administration of the Indian Reorganization Act, 1934–1945* (Lincoln: University of Nebraska Press, 1980); Felix S. Cohen, *On the Drafting of Tribal Constitutions*, ed. David E. Wilkins (Norman: University of Oklahoma Press, 2007); Elmer R. Rusco, *A Fateful Time: The Background and Legislative History of the Indian Reorganization Act* (Reno: University of Nevada Press, 2000); Wilcomb E. Washburn, "A Fifty-Year Perspective on the Indian Reorganization Act," *American Anthropologist* 86, no. 2 (June 1984): 279–89; McLerran, *New Deal for Native Art*.

50. See Deloria and Lytle, *Nations Within*, 80–153; Vine Deloria Jr., ed., *The Indian Reorganization Act Congresses and Bills* (Norman: University of Oklahoma Press, 2002). Like the Meriam Report, the Indian Reorganization Act may have been coauthored by Henry Roe Cloud. See Renya K. Ramirez, *Standing Up to Colonial Power: The Lives of Henry Roe Cloud and Elizabeth Bender Cloud* (Lincoln: University of Nebraska Press, 2018); 3, 121–49.

51. Theodore H. Haas, *Ten Years of Tribal Government Under I.R.A.* (United States Indian Service Haskell Institute Printing Department, 1947), 1.

52. Deloria, *Indian Reorganization Act*, xv.

53. John Collier, "Facts about the New Indian Reorganization Act: An Explanation and Interpretation of the Wheeler-Howard Bill as Modified, Amended, and Passed by Congress," 9–10, folder 46u, ERH Papers, SHSI-DM.

54. Deloria and Lytle, *Nations Within*, 141; Haas, *Ten Years of Tribal Government*, 3.

55. Johnathan L. Buffalo, "Historical Overview of the Adoption of the Indian Reorganization Act of 1934 by the Sac and Fox of the Mississippi in Iowa," 1, IRA, MHPO, 15-17.

56. Edgar Harlan to Collier, September 25, 1934, folder 49u, ERH Papers, SHSI-DM.

57. Collier, "Facts about the New Indian Reorganization Act," 16.

58. Jack Old Bear, Joe Peters, Harrison Kapayou, and John Tataposh to Ickes, December 18, 1934, IRA, MHPO.

59. Collier to Jack Old Bear, January 21, 1935, IRA, MHPO.

60. Edward Davenport, George Young Bear, Horace Poweshiek, and William Poweshiek to Collier, June 29, 1937; Young Bear, Charles Davenport, C. H. Chuck, Peter Morgan, John Tataposh, and Sam Slick to Collier, December 13, 1937; Jack Old Bear, Joe Peters, Harrison Kapayou, and John Tataposh to Harold L. Ickes, December 18, 1934, all in IRA, MHPO. See also Daubenmier, *Meskwaki and Anthropologists*, 40-46; Douglas E. Foley, *The Heartland Chronicles* (Philadelphia: University of Pennsylvania Press, 1995), 151.

61. Collier to Jack Old Bear, January 21, 1935.

62. Ira D. Nelson to Collier, May 18, 1935; Collier to Nelson, May 24, 1935; Collier to Nelson, June 11, 1935, all IRA, MHPO.

63. Nelson to Collier, June 15, 1935, IRA, MHPO.

64. Daubenmier, *Meskwaki and Anthropologists*, 43. See also Buffalo, "Historical Overview," 17-18.

65. Benjamin Reifel to Collier, March 5, 1937, IRA, MHPO.

66. Nelson to Collier, March 19, 1936, IRA, MHPO.

67. F. H. Daiker to Nelson, May 18, 1936, IRA, MHPO. See also Indian Reorganization Act of June 18, 1934, ch. 576, § 17, 48 Stat. 984.

68. Daubenmier, *Meskwaki and Anthropologists*, 40; *Cedar Rapids Gazette*, May 17, 1936.

69. Charlotte T. Westwood, "Memorandum for Mr. Collier, Commissioner of Indian Affairs," January 29, 1937; Reifel to Ed Davenport, March 5, 1937; Reifel to Collier, March 1, 1937; Westwood, "Memorandum to Organization Division of the US Department of the Interior," March 16, 1937, all in IRA, MHPO. See also Daubenmier, *Meskwaki and Anthropologists*, 40-41.

70. Westwood, "Memorandum for Mr. Collier."

71. Daubenmier, *Meskwaki and Anthropologists*, 43-46; D'Arcy McNickle, "Memorandum to Mr. Harper, Re: Sac and Fox Indians, Tama, Iowa," December 30, 1936; Westwood, "Memorandum to Mr. Collier," both in IRA, MHPO. See also Meskwaki Constitution, Art. X, Sec. 1 and Art. XI.

72. Westwood, "Memorandum for Mr. Collier," notes that there was little intermarriage between Meskwaki people and whites, although some Meskwaki people had married partners from Ho-Chunk, Potawatomi, and other Native tribes.

73. See "Minutes, January 8, 1935," folder "749 Community Meetings—Minutes of Meetings and Related Correspondence"; "Memo Re: Sac and Fox Indians of Iowa: Washington, Feb 4, 1931," folder "771 Charities and Benevolences—Rations (Food and Clothing), Misc. Correspondence, 1931–1933," both in box 293, SFA, RG 75, NARA-CH. See also Meskwaki Constitution, Art. II. See also Daubenmier, *Meskwaki and Anthropologists*, 48.

74. Foley, *Heartland Chronicles*, 173–74.

75. See Meskwaki Constitution, Art. II and Art. IV, Sec. 4.

76. Westwood to William Zimmerman, February 20, 1937; Zimmerman to Nelson, September 22, 1937; Nelson to Collier, September 30, 1937, IRA, MHPO.

77. Daubenmier, *Meskwaki and Anthropologists*, 45; Buffalo, "Historical Overview," 25.

78. "Studies Tama Tribe Election," n. p., 1938, news clipping, folder "Tribal Council Elections Jan. 18, 1938," box "Tribal Council Elections," BA.

79. John Tataposh to Franklin Delano Roosevelt, February 2, 1938, IRA, MHPO. See also Buffalo, "Historical Overview," 29–31.

80. Several community members recounted the story about the destroyed ballots in informal conversations. See also Theresa Essman Mahoney, "Practical Tips for Advocates of Indian Children: A Tribal Perspective," 3–4, slideshow presented at the 2011 Iowa State Bar Association's Juvenile Law Seminar, May 6, 2011.

81. Lisa Peattie, "Being a Mesquakie Indian," in *Documentary History of the Fox Project, 1928–1959: A Program in Action Anthropology Directed by Sol Tax*, ed. Fred Gearing, Robert McC. Netting, and Lisa R. Peattie (Chicago: University of Chicago Press, 1960), 75; Donald Wanatee, "The Lion, Fleur-de-lis, the Eagle, or the Fox: A Study of Government," in *The Worlds between Two Rivers: Perspectives on American Indians in Iowa*, ed. Gretchen M. Bataille, David M. Gradwohl, and Charles L. P. Silet (Ames: Iowa State University Press, 1978), 81; Daubenmier, *Meskwaki and Anthropologists*, 47.

82. Wanatee, "The Lion, Fleur-de-lis, the Eagle, or the Fox: A Study of Government," 80.

83. Peattie, "Being a Mesquakie Indian," 75.

84. Bertha Waseskuk to Mr. Life, September 13, 1950, copy in the author's possession.

85. Daubenmier, *Meskwaki and Anthropologists*, 48.

86. Foley, *Heartland Chronicles*, 150.

87. Buffalo, "Historical Overview," 29–30. On the tribe's inability to "get together," see "Miller, Bob Waseskuk," August 5, 500–505; "Fallers, Interview with Dan Youngbear," July 22, 1948, 532–33; "Fallers and Peattie, Interview with Mary Young Bear," August 1, 544, all on Reel 2, STP.

88. Frank C. Moorhead to Nelson Kraschel, May 5, 1938, folder "Tribal Council Elections Jan. 18, 1938," box "Tribal Council Elections," BA.

89. Moorhead to Kraschel, May 5, 1938; Buffalo, "Historical Overview," 31.

90. Moorhead to Kraschel, May 5, 1938; Buffalo, "Historical Overview," 31.

91. Moorhead to Kraschel, May 5, 1938.

92. Kennedy, "What the New Deal Did," 253–54.

93. Kennedy, "What the New Deal Did," 252, 267; Margot Canaday, *The Straight State: Sexuality and Citizenship in Twentieth-Century America* (Princeton, NJ: Princeton University Press, 2011), 18. Officially known as "Emergency Conservation Work," the program became the "Civilian Conservation Corps" in 1937.

94. C. N. Alleger and C. A. Alleger, *Civilian Conservation Corps, Iowa District History* (Rapid City, SD: Johnston and Bordewyk, 1935). See also Lea Rosson Delong and Gregg R. Narber, *A Catalog of New Deal Mural Projects in Iowa* (Des Moines: Iowa Humanities Board, 1982); Gregg R. Narber, "These Murals Were a New Deal," *Iowan* 32 (Spring 1984): 8–17; "States and Cities, Iowa," *Living New Deal*, accessed December 17, 2015, https://livingnewdeal.org/us/ia. See also Neil M. Maher, "A New Deal Body Politic: Landscape, Labor, and the Civilian Conservation Corps," *Environmental History* 7, no. 3 (July 2002): 435–62.

95. Calvin W. Gower, "The CCC Indian Division: Aid for Depressed Americans, 1933–1942," *Minnesota History* 43, no. 1 (April 1972): 4, 12. See also Mindy J. Morgan, "'Working' from the Margins: Documenting American Indian Participation in the New Deal Era," in *Why You Can't Teach US History Without American Indians*, ed. by Susan Sleeper-Smith, Juliana Barr, Jean M. O'Brien, Nancy Shoemaker, and Scott Manning Stevens (Chapel Hill: University of North Carolina Press, 2015), 181–96; Moore, *Proud Raven, Panting Wolf.*

96. "Work for Uncle Sam Started by Tama Indians," *Tama News-Herald,* July 20, 1933; Gower, "CCC Indian Division," 5.

97. Breid to Collier, March 8, 1934; Ira D. Nelson to Collier, May 31, 1934, both in folder "Correspondence, Letters Sent, CCC-ID, April 21, 1933–December 1933," hereafter "AD-1933," box 306, "CCC-ID Records, Letters Sent, 1933–1942," SFA, RG 75, NARA-CH.

98. Donald L. Parman, "The Indian and the Civilian Conservation Corps," *Pacific Historical Review* 40, no. 1 (February 1971): 45–46. See also Roger Bromert, "The Sioux and the Indian-CCC," *South Dakota History* 8, no. 4 (Spring 1978): 345.

99. Breid to Collier, February 12, 1934; Breid to Collier, July 3, 1933, both in AD-1933. On salaries for regular CCC enrollees, see Canaday, *Straight State*, 118.

100. Kennedy, "What the New Deal Did," 253–54.

101. Nelson to Heritage, April 25, 1942, folder "Correspondence—Letters Sent—CCC-ID, January–September 1942," Box 306, SFA, RG 75, NARA-CH.

102. Randolph W. Hellwig to Collier, July 13, 1942, folder "Letter to Commissioner of Indian Affairs over Close of CCC Program at Sac and Fox Sanatorium, July 13, 1942," box 308 "CCC-ID Handbooks, Safety Correspondence, Property Inventory, Etc., 1933–1942"; Victor L. Rushfeldt to William Heritage, January 7, 1939, folder "Correspondence, Letters Sent, CCC-ID, 1939," box 306, both in SFA, RG 75, NARA-CH.

NOTES TO CHAPTER 7   305

103. Hellwig to Collier, July 13, 1942; "Original Tama Indian Team Organized"; "Indian Ball Park Is Being Remodeled; To Be Ready by May 26," both in *Tama News-Herald*, May 23, 1935. The annual Meskwaki Powwow was a major economic boon to the tribal economy, bringing over five thousand spectators in 1934 alone. See also "Road Maintenance at Sac and Fox Sanatorium," *Indians at Work* 3 (June 15, 1936): 50; "Over 5,000 See Indian Pow Wow; Willford Speaks: Young Bear Leaves Sick Bed and Speaks on Sunday," *Tama News-Herald*, August 23, 1934; Warren, "To Show the Public," 21. See maps in folder "Conservation Work Program Report, April 1, 1935, Sac and Fox Reservation, Iowa, R. W. Hellwig, Junior Forester, April 18, 1935," box 311, both SFA, RG 75, NARA-CH.

104. Nelson to Charles Evans, March 29, 1941; Nelson to Heritage, April 3, 1941; "Agreement for the Use of Tribal Lands for a Proposed Roadside Park on the Sac and Fox Reservation, Tama, Iowa," March 21, 1941, all in folder "Project Plans 1940–1941," box 313, "CCC-ID Reports, Program Records, Enrollment Program, Project Plans, 1935–1942," SFA, RG 75, NARA-CH. See also "Rustic Shelter House Being Built by CCC on Indian Reservation," *Tama News-Herald*, May 8, 1941.

105. Roger Bromert, "The Sioux and the Indian-CCC," *South Dakota History* 8, no. 4 (Spring 1978): 344.

106. "Weekly Group Progress Report," September 7, 1934; Fred Anderson to Collier, February 18, 1935, both in folder "Forms 8 & 9 IECW, FY 1935," hereafter "IECW 1935," box 309, SFA, RG 75, NARA-CH.

107. "Weekly Group Progress Report," April 5, 1935; "Weekly Group Progress Report," April 26, 1935, both in IECW 1935.

108. Nelson to William Heritage, September 29, 1938, folder "CCC-ID Miscellaneous Correspondence, 1938–1940," box 307, "CCC-ID Records," SFA, RG 75, NARA-CH.

109. Nelson to Gabe E. Parker, November 15, 1938, folder "Correspondence, Letters Sent, CCC-ID 1938," box 306, "CCC-ID Records, Letters Sent, 1933–1942," SFA, RG 75, NARA-CH.

110. "Agreement on Work Order for a Proposed Roadside Park on the Sac and Fox Reservation, Tama, Iowa," folder "CCC-ID Project FY 1940-1941," box 313, "CCC-ID Records, Program Records, Enrollment Program, Project Plans, 1935–1942," SFA, RG 75, NARA-CH. Two documents in this folder share this title. The first is an agreement between the tribal council and Peter Morgan. The second is an agreement between the council and the US government.

111. Jacob Breid to Russel E. Getty, October 6, 1933, folder "Correspondence, Letters Sent, CCC-ID April 21, 1933–December 1934," box 306, SFA, RG 75, NARA-CH.

112. Nelson to D. E. Murphy, October 9, 1937, folder "Correspondence, Letters Sent, CCC-ID 1937," box 306, SFA, RG 75, NARA-CH.

113. Donald L. Fixico, *Termination and Relocation: Federal Indian Policy, 1945–1960* (Albuquerque: University of New Mexico Press, 1986), 4, 6.

114. Mark Harrison, *The Economics of World War II: Six Great Powers in International Comparison* (New York: Cambridge University Press, 1998), 81. See also Richard H.

Owens, *The Neutrality Imperative* (Lanham, MD: University Press of America, 2009); Katherine M. Osburn, *Choctaw Resurgence in Mississippi: Race, Class, and Nation Building in the Jim Crow South, 1830–1977* (Lincoln: University of Nebraska Press, 2014), 132.

115. Jonas Poweshiek, "Indians Again on the Warpath," *Annals of Iowa* 26, no. 4 (April 1945): 291. See also "Sac and Fox Tribe Work on Farms, In Defense Plants for Victory," *Tama News-Herald*, July 29, 1943.

116. "Eight Sac-Fox Indians Enlist in Nat'l Guard," *Tama News-Herald*, February 13, 1941. See Samuel Holiday and Robert S. McPherson, *Under the Eagle: Samuel Holiday, Navajo Code Talker* (Norman: University of Oklahoma Press, 2013); Noah J. Riseman, *Defending Whose Country?: Indigenous Soldiers in the Pacific War* (Lincoln: University of Nebraska Press, 2012), 169–94. Fixico, *Termination and Relocation*, 4-5.

117. "Eight Tama Indian Boys Operate Walkie-Talkie Radio Units in Army," *Tama News-Herald*, February 27, 1941.

118. "Harkin Introduces Legislation to Honor Sac and Fox World War II Veterans," June 21, 2002, news clipping in folder "Meskwaki Code Talkers," box "Military Service," BA.

119. "A Message from the Chairman," n.d., news clipping in folder "Meskwaki Code Talkers"; "Indian Promoted at Tank Destroyer Center," October 19, 1944, news clipping in folder "World War Two," both in box "Military Service," BA. See also George Shane, "War Scatters Tama Indians," *Des Moines Register*, October 11, 1942.

120. Poweshiek, "Indians Again on the Warpath," 292–97; "3 Indian Boys Freed from Nazi War Prison Camps," *Tama News-Herald*, May 17, 1945.

121. Jenny Welp, "Harkin Presents Medals to Meskwaki Code Talker," *Marshalltown Times-Republican*, August 11, 2002; "Honor Code: Meskwaki, US Marine Vet Working to Win Recognition for 'Code Talkers,'" *Waterloo Courier*, December 11, 2004. James Q. Lynch, "Meskwaki 'Code Talkers' Receive Congressional Gold Medal," *Cedar Rapids Gazette*, March 28, 2014.

122. "Tama's Indians Plan on Remote Axis Scalpings," *Waterloo Courier*, June 14, 1942.

123. Shane, "War Scatters Tama Indians"; "Indian Reservations Contribute Scrap Metal," n.p., n.d., news clipping, folder "Home Front World War Two," box "Military Service," BA.

124. Hoyt, "Tama: An American Conflict," ch. 4, pg. 6. "Sac and Fox Tribe Work on Farms, in Defense Plants for Victory."

125. William Poweshiek quoted in Shane, "War Scatters Tama Indians."

126. George Shane, "From Beadwork to Ammunition," n.p., n.d., news clipping, folder "Home Front World War Two," box "Military Service," BA.

127. "First Indian Nurse," *Tama News-Herald*, July 26, 1945.

128. George Young Bear quoted in Shane, "War Scatters Tama Indians."

129. "1937 Annual Report," 5, folder "Annual Statistical Report, Census, 1937," box 112, SFA, RG 75, NARA-CH; Sac and Fox of the Mississippi in Iowa, "An Overall Economic Development Plan Prepared by the Sac and Fox of the Mississippi in Iowa

NOTES TO CHAPTER 7   307

for the Economic Development Administration," 6, folder "An Overall Economic Development Plan of the Sac and Fox of the Mississippi in Iowa, 1978," box 108, MHPO.

130. See "Annual Income Report, Fiscal Year Ended June 30, 1940," folder "Statistics 1941 Annual Report," box 112, "Decimal File, Annual Reports 051, 1925–1930," both in SFA, RG 75, NARA-CH; Farver, "Reservation Post-War Program," 7. I calculated this decrease by totaling incomes in the Indian Office's 1940 report, estimating there were 95 families on the Settlement at that time (there were 97 in 1942 and 113 in 1944), and comparing it to the 1944 report. Income from Meskwaki military personnel or laborers who sent money back to their families may have gone unreported.

131. George Pierre Castile, *To Show Heart: Native American Self-Determination and Federal Indian Policy, 1960–1975* (Tucson: University of Arizona Press, 1998), xxi. "Indian Pow Wow September 13–16," *Tama News-Herald*, August 30, 1945.

132. Shane, "War Scatters Tama Indians."

133. "Horrors! Nazis Among Our Indians," *Tama News-Herald*, November 10, 1938.

134. Frederick O. Gearing, *The Face of the Fox* (Chicago: Aldine Publishing Company, 1970) offers a detailed discussion of race relations in Tama County; Hoyt, "Tama: An American Conflict," ch. 1, pg. 7.

135. Collier, Circular #3514, July 9, 1943, folder "Postwar Reservation Program 1943–1944," box 303, SFA, RG 75, NARA-CH.

136. "Indian Agent at Tama Sent to New Mexico," *Tama News-Herald*, August 6, 1942.

137. Lykins, "Curing the Indian," 10; "Indian Agent at Tama Sent to New Mexico," *Tama News-Herald*, August 6, 1942. Daubenmier, *Meskwaki and Anthropologists*, 59.

138. Daubenmier, *Meskwaki and Anthropologists*, 58.

139. R. M. Nygaard, "Proposed Sac & Fox Post-War Program Projects," May 1, 1944, 2–4., folder "Proposed Sac and Fox Post-War Program Projects, May 1, 1944, Sac-Fox Sub. Agency," box "US Treaties, Cong. Acts," BA.

140. "Bi-Weekly Report for Period Ending June 27, 1947," folder "14683-47, Minneapolis District Office, 032," box 1, "Central Classified Files 1940–1957, Minneapolis District Office," RG 75, NARA-DC; "26 Indian Families Flee from Flood on Reservation," *Tama News-Herald*, January 10, 1946.

141. Nygaard, "Proposed Sac & Fox Post-War Program Projects," 1–4.

142. Farver, "Reservation Post-War Program," 6; Buchanan to Friley, February 22, 1943.

143. Farver to Charles I. Gruber, May 7, 1943, folder "Postwar Reservation Program 1943–1944," box 303, SFA, RG 75, NARA-CH.

144. "Report of a Survey of Possibilities of Withdrawal of Federal Supervision and Services in Affairs of the Sac and Fox Indians of Tama, Iowa," August 1951, 5–6, folder "5993-1952, 077 (1 of 2)," box 5, "Central Classified Files, 1940–1957," MAO, RG 75, NARA-DC.

145. Nathan and Matt Bear, in discussion with the author, September 9, 2014.

146. "Report of a Survey of Possibilities of Withdrawal," 5–6. Hoyt, "Tama: An American Conflict," ch. 1, pg. 7.

147. See Fixico, *Termination and Relocation*; Donald L. Fixico, *The Urban Indian Experience in America* (Albuquerque: University of New Mexico Press, 2000), 8–25; Julie L. Davis, *Survival Schools: The American Indian Movement and Community Education in the Twin Cities* (Minneapolis: University of Minnesota Press, 2013); Douglas K. Miller, "Willing Workers: Urban Relocation and American Indian Initiative, 1940s–1960s," *Ethnohistory* 60, no. 1 (Winter 2013): 51–76. See also Douglas K. Miller, *Indians on the Move: Native American Mobility and Urbanization in the Twentieth Century* (Chapel Hill: University of North Carolina Press, 2019); Kiel, *Unsettling Territory*.

148. Fixico, *Termination and Relocation*, 183.

149. Mary Young Bear, in discussion with the author, May 28, 2015.

150. See Daubenmier, *Meskwaki and Anthropologists*, 221–23; Douglas E. Foley, "The Fox Project: A Reappraisal," *Current Anthropology* 40, no. 2 (April 1999): 175, 180.

151. Nathan and Matt Bear, in discussion with the author, September 9, 2014.

152. See for example "Two Brothers Dead in Shooting Incident at Youngbear Home on Tama Settlement," *Tama News-Herald*, January 3, 1970; "Timothy Youngbear," *Tama News-Herald*, October 19, 1995. Informal conversation with [name redacted], July 7, 2015.

153. Daubenmier, *Meskwaki and Anthropologists*, 4.

154. See Daubenmier, *Meskwaki and Anthropologists*, 196; Foley, "Fox Project Reappraisal," 171–92; Gearing, *The Face of the Fox*.

155. Fred Gearing, "Why We'd Just as Soon Not Farm Much," in *Documentary History of the Fox Project, 1928–1959: A Program in Action Anthropology Directed by Sol Tax*, ed. Fred Gearing, Robert McC. Netting, and Lisa R. Peattie (Chicago: University of Chicago Press, 1960), 209. Emphasis in original.

156. Lloyd Fallers, "interview with John Bear," August 6, 1948, 22-3, Reel 2, STP. Other tribal members believed that even if they wanted to farm, the tribal council would refuse to divide up the Settlement land appropriately. See "Interview with Adeline Wanatee, July 15, 1949, 451, Reel 2, STP.

157. Fred Barth, "Interview with Ed Davenport," July 18, 1948, D1989; "Interview with Adeline Wanatee," July 15, 1949, 451, both on Reel 2, STP. See also "Fallers, Interview with John Bear," August 6, 1948, B24, Reel 2, STP.

158. Hoyt, "Tama: An American Conflict," ch. 4, pg. 6.

159. "Harry Lincon [*sic*], Miller Bott," August 13, 1948, 2155, Reel 3, STP.

160. "Population of Iowa Placed at 2,543,502," *Tama News-Herald*, September 18, 1947; Sol Tax, "Diagnosis for Action," paper given at University of Chicago Symposium titled "The Fox Project," 1956, in *Documentary History of the Fox Project, 1928–1959: A Program In Action Anthropology Directed by Sol Tax*, ed. Fred Gearing, Robert McC. Netting, and Lisa R. Peattie (Chicago: University of Chicago Press, 1960), 314.

161. Cornelia F. Mutel, *The Emerald Horizon: The History of Nature in Iowa* (Iowa City: University of Iowa Press, 2008), 25–26.

NOTES TO CHAPTER 8

162. Nygaard, "Proposed Sac & Fox Post-War Program Projects," 2.
163. "Report of a Survey of Possibilities of Withdrawal," 27.

CHAPTER 8

1. Donald L. Fixico, *Termination and Relocation: Federal Indian Policy, 1945–1960* (Albuquerque: University of New Mexico Press, 1986), ix; Elmer R. Rusco, *A Fateful Time: The Background and Legislative History of the Indian Reorganization Act* (Reno: University of Nevada Press, 2000), 86–90; George Pierre Castile, *To Show Heart: Native American Self-Determination and Federal Indian Policy, 1960–1975* (Tucson: University of Arizona Press, 1998), xxi.

2. Castile, *To Show Heart*, xxii–xxvii.

3. Roberta Ulrich, *American Indian Nations from Termination to Restoration, 1953–2006* (Lincoln: University of Nebraska Press, 2010), 13; See also Daniel M. Cobb, *Native Activism in Cold War America: The Struggle for Sovereignty* (Lawrence: University Press of Kansas, 2008), 13; Castile, *To Show Heart*, xxii.

4. Ulrich, *American Indian Nations*, 14.

5. Fixico, *Termination and Relocation*, 183.

6. Ulrich, *American Indian Nations*, 100–105.

7. "Indian Office Closed; King is Transferred," *Tama News-Herald*, August 7, 1947; K. W. Dixon to Glenn L. Emmons, memorandum, April 1, 1954, folder "00-1954, 032," box 3, "Central Classified Files, 1940–1957," MAO, RG 75, NARA-DC; "MAO Annual Report, Fiscal Year 1970," 1–2, folder "216, MAO, 1968, 031," box 1, "Central Classified Files, 1958–1975," MAO, RG 75, NARA-DC.

8. Judith Daubenmier, *The Meskwaki and Anthropologists: Action Anthropology Reconsidered* (Lincoln: University of Nebraska Press, 2008), 59; "Report of a Survey of Possibilities of Withdrawal of Federal Supervision and Services in Affairs of the Sac and Fox Indians of Tama, Iowa," August 1951, 5–6, folder "5993-1952, 077 (1 of 2)," hereafter "5993-1952," box 5, "Central Classified Files, 1940–1957," MAO, RG 75, NARA-DC.

9. "Report of a Survey of Possibilities of Withdrawal," 4, 21. The report lists 579 Meskwaki people in 1951. Total federal spending, not including BIA employee salaries, totaled $66,409.01.

10. "Report of a Survey of Possibilities of Withdrawal," 19, 34.

11. "Relief Issue Splits Tribe, County Officials Take Stand," *Tama News-Herald*, May 18, 1944.

12. "Relief Issue Splits Tribe."

13. "Relief Issue Splits Tribe."

14. "Relief Issue Splits Tribe"; "Study Indian Aid Problem," n.p. April 13, 1944, news clipping in folder "adc Relief Issue, 1943–45," hereafter "ADC relief," box "ADC Meskwaki Family Services," BA.

15. "Relief Issue Splits Tribe."

16. "Relief Issue Splits Tribe."

17. "Relief Issue Splits Tribe."

18. "Relief Issue Splits Tribe."

19. "Bill on Aid to Indian Children on Reservation Passed by State Senate," *Tama News-Herald*, March 8, 1945.

20. "Indian Children Aid Bill Signed by Iowa Governor Robt. Blue," *Tama News-Herald*, March 23, 1945.

21. "Bill on Aid to Indian Children on Reservation Passed by State Senate"; "First Grants of Aid to Indians," n. p., August 2, 1945, news clipping, ADC Relief.

22. For the quote, see Nelson to Louis C. Mueller, July 7, 1936, folder, "Liquor Suppression Year of 1936," box 109, SFA, RG 75, NARA-CH. See also A. M. Ellis to Robert L. Russell, April 2, 1919, folder "Intoxicating liquors 1916–1926," box 109, "Decimal Files, Miscellaneous Correspondence 027-030, 1916–1942," SFA, RG 75, NARA-CH. See also box 109, SFA, RG 75, NARA-CH. On the broader history of peyote prohibition, see Thomas Constantine Maroukis, *The Peyote Road: Religious Freedom and the Native American Church* (Norman: University of Oklahoma Press, 2010); Jere Bishop Franco, *Crossing the Pond: The Native American Effort in World War II* (Denton: University of North Texas Press, 1999), 196–99.

23. Douglas E. Foley, *The Heartland Chronicles* (Philadelphia: University of Pennsylvania Press, 1995), 23.

24. Daubenmier, *Meskwaki and Anthropologists*, 53.

25. "Evening," June 29, 1948, 1598, Reel 2, STP; Foley, *Heartland Chronicles*, 21; F. F. Faville to Henry N. Graven, May 18, 1945, folder "Henry Graven, Jurisdiction over Sac and Fox, 1956," box "Land," BA.

26. Daubenmier, *Meskwaki and Anthropologists*, 51.

27. Foley, *Heartland Chronicles*, 21–22; Daubenmier, *Meskwaki and Anthropologists*, 51; "Mesquakies Now Have Their Own Judge and Court," *Toledo Chronicle*, March 27, 1941.

28. Walter B. Miller, "Authority and Collective Action in Fox Society," in *Documentary History of the Fox Project, 1928–1959: A Program in Action Anthropology Directed by Sol Tax*, ed. Fred Gearing, Robert McC. Netting, and Lisa R. Peattie (Chicago: University of Chicago Press, 1960), 141.

29. Daubenmier, *Meskwaki and Anthropologists*, 50.

30. "Testimony of Walter J. Willett, Prosecutor, Tama County, Iowa," *Hearings before a Subcommittee of the Committee on Indian Affairs House of Representatives, 2nd Sess., Pursuant to H. Res. 166., Part 3. Hearings in the Field* (1945), partially reprinted in Johnathan L. Buffalo, "1937–1951: Replacements Rather Than Losses," MHCD.

31. Daubenmier, *Meskwaki and Anthropologists*, 52-54.

32. "Wolffson Journal," July 23, 1948, 1641, Reel 2, STP.

33. "Law and Order on Reservation to Be Discussed," *Tama News-Herald*, September 18, 1947.

34. "Roy Houdyshell Badly Beaten Up on Road in Reservation by Young Indian Crazed with Fire Water—Jackie Wolf Insists He Is Not the Man Who Shouted He Was Jackie Wolf," *Tama News-Herald*, October 16, 1947.

NOTES TO CHAPTER 8

35. "Grand Jury Condemns Lawlessness on Reservation; Wants Indians Placed under State and County Rule," *Tama News-Herald*, October 30, 1947.

36. Daubenmier, *Meskwaki and Anthropologists*, 54-55.

37. Bertha Waseskuk, quoted in Daubenmier, *Meskwaki and Anthropologists*, 56.

38. Thomas W. Cowger, *The National Congress of American Indians, the Founding Years* (Lincoln: University of Nebraska Press, 199), 103. See also Daubenmier, *Meskwaki and Anthropologists*, 54.

39. Daubenmier, *Meskwaki and Anthropologists*, 55; "Confer Jurisdiction on the Courts of Iowa over Offences Committed by Indians, June 4, 1948," folder "Report to Accompany S. 1820, Mr. Butler, from the Committee on Interior and Insular Affairs, Calendar No. 1541, Report No. 1490, 1948," box "US Treaties and Cong. Acts," BA.

40. Daubenmier, *Meskwaki and Anthropologists*, 56–57; "Report of a Survey of Possibilities of Withdrawal," 37; "Comparative Review of Situation Data," June 22, 1955, 11, 5993-1952, box 5, MAO, RG 75, NARA-DC. See for example "Billy Waseskuk Charged with O.M.V.I, 2nd Offense," *Tama News-Herald*, January 10, 1952; "To File Charge of Drunken Driving on Arthur Blackcloud," *Tama News-Herald*, August 30, 1951.

41. *The Whole Town's Talking: Tama 1952*, directed by Charles Guggenheim (Ames, IA: WOI-TV, 1952), DVD; Charlotte M. Wright, "Wanatee, Jean Adeline Morgan," in *Biographical Dictionary of Iowa* (University of Iowa Press Digital Editions, 2009), accessed December 25, 2015, http://uipress.lib.uiowa.edu/bdi/DetailsPage.aspx?id=393.

42. Adeline Wanatee, "Education, the Family, and the Schools," in *The Worlds between Two Rivers: Perspectives on American Indians in Iowa*, ed. Gretchen M. Bataille, David M. Gradwohl, and Charles L. P. Silet (Ames: Iowa State University Press, 1978), 101. See also "Jean Adeline Morgan Wanatee, 1993 Iowa Women's Hall of Fame Honoree (1910–1996)," Iowa Department of Human Rights, accessed July 28, 2023, https://humanrights.iowa.gov/icsw/jean-adeline-morgan-wanatee.

43. John M. Byrd, "Educational Policies of the Federal Government toward the Sac and Fox Indians of Iowa, 1928–1937, with Resulting Changes in Indian Educational Attitude: A Study in the Process of Assimilation" (MS thesis, State University of Iowa, 1938), 23; "Tama Indian School is Different," *Cedar Rapids Gazette*, November 27, 1938. See also Daubenmier, *Meskwaki and Anthropologists*, 35–36.

44. Daubenmier, *Meskwaki and Anthropologists*, 160–64.

45. "Monthly Progress Report for the Month of August 1953," memorandum, folder "4091-1952," box 3, "Central Classified Files, 1940–1957," MAO, RG 75, NARA-DC; Daubenmier, *Meskwaki and Anthropologists*, 172.

46. Dillon S. Myer to Foster, August 7, 1952, folder 5993-1952, box 5, MAO, RG 75, NARA-DC.

47. "Will Send Indian 8th Graders to Tama Public School," *Tama News-Herald*, August 27, 1953.

48. "42 Indians Enrolled in Tama Public Schools," *Tama News-Herald*, September 17, 1953; "Monthly Progress Report, August 1953"; Daubenmier, *Meskwaki and Anthropologists*, 172.

49. "The Minneapolis Area Office," report dated 1961, hereafter "MAO, 1961," folder "15673-57," box 6, "Central Classified Files, 1940–1957," MAO RG 75, NARA-DC. See also Wanatee, "Education, the Family, and the Schools," 100–103; "Monthly Narrative Report, February 1958," memorandum, folder "00-1955," box 3, "Central Classified Files, 1940–1957," MAO RG 75, NARA-DC.

50. "Sac and Fox Tribal Resolution No. 1, 1966," folder "1156-1966, Sac & Fox A.F.O. 054 (3 of 3)," box 1, "Central Classified Files, 1958–1975," SFAFO, RG 75, NARA-DC, emphasis original.

51. "Report of a Survey of Possibilities of Withdrawal," 23; "Monthly Narrative Report for February 1959," memorandum, folder "00-1955," box 3, "Central Classified Files, 1940–1957," MAO, RG 75, NARA-DC.

52. "Report of a Survey of Possibilities of Withdrawal," 25.

53. "Report of a Survey of Possibilities of Withdrawal," 23–25; Daubenmier, *Meskwaki and Anthropologists*, 128.

54. "Report of a Survey of Possibilities of Withdrawal," 23–24.

55. Daubenmier, *Meskwaki and Anthropologists*, 173–75; "House Subcommittee on Indian Affairs Hearing on House Concurrent Resolution 108, July 10, 1953," meeting transcript, folder "H. Con. Res. 108, July 10, 1953," box "US Treaties and Cong. Acts," BA.

56. In a popular textbook for Native American history courses, Colin G. Calloway helpfully refers to enrolled members of Native Nations as "triple citizens." See Colin G. Calloway, *First Peoples: A Documentary Survey of American Indian History*, 6th ed. (New York: Bedford/St. Martin's, 2019), 585. See also Harvard Project on American Indian Economic Development, *The State of the Native Nations: Conditions under US Policies of Self-Determination* (New York: Oxford University Press, 2007), 188–92.

57. Leo A. Hoegh, transcript of speech, January 1957, folder "Speeches—Iowa and Midwestern Politics, Oct. 1955 to Jan. 1957," box 6, LAH Paper, UISC. See also Lizabeth Cohen, *A Consumer's Republic: The Politics of Mass Consumption in Postwar America* (New York: Vintage, 2003), 112–64; Charles Wilkinson, *Blood Struggle: The Rise of Modern Indian Nations* (New York: W. W. Norton, 2005), 271.

58. United States Department of Labor, Bureau of Labor Statistics, accessed August 18, 2015, http://data.bls.gov/pdq/SurveyOutputServlet. On the GI Bill, see Edward Humes, *Over Here: How the G.I. Bill Transformed the American Dream* (New York: Diversion, 2006). "Report of a Survey of Possibilities of Withdrawal," 27.

59. See Elizabeth Hoyt, "Tama: An American Conflict," ch. 2, p. 7, folder "Final Manuscript—Tama: An American Conflict, 1970," box 18a, EH Papers, ISUSC. This is a manuscript for Hoyt's book, *Tama: An American Conflict* (Ames: Iowa State University, 1964), which had a limited print run. ch. 1, p. 1; "Report of a Survey of Possibilities of Withdrawal," 12–13.

60. Hoyt, "Tama: An American Conflict," ch. 1, 6, 18.

61. Hoyt, "Tama: An American Conflict," ch. 1, 10.

62. Hoyt, "Tama: An American Conflict," ch. 6, 18.

63. "Monthly Narrative Report for December 1959," memorandum, folder "00-1955," box 3, "Central Classified Files, 1940–1957," MAO RG 75, NARA-DC.

64. Bonnie Buffalo to the Tama County Board of Supervisors, December 3, 1958, folder "14-1956, 720, (1 of 2)," hereafter "14-1956," box 16, "Central Classified Files, 1940–1957," MAO RG 75, NARA-DC

65. Emmons to H. R. Gross, January 9, 1959, 14-1956.

66. "State of Iowa Plan of Operation for Foster Care Contract # 14-20-0650-967," folder "4364-1958," box 18, "Central Classified Files, 1958–1975," MAO, RG 75, NARA-DC.

67. "Tribal Operations Officer's Report," memorandum dated July 19, 1967, folder "2493-1966 (2 of 2)," box 3, "Central Classified Files, 1958–1975," MAO, RG 75, NARA-DC.

68. "Monthly Narrative Report for April 1959," memorandum, folder "00-1955," box 3, "Central Classified Files, 1940–1957," MAO RG 75, NARA-DC; "MAO, 1961," 14.

69. Daubenmier, *Meskwaki and Anthropologists*, 234. See folder "Fox Cooperative Tractor Co., 1944–45," box 1, "Records of the Fox Cooperative Tractor Company, 1937–1947," SFA, RG 75, NARA-CH; "Interview with Kenneth Youngbear," 570, Reel 2, STP.

70. Daubenmier, *Meskwaki and Anthropologists*, 235–36.

71. Daubenmier, *Meskwaki and Anthropologists*, 251–52; Douglas E. Foley, "The Fox Project: A Reappraisal," *Current Anthropology* 40, no. 2 (April 1999): 176–80.

72. Gertrude Morris to Consuello Gosnell, July 24, 1962, folder "2033-1961 (Part 1, 2 of 3)," box 16, "Central Classified Files, 1958–1975," MAO, RG 75, NARA-DC; James E. Hawkins to Nash, July 10, 1962, folder "4364-1958 (Part 1, 1 of 3)," box 17, "Central Classified Files, 1958–1975," MAO, RG 75, NARA-DC.

73. "Resume of Superintendents Meeting Held of the Minneapolis Area Office, February 19 and 20, 1963," 12, folder "00-1960," box 6, "Central Classified Files, 1958–1975," MAO, RG 75, NARA-DC.

74. See Daubenmier, *Meskwaki and Anthropologists*, 54–55. See also "Civil Jurisdiction over Sac & Fox Reservation, Iowa," memorandum dated November 14, 1966, folder "7133-1964," box 6, "Central Classified Files, 1958-1975," MAO, RG 75, NARA-DC. On Public Law 280, see Duane Champagne and Carole E. Goldberg, *Captured Justice: Native Nations and Public Law 280* (Durham, NC: Carolina Academic Press, 2012).

75. "Tribal Operations Officer's Report," July 19, 1967.

76. "Civil Jurisdiction over Sac & Fox Reservation, Iowa," November 14, 1966.

77. "House Votes Indian Bill," *Des Moines Register*, March 1, 1967.

78. "Sac and Fox Tribal Council Minutes," memorandum dated December 30, 1969, in folder "1156-1966 (1 of 3)," hereafter "1156-1966 #1," box 1, "Central Classified Files, 1958–1975," Sac & Fox A.F.O.," RG 75, NARA-DC.

79. Castile, *To Show Heart*, xiv and 3–21. On the New Frontier more generally, see Irving Bernstein, *Promises Kept: John F. Kennedy's New Frontier* (New York: Oxford University Press, 1991).

80. Cobb, *Native Activism in Cold War America*, 3, 30–57; Daniel M. Cobb, "The War on Poverty in Mississippi and Oklahoma: Beyond Black and White," in *The War on Poverty: A New Grassroots History, 1964–1980*, ed. Annelise Orleck and Lisa Gayle Hazirjian (Athens: University of Georgia Press, 2011), 387–88. See also Wilkinson, *Blood Struggle*, 191–94; M. Milkis and Jerome M. Mileur, eds., *The Great Society and the High Tide of Liberalism* (Amherst: University of Massachusetts Press, 2005).

81. Nixon, Richard M, "Special Message to the Congress on Indian Affairs" (full text), July 8, 1970, The American Presidency Project, Gehard Peters and John T. Wooley, eds. (University of California–Santa Barbara), https://www.presidency.ucsb.edu/documents/special-message-the-congress-indian-affairs.

82. Wilkinson, *Blood Struggle*, 191–95; Daniel M. Cobb and Loretta Fowler, "Introduction," in *Beyond Red Power: American Indian Politics and Activism since 1900*, eds. Daniel M. Cobb and Loretta Fowler (Santa Fe: School for Advanced Research Press, 2007), xvi.

83. Castile, *To Show Heart*, 147. See also Gyorgy Ferenc Toth, *From Wounded Knee to Checkpoint Charlie: The Alliance for Sovereignty between American Indians and Central Europeans in the Late Cold War* (Albany: State University of New York, 2016).

84. Cobb and Fowler, "Introduction." On American Indian self-determination, see Wilkinson, *Blood Struggle*, 177–241; Kenneth R. Philp, *Termination Revisited: American Indians on the Trail to Self-Determination, 1933–1953* (Lincoln: University of Nebraska Press, 1999).

85. "The Minneapolis Area Office," 9, report dated 1961, folder "15673-57," box 6, "Central Classified Files, 1940–1957," Minneapolis Area, RG 75, NARA-DC.

86. Cobb, "War on Poverty in Mississippi and Oklahoma," 388.

87. Ira Katznelson, "Was the Great Society a Lost Opportunity?" in *The Rise and Fall of the New Deal Order, 1930–1980*, ed. Steve Fraser and Gary Gerstle (Princeton, NJ: Princeton University Press, 1989), 202; Wilkinson, *Blood Struggle*, 128.

88. Castile, *To Show Heart*, 25.

89. Paul L. Winser to Philleo Nash, March 31, 1964, folder "7464-1963," box 9, "Central Classified Files, 1958–1975," MAO, RG 75, NARA-DC.

90. "Area Staff Officer's Report," report dated September 20, 1966, folder "7133-1964," box 6, "Central Classified Files, 1958–1975," MAO, RG 75, NARA-DC; Hoyt, "Tama: An American Conflict," ch. 4, pg. 8.

91. Newman L. Groves to Owen D. Morken, May 13, 1969, 1156-1966 #1.

92. "Sac and Fox Tribal Council Meeting," memorandum dated October 6, 1969, 1156-1966 #1.

93. "Sac and Fox Tribal Council Minutes," memorandum dated December 30, 1969; "Sac and Fox Tribe of the Mississippi in Iowa Council Meeting," minutes of meeting held on November 4, 1969, both 1156-1966 #1.

94. "Minneapolis Area Office Annual Report, 1970," 1, hereafter "MAO, 1970."

NOTES TO CHAPTER 8

95. MAO, 1970, 2.

96. "Indian Industrial Development Program," December 31, 1963, in folder "1601-1963, MAO, 032, Part 1 of 2," box 2, "Central Classified Files 1958–1975," MAO, RG 75, NARA-DC.

97. Hoyt, "Tama: An American Conflict," ch. 5, pg. 1.

98. "MAO, 1970," 4; Hoyt, "Tama: An American Conflict," ch. 4, pg. 8.

99. Georgia Pushetonequa to Mrs. Goldsworthy, March 14, 1968, folder "MS 456," box 1, RHMP Papers, ISUSC.

100. Hoyt, "Tama: An American Conflict," ch. 2, p. 4; ch. 1, pg. 8; US Department of Labor, Bureau of Labor Statistics, "Databases, Tables, and Calculators by Subject," accessed August 20, 2015, http://data.bls.gov/pdq/SurveyOutputServlet.

101. Hoyt, "Tama: An American Conflict," ch. 4, pg. 9.

102. Hoyt, "Tama: An American Conflict," ch. 4, pg. 8.

103. "Sac and Fox Tribal Council Minutes," memorandum dated January 21, 1970, 1156-1966 #1.

104. "Sac and Fox Tribe of the Mississippi in Iowa Council Meeting," minutes of meeting held on December 5, 1969, 1156-1966 # 1.

105. "Sac and Fox Tribe of the Mississippi in Iowa Council Meeting," minutes of meeting held on May 26, 1969; "Sac and Fox Resolution No. 5-69," both 1156-1966 #1.

106. Halla M. Rhode to Harlan, January 20, 1932, folder 49s, ERH Papers, SHSI-DM; Helen Hornbeck Tanner, "In the Arena: An Expert Witness View of the Indian Claims Commission," in Cobb and Fowler, *Beyond Red Power*, 180–81. See also Harvey D. Rosenthal, "Their Day in Court: A History of the Indian Claims Commission" (PhD diss., Kent State University, 1976).

107. See also David Agee Horr, ed., *Sac, Fox, and Iowa Indians III: Commission Findings on the Sac, Fox, and Iowa Indians, United States Indian Claims Commission* (New York: Garland, 1974).

108. "Indians Confident Will Get Something from Claims Suit," n. p., n. d., news clipping; Columbus Keahna, "Notice of Special Meeting of the Sac and Fox Tribe in Iowa," both in folder "Special Claims Meeting, March 13, 1950," box "Indian Claims Commission," BA.

109. "Sac and Fox Tribal Resolution No. 4, 1970," folder "1156-1966 Part 2," hereafter "1156-1966 #2," box 1, "Central Classified Files, 1958–1975," SFAFO, RG 75, NARA-DC.

110. "Sac and Fox Tribal Resolution No. 5-1970," 1156-1966 #2; "Sac and Fox Tribal Council Resolution No. 9-69," resolution dated April 14, 1969; "Sac and Fox Tribe of the Mississippi in Iowa Council Meeting," minutes for meeting held on May 16, 1969, both in 1156-1966 #1. See also Hoyt, "Tama: An American Conflict," ch. 2, p. 4. The three tribes did not share dockets after 1967 and legal battles carried on for several years.

111. "Tama Indian Wins Squirrel Hunting Case," *Cedar Rapids Gazette*, n.d. 1968, news clipping in folder "Hunting Rights Suit—Squirrel Case, 1968," box "Natural Resources," BA.

112. "Treaty with the Sauk and Foxes, 1804," Northern Illinois Digital Library, accessed January 12, 2023, https://digital.lib.niu.edu/islandora/object/niu-lincoln%3A34785.

113. "Sac and Fox Treaty, 1842," State Historical Society of Iowa, accessed January 12, 2023, https://iowaculture.gov/history/education/educator-resources/primary-source-sets/right-to-vote-suffrage-women-african/treaty-sac-and-fox-tribe-1842. The specific parcel of land on which Lasley had been hunting had been added to the Settlement in 1909.

114. "Tama Indian Wins Squirrel Hunting Case," *Cedar Rapids Gazette*, n.d. 1968, news clipping in folder "Hunting Rights Suit—Squirrel Case, 1968," box "Natural Resources," BA.

115. "Indians-State Enter Battle to Settle Hunting Rights," *Waterloo Courier*, October 3, 1968.

116. "Case of Tama Indians Hunting on Land Out of Season Is Set for Nov. 26," *Traer Star-Clipper*, October 25, 1968; Otto Knauth, "Indian Wins Hunting Case, But Doesn't Get Squirrel," *Des Moines Register*, November 28, 1968.

117. See Sherry L. Smith, *Hippies, Indians, and the Fight for Red Power* (New York: Oxford University Press, 2012), 21–24; Larry Nesper, *The Walleye War: the Struggle for Ojibwe Spearfishing and Treaty Rights* (Lincoln: University of Nebraska Press, 2002); Joane Nagel, *American Indian Ethnic Renewal: Red Power and the Resurgence of Identity and Culture* (New York: Oxford University Press, 1996), 161–69; Nick Estes, Melanie K. Yazzie, Jennifer Nez Denetdale, and David Correia, *Red Nation Rising: From Bordertown Violence to Native Liberation* (Binghamton, NY: PM Press, 2021).

118. Foley, *Heartland Chronicles*, 23, 26, 30–36; "Tribal Operations Officer's Report," memorandum dated July 19, 1967, folder "2493–1966 (2 of 2)," box 3, "Central Classified Files, 1958–1975," Minneapolis Area Office, RG 75, NARA-DC.

119. See Foley, *Heartland Chronicles*, 23, 26.

120. Foley, *Heartland Chronicles*, 46.

121. On the 1968 school dispute, see Foley, *Heartland Chronicles*, 46–48.

122. Story quoted in Foley, *Heartland Chronicles*, 47; Donald Wanatee in discussion with the author, June 27, 2014.

123. Foley, *Heartland Chronicles*, 40–47.

124. "US Sues Iowa over Indian Fishing, Hunting," *Cedar Rapids Gazette*, August 18, 1975.

125. "Rules against Indians in Fishing Rights Case," n. p., July 20, 1977, news clipping in folder "Hunting Suit, 1977," box "Natural Resources," BA. See also Sac & Fox Tribe of the Mississippi in Iowa v. Licklider 576 F.2d 145 (8th Cir., 1978).

EPILOGUE

1. Johnathan L. Buffalo, in discussion with the author, July 16, 2014.
2. Buffalo, in discussion with the author, July 16, 2014.

3. Buffalo, in discussion with the author, July 16, 2014; Joshua Sales, "Meskwaki Topography," map by Meskwaki Nation GIS, copy in the author's possession.

4. Sac and Fox of the Mississippi in Iowa, "An Overall Economic Development Plan Prepared by the Sac and Fox of the Mississippi in Iowa for the Economic Development Administration," 2, 17, folder "An Overall Economic Development Plan of the Sac and Fox of the Mississippi in Iowa, 1978," box 108, MHPO.

5. Jefferson Cowie, *Stayin' Alive: The 1970s and the Last Days of the Working Class* (New York: New Press, 2010), xxv; Dorothy Schwieder, *Iowa: The Middle Land* (Iowa City: University of Iowa Press, 1996), 316.

6. "Overall Economic Development Plan, 1978," 18.

7. "Overall Economic Development Plan, 1978," 18.

8. "Overall Economic Development Plan, 1978," 24.

9. "Overall Economic Development Plan, 1978," 19–25.

10. "Overall Economic Development Plan, 1978," 18, 24.

11. "Overall Economic Development Plan, 1978," 15, 17.

12. Matthew Wilde, "Meskwaki School Bell Finally Rings," *Waterloo-Cedar Falls Courier*, October 13, 1998.

13. Douglas Foley, "*The Heartland Chronicles* Revisited: The Casino's Impact on Settlement Life," *Qualitative Inquiry* 11, no. 2 (2005): 297.

14. Donald L. Fixico, *Indian Resilience and Rebuilding: Indigenous Nations in the Modern American West* (Tucson: University of Arizona Press, 2013), 178–85. See also Jessica R. Cattelino, *High Stakes: Florida Seminole Gaming and Sovereignty* (Durham, NC: Duke University Press, 2008); Steven Andrew Light and Kathryn R. L. Rand, *Indian Gaming and Tribal Sovereignty: The Casino Compromise* (Lawrence: University Press of Kansas, 2005); Kenneth N. Hansen and Tracy A. Skopek, eds., *The New Politics of Indian Gaming: The Rise of Reservation Interest Groups* (Reno: University of Nevada Press, 2011).

15. Fixico, *Indian Resilience and Rebuilding*, 178–85. For the quote, see 182. See also Jeff Corntassel and Richard C. Witmer II, *Forced Federalism: Contemporary Challenges to Indigenous Nationhood* (Norman: University of Oklahoma Press, 2008), 107–33.

16. See "State of Iowa, Meskwaki Tribe Settle Compact," *Waterloo-Cedar Falls Courier*, September 19, 2004; "Compact between the Sovereign Indian Nation of the Sac and Fox Tribe of the Mississippi in Iowa and the Sovereign State of Iowa," October 21, 2004, http://www.meskwakigc.com/doc/compact_10_21_04.pdf. While states cannot tax tribal gaming revenues, some have been able to secure large "donations" from tribes in exchange for approval of a tribal-state gaming compact. See Brian Klopotek, *Recognition Odysseys: Indigeneity, Race, and Federal Tribal Recognition Policy in Three Louisiana Indian Communities* (Durham, NC: Duke University Press, 2011), 98–99.

17. Cattelino, *High Stakes*, 128.

18. See Cattelino, *High Stakes*, 104. On Meskwaki per caps and employment, see Foley, "*Heartland Chronicles* Revisited," 299–300.

19. Judith Daubenmier, *The Meskwaki and Anthropologists: Action Anthropology Reconsidered* (Lincoln: University of Nebraska Press, 2008), 275.

20. Meskwaki, Inc, accessed October 29, 2010, http://www.meskwakiinc.com; "You're Invited," *Meskwaki Nation Times*, July 12, 2009; Ken Black, "Local Bank Sold to a Meskwaki Corporation," *Marshalltown Times-Republican*, February 10, 2009; Ray Young Bear, "Letter to the Editor," *Tama News-Herald*, March 12, 2009.

21. Foley, "*Heartland Chronicles* Revisited," 296.

22. Foley, "*Heartland Chronicles* Revisited," 301–303, 306–310; Daubenmier, *The Meskwaki and Anthropologists*, 282. See also Cattelino, *High Stakes*, 90–94; J. Kēhaulani Kauanui, *Hawaiian Blood: Colonialism and the Politics of Sovereignty and Indigeneity* (Durham, NC: Duke University Press, 2008), 165–75; Klopotek, *Recognition Odysseys*, 97–109; Kim Tallbear, *Native American DNA: Tribal Belonging and the False Promise of Genetic Science* (Minneapolis: University of Minnesota Press, 2013).

23. See Margaret Cowell, *Dealing with Deindustrialization: Adaptive Resilience in American Midwestern Regions* (New York: Routledge, 2015); Michael Steward Foley, "'Everyone Was Pounding on Us': Front Porch Politics and the American Farm Crisis of the 1970s and 1980s," *Journal of Historical Sociology* 28, no. 1 (March 2015): 104–24; Jenny Barker Devine and David D. Vail, "Sustaining the Conversation: The Farm Crisis and the Midwest," *Middle West Review* 2, no. 1 (Fall 2015): 1–9; Denise O'Brien, "Memories of the Crisis," *Middle West Review* 2, no. 1 (Fall 2015): 51–68.

24. Daubenmier, *Meskwaki and Anthropologists*, 280.

25. Foley, *Heartland Chronicles*, vii.

26. Foley, "*Heartland Chronicles* Revisited," 301–303.

27. For other discussions of "special rights" language, see Jeffrey R. Dudas, *The Cultivation of Resentment: Treaty Rights and the New Right* (Redwood City, CA: Stanford University Press, 2008), esp. 17–38, 95–136; Cattelino, *High Stakes*, 199–202; Douglas Metoxen Kiel, *Unsettling Territory: Oneida Nation Resurgence and Anti-Sovereignty Backlash*, forthcoming from Yale University Press, 2024, manuscript shared with the author.

28. Foley, "*Heartland Chronicles* Revisited," 301–303.

29. See Klopotek, *Recognition Odysseys*, 98.

30. Dalyn Wabaunasee, email message to the author, November 3, 2015.

31. Foley, "*Heartland Chronicles* Revisited," 301–303.

32. The tribe continued to pay taxes on the 775-acre property near West Bend, which was not in trust, as well as more recently acquired parcels that are in the process of being placed in federal trust.

33. Diane K. Rosen to Adrian Pushetonequa, May 5, 2010, in folder "Notice of Decision on Trust Application, 2010," box "Land," BA.

34. Daubenmier, *Meskwaki and Anthropologists*, 278. Foley, "*Heartland Chronicles* Revisited," 300.

35. Buffalo, in discussion with the author, July 16, 2014. See also Meskwaki, Inc, accessed January 13, 2023, https://meskwakiinc.com/.

36. Joshua Sales, email message to the author, October 28, 2015.

NOTES TO EPILOGUE

37. Sales, email message to the author, October 28, 2015. See also "CRP Can Boost Pheasant Habitat," Farmprogress.com, August 2011, http://magissues.farmprogress.com/WAL/WF08Aug14/wal060.pdf.

38. "Iowa Couple Entrust Their Land to Indians," *Des Moines Register*, March 3, 1990; Sales, email message to the author, October 30, 2015.

39. John Speer, "High Speed Internet on Fast Track for Meskwaki Settlement," *Tama News-Herald*, May 4, 2012.

40. "Meskwaki Food Sovereignty," Meskwaki Nation, accessed November 27, 2023, http://meskwaki.org/mfsi.

41. "Today's Success and Our Future," Meskwaki Nation, accessed November 27, 2023, https://www.meskwaki.org/history/.

42. John Speer, "Plan $21 Million Expansion of Meskwaki School," *Toledo Chronicle*, June 6, 2007; "Meskwaki High School Grand Opening," *Meskwaki Nation Times*, October 1, 2009; Yolanda Pushetonequa, "Meskwaki Language Research"; and Jacob Manatowa-Bailey, "Language Revitalization and Youth," papers presented at the 2015 Meskwaki Symposium, Meskwaki Settlement, Iowa, October 13, 2015; Nancy Dostal, "STC Students Walk Out; Communication Will Be Key to Resolving Conflict," April 30, 1998; Peter Comings, "Students Walk Out at South Tama," September 22, 1999, both news clippings, n.p., folder "Indian Student Walkout 1999," box "Education, Sac and Fox Day School, Meskwaki Settlement School," BA.

43. See David Mayer Gradwohl, Joe B. Thompson, and Michael J. Perry, *Still Running: A Tribute to Maria Pearson, Yankton Sioux* (Iowa City: Iowa Archaeological Society and Office of the State Archaeologist, 2005).

44. Jerome Thompson, "Turn of the Century History and the Meskwaki Tribe/State Historical Society of Iowa," paper presented at the 2015 Meskwaki Symposium, October 2015, Meskwaki Settlement.

45. "State of Iowa and Sac & Fox Tribe of Iowa Sign Intergovernmental Agreement for the Regulation of Hunting and Fishing on the Meskwaki Indian Settlement," press release, February 27, 2002, folder "Intergovernmental Agreement Hunting and Fishing 2-2-2002," box "Natural Resources," BA. See also Daubenmier, *Meskwaki and Anthropologists*, 281.

46. "Study Reports Are Readied for Tama Settlement," *Cedar Rapids Gazette*, January 29, 1963.

47. "Sac and Fox Tribal Resolution No. 13, 1977," folder "Tribal Court System Development, 1977–1980," box "Tribal Court," BA. See also Johnathan L. Buffalo, "Meskwaki Tribal Court: A Historical Overview of Development," Meskwaki Historic Preservation Office, 2005, folder "Meskwaki Tribal Court: A Historical Overview," box "Tribal Court," BA.

48. Daubenmier, *Meskwaki and Anthropologists*, 281.

49. Buffalo, "Meskwaki Tribal Court," 47.

50. "Meskwaki Nation Police Department," Meskwaki Nation, accessed November 27, 2023, http://www.meskwaki.org/police-department.

51. Ken Black, "Judge: Meskwaki Officers Are Legal Law Enforcement in Iowa," *Marshalltown Times-Republican*, March 23, 2011.

52. "Iowa Lawmakers Back Repeal of Jurisdiction Over Meskwaki Tribe," *Z News*, June 12, 2015, http://www.indianz.com/News/2015/017838.asp.

53. Anna Spoerre, "Iowa Supreme Court Rules Crimes on Meskwaki Settlement Not Involving Tribe Members Should Be Prosecuted By State," *Des Moines Register*, September 13, 2019, https://www.desmoinesregister.com/story/news/crime-and-courts/2019/09/13/iowa-supreme-court-jurisdiction-non-tribal-crimes-settlements-goes-state/2310546001/.

54. Jennifer Hemmingsen, "Marshals Close Meskwaki Casino," *Indian Country Today Media Network*, May 30, 2003, http://indiancountrytodaymedianetwork.com/2003/05/30/marshals-close-meskwaki-casino-88833; Daubenmier, *Meskwaki and Anthropologists*, 276.

55. "Closing Shocks Meskwaki Casino Workers," *Sioux City Journal*, May 24, 2003, http://siouxcityjournal.com/news/state-and-regional/closing-shocks-meskwaki-casino-workers/article_2c86d7df-62e1-5923-baf4-3ddc519979d1.html; "NIGC Reaffirms Shutdown of Meskwaki Casino, *Z News*, September 12, 2003, http://www.indianz.com/News/archives/001420.asp; Daubenmier, *Meskwaki and Anthropologists*, 276.

56. Foley, "*Heartland Chronicles* Revisited," 312.

57. Daubenmier, *Meskwaki and Anthropologists*, 276.

58. Daubenmier, *Meskwaki and Anthropologists*, 276.

59. Foley, "*Heartland Chronicles* Revisited," 313–17.

60. Daubenmier, *Meskwaki and Anthropologists*, 277.

61. Kiel, *Unsettling Territory*.

62. Keith C. Davenport and Harvey Davenport Jr., "Meskwaki Nation's Proclamation Day," May 27, 1992, https://www.meskwaki.org/wp-content/uploads/2021/03/Meskwaki-Nations-Proclamation-Day.pdf.

Artist's Statement

The drawings that open each part of this book were done by Mary Young Bear, a Meskwaki artist, conservator at the tribal museum, and 2020 inductee to the Iowa Women's Hall of Fame.

Part I. Thunderbird, 4 in. x 6 in., ink on watercolor paper
This was a challenge for me because of the stature this being has in our culture. I also knew I had to keep in mind the image would ultimately be smaller. I tried to keep the lines simple and not too detailed so the final image would not become a blur.

Part II. Pipe Carving, 4 in. x 6 in., ink on watercolor paper
This was a challenge because of the straight lines I used in this design. I wanted to do something geometric and I started to put lines on my paper, I was reminded of not only the pipe, but the long wooden stems that were made for them.

Part III. Underwater Panther, 4 in. x 6 in., ink on watercolor paper
The Underwater Panther is also a part of our culture and is the counter of the Thunderbird. Some people equate the two beings as powerful counter forces of good versus evil, however I was taught that they have different responsibilities in our world. I found this drawing to be the most challenging, and the most fun I've had in a long time. I had to make myself stop working on it.

Part IV. Beadwork #3, 4 in. x 6 in., ink on watercolor paper
The beadwork design was created from the same template as the pipe carving, with a couple of adjustments to each one. This design could actually be used in almost any project from applique, beadwork, woodcarving and pipe stems, depending on what an artist was working on.

Mary Young Bear
Bonabiga

Index

Italicized references indicate illustrations.

action anthropology, 199–200. *See also* anthropology, as discipline
Agricultural Adjustment Act (AAA), 175
agricultural extension programs, 178. *See also* farming
Aid to Dependent Children (ADC), 204–6, 214. *See also* child welfare programs
Alaska, 4, 217
Alaska Native Claims Settlement Act (1971), 217
Alcatraz Island, 224
alcohol, 206, 208
Algonquin language family, 28, 31
alliances, 33–35
Allison, William B., 121
allotment, 112–14, 142, 144–46, 166
Amana Colonies, 86
American colonists, 37–41; conflicts with Sauk, 35–38, 48–49; land purchases and dispossession by, 49–56, 63, 73–78; reservation system of, 63, 81–84; treaty-making by, 50–57; violent conflicts with, 85
American Fur Company, 59
American Indian Movement (AIM), 224–25
Americorps, 236
animal husbandry, 178, 179, *180*
Anishinaabe (Ojibwe), 28, 59
Anishinaabewaki, 26, 28–38. *See also* Meskwaki Nation, overview; Sauk Nation, overview
annuities, 115, 150, 168, 178
annuity rolls, 107, 112–14

anthropology, as discipline, xxi, 140, 199–200
anti-slavery party, 88–89
Appanoose, 67, 73
Arapaho, 103
Arikara villages, 42
arrests of anti-assimilationists, 130–32. *See also* assimilation
Articles of Confederation, 39
Asakiwaki Nation. *See* Sauk Nation, overview
assimilation: as concept, 55, 88, 108, 113, 126; farming and, 102; forced policies of, 16, 54, 82, 106, 119–22, 166; resistance to, 31, 130–32; through religious conversion, 63; village burning and, 139; wage work and, 195. *See also* Indian removal policy

Bad Soldier-Snow, Stephanie, 4–5
Banzhof & Reimer, 127
Barona Band of Mission Indians, 11
Bde Maka Ska, as name, 6
Beach, John, 73, 81
Bear, John, Jr., *150*
Bear, Nathan, 197, 198
Bear City, 102
Bear clan, 31–32
bear claw necklace, 69, 92, 169, *238*
Bear Ears National Monument, 8
Benson, Dale, 199
Benson, Edward, 193
BIA (Bureau of Indian Affairs), 3–4, 202–4, 209–11, 214, 216, 218, 220, 240. *See also* Office of the Indian Affairs

323

Biden administration, 8
birthing practices, 173
Black Cloud, Mary, 179
Black (Sparrow) Hawk. *See* Makataimeshekiakiak
Black Hawk Purchase (1833), 63–64, 67, 77
Black Hawk War, 60–63
Black Wolf, 104–6
boarding schools, 3, 120, 125, *127*, 127–30, 153, 166. *See also* schools
Boaz, Franz, 140
Boston, Grace, 159
Breid, Jacob, 160–61, 168, 177
British colonists, 34–39, 55
broadband fiber project, 236
Brookings Institution, 165–66
Brothertown Indian Nation, 10–11
Buffalo, Bonnie, 214
Buffalo, George, *150*
Buffalo, Johnathan: on Americans and War for Independence, 37, 38; on British relationship, 34; on creation of Sac and Fox Tribe, 51; European–Meskwaki meeting, 28; on Fox Wars, 29; on Kansas, 82; on Lewis and Clark, 47; on Meskwaki leadership, 32, 155; on Settlement changes, 228–29; on Wisaka, 25, 27
Buffalo Bill's Wild West Show, 149
Burge, James, 102
burning of the Settlement Village, 137–39
business development, 233–35. *See also* economic strategies; gaming
Butler, David, 93
Butler, Isaac, 1–2, 90, 92–93
Butler, Philip, 93
Butler, Sam, 1–2, 92–93
Butler, Susan, 90
Butlerville, 90–91
buy-back program, 3–4, 9–10. *See also* economic strategies; Landback movement

California, 2, 3
casino, 229, 231–32, 239–40
census, 68, 106–9, 114, 185
Chakotakosee, 123
Chalkkalamah, 93
Chambers, John, 71, 73–75
Chequamegon Bay, 28

Cherokee Nation, 5, 11
Chicago & Northwestern Railway Company, 117, 119
child welfare programs, 204–6, 214, 215, 238–39
Chippewa Indians, 11
cholera, 82
Christianity, 63, 86
Circular 1665 (1923), 164
citizenship, 114
Civilian Conservation Corps, 174
Civilian Conservation Corps–Indian Division (CCC-ID), 189–90
Civil War, 98, 101. *See also* US Army
clan groups, 31–32
Clark, Leander, 101
Clark, William, 36, 41–42, 45–47, 56, 102
clothing, 139
Cloud, Henry Roe, 166
Cobell v. Salazar, 3
code talkers, 193
Cole, Cyrenus, 157
Collier, John, 174–75, 182, 191, 196, 202
Comanche, 103
Confederated Salish and Kootenai Tribes, 3
Confederated Tribes of the Warm Springs Reservation, 11
constitutional committee, 184–86
Coolidge, Calvin, 165
Corps of Discovery, 45–47
COVID-19 pandemic, 136–37
crafts, *181*, 215
Crawford, Hartley, 71, 73–74
creation, 23, 25
creative autonomy, 16, 161–62
Creek Nation, 6
cultural sovereignty, 128–29. *See also* sovereignty
Cummins, A. B., 138, 143, 144

Dakota Access Pipeline, 5–6
Dakota Nation, 3, 28, 36, 37, 59–60, 85
dancing, 148–49, 164
Davenport, Albert, *150*
Davenport, Charles, 167–68, 188
Davenport, Charlie, 155
Davenport, Edward, *150*, 185, 192
Davenport, George L'oste, 107
Davenport, Mary, 167–68
Dawes Act (1887), 9, 11, 112–14, 115, 140

INDEX

Depression, 169–70, 176–77, 180, 189–90
Des Moines Register (publication), 204
Dey, Peter, 114
disease, 134–39. *See also* smallpox epidemic
dispossession, 49–56, 63, 73–78, 202–4. *See also* Indian removal policy
Doctrine of Discovery, 8, 34
Drake, Francis M., 117, 118–19
Dubuque, Julien, 43
Duncan, Preston, 173

Eastman, Charles A., 128
Economic Development Administration (EDA), 230
economic strategies, 115–16, 149–50, 168–70, 178–81, 187, 218–19, 222–23, 230–36. *See also* sovereignty
eminent domain, 117–19
enrollment, tribal, 106–9
environmental governance, as term, 5
Esselen Tribe, 3

farming, 102, 112–13, 115, 120, 141, 175, 194, 200, 236–37. *See also* gardening
Farver, Peru, 196–97, 200
federal recognition, as concept, 99–101. *See also* Sac and Fox Tribe, as federal designation
fish-in protests, 224
Flathead Reservation, 3
flooding, 196–97
Foley, Douglas, 233, 234
food sovereignty, 236. *See also* sovereignty
forced assimilation. *See* assimilation
forced removal. *See* dispossession; Indian removal policy
Ford, Gerald, 218
Fort Sumter, 98
Fox clan, 32
Fox Project, 215
Fox Wars, 19, 29, 33, 141
The Fox Wars: The Mesquakie Challenge to New France (Edmunds and Peyser), 12
French colonists, 34, 35, 45
French trade, 29–30, 35, 42
fur trade, 42, 58–59, 66–67. *See also* trade economy

galena, 42
gaming, 229, 231–39. *See also* casino

gardening, 33, 71, 83, 91, 94–96, 141, 142, 147, 153–54, 177–78, 190, 197–98, 236. *See also* farming
gender roles and work, 95–96
German immigrants, 86
Gisha Manitou, 25
Grand Staircase-Escalante National Monument, 8
Grand Traverse Band of Ottawa and Chippewa Indians, 11
Grand Village of the Meskwaki, 28
Great Depression, 169–70, 176–77, 189–90
Great Sioux Nation, 3
Great Society programs, 217, 218–19
Green, Orville J., 145, 151
Grimes, James, 71, 73, 86–87, 88, 89, 92
Grinnell, George Bird, 112
Grinnell, Josiah, 89

Half-Breed Tract, 263n112, 267n31
Hapayasha, 92
Harlan, Aaron W., 158
Harlan, Edgar, 158–61, 167, 169, 177, 182–83, 295n60
Harrison, William Henry, 49–50
Haudenosaunee (Iroquois), 28
hemp farming, 237. *See also* farming
Hitchcock, Ethan A., 136
Ho-Chunk (tribal group), 28, 42, 58, 59, 96, 126
Hoegh, Leo A., 213
Homestead Act (1862), 2, 11, 95
Hoover, Herbert, 174
House Concurrent Resolution (HCR-108), 211–12
hunting, 65, 95, 96, 148, 177, 178, 197–98, 223–24

Ickes, Harold, 183
Illini Nations, 28
Indian, as term, xxiii
Indian Citizenship Act (1924), 165
Indian Claims Commission (ICC), 127, 221–22
Indian Gaming Regulatory Act (IGRA), 232
Indian Industrial School, *127*
Indian Land Tenure Foundation, 9
Indian New Deal, 174–76, 181–82, 217, 222
Indian Relief and Rehabilitation Act, 175
Indian Relief program, Iowa, 214

Indian Removal Act (1830), 63, 112
Indian removal policy, 62–63, 75–78, 83, 98, 106–9. *See also* assimilation; Dawes Act (1887); land purchases and dispossession
Indian Reorganization Act (1934), 11, 181–84
Indian Rights Association, 120–22, 127, 133
Indian Self Determination and Education Assistance Act (1975), 218
Indian Territory, 11, 81, 94
Indiantown, 91
Indigenous boarding schools, 3, *127*, 127–30
Indigenous power, 19, 20, 38–41, 69–70
industrial education, 128. *See also* boarding schools
influenza pandemic, 136
infrastructure improvements, 117–19, 149–51, 189–90, 213, 235. *See also* road infrastructure
Institute for Government Research, 165–66
intermarriage, 31, 43, 129, 162–63, 185, 204, 302n72
Intertribal Sinkyone Wilderness Council, 2
Iowa. *See* State of Iowa
Iowa Committee on Indian Affairs, 214
Iowa Department of Social Welfare, 215
Iowa River, 1–2, 65, 75, 83, 90–91, 104, 134, 178, 191, 228
Ioway Nation, 36, 56
IRA. *See* Indian Reorganization Act (1934)
Iroquois, 27–28
#IslandBack, 2–3

Jackson, Frank D., 116
Jamestown S'Klallam Tribe, 11
Jay's Treaty (1795), 45
Jefferson, Marie, 194, *195*
Jefferson, Thomas, 45–47
Jiwere (Otoe) people, 36, 37
Johnson, Lyndon B., 217, 218
Johnson v. McIntosh, 9
Jones, John, *150*
Jones, William, 79, 140, 141

Kansas, reservation in, 19, 81–84
Kapayou, Kenneth, *150*
Katwaya, 161
Kawkawke, 74
Keliiaa, John B., 211
Kennedy, John F., 217
Keokuk, 61, 67, 73, 74

Keokuk's Reserve, 64
Kickapoo, 28
Kiowa, 103
Kiowa-Apache, 103
Kishkekosh, 72
Kraschel, Nelson G., 186, 188
Kuwesuwi Monihq (Pine Island), 2–3, 5

Lake Calhoun, as name, 6
Lakota, 3
land acknowledgments, 6–7
land allotment, 112–14, 142, 144–46, 166
#Landback, 2
Landback movement, 2–7, 9–10, 16.
"Land Buy-Back Program for Tribal Nations" program (BIA), 3–4, 9
land preemption, 8, 44–45, 114
land purchases and dispossession, 49–56, 63, 73–78, 87–89. *See also* Indian removal policy
land tenure model, 142–44, 212
Lasley, Orrie, 223, 224
law enforcement and lawlessness, 206–9, 239
lead mining and exchange, 42–44, 58
lead sulfide, 42
leases of tribal land, 115–16, 150
Lesser, Wallace R., 115–16
Lewis, Meriwether, 45–47, 76
Licklider, Les, 226
Linn, A. M., 135, 138
Lone Wolf v. Hitchcock, 127
Louisiana Purchase (1803), 40
Louisiana Territory, 45, 47

MacMartin, W. G., 207
Major Crimes Act (1885), 105, 131–32, 206
Makaka, 95
Makataimeshekiakiak, 52, 60–62, 158
Makatawahquahtwa, 130
Malin, William, 131, 132–33, 135, 136, 138, 140, 145
Mamiwanige, 92, 95, 100, 102, 110, 111, 161
maple syrup, 179
marriage, 31, 43, 129, 162–63, 185, 204, 302n72
Marshalltown Canning Factory, 177
Mascouten Nation, 28
Mashpee Wampanoag, 8
Mason-Dixon Line, 58

INDEX

Masqasee, 125, 131–32, 251n5, 283n1
Massachusetts Bay Colony, 28
Matauaquah, 93, 118, 274n61
Mathanuh, 93
Mauskemo, Clement, 193
McGirt v. Oklahoma, 6
McNickle, D'Arcy, 154–55
medicine, 130–31, 135. *See also* plants
Menominee (tribal group), 59, 96, 217
Menominee Restoration Act (1971), 217
Meriam Report (1928), 165–67, 175
Merritt, E. B., 156
Meskwaki Bingo Casino Hotel (MBCH), 229, 231–40
Meskwaki Booster (publication), 148
Meskwaki Children's Poultry Club, *180*
Meskwaki code talkers, 193
Meskwaki Constitution, 184–88
Meskwaki Food Sovereignty Initiative (MFSI), 236
Meskwaki Historic Preservation Office, 164, 229
Meskwaki Inc., 233
Meskwaki Indian Powwow Association. *See* Powwow Association
Meskwaki Nation, overview, xxiii, 1–2, 12–21. *See also* Sac and Fox Tribe, as federal designation
Meskwaki Nation Day, 241
Meskwaki Police Department, 239
Meskwaki Settlement, *15*, 19; burning of, 137–39; CCC-ID of, 189–90; death and disease on, 134–37, 139; economic strategies of, 115–16, 149–50, 168–70, 178–81; expansion of, 101–3; federal status of, 10, 120–22, 127, 212–13; Great Depression on, 169–70, 176–77; Harlan as ally to, 158–61; land allotment on, 142, 144–46; land and resource use on, 95–96, 147–51; land leases of, 115–16; land rights and politics on, 119–22; land tenure model on, 142–44; law enforcement and lawlessness on, 206–9; leadership of, 110–12; location of, 83–84; population statistics of, 95; as proposed state park, 157; purchase of, 2, 11, 13, 87–89, 114; railroad fire on, 117, 119; as reclamation, 97–98; recognition and coercion and, 99–101; road construction and eminent domain on, 117–19; State of Iowa and, 98–99, 120; Tama Agency, as name for, 101; as trade center, 104; tribal enrollment policy on, 106–10; village reconstruction of, 139–42. *See also* sovereignty
Meskwapuswa, 118
migrations, *26*; of American settlers, 57–60; of Meskwaki people, 19, 25–28, 89–90
military service, 20
Millard, Isaac C., 149
mining, 42–44, 58
missionaries, 128
Mission Indians, 232
Missouria, 36
Missouri Nation, 37
Mitchell, George, *150*
Mixed-Race Reserve, 59–60
money chiefs, 67
Moquibushito, 110, 119
Morgan, Amos and Cora, 179
Morgan, Peter, 192
Morgan, Robert, 193
Mount McKinley, as name, 6
Mucqua clan, 31–32
murder, 104–5
Myaamiaki (Miami), 28

National Bison Range, 3
National Congress of American Indians, 209
Native American Graves Protection and Repatriation Act of 1990 (NAGPRA), 237
Native American Rights Fund (NARF), 226
NDN Collective, 2, 4
necklace, 69, 92, 169, *238*
Nellis, George, 129–30
Nelson, Ira D., 177, 183–84
Neneemekee clan, 32
Ne-No-Tal Indian Girls 4-H Club, 179
Netwatwytuk, 118
Neutral Ground, 60, 65, 75
New Deal programs, 20, 174–76, 181–82, 217, 222
New France, 26–27
Niutachi (Missouria) people, 36
Nixon, Richard, 217–18, 220
"No Dancing Letter" (US Department of Interior), *xvi*, 164
#NODAPL movement, 5–6
Northwest Indian War (1786–1795), 39
Northwest Ordinance (1787), 39–40
Northwest Territory, 27, 39, 40

Obama administration, 6, 8
Oceti Sakowin, 3, 103
Office of Economic Opportunity (OEO), 218–19, 220
Office of the Indian Affairs: fire cleanup by, 137–39; Meriam Report on, 166; Meswaki land transfer by, 122, 127; "No Dancing Letter" by, *xvi*, 164; termination policy of, 202; on tribal land leases, 116. *See also* BIA (Bureau of Indian Affairs); US Department of Interior
off-Settlement life, 194–99. *See also* wage work (off-Settlement)
Ojibwe. *See* Anishinaabe (Ojibwe)
Oklahoma v. Castro-Huerta, 6
Old Age Assistance program, 175
Old Bear, Ada, 194, *195*
Old Bear, Jack, 161–62, 166, 281n32
Old Northwest, 27, 31, 35, 56, 59, 61
Oneida Tribe of Wisconsin, 6
Osage Nation, 11, 36, 37, 48, 56, 81
Osage River reservation, 81–83
Ottawa Tribe in Michigan, 11
Ottawa Tribe in Oklahoma, 11
overhunting, 36
Owen, Mary Alecia, 69–70

Painted Rocks, 75
Paquesheka, 95
Passamaquoddy Tribe, 2–3, 5, 219
Patagoto, 92, 93
pays d'en haut, 26–27
peace chiefs, 31–32
Pearson, Maria, 237
Pemoussa, 33
People of the Red Earth, as term, 5. *See also* Meskwaki Nation, overview
Peoria (tribal group), 30
Pe' Sla, 3
Peters, Jim, 125, 131–32, 139, 289n73
Peters v. Malin, 132–33, 143, 145, 155, 157, 168, 206
peyote, 206
pheasant sanctuary, 236
Pierce, Franklin, 86
Pike, Zebulon, 66, 68
Plains Apache, 103
plants, 95–96, 104. *See also* traditional medicine
plenary power, 126–27

Pontiac, 35
Pontiacs' War, 35
population statistics, *14*, 27, 33, 57, 68, 95, 125–26, 173–74, 269n64, 307n130
Potawatomi, 28, 61, 102
poultry club, 179, *180*
Poweshiek, 72–75, 83
Poweshiek, Horace, 152–53, 185
Poweshiek, Ida Snowball, 67, *154*
Poweshiek, James "Old Jim," 83, 110, 151–52
Poweshiek, Jonas, 152, *153*, 159, 193
Poweshiek, Mary, 151
Poweshiek, Ruth, 152, *153*
Poweshiek, William, 152–53, 167
powwow, 149, *150*, 163–65
Powwow Association, *150*, 163–65
Prairie du Chien, Wisconsin, 28–29, 59
preemption, 8, 44–45, 114. *See also* land purchases and dispossession
Presbyterian mission, 128
Price, Hiram, 109, 114
Proclamation Day, 241
property taxes, 115, 121, 235, 236, 318n32
Public Law 280 (PL-280), 216
Pueblos, 10
Pushetonequa, 110, *111*, 112, 115, 116, 118–19, 129–30, 154–56, 160
Pyepaha, 125

Quakers, 128
quarantine, 135–37, 138
Quashquame, 49

racial violence, 224–25
racism, 97, 135–36, 176, 196, 204, 267n31
railroad fire, 117
Rebok, Horace M., 119–20, 122, 129, 130, 282n53
Red Rock Line, 76
Reifel, Benjamin, 185
Remley, Milton, 116
Removal Treaty of 1842. *See* Sac and Fox Treaty (1842)
Renegade Period (1845–1856), *14*
renegades, 83–85
reparations, 127
repatriation, 237
reservation system, 63, 81–84, 122
resources from the land, 41–44, 64–65, 95–96, 147–51

INDEX

Revolutionary War, 37–38
road infrastructure, 117–19, 181, 235. *See also* infrastructure improvements
Roberts, John, *150*
Roberts, Terry, 199
Roosevelt, Franklin Delano, 174, 175, 186
Roosevelt, Theodore, 140, 141
Rosebud Sioux Tribe, 11
Royal Proclamation (1763), 37
Russell, Robert L., 155, 160, 162

Sac and Fox Indian Poultry Club, 179, *180*
Sac and Fox Removal Treaty (1842), 21, *50*, 63, *66*, 66–77, 82, 84, 87, 93, 99, 102, 223, 226, 241, 270n95
Sac and Fox Treaty (1804), 50–52, 61, 67–68, 263n112
Sac and Fox Tribe, as federal designation, xxiii, 50–52, 56–57, 83–84, 114, 132, 264n121. *See also* federal recognition, as concept; Meskwaki Nation, overview; Sauk Nation, overview
Sac and Fox Tribe of the Mississippi in Iowa v. Licklider, 226, 227, 232, 237
sáhniš, 42
Sanache, Frank, 193
Santa Ana Pueblo, 10
Saukenauk, 41
Sauk Nation, overview, 28, 30–32, 251n5. *See also* Sac and Fox Tribe, as federal designation
Save the Redwoods organization, 2
schools, 3, 120, 125, *127*, 127–30, 153, 166, 209–11, 225, 230, 237
Scott, Tom, *150*
self-determination, xxiv, 216–18, 241. *See also* sovereignty
self-governance. *See* sovereignty
Seminole Tribe of Florida, 231
Settlement. *See* Meskwaki Settlement
Seven Years' War, 34, 35, 37, 38, 45
Shaw, James, 138
Shaw, Leslie M., 117, 136
Sherman, Buren R., 109
Slick, Moses, *150*
Slick, Sam, 167, *169*, 170, 237, *238*
smallpox epidemic, *14*, 36, 134–39, 287n47
Society of American Indians (SAI), 165
Southern Cheyenne, 103

South Farm, 15, 115, 150, 152, 191, 236, 282n45
sovereignty, xxiii, 4, 19, 69–70, 105, 128–29, 156, 161–62, 188–92, 218–20, 233. *See also* economic strategies; Meskwaki Settlement; termination policy
Spanish colonists, 10, 34, 38, 44–45
spirituality, 17
squirrel case, 223–24, 226
Standing Rock Reservation, 5–6
State Board of Education, Iowa, 209, 210
State Historical Society of Iowa, 153
State of Iowa, 87, 93, 97, 98, 121–22, 132, 158, 189, 206, 214–16, 226–27, 237–40
Stevens, E. S., 107
Student-Parents Association, 209
summer homes, 94–95
Svacina, Joseph, 158

Tamacraft, 215
Tama News-Herald (publication), 195–96, 199
Tama Water Power Company, 118
Tataposh, John, 171, *171*
Tax, Sol, 199, 210
taxes, 115, 121. *See also* property taxes
Tc'ih-Léh-Dŭñ (Fish Run Place), 2
Tecumseh, 62
Teller, Henry M., 109
Tenskwatawa, 54
termination policy, 202–4, 211, 216–17. *See also* sovereignty
Tesson, Joseph, 118
Thunder people, 32
Toledo sanitorium, 196
Trade and Intercourse Act (1790), 8–9, 47
trade economy, 29–30, 35–36, 42, 58–59, 66–67, 96–97
traditionalism, 187
traditional medicine, 130–31. *See also* plants
Trail of Tears, 62–63
treaty-making, 50–57. See also *names of specific treaties*
Treaty of Ghent (1815), 54, 56
Treaty of Laramie (1868), 103
Treaty of Medicine Lodge (1867), 103
Treaty of Paris (1763), 34, 37
tribal constitution, 184–88
tribal councils, 166–67, 228, 230, 238–40
tribal enrollment, 106–10

Tribal Historic Preservation Department, 237
Tribal Housing Authority (THA), 221
Tribal Land Enterprise Office, 11
tribal statistics, 10, *14*, 27, 33
True Inspirationists, 86
Trump administration, 6, 8
trust status, 9–10, 120–22, 212–13. *See also* Meskwaki Settlement
Tucker, Jonathan B., 134
Twin, Melvin, 193

Udall, Stewart, 217
unemployment, 164, 174, 213, 220–21, 230. *See also* wage work (off-Settlement)
United Nations, 16–17
University of Iowa hospital, 203
Upper Country, 26–27
Upper Mississippi, 32–33
US Army, 85, 104. *See also* Civil War
US Constitution, 8, 40
US-Dakota War (1862), 97
US Department of Agriculture, 8, 236
US Department of Interior, 3, 8, 186. *See also* Office of the Indian Affairs
use-rights system, 142, 177
US House of Representatives, 109
US–Sauk War, 60–63, 69–70, 83, 158
US v. Kagama, 133

vaccination programs, 134, 287n47. *See also* smallpox epidemic
Valentine, Robert G., 145–46
Variola major. See smallpox epidemic
Vieja Band of Mission Indians, 11
village reconstruction, 139–42
Volunteers in Service to America (VISTA), 218, 220, 236

wage work (off-Settlement), 20, 177, 194–96, 201, 213, 220. *See also* off-Settlement life; unemployment
Wahgohagi clan, 32

Wahpekute Dakota, 87
Wakumo, 110
Wallace, Anthony F. C., 51
Wanatee, Adeline, *208*, 209
Wanatee, Donald, *xx*, xxiv, 27, 90
Wanatee, Frank, 159
Wapanuka, 95
Wapello, 21, 61, 67, 73, 77, 241
war chiefs, 32
Ward, Nell G., 194
warfare, 33–37
War for Independence, 37–38
War of 1812, 53–57, 67
Waterloo Daily Courier (publication), 167
Waterloo Drum and Bugle Corps, 181
Waukano, 93
Wayne, Judy, 193
Whiskey Bottom, 144–45
Wick, B. L., 162–63
wickiups, 73, 92, 135, *137*, 141
Wilcox, E. I., 130
Willett, Walter J., 207
Willford, Albert C., 167
Wilson, George A., 181
Wilson, Jesse E., 143
Wisaka's arrow, 25–27, 89, 241
Wishecomacquet, 72, 75
Wishewahka, 72
Workforce Development Office, Meskwaki Nation, 4–5
World War II, 193, 195, 206
Wounded Knee protest (1973), 224

Young Bear, 158–59, *160*, 167–68, 177
Young Bear, Dan, *150*
Young Bear, Dewey, 193
Young Bear, George, *150*, 167, 184–85, 194
Young Bear, John, *150*
Young Bear, Kenneth, *150*
Young Bear, Mary, xix, 198, 247, 321–22
Young Bear, Richard, 199
Young Bear, Robert, *150*, 159
Ytatahwah, 130–31

www.ingramcontent.com/pod-product-compliance
Lightning Source LLC
Chambersburg PA
CBHW021335230426

43666CB00006B/301